D.W. Winnicott and Political Theory

Matthew H. Bowker • Amy Buzby
Editors

D.W. Winnicott and Political Theory

Recentering the Subject

palgrave
macmillan

Editors
Matthew H. Bowker
Medaille College
Buffalo, New York, USA

Amy Buzby
Arkansas State University
Jonesboro, Arkansas, USA

ISBN 978-1-349-95418-6 ISBN 978-1-137-57533-3 (eBook)
DOI 10.1057/978-1-137-57533-3

This Palgrave Macmillan imprint is published by Springer Nature
The registered company is Nature America Inc.
The registered company address is: 1 New York Plaza, New York, NY 10004, U.S.A.

For Isabelle and Zoe

Contents

Notes on Contributors

C. Fred Alford is a Professor of Government and Distinguished Scholar-Teacher at the University of Maryland, College Park. A recipient of three awards from the Fulbright Commission, he is an author of more than a dozen books in moral psychology and psychoanalytic political theory, including, most recently, *Trauma, Culture, and PTSD* (Palgrave), *Trauma and Forgiveness: Consequences and Communities* (Cambridge), *Psychology and the Natural Law of Reparation* (Cambridge), *Narrative, Nature and the Natural Law: From Aquinas to International Human Rights* (Palgrave), and *After the Holocaust: The Book of Job, Primo Levi, and the Path to Affliction* (Cambridge). Professor Alford is the Executive Director of the Association for Psychoanalysis, Culture and Society, past president of the Political Psychology Section of the American Political Science Association, Coeditor of the *Psychoanalysis and Society* Book Series, published by Cornell University Press, and sits on the editorial boards of numerous professional journals.

Matthew H. Bowker is Clinical Assistant Professor of Humanities at Medaille College in Buffalo, NY. Educated at Columbia University and the University of Maryland, College Park, he brings literary, intellectual-historical, and psychoanalytic approaches to his research in political theory. He is the author of several books on the psycho-politics of contemporary life, including *A Dangerous Place to Be: Identity, Conflict, and Trauma in Higher Education* (with David Levine, Karnac), *Ideologies of Experience: Trauma, Failure, Deprivation, and the Abandonment of the Self* (Routledge), *Rethinking the Politics of Absurdity: Albert Camus,*

Postmodernity, and the Survival of Innocence (Routledge), *Escargotesque, or, What Is Experience?* (Punctum Books), *Albert Camus and the Political Philosophy of the Absurd: Ambivalence, Resistance, and Creativity* (Rowman & Littlefield), and *Ostranenie: On Shame and Knowing* (Punctum Books). He has published numerous papers on psycho-politics, ethics, and pedagogical theory.

Amy Buzby is Associate Professor of Political Science at Arkansas State University. She obtained her Ph.D. in political science from Rutgers University in 2011. She is the author of numerous articles, and her books include *Subterranean Politics and Freud's Legacy* (2013) and *Communicative Action* (2010).

Robert C. Chalwell is an Assistant Professor of Political Science, International Relations, and Comparative Politics at Broward College in Pembroke Pines, Florida, USA. He specializes in postcolonial development in Latin America and the Caribbean, youth marginalization, and the development pursuits of historically marginalized groups broadly. Recent publications look at Monetary Policy in Developing Countries, Voter Demobilization, Minority Male Academic Success, and the Intersectional Dynamics of Tourism-Driven Economies.

Michael A. Diamond is Professor Emeritus of Public Affairs and Organization Studies and Director Emeritus of the Center for the Study of Organizational Change at the Truman School of Public Affairs, University of Missouri. His research is focused on the nexus of psychoanalysis, organizational politics, and culture. Diamond was awarded the 1994 Harry Levinson Award for Excellence in Consulting Psychology from the American Psychological Association, the 1999 William T. Kemper Fellow for Excellence in Teaching, and the 2005 Faculty-Alumni Award from the University of Missouri. He has published extensively in peer-reviewed journals and has authored and coauthored five books, including, most recently, *Discovering Organizational Identity: Dynamics of Relational Attachment* (University of Missouri) and *Private Selves in Public Organizations* (with S. Allcorn, Palgrave). He is a practicing organizational analyst and has consulted with public, private, and nonprofit organizations, including several Fortune 100 companies. He is past coeditor-in-chief of the *American Review of Public Administration* and serves on the editorial boards of *Administration & Society*, *Psychoanalysis, Culture, & Society*, and *Organisational and Social*

Dynamics. He is past-president and founding member of the International Society for the Psychoanalytic Study of Organizations (ISPSO).

Jeremy Elkins is Professor in Political Science at Bryn Mawr College. He has taught at the University of California, Berkeley, and the University of California, Santa Cruz, where he served as chair of the Legal Studies Program. His interests are in the area of moral, political, and legal philosophy, social and political theory, public law, law and politics, and the administrative state. He has published in the areas of constitutional theory and jurisprudence, and is currently working on a book on the relationship between state, society, and law.

Gal Gerson is Associate Professor in the Department of Government and Political Theory, School of Political Sciences, University of Haifa. He has published books on British liberalism, such as *Margins of Disorder: New Liberalism and the Crisis of European Consciousness* (SUNY Press) as well as articles on liberalism, nationalism, feminism, and the interface between psychoanalysis and political theory. He has contributed to an anthology on R.D. Fairbairn, entitled *Fairbairn and the object relations tradition* (Karnac), edited by David Scharff and Graham Clarke.

Bonnie Honig is Nancy Duke Lewis Professor in the departments of Modern Culture and Media (MCM) and Political Science at Brown University and Affiliated Research Professor with the American Bar Foundation, Chicago. She is author of *Political Theory and the Displacement of Politics* (Cornell), *Democracy and the Foreigner* (Princeton), *Emergency Politics: Paradox, Law, Democracy* (Princeton), and *Antigone, Interrupted* (Cambridge). She has edited or coedited: *Feminist Interpretations of Hannah Arendt* (Penn State), *Skepticism, Individuality and Freedom: The Reluctant Liberalism of Richard Flathman* (Minnesota), the *Oxford Handbook of Political Thought* (Oxford), and *Politics, Theory, and Film: Critical Encounters with Lars von Trier* (Oxford). Her book *Public Things* appears with Fordham University Press in 2017.

John LeJeune is an Assistant Professor of Political Science in the Department of History and Political Science at Georgia Southwestern State University. His research interests include the political thought of Hannah Arendt, the nature and sources of human flourishing, and the normative and empirical study of revolutions. His recently published research includes "Hannah Arendt's Revolutionary Leadership" in HannahArendt.net, Vol. 7, No. 1 (2013), and "Revolution" in Wiley-Blackwell's *Encyclopedia of Political Thought* (2014).

David P. Levine is Professor Emeritus of Economics at the Josef Korbel School of International Studies at the University of Denver. In 1994, he was awarded a Certificate in Psychoanalytic Scholarship from the Colorado Center for Psychoanalytic Studies. In addition to his work in political economy, he has published numerous books in the field of applied psychoanalysis, including most recently *Psychoanalysis, Society, and the Inner World: On Embedded Meaning in Politics and Social Conflict* (Routledge), *Psychoanalytic Studies of Creativity, Greed, and Fine Art: Making Contact with the Self* (Routledge), *Object Relations, Work, and the Self* (Routledge), *The Capacity for Civic Engagement: Public and Private Worlds of the Self* (Palgrave), and *The Capacity for Ethical Conduct: On Psychic Existence and the Way We Relate to Others* (Routledge). He is a member of the International Society for the Psychoanalytic Study of Organizations and served for several years as a member of the Executive Board of the Colorado Society for Psychology and Psychoanalysis.

David W. McIvor is Assistant Professor of Political Science at Colorado State University. He has recently published or forthcoming work in a variety of journals including *Contemporary Political Theory*, *Constellations*, and *New Political Science*. His first book *Mourning in America: Race and the Politics of Loss* will be published in 2016 by Cornell University Press.

Zehra Mehdi is a psychoanalytic psychotherapist from Delhi, India with an M.Phil. in Psychotherapy and Clinical Thinking from Ambedkar University Delhi. In her work, she explores the relationship between psyche and politics, religion, violence, and identity. She is beginning her doctoral research at Graduate School of Arts and Sciences, Department of Religion at Columbia University in Fall 2016 where she has been appointed the Dean's Fellow for 2016–2017. She has written on the transgenerational trauma of Partition, religious and political identity within the clinic, psychotherapy as a means for social justice as well as on cultural reading of India cinema around themes of stammering, memory as history, political violence, and popular representations. Her essays are forthcoming in Routledge, Brill, and Karnac Books.

Melissa A. Orlie's writing engages tensions and convergences among political, ecological, psychoanalytic, and ethical concerns. She received her B.A. from the University of California, Santa Cruz and her M.A. and Ph.D. from Princeton University. She teaches political theory at the University of Illinois, Urbana-Champaign.

Alex Zamalin is Assistant Professor of Political Science and the Director of the African American Studies Program at University of Detroit Mercy. His areas of expertise include African American political thought, American politics and political theory. He has written on topics such as politics and literature, ethics, social justice, and race and politics in journals like *Women's Studies Quarterly* and *New Political Science*. He is the author of *African American Political Thought and American Culture* (Palgrave, 2015) and coeditor of the forthcoming collection, *American Political Thought: An Alternative View* (Routledge, 2017). He is currently completing a book manuscript tentatively entitled *The Political Thought of African American Resistance* with Columbia University Press.

List of Figures

CHAPTER 1

Introduction

Matthew H. Bowker and Amy Buzby

This volume has been written for diverse audiences: political theorists interested in psychoanalysis, psychologists interested in political theory, object-relations theorists wishing to consider how D.W. Winnicott's work may be applied to phenomena in the wider world, and interdisciplinarians and generalists intrigued by the prospect of discovering new and fruitful connections between what may be otherwise imagined as discrete disciplines and professional fields. We, the editors, consider the book an *ouverture*, in both senses: an opening act that sets the stage, as it were, for what may follow, and an opening up of Winnicott's thought. The following 14 chapters explicate some of Winnicott's best-known, but often least-carefully considered, concepts, such as holding, transitional space, creativity, the true and false self, the use of objects, and the meaning(s) of aggression and destruction. These concepts, and more, receive detailed examination here, not only in their own right, but in connection with

M.H. Bowker (✉)
Medaille College, Buffalo, NY, USA

A. Buzby
Arkansas State University, Jonesboro, AR, USA

M.H. Bowker, A. Buzby (eds.), *D.W. Winnicott and Political Theory*,
DOI 10.1057/978-1-137-57533-3_1

debates, discourses, and sociopolitical phenomena where they hold great relevance but have been less frequently applied.

Winnicottian thought has found a place of prominence in some of the most interesting recent work in contemporary political theory, including that of Bonnie Honig (2013, 2015, 2016), C. Fred Alford (2005, 2009, 2013), and Axel Honneth (1995). A broader claim may even be made that political theorizing, or at least a certain important kind of political theorizing, is no longer separable from psychological and/or psychoanalytic theorizing. Several years ago, when we conceived of creating the first volume of scholarly essays devoted to the intersections between Winnicott's work and the field of political theory, we were excited about offering readers focused demonstrations of how their research, teaching, and organizational, clinical, or political work might be enriched by Winnicott's thought. We were equally eager to see what would happen when many of the world's most renowned psychoanalytically inclined political theorists—two of the three aforementioned are featured in this volume—focused their attention specifically on the intersections between Winnicott's concerns and those of political theorists.

We believe that the chapters that follow succeed in demonstrating that Winnicott's thought, in particular, and psychoanalytic object-relations theory, more generally, may be usefully applied to traditionally "political" issues, such as the foundations of political community, democratic processes and conflicts, civic action and civil society, discrimination and injustice, violence and warfare, socioeconomic development, and the underpinnings of law and rights. What is more, we feel confident that, from these chapters, readers will derive not only an enriched knowledge of some of the most pressing political theoretical issues of our time, but a deeper and more nuanced understanding of Winnicott's thought.

Indeed, as our work progressed, we realized that an even more precise aim might be achieved: that the thought of D.W. Winnicott may be shown to contain, within itself, a rudimentary political theory of the subject, the uncovering, elaboration, and extension of which could be of momentous import in advancing the contemporary theories not only of politics but of a wide range of disciplines within the humanities and social sciences. This Winnicottian political theory of the subject revolves around the psychic needs of the nascent subject and the premise that healthy, developed subjectivities, subjective capacities, and intersubjective norms are defensible political ideals.

Recentering the Subject

Close readings of Winnicott's *oeuvre* and of much contemporary political theory show that the capacities most feared and hated in the monadic political subject—namely, the subject's potential for withdrawal and isolation, for aggression, for a kind of domineering self-sovereignty, and for the use and abuse of others—are close to (although not identical to) those capacities that *must* be cultivated in developing a psychologically healthy subject. This is not a paradox. The experiences most needed by nascent subjects—experiences such as non-impingement, impulsive aggression or motility, holding and handling that permits of "creating" the world, and illusions of omnipotence—are also precarious, difficult, and almost universally thwarted or lost in the process of individual maturation. While the lack or too-early loss of such experiences can be devastating for the emerging subject, eventual and timely losses of such experiences are both necessary parts of development and, at the same time, the earliest forms of victimization or, in some cases, trauma. There is an important difference here, between privation and deprivation, that will be taken up in more detail below and in Part II of this volume.

For now, we may say that loss, impingement, deprivation, suffering, and even disaster recur in various forms throughout life. These unhappy realities challenge subjects to hold onto, re-create, or in other ways preserve contact with an inner vitality or real self. To be incapable of meeting this challenge, for any number of reasons, is to be forced to manage life by resorting to often rigid defenses, including an overreliance on projection or psychic expulsion and a predominance of ingenuine and self-degrading patterns of being, doing, and relating.

If the very qualities on which healthy subjectivity depends are either absent from the start or are precariously held onto, frequently threatened, and sometimes lost, then it is no stretch of (psycho)logic to suggest that unconscious motives such as envy and hate may drive us to suspect or disparage them. Put another way, discourses of the disruption, decentering, and even "death" of the subject (see, e.g., Lyotard 1984) mirror psychic processes that undermine the development of budding subjects. If these discourses are representative of general attitudes toward subjects (i.e., persons), then to the extent that they are prominent in political, cultural, and intellectual life, the "environment" that would facilitate healthy subjectivities and intersubjectivities will be considerably jeopardized.

By and large, contemporary political theorists have been deeply concerned with the fact that subjects are "already affected" by other people, things, contexts, and more, which, while perhaps not entirely determining of the subject, are thought to leave an indelible "impress" upon subjects and, what is worse, to do so in a way of which we cannot be fully aware because we are "not present for the process" of being affected. That is, the process of becoming an "I" involves that of which "I" am not aware, so much that to say "I am" is "to occupy an impossible position" (Butler 2015, 2–4).

If we enter into these discourses, we find that the question comes down to whether there is, or can be, such a thing as a healthy subject, or whether subjectivity as we know it must be abandoned in order for something else, something post-subjective and post-human, to arise in its place. If we take any sensible definition of subjectivity as a starting point, then this question is more than a semantic game. What is at issue is whether the subject—a creature that is partly isolated, partly related, partly autonomous, and partly dependent—ought to exist in our world.

To begin to answer this question, it must first be decided whether a distinction will be permitted between an ideal subjectivity and a politically and morally undesirable one. That is, does any form of subjectively intrinsically lead to those greedy, violent, "sovereign" attitudes and actions that are so universally derided? Or might it be that subjectivity, itself, is not the problem, but only some unfortunate (modern, western, acquisitive, etc.) versions of it? These versions of subjectivity are the primary objects of critique in the late modern and postmodern eras by theorists like Friedrich Nietzsche, Georges Bataille, Michel Foucault, Jean-Francois Lyotard, Jacques Derrida, Max Horkheimer, and Theodor Adorno. Consider Nietzsche's sweeping assertion that

> a quantum of strength is equivalent to a quantum of urge, will, activity, and it is only the snare of language (of the arch-fallacies of reason petrified in language), presenting all activity as conditioned by an agent—the "subject"—that blinds us to this fact. For, just as popular superstition divorces the lightning from its brilliance, viewing the latter as an activity whose subject is the lightening, so does popular morality divorce strength from its manifestations, as though there were behind the strong a neutral agent, free to manifest its strength or contain it. But no such agent exists; there is no "being" behind the doing, acting, becoming; the "doer" has simply been added to the deed by the imagination—the doing is everything. (1956, 178–179)

While a case could be made that Nietzsche, in other writings, advocates for a kind of *uber*-subject, a subject who exceeds in every way the psychology of the "neutral agent" imagined here, to apply the term "subject" to this "doer" would be to stretch the term beyond recognition and to gravely misconstrue Nietzsche's intent.

Attempts to rescue subjectivity either from its inherent flaws or prior bad acts (if you will) may be considered by some a reactionary attempt to salvage a relic of a rationalistic, chauvinistic, colonial (one could add any number of contemporary "bad words" here) era. Perhaps there is nothing about subjectivity we can save. Or perhaps there is nothing about subjectivity we wish to save, in which case we must embrace our subjective "un-doing" (Butler 2004) as an ethical mandate and, in the words of Lauro and Embry, "pull the trigger on the ego ... destroy the brain ... lay humanism and its legacy of power and oppression in the grave ... undo our primary systems of differentiation: subject/object, me/you" (2008, 107).

Do we concur that the end of subjectivity is the only way forward? Do we agree that "the only way to truly get posthuman is to become antisubject" (Lauro and Embry 2008, 87)? It is a complex problem. Nietzsche's assertion of non-subjectivity runs counter not only to modern philosophy but to the basic premises of psychoanalytic theory and, specifically, to Winnicott's well-known premise that in health there must always be a "doer," a "being" behind any creative and meaningful "doing." Would it surprise readers to learn that the following passage is not taken from Winnicott or one of his contemporaries, but from Dante Alighieri's *De Monarchia* (1957, 18), written in the early fourteenth century at the dawn of the "modern" era: "For in any action what is primarily intended by the agent ... is to make manifest his own image; hence an agent is delighted when he is thus active, for as all things desire their own being, and as an agent in acting unfolds his own being, a state of delight naturally arises."

This passage would not seem terribly out of place in Winnicott's famous essay on "living creatively" (1986, 39–54). It is even cited by Hannah Arendt (but in a different translation where "agent" is rendered "doer") in *The Human Condition* (1998, 175) to frame her well-known account of political action. But what Arendt does not include in her epigraph, and what Winnicott and likeminded thinkers would surely struggle with, is the omitted line that follows: "An agent acts, therefore, only because he is already the kind of thing which what he acts on is supposed to become" (Alighieri 1957, 18). There is the rub: a version of subjectivity that runs through modern philosophy from Francis Bacon to G.W.F. Hegel, challenged by critics of modernity from the theorists of the Frankfurt School to Emmanuel Levinas. There we find the most significant point of contention, and even opposition, between what might be termed a "modern" version of subjectivity and a psychoanalytically informed one. Winnicott offers us the grounds for making this distinction by showing that it is not essential to the nature of subjective being and doing to seek to impress the subject's qualities upon others (objects).[1] Indeed, Winnicott argues that the genuine presence of being that lies behind doing mitigates against the need to impose the subject's fears, desires, and demands upon its objects in ways that impinge upon their own real existence. The project of placing objects outside the realm of subjective control, even in opposition to subjective control, rather, is an achievement of subjectivity and, paradoxically perhaps, fails *not* because of a surfeit of subjectivity but because of the lasting impact of absences, losses, impingements, and other disturbances in the process of subjective development.

When Winnicott conjectures that "before a certain date it is possible that there was only very exceptionally a man or woman who achieved unit status in personal development. … A body of science was needed before men and women could become units integrated in terms of time and space, who could live creatively and exist as individuals," (1971, 70) we are tempted to condemn Winnicott, and perhaps with him all of psychoanalytic theory, to holding a "modern" attitude. But the distinction referred to here is precisely that which differentiates Winnicott, and those who apply and extend his work in this volume, from naively modernist views of subjectivity. To put it simply: The ills of subjectivity decried over the past century-and-half may be corrected by a careful understanding of Winnicottian subjectivity: a subjectivity grounded in the relinquishment of aggression, illusions of omnipotence, symbolic violence, and subjective control over others which is, itself, rooted in the healthy indulgence of the same in the emerging subject.

The alternative to this Winnicottian correction has been, by and large, the advocacy of subjective disruption and recognition of the profound interdependence, vulnerability, contingency, and precariousness of the subject's capacity to maintain contact with herself. While there are several limitations of Winnicott's perspective, as to anyone's, Winnicott is keenly aware of that which lies at the root of this line of argument, that which has come to compose the postmodernist's obsession: the tremendously influential role of the environment and of others in the life experience of the individual. For Winnicott, these elements are most influential in early life, in nurturing or thwarting the development of the self or subject. What we ask of readers, therefore, is a more careful, open-minded, and reflective consideration of the meaning and consequences of this influence. That is, to suggest that human beings are dependent, vulnerable, and precarious before others, particularly before elders, authorities, and "mothers" of various kinds is unquestionable.[2] But this fact of human existence may be taken to imply vastly different normative conclusions. Acknowledging the reality of dependence and vulnerability could suggest merely that we ought not to remain children forever, deluded by fantasies of omnipotence and self-sufficiency. Alternatively, it could mean that we ought never enjoy the intended product of the very nurturing on which we so profoundly depend because we must, for some reason, never forget just how dependent, vulnerable, contingent, and precarious we are.

We wish to argue—and we believe the chapters in this volume are exceedingly useful in problematizing, critiquing, explaining, and in many cases supporting this argument—that to make good use of our dependence, contingency, precarity, and so on, we must be capable *both* of acknowledging it and of not acknowledging it. Or, to say it a bit differently, we cannot make use of the capacities and potentialities afforded to us, both in light of and in spite of our precarious condition, if we are drawn toward ideologies of subject-disruption or even subject-destruction in which all that is becoming of the subject is feared and only the subject's violation or "death" will satisfy our putatively ethical and political (but unconsciously envious and hateful) demands.

"Do We Still Want to Be Subjects?"

The provocative question asked by Ute Guizzoni, "Do we still want to be subjects?" (1996, 201), is intended to remind us that we need not be "constrained" by "the particular ontological state of being subjected, caught within its histories and institutions, including its philosophical, anthropological and humanist embodiments" (Zuss 1998). And yet it would be curious if, within the modern construction of subjectivity, we saw *only* constraint. If Simon Critchley is right that the notion of subjectivity may be referred back to the Greek *hypokeimenon*, meaning "that which lies under," or "the substratum," then we may read in subjectivity the very idea that there is a being or entity "of which all other entities are predicated but which is itself not predicated of anything else" (1996, 13).

This notion clearly has both attractive and unlikeable aspects, along the lines of what has been discussed above: The subject as an end in itself is attractive on several counts, but the subject who denies dependency and "predication" of or by others seems dangerous. Since the denial of dependency is closely linked to mid-twentieth-century atrocity (see Bowker 2014) and to what Ihab Hassan calls our "revulsion against the western [modern] self" (1987, 5), our confrontation with the subject's involvement in enslavement, mass murder, colonization, and oppression may be conceived as an encounter with psychic trauma, not only for the victims—who suffered psychic and physical trauma on perhaps unprecedented scales—but also for those who identify with the presumed subjectivity of the victimizers.

Frederick Jameson reminds us that Sartre's term, "totalization," was "coined specifically to differentiate himself from Lukàcs and the latter's key word 'totality'. Unfortunately, the ideological connotation with which the Sartrean term has been more recently endowed pointedly conflates these two terms. … 'Totalizing' has thus become a slogan which identifies a claim to speak from above and for all of society, as opposed to the minoritarian and differential positions of this or that Foucauldian 'specific intellectual'" (in Sartre 1960, xx). This intellectual slippage reflects our desire to distance ourselves from, disidentify with, and decenter our own subjectivities, even as, in an underappreciated irony, our antipathy to "totalization" frequently implies that the subject is "totally" evil.

Emmanuel Levinas, the Lithuanian-French philosopher and Talmudic scholar who has been tremendously influential in postmodern political theory, is perhaps best-known for his account of relational violence, an account not entirely different from the type usually associated with Pierre Bordieu or Slavoj Žižek, although Bordieu and Žižek have more often attended to the ways that language and thought cover up violence by assimilating it into the order of the usual and the rational. For Levinas, violence occurs when subjects relate to and, therefore, reduce others' alterity, totalizing them, and making then foreign or alien to themselves (Levinas 1969). To prevent such violence, Levinas recommends what C. Fred Alford aptly calls "hostage-being" (2002, 29), a condition in which the subject is effectively a hostage to the other's demand, but is not related to this other in any usual sense. This mode of encounter thwarts the subject's temptation to ground its relation to the other in sameness, mutuality, or even recognition: all of which are thought to be totalizing approaches that risk the imposition or "impingement" of the subject's qualities upon the other, destroying the other *qua* other (Levinas 1969, 80). Levinas' hostage-being is presented as a way to stop imposing, impinging, and totalizing, as a protection for others against the self's temptation to reduce others to their roles in our own internal dramas.

While Levinas' thought is extraordinary complex—too complex to do it justice here—we would argue that subjects cannot be subjects if they are "hostages" to others, just as they cannot experience subjective being in any robust sense if they are to be constantly reminded that their subjectivity is dangerous, precarious, or ultimately contingent upon others. To use a term particularly *in vogue* of late, subjects cannot be subjects if they are asked, coerced, or even required to apologize for the "privilege" of being subjects, which is sometimes reduced to a matter of linking their own existence (and particularly those moment of existence when one forgets about others) to guilt for the suffering of others. What is implied here is that the subjective experience of even one person is, in fact, causally responsible for the injustice, injury, and suffering of others.

George Yancy's open letter in the *New York Times(2015)*, "Dear White America," comes at a difficult time in American racial politics and reflects both a sense of understandable moral indignation and longstanding trends in academic and popular discourse that assert a link between subjective being and complicity in violence perpetrated upon others. It does so in some subtle and some not-so-subtle ways. It begins by telling the reader to "listen with love," to "take a deep breath," to accept the letter as "a gift," and to be "silent" by "quiet[ing] your own voice." "If you are white," Yancy continues,

> [d]on't run to seek shelter from your own racism. Don't hide from your responsibility. Rather, begin, right now, to practice being vulnerable. Being neither a "good" white person nor a liberal white person will get you off the proverbial hook. Take another deep breath. I ask that you try to be "un-sutured." If that term brings to mind a state of pain, open flesh, it is meant to do so ...
>
> I can see your anger .... This letter is not asking you to feel bad about yourself, to wallow in guilt. That is too easy. I'm asking for you to tarry, to linger, with the ways in which you perpetuate a racist society, the ways in which you are racist .... I am asking you to enter into battle with your white self. I'm asking that you open yourself up; to speak to, to admit to, the racist poison that is inside of you ...
>
> What I'm asking is that you first accept the racism within yourself, accept all of the truth about what it means for you to be white in a society that was created for you ...

> White America, are you prepared to be at war with yourself, your white identity, your white power, your white privilege? …
>
> Perhaps the language of this letter will encourage a split—not a split between black and white, but a fissure in your understanding … enabl[ing] you to see the role that you play (even despite your anti-racist actions) in a *system* that continues to value black lives on the cheap.

It is not difficult to understand what Yancy means when he insists that every reader is inherently racist, in spite of the fact that she may not think, feel, or behave in ways that are racist, and even if she regularly undertakes "anti-racist actions," whatever those may be. The familiar logic here is that being "un-sutured," tarrying and lingering with guilt and shame concerning one's moral "responsibility" for the oppression of black Americans, is of value in itself. It is, rather plainly, the belief that being "at war" with oneself is a desirable state of being, and that provoking this internal war in others by asking them to experience "a state of pain, open flesh," is in keeping with the laudable aims of justice, equity, and ethical community. If one is not "at war" with oneself, then one is doing something wrong. If we are not "undone by each other … then we're missing something" (Butler 2004, 23).

While surely there are complex issues of unconscious or unacknowledged racism, as well as legacies of atrocious racial oppression and continuing systemic injustices, all of which are beyond the scope of this particular chapter, it is possible to see such commentaries as discursive attempts to thwart (to "split") the subjective experience (particularly the "understanding") of others, to inflict guilt, pain, and fear such that it becomes difficult to creatively and thoughtfully experience one's subjectivity. Subjects and subjects-to-be cannot experience those moments of solitary being, of "going on being," or of transitional being between the "me" and the "not me" if they must live in fear of "forgetting" their apparently ineradicable complicity with evil, to which they are bound, perhaps ironically, by nothing other than the color of their skin.

To take a more circumspect approach as an example, if we say, with Butler, that the "'I' remains in thrall to a prior transitivity, acted upon as it acts," then this "I" is less likely to feel like an "I" and is less likely to experience the very transitivity it appears to wish to acknowledge. That is, to admonish those who act "*as if* they were not formed by the matrix of relations that gives rise to the subject" may signify something more than an acknowledgment of the contexts of histories, languages, and relationships in which we find ourselves (2015, 8, *emphasis added*). It may signify an attempt to call us back to others as something not unlike "hostages," to focus not on the outcome of our subjective formation but to become preoccupied with our formation. If this occurs, then we are likely to fail to realize the positive side of this "as if."

If we sermonize about how dangerous it is to act "as if [we] were not formed," which is "to engage in a form of disavowal that seeks to wish away primary and enduring modes of dependency and interdependency, including those disturbed conditions of abandonment or loss registered at early ages that are not precisely overcome or transcended in the life that follows" (Butler 2015, 8), then we may implicitly or explicitly endorse the failure of the subject, for whom dependency and its disturbances (e.g., "abandonment or loss") are never integrated or forgotten, and, rather, must be forever attended to, deemed necessary or inevitable (e.g., "not precisely overcome or transcended"), or even treasured as "a gift."

Surmounting dependence and its vicissitudes is typically associated with the highly pejorative figure of the "sovereign 'I' ... supported by ... denial ... thoroughly brittle, [and] often displaying brittle insistence in symptomatic ways" (Butler 2015, 8–9). Thus, the questions we pose to the imagined "sovereign" subject are questions of its ruin, not of its recuperation: "When will that figure break of its own accord, or what will it have to destroy to support its image of self-sovereignty?" (9) Perhaps worse, such questions are framed as ethical matters, where ethical relations are misconstrued as relations occurring in a context of de-subjectification, where the call of the other always holds primacy over the calls of the self. "Already undone, or undone from the start, we are formed, and as formed, we come to be always partially undone by what we come to sense and know. What follows from this is that form of relationality that we might call 'ethical': a certain demand or obligation *impinges* upon me, and the response relies on my capacity to affirm this having been acted on, *formed into one who can respond to this or that call*" (11, *emphasis added*).

Such claims are fundamentally opposed to what a careful reading of Winnicott, and what we believe to be a more useful approach to the meaning of subjective, intersubjective, mature, and ethical relationship, suggests: that impingement and reaction can never stand at the center of mature being or relating because impingement and reaction to impingement can be nether subjective nor intersubjective. Actions arising in this way are, in Winnicott's words, mere "pattern[s] of reacting to stimuli" (1986, 39), undertaken not by a subject capable of ethical thought but by an object, an impinged-upon reactive organ who merely responds to "this or that call." On the contrary, genuinely ethical action, we argue, must begin with a subject who is a creator, author, or, to borrow Kohut's phrase, a "center of initiative" (1977, 99).

The alternative to conceiving of subjective and intersubjective action in this way is to assign asymmetrical and even logically impossible ethical duties to agents: The ethical actor must be "undone" before the other (Butler 2004, 23), but this other actor would, presumably, have reciprocal obligations to become "undone" by the other's others. In a world where all are undone by being *impinged upon* by others, and where all are merely *reacting* to these putatively "ethical" impingements, there can be no genuine subjective being and no willed, thought, or ethical action or relation. In Winnicott's language, there can be no "being" and no "doing that arises out of being" (1986, 39).

Guilt for Being and Not Being

Let us say something obvious that may, nevertheless, seem surprising: There is such a thing as excessive concern for others. If we are overly concerned with the needs of others, or if we are, at a discursive level, so concerned about possible denials of dependence or interdependence, we may find ourselves confusing impingement with ethical responsiveness, or confusing compliant, guilt-ridden, or self-destructive patterns of relating with authentic concerns for others. For Winnicott and like-minded thinkers, excessive concern for others may reflect an incapacity that is, itself, a remnant of disturbances related to dependence and vulnerability. Neglect, deprivation, abandonment, impingement, pseudo-confirmation, and other forms of what may become what Leonard Shengold famously calls "soul murder" of the developing subject, are disastrous precisely because they encourage the development of a false self system, in which the subject is replaced by an object of the other's desire (1989, 1999).

It is not prima facie unreasonable to assert that such a state of affairs—a state in which the subject is displaced by desire of the other, or of the "Other"—is inevitable. The incalculably influential work of Jacques Lacan is sufficient to establish as much (1977, 1988, 1998). But neither is it unreasonable to wonder whether the insistence upon the inevitability of subjective degradation, the urgency with which we have sought to ratify the decentered subject as a psycho-social "fact," and the vehemence with which critics of or opponents to this perspective are vilified as naïve or oppressive, may equally be read as symptoms in themselves, symptoms that reflect a broad system of defense. Defense against what? We suggest: defense against the possibility, or, in Winnicottian language, the potentiality, of subjective becoming.

Contra Lacan, at the center of the Winnicottian subject is *no other* in any of its manifestations: not the *objet (petit) a*, nor "other people," nor the (Big) Other, nor the other as symbolic order, nor the barred Other (Ⱥ), and so on. For Winnicott, at the center of the subject is a core of reality-feeling and being that composes the "secret self" which contains an "incommunicado" element that survives precisely by being isolated from all others and, so, from the potential for relations with objects to alter or deform it (1965, 187). This secret self in its inner citadel Winnicott finds necessary for genuine subjective emergence, since the alternative, the idea that *all* of the self may be available to or penetrable by others, is crushing. From these speculations Winnicott asserts a "right not to communicate," derived not from a rational ethical grounding so much as from an inner "protest" that arises in the core of the self against "the frightening fantasy of being infinitely exploited" (179).

One might immediately think of Melville's Bartleby (2004) or, perhaps, of Camus' Meursault (1988) as heroes defending this right not to communicate. And, if so, then one is likely to think of Giorgio Agamben's well-known essay on Bartleby and his defense of the intransigent scrivener, perhaps paradoxically, as a champion of contingency (1999). And while the idea of potentiality is linked, both in Winnicott and in Agamben, to the preservation of an authentic and incommunicado element of subjectivity, there is a difference between Winnicott's personal "right not to communicate" and the rather fantastical impact Agamben attributes to Bartleby's protest, which is nothing less than the establishment of a sphere in which "even the past would not be settled," for "Bartleby's experiment ... is possible only by calling into question the principle of the irrevocability of the past, or rather, by contesting the retroactive unrealizability of potentiality" (1999, 261). Both Bartleby and Meursault have, in their own ways, "given up" (Melville 2004, 60), not only on copying, in the case of the former, and on "playing the game" (Camus 1968, 335), in the case of the latter, but on subjective being, itself (see also Bowker 2014). Winnicott would not have us imagine that refusals to communicate rooted in deeper rejections of the burdens of subjectivation can undo the past. Rather, by protecting something precious within ourselves we may find a source of subjective fortitude or resilience when pressured to accept falsity, the idea of impossible subjectivity, or the necessity that subjective experience be linked with crime and guilt.

It is impossible, at this point, not to mention the extraordinary influence of discourses of trauma over the past four decades and the reification of psychic injury—and "moral injury" (see Bowker and Levine 2016)—that has come in its wake. Perhaps the most powerful explanation of the ascendency of "trauma talk" is captured in Judith Herman's concise assertion that every instance of traumatic injury "is a standing challenge to the rightness of the social order" (qtd. in Shay 1995, 3). Thus, not subjects but subjective absences are imagined to generate politically salient contention, opposition, and even rebellion. If the "social order" is false, then it is the putative "truth of traumatic experience," that gives trauma its political value. Cathy Caruth, still the best-known trauma theorist in the humanities, claims that although the "overwhelming occurrence" of trauma returns to the individual in delayed and incomplete forms, it remains "absolutely true to the event," and is, therefore, "not a pathology … of falsehood or displacement of meaning, but of history itself" (1995, 5).

The fantasy or ideology associated with trauma, then, is that of subjective dispossession by objective truth: that the traumatized "carry an impossible [yet true] history within them, or they become themselves the symptom of a history that they cannot entirely possess" (Caruth 1995, 5). If there is a fantasy (or wished-for experience) involved in trauma talk, it would seem to involve the same "formation" processes of which Judith Butler speaks, although taken in a more extreme direction. That is, if we seem stuck with, unable to move beyond, or preoccupied with having been dependent upon, "formed," and profoundly affected by others in ways over which we had little or no control or consciousness, then perhaps our preoccupation reflects a *wish* to return to or remain in this state, to accept or invite objects—even traumatic objects—to take up residence in the psychic space where a subject might have been.

While beyond the scope of this volume, it would seem that, from the affective turn to the turn to "body studies," or "corporeality," one may find evidence of a wish that bodies become privileged sites of analysis because bodies are, in some important sense, not our own. Teresa Brennan's work on the transmission of affect finds that "the psyche is, of course, also a physical or embodied thing. This has to be so if one accepts the premise that the psychical actually gets into the flesh …. It is these embodied psychical urges, these constellations of affects, that lead us to eat the wrong way, do the wrong things, push ourselves for the wrong reason, and so forth" (2004, 156). And, as Lisa Blackman writes, the body is "always *in process* ... made up from the diverse relays, connections and relationships between artefacts, technologies, practices and matter which temporarily form it as a particular kind of object" (2008, 2849–2855, *emphasis in original*). Parallel to the endeavor to demonstrate the precariousness and dependence of subjects, the body and its affects, too, have become things that are not possessed by the individual but are shared, exposed to others and to transmissions of experience by and through others.

We submit that such trends in political theory, and in several related branches of the humanities and social sciences, express an ambivalence, if not a form of terror, concerning the grounds for subjective being, for the subject's own reality-feeling, for the feeling that "I AM" (Winnicott 1965, 155). Such ambivalences and terrors are in some sense natural in the process of coming into being and making the world one's own. But a retreat from the position of subjective being altogether, along with continuing condemnations of subjective being, suggests something more: a defense against or *apologia* for a failure to be.

When Jacques Derrida asks, "by what right does subjectivity exist?" (1991, 100), a psychoanalyst may find it difficult not to hear a reverberation of depressive guilt. If we rephrase the question in the first person—"By what right do I exist?"—this emotion likely comes through more clearly to every reader. We might respond (although perhaps not in the consulting room) by asking: *Must* subjectivity exist by right? Must your very existence be permitted by other persons who exist, or by law, or by some other right-granting force, such as a god? Derrida's challenge is also wrong-headed because the notion of the subject is coincidental with, if not antecedent to, the concept of (legal, political, moral) right. That is, while this matter is now somewhat contested, we would argue that there can be no meaningful sense of "right" without subjects. To put it in a more evocative way: A world without subjects would be a world without right. This formulation may, again, help us hear the depressive fantasy beneath Derrida's question.

We contend that preoccupation with disturbance, affectedness, trauma, and suffering in general represents a need to demonstrate to ourselves and others the impossibility or groundlessness (*Grundlosigkeit*) of establishing a real, vital subject or self. This demonstration, with notes of *apologia*, would serve the purpose of reassuring ourselves that the destruction of subjectivity is inevitable, and that the identification with the needs of others is either necessary or ideal. (Perhaps, in this situation, there is no difference between ideal and necessity.)

While *apologia* is different from apology, both respond to guilt. That is, an ongoing *apologia* for subjective failure would only be necessary if there was something we needed to explain, something about which we felt disturbed, ambivalent, split, or guilty. If our incapacity *to be* stems from guilt, guilt about being that, itself, likely arises in the context of failures of the environment to facilitate being and make being safe, then anti-subjective discourses assuage not only this guilt but its correlate: the guilt of *not* being a subject, of having failed to achieve subjectivity for ourselves (see Bowker 2016, 60–61). If we offer explanations, defenses, and *apologias*, but can never quite be done with them, it is because they do not return us to the truth that the "I AM" moment is not given by right, and hence its taking is not righteous, justifiable, or even forgivable. To pay endless homage to all that has formed, shaped, impressed upon, impinged upon, and disturbed our senses of subjectivity is to undertake a kind of doing that arises from *not being*. It is to bracket or suspend the feeling of "I AM" and to attune ourselves to the needs of others by acknowledging their presence while apologizing for our own.

The subtitle of this volume, "Recentering the Subject," asks readers to consider and question the ideas that subjects require a right to exist, that subjects are inherently or "totally" malevolent, and that subjects are both inevitably and ideally penetrated by others and environments that form them. Among the challenges and novel possibilities we hope the reader will find within is the possibility of upturning what has become a cornerstone of contemporary political thought, replacing its suspicion of the subject with alternative, constructive possibilities for developing healthy subjectivities and intersubjectivities.

Winnicottian Interventions

The possibility that subjects will become closed-off, totalistic, or aggressive—in the usual sense of violence emanating from frustration—are real. But the solutions to these and other unfortunate possibilities lie not in dismantling the subject but in the facilitation and even fortification of healthy subjectivity, particularly in its earliest forms. That is, tolerance and facilitation of aggression, isolation, and destruction—in the senses in which Winnicott defines these terms—are needed in order for the healthy subject to come into existence.

To be clear, it is no one's hypothesis that political subjects, who are typically presumed to be "developed," "adult," or in some other sense "mature," ought to expect the indulgences afforded to infants, nor that they ought to adopt childlike characteristics, no matter how useful or pleasant such indulgences or characteristics may have been in the first years of life. Instead, the argument that runs throughout this volume is that Winnicott's thought helps us to clarify how healthy, progressive, and ethical political communities begin and end with healthy subjects. If the needs of nascent subjects are neglected, or, worse, are met with anxiety- or distress-provoking reactions, which are themselves forms of impingement and disruption, then we find ourselves in a world of would-be subjects whose aggression is mobilized *not* for the sake of discovering spontaneous movement or the joy of reaching out to meet that which offers resistance, but, instead, for imposing suffering on the self and others to compensate for scarcely understood senses of loss, deprivation, anger, and unreality.

Subjects who are healthy in a Winnicottian sense are more likely to be capable of engaging with and ("agonistically") opposing others, of ethically relating, of meaningfully participating in political life, and, lest we forget what, of being part of healthy families which, one day or another, may generate new nascent subjects. One finds defenses of claims not terribly distinct from these in the pages of *Political Theory* and other prominent journals in the field (see, e.g., Rosenthal 2016). Readings of recent scholarship in this area will likely prove to be persuasive to political thinkers.

But, for Winnicott, and for others, such activities are not the end (*telos*) of the subject. To subordinate the life of the subject to aims or ends of others, of communities, of families, or of nation-states, especially when doing so means rendering the subject more vulnerable than she may be already, is to encroach upon that which permits subjects to enrich their own experience of themselves and of the world, and, subsequently, to contribute part (but not *all*) of themselves to their communities and polities. Thus, it is fitting to begin this volume with three chapters focused primarily on the nascent subject and her needs.

Part I: The Subject's Creation: Aggression, Isolation, and Destruction

The first part of this volume, "The Subject's Creation: Aggression, Isolation, and Destruction," is so titled in order to draw attention to what is unique about Winnicott's view of subjective development and what may, at first, seem perplexing or even bizarre. The emergence of a human subject depends upon its exercise of, as well as its caregiver's facilitation of, qualities that seem undesirable in the developed or mature subject:

the isolation of the true self from others, the capacity to withdraw and protect what is most genuine about the self when relating, the exercise of spontaneous aggression or motility, the coalescence of reality-feeling and self-sense around aggressive or motile action, and nearly constant fantasies involving the destruction of the (internal) other or object.

This part commences with Jeremy Elkins' remarkable essay, "Being and Encountering: Movement and Aggression in Winnicott," which carefully examines elements of Winnicott's thought that Winnicott, himself, left obscure. Elkins locates aggression at the very center of Winnicott's thought, at the heart of thinking about what it means to be a subject, and, by extension, at a focal point in contemporary political theorizing. Of the two types of errors that bring individuals into consulting rooms or, barring that, leave individuals in unfortunate situations—one being a loss of contact with the outer world; the other being a loss of contact with the inner world—Elkins makes a persuasive case that *both* may be best understood as failures of aggression.

The facilitated use of aggression—which, Elkins reminds us, begins *in utero*—when understood in distinction to its more typical associations with hatred or violence, helps creates a subject whose experience of the world is also an experience of herself and whose destructiveness, in a later development, permits for the possibility of finding real others in that world who may also be imbued with subjectivity. Fantasized destruction of internal objects permit buddings subjects to let go of subjective control and, then, to discover an external world whose objects exist in their own right.

The idea that fantasized destruction is inseparable from what might be called "creating" objects in the external world is a complex one, one that Winnicott described in brief sketches in which, for instance, the subject says: "'Hullo object!' 'I destroyed you.' 'I love you.' 'You have value for me because of your survival of my destruction of you.' 'While I am loving you I am all the time destroying you in (unconscious) fantasy'" (1971, 90). Aggressing without hate, then, creates a feeling of realness in the self, the foundation for subjectivity, just as destructiveness of a sort creates, for the growing subject, the possibility of living in a world with real others and real things, not just projections or illusions.

If it seemed odd that aggression and destruction were necessary, but perhaps not sufficient, conditions for subjective development and the capacity for healthy contact with the world, David Levine's exceptional essay, "The Isolation of the True Self and the Problem of Impingement:

Implications of Winnicott's Theory for Social Connection and Political Engagement," advances with force and clarity the somewhat paradoxical idea that *not* relating is, in fact, fundamental to healthy political engagement. Levine emphasizes the capacity of the subject to protect her original vitality from damaging forms of relating, which, in turn, helps the subject resist the urge to create simulacra of the (disrupted, lost) holding environment in object relating.

Levine's essays follows logically from Elkins' if we acknowledge that aggression plays its part not only in discovering the impulsive and spontaneous center of initiative and in destroying in fantasy those objects we wish to survive in external reality, but in defending and isolating the true self. Aggression, that is, is implied in the need Levine elaborates: to protect the core self against impingements and impositions that would alter or disrupt it. An enjoyable "cognitive music" is created in the juxtaposition between Elkins' and Levine's essays, as they point to two equally important and yet in some sense competing needs in subjective development: in Elkins' case, the subject's need to create (through aggression and destruction) an external world; in Levine's case, the subject's need to create (through isolation and, perhaps, a form of aggression) an internal world.

Ultimately, Levine courageously draws out a difficult consequence of Winnicott's thought on the isolation of the true self as it relates to civil life. In civil relating—what he calls a "modality of relating" that is distinct from and in some sense superior to object relating—object relations are largely absent, as are the defining qualities of the individual's unique being. Civility, then, is the expression of an ability to accomplish a subjective investment and disinvestment simultaneously: The subject's true self is not engaged in civil relating, but the subject is therefore able to relate to others as more than objects serving either to gratify or frustrate. While perhaps a surprising claim, consider the alternative: a situation in which the true self knows no isolation or privacy and, therefore, can only seek to re-create in the world a facsimile of the holding environment that failed to protect it, an environment in which others must be attuned to us and our needs. Such a fantasy generates political dramas based on competition over the right to act omnipotently and to "create" a new world in one's own image, as it were. More mature forms of politics, Levine argues, depend on the ability of the polity and the families in it to leave its subjects with the residue of a good enough holding environment, one that kept a part of the subject separated from excessive or too-early relating and from other social and political realities.

Melissa Orlie's exhaustively researched chapter, "The Psychoanalytic Winnicott We Need Now: On the Way to a Real Ecological Thought," offers detailed readings not only of Winnicott but of several crucial secondary texts, such as those of Masud Khan, Hans Loewald, and Marion Milner. Orlie does not limit herself to one particular Winnicottian concept but seeks first to clarify and then to re-present central Winnicottian insights, particularly those concerning the presence/absence of "a baby" and the relationship between mother and child, as needed correctives to return to an embrace of what Orlie calls "earthly life." The term, "earthly life," of course, harkens not only to religious thought in general but to Nietzsche, in particular, and implies the repudiation of fantasies both spiritual and secular. Orlie asks us to consider an "impersonal narcissism" as a potential antidote to pathological and personal narcissisms that interfere with our ability to be ourselves and to care for others (and even to care for Earth). Like the chapters that precede it, Orlie does not hesitate to provoke and challenge the reader to accept the usefulness of capacities and attributes that are traditionally treated pejoratively.

Finally, all three chapters ask what attitudes toward political and social life are likely to be generated by different experiences of and accounts of subjective becoming. Elkins asks: If aggression is only understood as a defense against frustration, are we likely to conceive of political life primarily as a contest for frustration-reduction, as a "system of needs" featuring competition over "primary goods"? If, as Levine contends, we neglect to protect and preserve the subject from relating then, shall we end with a political system that more closely resembles (the fantasy of) a family? If, as Orlie wonders, we do not embrace the difficult challenges posed by Winnicott, such as permitting ourselves to be made use of (and surviving use) as well as using others (such that they survive our use), then shall we have difficulty facing the inevitable losses and tragedies of "earthly life" both as subjects and as societies? These questions, particularly how we face, encounter, fantasize about, and forgive loss, injury, and tragedy are the subjects of the second part of this volume: "The Subject Faced with Deprivation and Disaster."

Part II: The Subject Faced with Deprivation and Disaster

Early in this chapter, we examined some of the ways that discourses of suffering and trauma may lead to undue emphases, preoccupations, or even obsessions with subjective suffering, disruption, and "undoing," such that a healthy subject may find no place. Nevertheless, it is undeniable that suffering, disruption, and "undoing" are real experiences for subjects, families, communities, and societies. What is more, some form of response (conscious or unconscious, productive or regressive) to unfortunate occurrences must be undertaken. Winnicott was no stranger to suffering and deprivation, having devoted years of his life and several key pieces of writing to contending with both the theoretical and the practical consequences of war and family-separation (see e.g., 1984). Perhaps even more importantly, Winnicott was aware that disasters need not always be spectacular in order to be disastrous, as he reminds us in what may be considered his (less poetic and less dualistic) version of Blake's famous couplet: "Some are Born to sweet delight,/Some are Born to Endless Night" (1982, 492, lines 123–124):

> I find it useful to divide the world of people into two classes. There are those who were never let down as babies and who are to that extent candidates for the enjoyment of life and living. There are also those who did suffer traumatic experience of the kind that results from environmental let-down, and who must carry with them all their lives the memories (or the material for memories) of the state they were in at moments of disaster. These are candidates for lives of storm and stress and perhaps illness .... There is a middle group, however .... [W]e would include those who carry round with them experiences of unthinkable or archaic anxiety, and who are defended more or less successfully against remembering such anxiety, but who will nevertheless use any opportunity that turns up to become ill and have a breakdown in order to approach that which was unthinkably terrible. (1986, 31–32)

Winnicott's initial dichotomy here may draw our attention to the difference between persons who have been subjected to privation and those who have been *de*prived, since what is meant by "environmental let-down" is not entirely clear. (The question of privation and deprivation is a focal point of Bowker's chapter, to be discussed momentarily.) Winnicott's "middle group" alludes to a category of persons who are neither damned nor saved, who are closer to mental health than those of the second "class," but who certainly do not enjoy optimal health.

Everyone suffers deprivation—if not *structurally* then at least seemingly unavoidably—throughout life. Without deprivation, we might say, the infant would never grow up. Of course, there are necessary deprivations and unnecessary deprivations, moderate and severe deprivations, tolerable and intolerable deprivations, and even, as Herbert Marcuse might put it, "basic" and "surplus" deprivations. An important difference between privation and deprivation is that deprivation implies a loss of something already had, whereas privation implies an absence from the beginning. The important caveat then, to the claim that *everyone* suffers deprivation is the possibility that the only "class" of persons who do not suffer deprivation are those who have suffered extreme privation. These persons have already lost all there is to lose, and so may seem both damned and saved, ambivalently immune to further loss.

Faced with deprivation, we may play games to reencounter the traumas we have suffered, to master them, to trade roles with our aggressors, and more. We open this part with Zehra Mehdi's mesmerizing depiction of her work with children at the Kandhla relief camp after the 2013 ethno-religious riots in Muzaffarnagar, a district in Northern India. Her essay, "Playing 'Riot': Identity in Refuge: Absent Child Narratives in the 2013 Hindu Muslim Riots in Muzaffarnagar, India," recounts Mehdi's observations and reflections on questions of identity, trauma, and recovery during and after the riots, riots in which Muslims were brutally attacked and displaced by their neighbors. Fascinated by the games designed by the children in the camp, Mehdi deploys Winnicott's work expertly, particularly his understanding of the meaning of games and play. In doing so, she allows these children to communicate that which might seem incommunicable, even opening avenues for reconceptualizing play as a kind of (pre-) political subjective agency that developing subjects (children) may access.

Following this detailed examination of various forms of play involving destruction, death, and the repetition of traumatic experience, Matthew Bowker's essay, "Safety in Danger and Privacy in Privation: Ambivalent Fantasies of Natural States Invoked in Reaction to Loss," turns to two theoretical sources to explore the role that fantasies of privation (we might even call them "dramas" of, or "playing" with, privation) take on in the wake of disasters personal and collective. Bowker argues that state-of-nature fantasies, while not categorically distinct from Edenic and Arcadian ideals known since antiquity, express a wish to return to a "psychic state of nature," where what is real is the absence and not the presence of subjectivity. Fantasies of non- or anti-subjectivity operative in disaster-narratives such as the state of nature tend to throw out the subject with the ills of civilization.[3] Such fantasies, given the influence of social contract theory on liberal political ideology, not to mention the growing popular fascination with apocalypse and disaster, are morally and politically suspicious, for they suggest that the state of extreme privation is a state of moral "safety" or innocence, one ill-suited to subjective or intersubjective being.

On the other hand, in anticipation or response to disaster, it may be that although we feel the regressive, "gravitational" pull (to invoke images from Bonnie Honig's delightful chapter on von Trier's "Melancholia") to an antecedent condition or former "world" constituted by childish fantasy or grandiose illusion, we also find or create in moments of crisis opportunities for subjective growth. Of course, we can only find or create such opportunities if we have the inner and outer resources needed not exactly to "survive" but to surpass, pass through, and emerge renewed. Honig's provocative essay, "'Out Like a Lion': *Melancholia* with Euripides and Winnicott," on *The Bacchae*, and Lars von Trier's popular apocalyptic film, "Melancholia," hinges on the question of what issues from the "end" of worlds, particularly the "world" of the immature subject. Thus, Honig opposes a version of childishly "sovereign" subjectivity with a mature version of subjectivity facilitated by only one of two mother figures in von Trier's film, both of whom are facing (either literally or metaphorically) a world-ending event.

If, in apocalypse, we often find the hope for renewal and rebirth—"Apocalypse" always, in some sense, implies rebirth, as the term derives from *apo + kalyptein*, meaning to uncover—then it is reasonable to imagine that the falsely sovereign subjectivity of a child must be shed (or uncovered) to reveal a more genuine yet more vulnerable subjectivity underneath. This uncovering may, indeed, be experienced as an annihilation or as the end of a world and it is possible to be unduly fascinated with apocalyptic thinking and fantasy (see, e.g., Jay 1993). But Honig does not glamorize apocalypse for the suffering it entails, nor does she locate the idea of disaster, in itself, at the center of the mature subjective potentialities that issue from the facilitative work of those who bear developing subjects through it. Both the child, Leo, in von Trier's film, and the young king, Pentheus, in Euripides' tragedy, navigate their way through a developmental period that, on Winnicott's account, involves violence, aggression, despair, and murder (of self, of other). But only von Trier's Leo is possessed of a "good enough" mother, one who can "create the in-between needed to transition to a possible adulthood."

Finally, in C. Fred Alford's frank yet hopeful essay, "Forgiveness and Transitional Experience," we are invited to explore the possibility that the process of contending with loss, injury, injustice, or disaster affords an opportunity to enter transitional space, from which forgiveness may arise but, at the same time, from which forgiveness becomes less significant.

Alford leverages his decades of engagement with Winnicott's work to offer a surprising insight into how we may or may not get on in the world after suffering something terrible. It may be, he contends, that it is well if we decide (whether consciously or unconsciously) not to forgive, or rather not to think about forgiveness. That is, the alternative to forgiveness, Alford argues, is residing in transitional space, where the other's offense is no longer the center of the victim's world. One problem with discussions of forgiveness today, he finds, is the tendency to use forgiveness to seek power instead of reunion, either with the offender or the holding community. By "power," Alford means that temptation noted in different ways in earlier chapters (e.g., Levine's and Bowker's) to re-create in the world a holding environment that never was, and to impose a wholeness without room for otherness. The primary virtue of forgiveness, we might say, is the enjoyment, by the offended party, of transitional space, which then makes forgiveness itself unimportant. For Alford, and for Winnicott, the subject's enjoyment of transitional space is its own reward.

Part III: Revitalizing the Subject of Political Theory

The third part of this volume, "Revitalizing the Subject of Political Theory," gathers three chapters that apply Winnicott's work to well-known debates and topics in contemporary political theory. Each author shares the goal of extending Winnicott's thought to revitalize political theory and to reinvigorate our ability to build connections between theory and constructive praxis. The diversity of these chapters and their subjects underscore our central contention that Winnicott has a broad and rich contribution to make to political theory as a discipline. This part builds on the insights gleaned in Part I—questions of the constituent elements of healthy subjectivity—and Part II—experiences of and potential responses to disruptions and deprivations faced by both children and adults.

By applying several of the Winnicottian concepts and categories elaborated thus far, the authors of these three chapters provide the subject elucidated in this text with firmer moorings, both external and internal. Winnicott's work lends itself immediately to such applications, not least because Winnicott himself worked to build conversations and connections with professionals in other fields. A forebear of interdisciplinarity, Winnicott embraced opportunities to reflect on the relevance of his thought and practice to these fields, mostly through talks before professional associations and on wider platforms like radio addresses given during the Second World War. These talks never aimed at indoctrinating the audience on psychoanalytic concepts and principles, as Winnicott was no systematizer and eschewed any pretense of orthodoxy. Instead, Winnicott reached out collaboratively to his audiences, encountering them as valuable in their own experience and expertise, to offer whatever insight he thought might make them more effective and productive versions of themselves. This is commensurate with his belief in the possibility of a community composed of true selves, capable of holding struggling members of society as they worked through the difficult processes of integration.

At Paddington Green Children's Hospital, where he worked for most of his professional life, Winnicott opened his time to parents of struggling children, providing single assessments that were meant to identify fundamental issues and to enable the healing process to begin. Winnicott's immediate goal was not to influence the thinking of a larger population of parents and children, but rather to bring those families relief from their internal, unseen struggles. A significant component of this praxis, indeed, was the simple encounter with Winnicott himself—the other grounded in a standpoint of creative compassion, representative of a world capable and desirous of holding the wounded subject. It is this Winnicott, the practitioner who built his theory into his methods and work because he simply could not do otherwise when confronted with a world full of hurt, even despite the personal toll of his taxing work, that these authors call forth to hold political theory itself now. It is consistent with Winnicott's legacy, therefore, that the authors gathered into this part share the hope that the use of Winnicott will revitalize not only extant discourses in various corners of political theory, but also (and more importantly) the real subjects considered within those scholarly conversations.

The part commences with David McIvor's masterful essay, "In Transition, but to Where?: Winnicott, Integration, and Democratic Association," which reconsiders the foundations of democratic theory. McIvor contends that Winnicott is useful for understanding both the facilitating democratic environment and the process of democratic integration in ways deeper than have previously been considered. McIvor draws on Winnicott to argue that democratic association requires both antagonism and collaboration if integration is to be achieved, and to warn that models of civic volunteerism risk feeding false selfhood by ignoring the pressing need for integration.

Amy Buzby's "Vanquishing the False Self: Winnicott, Critical Theory and the Restoration of the Spontaneous Gesture" questions how the critical theory of the Frankfurt School can overcome its mobilization problem. Buzby contends that, despite its powerful criticism, critical theory falls short in providing methods that the subject can use to contest alienation as it manifests both inside and out. Winnicott's thought and methods, which are centered in many ways on fostering creativity, spontaneity, and authenticity are called forth to fill this gap.

In the final chapter of the part, "Adults in the Playground: Winnicott and Arendt on Politics and Playfulness," John LeJeune questions both Arendt's formulation of vital citizenship and Winnicott's own tenuous relation to politics. LeJeune offers a way of understanding Winnicott's thinking as deeply political, and politics as a site for the kind of playful and rewarding form of citizenship that can animate democratic associations. Each of these chapters models Winnicott's potential to spark fresh directions and work in political theory. Collectively, they point to the broad and salutary impact his legacy offers to the discipline and the subjects political theorists turn to and return to in their work.

Part IV: Intersubjectivity, Justice, and Equality

The final part of this volume, "Intersubjectivity, Justice, and Equality," applies Winnicott's work to a broad set of sociopolitical concerns—including racism, organizational culture, the welfare state, postcolonialism, and contemporary international relations. While we do not see a bright line between theory and practice, nor a priority of one over the other, it is fair to say that the chapters in this part tackle what might be called "real-world" political, economic, organizational, and cultural phenomena. It is a formidable task: to stretch and extend Winnicott's thought into domains where it has been least often addressed. Nevertheless, these incisive essays clarify relationships and trends, from the local to the global, that threaten to impinge on and pressure subjects, as individuals and as collectivities, to adopt positions akin to the false self. Indeed, although looking through a somewhat wider lens, these chapters identify areas where the pressures to falsity are at their most intense.

Democratic life has always been something of a minefield for the subject, as even in the ideal, one has to be willing to share her views with others who might reject, or even revile, the subject for her thinking. It requires the confidence of the true self—playful, creative, and autonomous—to negotiate citizenship even in the healthiest society (which, in Winnicott's terms, is the one most capable of holding its vulnerable and troubled members). In the real world, societies fall, in varying degrees away, from Winnicott's standards, making citizenship even more challenging. A host of broader, international, and global patterns also complicate the world we inhabit and our relationships to it and to the other subjects who share it. The question thus becomes: How can we support and facilitate the development of healthy subjects (in every sense of the term) in the context of a world that so often fails so many? Each author in this final part works with Winnicott to clarify "real-world" political trends that threaten intersubjective norms, particularly those of justice and equality, in practice. In so doing, each reaches out actively, in the hope of impacting our means of understanding and experiencing sociopolitical life.

Alex Zamalin's powerful chapter, "D.W. Winnicott, Ethics, and Race: Psychoanalytic Thought and Racial Equality in the United States," uses Winnicott's ideas concerning freedom, creativity and environmental holding in tandem with analysis of the historical experiences of the Greensboro Truth and Reconciliation Commission and the Mississippi Truth Project to develop new normative tools for the pursuit of racial justice. By providing Winnicottian strategies toward adding a normative aspect to critical race studies, Zamalin also provides a foundation upon which the damage done by racism to all subjects can be freshly experienced and mediated.

Michael A. Diamond's "Winnicott at Work: Potential Space and the Facilitating Organization" is a thoughtful meditation of the dynamics of organizational life that explicates Winnicott's concepts of transitional objects and potential space in the context of progressive organizational politics. Winnicott's theories of good enough mothering and the holding environment represent, for Diamond, normative foundations for good governance and democratic politics (and micro-politics) rooted in authenticity and agency. From Winnicott's writing we learn of thirdness, the in-between (self and other; subject and object; me and not-me) position; out of which evolve the contemporary psychoanalytic ideas of intersubjectivity and attentiveness to experience. And, from this conceptual turn emerges an ethic and politic for mutual understanding and cooperation.

Gal Gerson's persuasive essay, "Winnicott and the History of Welfare State Thought in Britain," demonstrates that, although it is primarily appreciated for its contribution to the internal development of psychoanalytic theory and practice, Winnicott's work may also be seen in the light of broader political and economic debates within British society. Since the end of the Victorian era, Gerson argues, liberal thinkers searched for theoretical anchors to ground their project of expanding rights from entitlement to life, liberty, and property to social welfare. These expansions required a reformulation of the relationship between individual and society. Winnicott and the other object-relations thinkers, Gerson claims, provided such thinkers with insights about the social determination of individuality at a crucial junction when the institutional foundations of the welfare state were being established, and when alternative explanations of social determination, such as those based on evolutionary biology, seemed to weaken.

The final essay in this collection, Robert Chalwell's "Vulnerability, Dependence, Sovereignty, and Ego-Distortion Theory: Psycho-Analyzing Political Behaviors in the Developing World," employs Winnicott's theories of development and the true self/false self dichotomy to understand the relationship between former mother-countries and former colonies in the developing world. Chalwell theorizes that these former colonies are ensnared in the position of the false self, and suggests that Winnicott's though offers solutions to bring them to a fuller realization of both independence and integration. The Winnicott invoked in these chapters evinces an ability to make contact with and even to hold subjects, as individuals interpellated with organizations, cultures, nations, and global trends. In this sense, the final part of the volume represents a moment in which political theory reaches out actively and constructively to meet the political world we share.

Postscript on the Life and Work of D.W. Winnicott

Readers typically find Winnicott to be a persuasive source of insight about psychological dynamics and developmental processes because his conclusions are drawn from, or are at least readily referred back to, case illustrations and lessons learned in his own clinical practice. This volume, we hope, reflects this shared attention to the abstract and the concrete. It includes chapters psychological, philosophical, and theoretical, but also chapters ethnographic, historical, and political.

It is also fair to say that readers find Winnicott persuasive for his nonchalance, his wit, and his colloquial style. Winnicott advocated the use of plain language, and those who study and comment on his work often strive for the same. We have asked ourselves and all contributing authors to clarify, to the greatest extent possible, the meanings of terms and the thrust of ideas advanced in our essays. This has made for a volume with relatively little jargon and with many novel and pleasantly frank conceptual formulations. As mentioned above, a fair number of Winnicott's best-known ideas were conceived and delivered as lectures or talks: They appear casual, simple, even playful.

And yet there are moments in Winnicott's work when, upon close examination, one finds that things are not so simple after all, that at the center of one or another of his ideas lies a mystery, an obscurity, even an opacity. It is true, of course, that Winnicott relied heavily on the notion of tolerating paradox, and it is possible that he over-relied on this notion when additional clarity could have saved the reader from undue perplexity. In any case, readers must undertake some active and creative work themselves if they wish to make sense of all of Winnicott's thought, and the editors feel it is well to point out that if at first something seems simple within the chapters that follow, it generally becomes less so the more deeply it is considered by both author and reader.

Those who come to this volume with extensive knowledge of Winnicott's work are likely well aware of what has been said so far. For others, however, Winnicott may be new. For any wishing to gain a richer and more detailed understanding of Winnicott, the person and his work, we cannot recommend anyone's work more highly than Jan Abram's (2007, 2013). Barring a thorough review of her work, and keeping in mind that the present volume is not a biography, nor even intellectual biography, we believe it may be helpful to very briefly (re)introduce Winnicott to all.

D.W. Winnicott was born in Plymouth, England in 1896, although he would grow up in Rockville after a move in 1899, the youngest child and only son of a fairly prosperous merchant family. From a young age, Winnicott faced steady pressure from his father, who seems to have been an overbearing presence in his son's life, to someday take over the family business, despite his genuine and early interest in the medical sciences. He also faced protracted personal struggles due to his efforts to gladden his chronically depressed mother (Rodman 2003), which perhaps influenced his later theories on good enough mothering, the holding environment, and the factors that lead children to develop false self formations.

Winnicott's process of becoming Winnicott was not only shaped, of course, by his childhood familial experiences. His education began at the Leys, a boarding school, before he continued on to a course in biology at Jesus College, Cambridge, where he was a popular (if uneven) student.

After a brief foray in the Royal Navy in 1917, Winnicott resumed his education at St. Bartholomew's Hospital Medical College that fall. It was here that his interest in psychoanalysis bloomed, particularly as he began to take and study case histories of his patients and discovered the writings of Sigmund Freud (Rodman 2003, 38–39). Winnicott graduated medical school in 1920, and, already heavily influenced by the psychoanalytic concepts that would shape his thought and work, began to take hospital appointments, most notably at Paddington Green Children's Hospital, where he would work until his retirement in 1963.

He would become a candidate at the British Institute for Psycho-Analysis in 1927 and would develop a complicated relationship with the British Psychoanalytic Association, which was primarily centered on the figure and ideas of Melanie Klein. Winnicott famously disagreed with Klein on a host of issues, most notably in his belief that aggression can play a role in healthy development and in his rejection of her famous conceptualization of the depressive position. As something of a maverick, an analyst who tended to reject orthodoxy, someone willing to revise even the most accepted concepts, and someone rarely afraid to advance his own thought and methods, Winnicott became a noteworthy force in the British Independent Group, often called the "Middle School," of British Psychoanalysis.

Winnicott's personal life, however, continued to interfere with his professional and personal success. In 1923, he entered into a passionless, and potentially unconsummated, marriage with Alice Taylor. It was not until he met and began an affair with his second wife, the social worker and theorist Clare Britton, that Winnicott truly began to flourish in his own right. In the playful and creative space provided by this relationship, Winnicott finally found something like the facilitating care that is often the focus of his work. The Second World War also solidified many of his core ideas, as Winnicott worked to help children and families struggling with the traumas of war and separation caused by the relocation programs started in response to the Blitz. Through his work with displaced children and his radio addresses directed at families trying to navigate nearly impossible circumstances, Winnicott came to understand how difficult the achievement of the true self is, even when environmental and relational factors are good enough. After the war, Winnicott began writing the essays and books that are discussed at length in this volume. These texts include *The Child and the Family, The Family and Individual Development, Playing and Reality,* and *The Piggle: An Account of the Psychoanalytic Treatment of a Little Girl* (another major work, *Deprivation and Delinquency*, was published posthumously).

Winnicott died in 1971, after a productive career and long struggle with poor health. In his unfinished (in fact, barely started) autobiography, Winnicott left behind the prayer, "God, let me be alive when I die!" (Ulanov 2005, 88).

Notes

1. Here, and in chapters throughout this volume, the word "object" may be employed in its psychoanalytic sense, which refers to other persons and to internal representations of persons, groups, and abstractions, including even a "country, liberty, [or] an ideal" (Freud 1957, 243) with which one may relate. While the common use of the term is guided by object-relations theory, the term itself arose out of Freud's terminology of drives and their "objects." For object relations theorists, objects are others, internal representations of others, and even parts of others and of the self. "People react to and interact with not only an actual other but also an internal other, a psychic representation of a person which in itself has the power to influence both the individual's affective states and his overt behavioral reactions" (Greenberg and Mitchell 1983, 10). The history, dynamics, and patterns of an individual's relationships with internal and external objects are, in some sense, the very content of the individual's psychic experience of her inner and outer worlds.
2. There are moments when Winnicott's use of the term "mother" does not seem necessarily sex- or gender-specific. When not speaking about the mother as woman, or as female, or in relation to the breast, or in distinguishing primary maternal preoccupation with the baby, one might suppose that the "mother" could be any parent or primary caregiver, a father, or a nanny, or a relative. At the same time, Winnicott did offer, in several essays, distinctions between the roles of mother and father, man and woman, not only in terms of parenting care and relations to children, but in terms of social and political roles. Furthermore, Winnicott lived in a time and place where "mothers" were not typically abstract, where, more often than not, cis-gendered female birth-parents were "mothers," and bore the primary responsibility of being so. "At the very beginning everyone was dependent on a woman.…This means sensitive initial adaptation on the part of a human being. That human being is woman, and usually mother" (1986, 191). While it is beyond the scope of this volume to address this issue, it would be foolish to err in either direction: foolish to assume that when Winnicott speaks of "mother" he is only speaking about a female parent and

her capacities as a female, and foolish to assume that he is, or we are, free of temptation to imagine a woman, a female, and a mother when called upon to imagine "mother" in the abstract.

3. One is tempted to say here that such fantasies "throw out the baby with the bathwater," in what would be a pregnant phrase in a Winnicottian context. Of course, the phrase, "a pregnant phrase," is also in some sense a pregnant phrase in this context.

References

Abram, J. 2007. *The Language of Winnicott: A Dictionary of Winnicott's Use of Words*. London: Karnac.

———., ed. 2013. Donald Winnicott Today. In *Series: The New Library of Psychoanalysis*, ed. A. Lemma. New York: Routledge.

Agamben, G. 1999. *Potentialities: Collected Essays in Philosophy*. Trans. and Ed. D. Heller-Roazen. Stanford, CA: Stanford University Press.

Alford, C.F. 2002. *Levinas, the Frankfurt School, and Psychoanalysis*. Middletown, CT: Wesleyan University Press.

———. 2005. *Rethinking Freedom: Why Freedom Has Lost Its Meaning and What Can Be Done to Save It*. New York: Palgrave.

———. 2009. *After the Holocaust: The Book of Job, Primo Levi, and the Path to Affliction*. New York: Cambridge University Press.

———. 2013. *Trauma and Forgiveness: Consequences and Community*. New York and Cambridge: Cambridge University Press.

Alighieri, D. 1957. *On World-Government, or, De Monarchia*. Trans. H.W. Schneider. New York: Liberal Arts/Wildside Press.

Arendt, H. 1998. *The Human Condition*. 2nd ed. Chicago and London: University of Chicago Press.

Blackman, L. 2008. *The Body: The Key Concepts*. Electronic ed. Oxford: Berg.

Blake, W. 1982. *The Complete Poetry and Prose of William Blake*. Ed. D.V. Erdman, Newly Rev. ed. Berkeley, CA: University of California Press.

Bowker, M.H. 2014. *Rethinking the Politics of Absurdity: Albert Camus, Postmodernity, and the Survival of Innocence*. New York: Routledge.

———. 2016. *Ideologies of Experience: Trauma, Failure, Deprivation, and the Abandonment of the Self*. New York: Routledge.

Bowker, M.H., and D.P. Levine. 2016. Beyond the Battlefield: 'Moral Injury' and Moral Defense in the Psychic Life of the Soldier, the Military, and the Nation. *Organisational and Social Dynamics* 16(2): 85–109.

Brennan, T. 2004. *The Transmission of Affect*. Ithaca and London: Cornell University Press.

Butler, J. 2004. *Precarious Life: The Powers of Mourning and Violence*. London: Verso.

———. 2015. *Senses of the Subject*. New York: Fordham University Press.

Camus, A. 1968. *Albert Camus: Lyrical and Critical Essays*. Ed. P. Thody, First American ed. New York: Alfred A. Knopf.

Camus, A. 1988. *The Stranger*. Trans. M. Ward, First Vintage International ed. New York: Vintage.

Caruth, C. (ed). 1995. *Trauma: Explorations in Memory*. Baltimore, MD: Johns Hopkins University Press.

Critchley, S. 1996. Prolegomena to any Post-Deconstructive Subjectivity. In *Deconstructive Subjectivities*, ed. S. Critchley, and P. Dews, 13–46. Albany, NY: SUNY Press.

Derrida, J. 1991. 'Eating Well,' or the Calculation of the Subject: An Interview with Jacques Derrida. In *Who Comes After the Subject?* ed. E. Cadava, P. Connor, and J.-L. Nancy, 96–119. New York: Routledge.

Freud, S. 1957. Mourning and Melancholia. In *On the History of the Psychoanalytic Movement, Papers on Metapsychology, and Other Works*, ed. J. Strachey, 243–258. *Standard Edition of the Complete Psychological Works of Sigmund Freud*, 14. London: Hogarth.

Greenberg, J., and S. Mitchell. 1983. *Object Relations in Psychoanalytic Theory*. Cambridge, MA: Harvard University Press.

Guizzoni, U. 1996. Do We Still Want to be Subjects? In *Deconstructive Subjectivities*, ed. S. Critchley, and P. Dews, 201–216. Albany, NY: SUNY Press.

Hassan, I. 1987. *The Postmodern Turn: Essays in Postmodern Theory and Culture*. Columbus, OH: Ohio State University Press.

Honig, B. 2013. The Politics of Public Things: Neoliberalism and the Routine of Privatization. *No Foundations* 10: 59–76. Also available at: Thinking Out Loud Series, Monday, April 15, State Library of NSW, Lecture one available fromBig Ideas, Radio National.

———. 2015. Public Things: Jonathan Lear's Radical Hope, Lars von Trier's Melancholia, and the Democratic Need. *Political Research Quarterly* 68(3): 623–636.

———. 2016. What Kind of Thing Is Land? Hannah Arendt's Object Relations, or The Jewish Unconscious of Arendt's Most 'Greek' Text. *Political Theory* 44(3): 307–336.

Honneth, A. 1995. *The Struggle for Recognition: The Moral Grammar of Social Conflicts*. Cambridge, MA: MIT Press.

Jay, M. 1993. *Force Fields: Between Intellectual History and Cultural Critique*. New York: Routledge.

Kohut, H. 1977. *The Restoration of the Self*. Chicago: University of Chicago Press.

Lacan, J. 1977. *Écrits: A Selection*. Trans. A. Sheridan. London: Tavistock.

———. 1988. *The Seminar of Jacques Lacan: Book I, Freud's Papers on Technique, 1953–54*. Ed. J. Miller and Trans. J. Forrester. Cambridge: Cambridge University Press.

Lacan, J. 1998. *The Seminar of Jacques Lacan: Book XI, The Four Fundamental Concepts of Psychoanalysis.* Ed. J. Miller and Trans. A. Sheridan. New York: W.W. Norton.

Lauro, S., and K. Embry. 2008. A Zombie Manifesto: The Nonhuman Condition in the Era of Advanced Capitalism. *Boundary 2* 35(1): 86–108.

Levinas, E. 1969. *Totality and Infinity: An Essay on Exteriority.* Trans. A. Lingis. Pittsburg, CA: Duquesne U. Press.

Lyotard, J.-F. 1984. *The Postmodern Condition: A Report on Knowledge.* Trans. G. Bennington and B. Massumi. Minneapolis, MN: University of Minnesota Press.

Melville, H. 2004. Bartleby, the Scrivener. In *The Great Short Works of Herman Melville*, Perennial Classics ed., 39–74. New York: Harper Collins.

Nietzsche, F. 1956. *The Birth of Tragedy and the Genealogy of Morals.* Trans. F. Golffing. New York: Doubleday.

Rodman, F. Robert. 2003. *Winnicott: Life and Work.* Cambridge: Da Capo Press.

Rosenthal, I. 2016. Aggression and Play in the Face of Adversity: A Psychoanalytic Reading of Democratic Resilience. *Political Theory* 44(3): 337–362.

Sartre, J.-P. 1960. *Critique of Dialectical Reason*, vol. II. Trans. Q. Hoare. London: Verso.

Shay, J. 1995. *Achilles in Vietnam: Combat Trauma and the Undoing of Character.* New York: Simon and Schuster.

Shengold, L. 1989. *Soul Murder: The Effects of Childhood Abuse and Deprivation.* New York: Random House.

———. 1999. *Soul Murder Revisited: Thoughts About Therapy, Hate, Love, and Memory.* New Haven and London: Yale University Press.

Ulanov, A.B. 2005. *Finding Space: Winnicott, God, and Psychic Reality.* Westminster: John Knox Press.

Winnicott, D.W. 1965. *The Maturational Processes and the Facilitating Environment: Studies in the Theory of Emotional Development.* Ed. M. Khan. London: Hogarth and the Institute of Psycho-Analysis.

———. 1971. *Playing and Reality.* London: Routledge.

Winnicott, D.W. 1984. *Deprivation and Delinquency.* Eds. C. Winnicott, R. Shepherd, and M. Davis. London and New York: Routledge.

Winnicott, D. W. 1986. *Home Is Where We Start From: Essays by a Psychoanalyst.* Eds. C. Winnicott, R. Shepard, and M. Davis. New York: W.W. Norton.

Yancy, G. 2015. Dear White America. *New York Times*, December 24. http://opinionator.blogs.nytimes.com/2015/12/24/dear-white-america/?_r=0. Accessed 1 January 2016.

Zuss, M. 1998. On the Futures of the Subject. Twentieth World Congress of Philosophy, Paideia Archive. http://www.bu.edu/wcp/Papers/PPer/PPerZuss.htm. Accessed 1 January 2016. See also: Zuss, M. 1999. Subject Present: Life-Writings and Strategies of Representation. *Counterpoints*78: 181–205.

PART I

The Subject's Creation: Aggression, Isolation, and Destruction

CHAPTER 2

Being and Encountering: Movement and Aggression in Winnicott

Jeremy Elkins

Winnicott's Question

In recent years, D.W. Winnicott has become a figure of interest to political theorists. In drawing on his work, a common strategy of political theorists has been to take up one (or more) of his particular ideas, generally one that comes packaged in a noted and notable phrase—the transitional object, the holding environment, and so on—and "apply" it to the political realm. This kind of venture (which has become a *modus operandi* within political theory) is one of appropriation and translation, and is motivated by the admirable desire to expand the resources of political thought. It can have its rewards. It can also at times feel too much like a trip back from the flea market. A charming table lamp in hand and the hope that it might spruce up the existing furniture, the risk is that even if it fits, it comes in too late to do more than add touches on a design mostly already set. If more than that is to be gotten from the trip and the transplant, there will need to be an account of why and how an idea developed elsewhere is applicable to politics, and this will almost of necessity require not merely an application, but an extension, of the theory, one that is attentive to the particularly political character of the problem.[1] Yet for those whose motivation for

J. Elkins (✉)
Dalton Hall, Bryn Mawr College, Bryn Mawr, PA, USA

M.H. Bowker, A. Buzby (eds.), *D.W. Winnicott and Political Theory*,
DOI 10.1057/978-1-137-57533-3_2

rummaging through new bins was just the hope of finding those answers to political questions, this may seem to demand just what the exercise was supposed to have accomplished.

I will pursue a different path here. I believe that Winnicott does offer us important resources for political thought, but that these need to come in much earlier to our thinking about the problems of politics. In this paper, I want to take up one central idea, or complex of ideas, in Winnicott's thought, though one that I believe is intricately connected with most or all of the other central components of his work. This idea is one that has been, I think, too much neglected in the secondary work on Winnicott, and I shall claim both that it deserves more attention within the psychoanalytic literature and that it ought to be of special concern for political theorists. The *reason* that it has not received more attention is that unfortunately Winnicott himself did not thematize it. And so it does not have the packaging of some of his other ideas. Indeed, it will require some work to make clear just what the idea is. My task here, then, is twofold. First, I shall need to describe the idea. Second, I shall need to show why those who are particularly concerned with political thought have reason to take it up.

The complex of ideas that I will be examining here revolves around aggression, and more specifically around what Winnicott would come to call "motility." For Winnicott, motility and the forms of aggression with which it is associated are central to the constitution of the self, and central to the relationship between individual minds and the external world. As with most psychoanalytic thinkers, Winnicott's focus was on individual health. Yet for Winnicott the question of motility was central to the project of understanding what it means to live an authentic life in relation to others. In this respect, motility was, for Winnicott, fundamentally a social matter.

I shall not aim to work out in a detailed way the implications of Winnicott's thinking in this area for political and social thought. In declining to do so, I am happy to claim as an excuse the limited space available here. But in truth this is only part of the reason. What I want to show is the direction in which Winnicott's thinking in this area might take us, and my view is that his contribution is indeed by way of a direction rather than a program. What Winnicott offers us is a way of thinking about human beings that resets the question of how to understand the very terms of a good social order.

In one of his later writings, Winnicott remarked that psychoanalytic thought has tended to focus so centrally on neuroses and the defenses connected with them that "we seldom reach the point at which we can start to describe what life is like apart from illness or absence of illness"

(1971b, 98). The aspects of human development and of the constitution of the individual with which I will be concerned were at the core of Winnicott's attempt to remedy this neglect: his lifelong project "to tackle," from a psychoanalytic perspective, the "question of what life itself is about" (98). In the long history of that field that has come to be designated "political theory," this question certainly has not been neglected. And yet within contemporary political theory it seems (to me) that it has largely fallen away as a central concern. Winnicott's work can return us to that question. My aim is to show how it does so, the special contribution it makes toward it, and the implication of those ideas for the fundamentally political question of the organization of social life.

In what follows, I describe what I take to be Winnicott's profound insight about the centrality of movement or motility in the development of the psyche–soma, its relation to aggression, and the significance of all of this for the constitution of the self and to what Winnicott sometimes calls *being*. *Being*, in Winnicott's use of the term, is not an ontological fact, but a possibility; or more precisely, it is (generally) a fact at the beginning of life, and a possibility in respect of its continuation. This can be a matter of degree. The question of being is, for Winnicott, linked with the question of what it is to live in a vital way, and that in turn with the question of "what life itself is about."

I shall present Winnicott's basic thinking about these matters; focusing first on his early formulation of the role of movement in the organization of the self, and then on what he came to see as the special significance of aggression in relation to (what he would now call) the motility impulse, an impulse that appears even before birth, when psyche and soma are hardly distinguished and when the emphasis is on the experience of physical movement. I then turn to what I shall refer to as "psychic motility," or the motility impulse when it is no longer directly tied to physical movement. For Winnicott, psychic motility (as I am calling it) plays a special role in creativity, and here I focus on Winnicott's concern with the psychic conditions for creative living. Finally, I suggest some of the political and social directions in which these ideas can take us.

Movement and Being

Winnicott's ideas about motility and aggression are developed in a number of papers. To my mind, one of the most important of these, and one to which I shall give special attention, is "Aggression in Relation to Emotional Development," a compilation of three talks that Winnicott delivered between the years 1950 and 1955. In the introduction to the first of these talks, Winnicott signals his own sense of the political-social significance of the phenomenon he is working to understand: “The main idea behind this study of aggression is that if society is in danger, it is not because of man’s aggressiveness but because of the repression of personal aggressiveness in individuals” (1950–1955, 204). In his typical fashion, Winnicott will never, in the course of that talk or the rest of the consolidated paper, fully return to take up this suggestion, and will only barely hint at the social implications of the ideas he describes. Nonetheless, Winnicott clearly believed that the three papers that he brought together for publication were working on the same path, and he believed—rightly, I think—that their social implications were potentially profound.

The significance of “Aggression in Relation to Emotional Development” (and other papers of Winnicott’s that follow some of the same threads) is that in it Winnicott is attempting a quite radical shift in the psychoanalytic understanding of human beings. On the one hand, Winnicott accepted the basic tenets of the classical model of the drives, or at least those drives for which that model had been worked out—the sexual drive being perhaps the prototype. In that model, drives are characterized by pressure and by the general aim of satisfaction through release of tension; they are distinguished by the particular source in the body where the pressure is experienced (the mouth, the anus, the genitals, etc.) and the particular aim and object through which satisfaction is sought. These are the drives that Winnicott is referring to when he describes primitive “erotic experience” as that which “can be completed by anything that brings relief to the erotic instinctual drive, and that allows of forepleasure, rising tension of general and local excitement, climax and detumescence or its equivalent, followed by a period of lack of desire” (1950–1955, 215).

Winnicott, however, had long thought that there was a different kind of primitive force, one that had found no place in this conception of drives. The primary significance of this other force is not that it worked in *opposition* to the erotic drives (as is the case with Freud’s early postulate of “ego-instincts” in relation to the sexual drives, or his later hypothesis of the death drive in opposition to Eros), but in its constitutive role in the development of that very self “which id-demands will be felt as part *of*” (1960, 141, *emphasis added*). This other force or impulse also has an erotic quality, but it is an “erotism … of a different order from that of the instinctual erotism associated with specific erotogenic zones” (1950–1955, 215). It is felt more generally in the muscles, it is not experienced as a local pressure, and it does not seek release or reduction of pressure in the way of the classical drives. It has "no climax ... [and] this distinguishes [it] from phenomena that have instinctual backing" (1971b, 98). Yet, it is a force that Winnicott insisted was absolutely central to early development, and central to the character of the self that it inaugurates.

Winnicott struggled somewhat in naming this other force. At times he referred to it in the language of aggression or "primary aggression." There was good reason for this, for it is connected with aggression in several respects: in being active, in the character of the pleasure that it seeks, and also in being at the root (or at least a primary root) of that more determinate impulse to which the term "aggression" is usually applied. But Winnicott believed that "aggression" in that more usual sense of the term—what is associated, for example, with anger and hate—was a later and complex development and only one outgrowth of this yet more basic and primitive impulse. Because of that, the use of the term "aggression" to describe the latter was bound to muddy the waters. So again for good reason, in 1955 Winnicott began to use instead the term "motility."[2]

What is this force that Winnicott found wanting in the existing theory, that is connected to the growth of aggression in these various respects, and that Winnicott came to associate with motility? For Winnicott it is, as I have said, a force no less basic than that which underlies the classical drives:

> Our task is to examine the pre-history of the aggressive element ... in the earliest id experience. We have at hand certain elements which date from at least as early as the onset of foetal movements—namely motility .... To get to something in terms of aggression corresponding to the erotic potential it would be necessary to go back to the[se] impulses of the foetus, to that which makes for movement rather than for stillness, to the aliveness of tissues and to the first evidence of muscular erotism. We need a term here such as life force. (1950–1955, 211–216)

Motility, as Winnicott typically would come to use the term, refers to the movement of a person in and through space and time. Roughly, we can understand it as movement that is attributable not merely to this or that component system within an organism, but to the organism itself. It arises from what Winnicott calls personal impulse, and it is at origin "almost synonymous with activity." In its earliest state, it is not anything as sophisticated as intentional: "A baby kicks in the womb [though] it cannot be assumed that he is trying to kick his way out. A baby of a few weeks thrashes away with his arms [though] it cannot be assumed that he means to hit. A baby chews the nipple with his gums [though] it cannot be assumed that he is meaning to destroy or to hurt" (1950–1955, 204). Motility begins "[p]rior to integration of the personality" (1950-1955, 204) and the integration of the personality goes hand-in-hand with the development and growing sophistication of motility.

Motility encompasses not merely the physical aspect of movement, but the psychic as well. Indeed, early on, "the body and the psyche develop together, at first fused," "not to be distinguished except according to the direction from which one is looking." Only "gradually [do they] becom[e] distinguishable the one from the other" (1949a, 191, 1949b, 244). At the core of motility is the somatic–psychic sense of "a personal going-along, a continuity of experiencing." This "personal continuity of existence" is "the beginnings of the self" (1949a, 191, 1971b, 97).

These ideas about the self and its relation to movement are central to Winnicott's thought. They underlie all of those more well-known Winnicottian concepts of the facilitating environment, the good-enough mother, the transitional object, and the true self. The significance of these ideas about motility will, however, be missed if they are reduced to the thought that motility is merely something that the infant *has*. That traditional way of thinking of motility is reflected, for instance, in Freud's formulation that among the "principal characteristics of the ego" (1938, 145) is that it "has voluntary movement at its command," that it "controls the approaches to motility" (1933, 75).

Winnicott's profound and striking thought is rather that the early self *is* this experience of "personal impulse," of "continuity of being," of a "personal going along." This movement—we may call it "free movement" (my term) or primitive motility (Winnicott's term)—is movement that is uninhibited, nondefensive, and that originates "in the centre" (1950–1955, 211) or core (see, e.g., 1950–1955, 211–214, 1959, 1963b, 184). The experience of this movement is the opposite of that which comes in on the infant from the outside, or what Winnicott calls "impingement." Free movement or motility is the infant's very "ownness" or *being*, and impingement, or the reaction to impingement, nothing less than an interruption of being. As Winnicott writes: "Let us assume that health in the early development of the individual entails continuity of being. The early psyche-soma proceeds along a certain line of development provided its continuity of being is not disturbed" (1949b, 245).

> This state of being belongs to the infant and not to the observer .... If one takes the analogy of a bubble, one can say that if the pressure outside is adapted to the pressure inside, then the bubble has a *continuity of existence* and if it were a human baby this would be called "being." If on the other hand the pressure outside the bubble is greater or less than the pressure inside, then the bubble is engaged in a *reaction to impingement.* It changes in reaction to the environmental change, not from personal impulsive experience. In terms of the human animal this means that there is an interruption of being, and the place of being is taken by reaction to impingement. The impingement over, the reacting is no longer a fact, and there then is a return to being. This seems to me to be a statement which not only can take us back to intra-uterine life without demanding a stretch of imagination but which can also be brought forward and applied usefully as an extreme simplification of very complex phenomena belonging to later life at any age. (1988, 127)

The "healthy development of the early psyche-soma" requires an environment that facilitates this sense of "on going being," allowing "the infant to experience spontaneous movement," protecting it against impingements that press against the infant's free movement through space and time and overwhelm the infant's own activity (1949b, 245, 1956, 303). As part of this, it is important that the caretaker not "introduce complications beyond those which the infant can understand and allow for," but rather try "to insulate [the] baby from coincidences and from other phenomena that must be beyond the infant's ability to comprehend." Slowly and over time, the "good-enough mother" (or other caretaker) allows for "the graduated failure of adaptation"—"negative care or an alive neglect"—"according to the growing ability of the individual infant to allow for [this] by mental activity" (1949b, 245). Through the infant's increasing capacity for understanding, "disruptions," including absences and the failure of immediate satisfaction, can be assimilated into (rather than disrupting) the infant's continuity of being. "Thus there appears in the infant a tolerance in respect of both ego need and instinctual tension" (1949b, 245–246). The "good (psychological) environment is" at first "a physical one, with the child in the womb or being held and generally tended." In "the course of time," with psyche and soma "gradually becoming distinguishable," and "involved in a process of mutual interrelation," the "experience of continuity" will gradually take on a more distinctly psychic character, still tied to the body, but less directly bound up with physical movement. As this occurs, "the environment develop[s] a new characteristic which necessitates a new descriptive term, such as emotional or psychological or social" (1949a, 191, 1949b, 244–245). But the primary function remains the same: to protect the free or spontaneous movement of the child from overwhelming impingements.

In the contrary case, the failures of adaption are too early, before the infant is capable of accommodating them. In this case, the environment is too "unpredictable since it has nothing to do with the life process of the individual," and it can only be experienced as an "impingement to which the psyche-soma (i.e., the infant) must react. This reacting disturbs the continuity of the going-on-being of the new individual" (1949b, 245, 1988, 128).

The Aggression of Being

The key ideas that I have just discussed—that the emergence of a self is bound up with the experience of psychic–somatic movement, that the character of the self thus arises in part from the character and quality of that movement (whether it is free or defensive), and that free movement, while it is natural, requires a supportive environment—are basic to Winnicott's thought. They pre-date "Aggression in Relation to Emotional Development," and they will remain central to his understanding of motility.

Beginning in the 1950s, however, along with the introduction of the term motility to describe what he had been discussing in other language, there was an important conceptual shift in Winnicott's thinking. This shift did not consist in a rejection of the earlier strand of thought, but in a crucial modification of it in respect to the importance of the environment. In the earlier accounts, Winnicott typically treated the environment as a background condition for the development of the infant's continuity of being, silently and inconspicuously adapting, in the optimal case, to the needs of the infant. What this account neglected, however, was the vital importance for the infant's development of the quality of the encounter *with* the environment. In the earlier line of thought, that is, the inclination was to think of *opposition* in relation to the environment primarily in terms of danger: the danger *from* the environment encroaching on the infant's own movement; the danger of impingement. What Winnicott came to see, however, was that if there is this experience of opposition which is a threat to health, there is a different kind of experience of opposition that is *constitutive* of health; that what matters is not *whether* there is opposition between the infant and the environment, but the *direction* of it. This insight would fundamentally alter both Winnicott's understanding of motility, and his understanding of aggression.

This crucial shift appears first in "Aggression in Relation to Emotional Development," although its presentation there gives all the indications of a thought still *in statu nascendi*. I have already quoted Winnicott's statement from that paper that "[t]o get to something in terms of aggression corresponding to the erotic potential it would be necessary to go back to the impulses of the foetus, to that which makes for movement rather than for stillness ... [for which we] need a term here such as life force." Immediately thereafter, Winnicott goes on to describe "the fate of the life force of the (prenatal) infant." In doing so, he once again characterizes "ill-health at this early stage" as the condition in which "it is the environment that impinges" such that "the life force is taken up in reactions to impingement" and there is no "early firm establishment of the Me":

> In the extreme there is very little experience of impulses except as reactions, and the Me is not established. Instead we find a development based on the experience of reaction to impingement, and there comes into existence an individual that we call false because the personal impulsiveness is missing.

But when Winnicott turns to the case of "health," he insists now that what matters is not only the absence of overwhelming impingement, but that

> the foetal impulses bring about a discovery of environment, this latter being *the opposition that is met through movement, and sensed during movement*. The result here is an early recognition of a Not-Me world, and an early establishment of the Me. (It will be understood that in practice these things develop gradually, and repeatedly come and go, and are achieved and lost). (1950–1955, 216–217, *emphasis added*)

This first active encounter with an environment is perhaps accidental. But very soon it comes to be part of the essential pleasure of movement. The erotism of movement, that is, has, or very early on comes to have, an aggressive quality. As Winnicott puts it in a later paper,

> [i]f we look and try to see the start of aggression in an individual what we meet is the fact of infantile movement. This starts even before birth, not only in the twistings of the unborn baby, but also in the more sudden movement of limbs that make the mother say she is feeling a quickening .... A part of the infant moves and by moving meets something .... [I]n every infant there is this tendency to move and to get some kind of muscle pleasure in movement, and to gain from the experience of moving and meeting something. (1964b, 233–234)

In fact, the motility impulse cannot "give any satisfactory experience *unless* there is opposition. The opposition must come from the environment, from the Not-Me which gradually comes to be distinguished from the Me" (1950–1955, 215, *emphasis added*). "The impulsive gesture reaches out and becomes aggressive when opposition is reached," writes Winnicott (1950–1955, 217).

But this is not to be understood according to the ordinary theory that "aggression is a reaction to frustration." In the usual account, aggression arises because there is

> frustration during erotic experience, during a phase of excitement with instinctual tension rising. That there is anger at frustration in such phases is only too obvious, but in our theory of the earliest feelings and states we need to be prepared for aggression that precedes the ego integration that makes anger at instinctual frustration possible, and that makes the erotic experience an experience. (1950–1955, 216)

The aggression that is felt when opposition is met is not born of frustration, but precedes it. It is aggression that is not from a failure to relieve instinctual tension, but that is pleasurable in itself: the pleasure in meeting an outside. "[T]he phenomena that I am describing have no climax. This distinguishes them from phenomena that have instinctual backing, where the orgiastic element plays an essential part, and where satisfactions are closely linked with climax. But these phenomena that have reality in the area whose existence I am postulating belong to the experience of relating to objects" (1971b, 98). (The term "object" here and throughout is used in the psychoanalytic sense—not in distinction from persons, who are central in "object relations" but, as in the grammatical case, in contrast to a subject.) Winnicott will emphasize that this aggressive experience is essential to the feeling of *real.* "There is reality in this experience" and while "it very easily fuses into the erotic experiences that await the new-born infant," "it is this impulsiveness, and the aggression that develops out of it, that makes the infant need an external object, and not merely a satisfying object." The impulsiveness that is motility, in other words, "*needs to find opposition* … it needs something to push against, unless it is to remain unexperienced and a threat to well-being" (1950–1955, 212, 217, *emphasis in original*).

What Winnicott, in other words, came to see is that from the beginning, or very nearly so, motility is bound up with aggression. This is true in more than one sense. There is, first, the idea, rather common by now, that "at origin, aggressiveness is almost synonymous with activity" (1950–1955, 204). But Winnicott's account points to a second sense as well in which motility can be said to be bound up with aggression, one that is less familiar and perhaps more extraordinary in its implications: that not only is aggression at origin activity, but that activity is, almost from its origin, aggressive; that the basic motility impulse needs (or very early on comes to need) a world to press against; that at a fundamental level, there is a need for, and pleasure in, opposition; and that this need for, and pleasure in, opposition, is not born of hatred and hostility, but is prior to them. Free movement, on this understanding, then, *is not movement that is unencumbered, but movement that is free (uninhibited) to discover the resistance of the world and to press against it.* In healthy development, "opposition" is central, but in this case the opposition is not encroachment from the environment (impingement), but rather the existence of an environment itself, that which is encountered, met up against, that which we as observers would call (and what the infant will come in time to experience as) an outside, that which resists and that can therefore be pushed against.

To appreciate the significance of this idea it is once again necessary to understand that, as in the earlier strand of his thinking about motility, Winnicott is not describing simply a pleasure *for* the self, but what is central to the constitution *of the self*. Developmentally, it is only *through* the experience of opposition, *through* the pleasure of meeting and pressing against the world that the "Me" comes to be distinguished from the "Not-Me." And the character of the self that emerges is a function of the *quality* of this early aggressive movement. There are, of course, other influences as well. But so central is the importance of the infant's own "impulses [that] bring about a discovery of environment," so significant is the feeling of "position that is met through movement," so crucial is the growth of aggression that has its "root in personal impulse, motivated in ego spontaneity" (1950–1955, 216–217), that Winnicott will characterize the authentic or "true self" just in terms of this kind of movement and will insist that only through this movement does the individual in the robust sense of the term start to exist at all. "Here [when things go well] each experience … emphasizes the fact that it is in the centre that the new individual is developing, and contact with environment is an experience of the individual." By contrast, "where impingement is too overwhelming, the result is a failure … to evolve an individual" and what predominates is a "false self": "instead of a series of individual experiences there is a series of reactions to impingement" and "[m]otility is then only experienced as a reaction to impingement" (1950–1955, 211–212). Put more succinctly if somewhat crudely, the early "me," or "me-ness,"[3] *is* aggressive, free motility: motility pressing against a world.

What is at stake in this early movement is not merely the emergence of the self, but the *quality* of the self that emerges. Will it be along the lines of "personal impulse, motivated in ego spontaneity" (1950–1955, 217), with an emphasis on the pleasures of probing, pressing, discovering? Will the "individual … enjoy going around looking for appropriate opposition" (1950–1955, 212)? Will encounters with "objects that get in the way" (1970b, 42) "feel like a part of life and real" (1988, 128) and bring about a feeling of being alive? Or will the self instead be organized "on the pattern of reacting to stimuli," "dependent on the experience of opposition" from without, or even "persecution" (1950–1955, 217), "reactive-doing" (1970b, 39)? Will the individual experience the world as demanding compliance, and the resistance of objects that "get in the way" as "detract[ing] from the sense of real living, which is only regained by return to isolation in quiet" (1988, 128)?

"In health," the self develops around and through the experience of aggression in relation to the environment, the experience of pushing up against the environment, of moving up against a world. This movement requires a world that can both resist and yield, a world that allows itself not only to be found, but to be pressed into, that is both solid enough and soft enough to hold and receive the infant's strivings. The Me *becomes* through pushing itself against an available world. The meaning of the opening provocation now becomes clear: "The main idea behind this study of aggression is that if society is in danger, it is not because of man's aggressiveness but because of the repression of personal aggressiveness in individuals."

Psychic Motility and Creativity

The early motility impulse—that "life force" "which makes for movement" and which brings with it a "sense of real" (1950–1955, 213)—is at first (beginning *in utero*) tied rather directly to physical movement and to the psychic aspect of the experience of that movement. Gradually, however, the psyche—though still, naturally, tied to the body—becomes distinguishable from physical movement; and with this, motility takes on as well a more distinctly psychic character. Winnicott only rarely uses the *term* motility in discussing this course of development (such as, e.g.,

1950–1955, 212); he tends rather more toward the language of aggression and personal impulse. But however it is named, this development is an outgrowth of the same basic impulse: that which comes "from the centre," is directed outward, and finds pleasure in discovering and moving up against an environment or a world. As with physical movement, this more distinctly "psychic motility" (as we may call it) is perhaps best described as a *reach*, an impulse toward a world that can be met and that can receive it. For the infant, for whom the delineation between a Me and Not-Me world is very much at issue, and for whom there is no sharp distinction between what is made and what is found, this reach, if it is genuinely along the lines of personal impulse and on the infant's own terms (as Winnicott insists it must be in health) is necessarily a creative one. It is the "gesture of a baby who reaches out for the mother's mouth and feels her teeth, and at the same time looks into her eyes, seeing her creatively" (1971b, 106). Through this creative gesture the infant "produces" the early objects that it finds. Winnicott offers this account from the perspective, as he imagines it, of the very young infant:

> Imagine a baby .... Hunger turns up, and the baby is ready to conceive of something; out of need the baby is ready to create a source of satisfaction, but there is no previous experience to show the baby what there is to expect. If at this moment the mother places her breast where the baby is ready to expect something, and if plenty of time is allowed for the infant to feel round, with mouth and hands, and perhaps with a sense of smell, the baby "creates" just what is there to be found .... The mother allows the infant to dominate ... [and] by fitting in with the infant's impulse ... the baby eventually gets the illusion that this real breast is exactly the thing that was created out of need, greed, and the first impulses of primitive loving. Sight, smell, and taste register somewhere, and ... gradually ... the baby uses perceived detail in the creation of the object expected. (1948, 163, 1964a, 90)[4]

Let us look at what this involves. We have a baby with a need. There is physical movement: "the infant ... feel[ing] round, with mouth and hands." But the action is not merely of physical movement. The impulsive gesture, which at first takes wholly the form of physical movement, now involves also a more distinctly psychic reach, "a gesture that [arises] out of need, the result of an idea that [rides] in on the crest of a wave of instinctual tension," a gesture that involves a creation of "nipple and ... milk," and everything else that is entailed by our use of the term "breast" (1988, 110). "The creative potential of the individual arising out of need produces readiness for an [*sic*] hallucination" (1952, 223). So there is the physical reach—for the actual breast that we as observers know has been presented; but there is also, from the perspective of the baby, a creative movement, a psychic reach: from the *here* of immediacy of need to the *there* of an other—what we call "breast for simplification of description" (1948, 163)—that can satisfy it. The primitive spontaneity of the physical gesture is now elaborated as a creative psychic gesture, one that is capable of producing a breast out of need. "A thousand times before weaning" this will be repeated, and when this goes well the happy "result [is] that … there [develops] a live relationship between inner reality and external reality, between innate primary creativity and the world at large which is shared by all" (1964a, 90).

Earlier, I noted Winnicott's key insight concerning the aggressive character of primitive motility: the pleasure of discovering an environment and pressing against it. At the "early stage," writes Winnicott, "when the Me and the Not-Me are being established, it is the aggressive component that more surely drives the individual to a need for a Not-Me or an object that is felt to be external," a need for "an external object and not merely a satisfying object" (1950–1955, 215), a "need[] to find opposition," for "something to push against." It is this same aggressive impulse that is at the core of the creative gesture that "produces" a breast. What is imaginatively produced (or we might just as well say, imaginatively found) in the creative reach is an otherness; not merely the idea of relief of instinctual tension, but an object that can be found in being made, that can receive the infant's pressure and its pressing need. This is a movement of personal impulse, a direct descendant of physical motility, still unmistakably bound to it, yet also distinguishable from it. Just as the aggressiveness of physical motility finds pleasure in a world that physically resists and that can be pressed against—the experience of physical body moving against physical body—the aggressiveness of this more distinctly psychic motility takes the form of an imaginative reaching that produces a world of objects, a first Not-Me that can be an object *for* me, a world of objects that can get "in the way [so that] there can be a relationship" (1970b, 41).

In the proper environment, this initial contact with exteriority originates from within. It requires "the infant's ability to use illusion," for only through illusion is "contact … possible between the psyche and the environment" in accordance with the infant's own movement and "without loss of sense of self" (1952, 222–223). Yet, there is an obvious difficulty here. For the motility impulse finds its satisfaction in the push against an external world, and if there is to be a genuine and creative relationship with the world, a baby cannot continue "feeding on the self," but must rather learn to "feed[ ] from an other-than-me source" (1971d, 89). Under good enough conditions, then, the early "capacity for illusion"—that the world has been produced from one's own need—can and must permit "gradual disillusioning" (1948, 163). But there must be a sequence here, else the discovery of the world as a fact comes in as itself an imposition, and the relationship to the world that grows up is one of compliance. It is the early experience of imaginative extension, of pressing toward a world that can meet the pressure, of producing a world that can be found, that "lay[s] down the foundation" for the capacity, crucial for vital living, to "reach to the world creatively" (1968a, 25), for the "retention throughout life of something that belongs properly to infant experience: the ability to create the world" even though at the same time we know that we can "only create what we find" (1970b, 39–40, 53).

For Winnicott, creative living is at the heart of the answer to the question "what life itself is about." And yet "creative living involves, in every detail of its experience, a philosophical dilemma" (1970b, 53) for just the reasons we have noted. On the one hand, being "alive," fully "exist[ing] and hav[ing] a feeling of existing," "impulse-doing over reactive-doing" (1970b, 39), entails the experience of extension of oneself outward, continually creating a world.

> It is creative apperception more than anything else that makes the individual feel that life is worth living. Contrasted with this is a relationship to external reality which is one of compliance, the world and its details being recognized but only as something to be fitted in with or demanding adaptation. Compliance carries with it a sense of futility for the individual and is associated with the idea that nothing matters and that life is not worth living. (1971a, 65)

And yet the motility impulse "need[s] an external object"; it can find its satisfaction only in a world of "actual presence … and survival" (1950–1955, 218). To find satisfaction in pressing against the world requires a world that is not merely in our mind and of our making. "[W]e cannot be creative into the blue unless we are having a solo experience in a mental hospital or in the asylum of our own autism" (1970b, 53). The "true self," the vital self, originates in the center, in personal impulse, in the creative gesture that necessarily entails a projection. And yet it can find satisfaction only when opposition is reached; for only then is there "the sense of reality or of existing" (1950–1955, 213).

Aggression and Destruction

Let us summarize where we have come thus far. I began by describing Winnicott's thought that in addition to the classical drives there is another "life force," one that is at the very origin of the self, that consists in what I have called free movement or motility, and that requires a proper environment for its protection ("continuity of being") against interruptions or impingements. I then described a second stage in Winnicott's thinking, in which he came to see that this movement could not be treated in isolation from the world, but entailed the aggressive pleasure of pressing up or pushing against a world. In the early stages, this aggressive motility is primarily physical, but as psyche and soma come to be distinguished, it takes on as well a more distinctly psychic form, one that is at the core of the capacity for a creative relationship to the world. In describing this, I have noted the tension inherent in the very idea of a kind of movement that to be free must originate from within and yet which finds its pleasure only in relation to an external world.

For Winnicott, this tension posed a special problem, one that he would struggle with for the remainder of his life. The problem was not the *fact* of a tension, the existence of a "philosophical dilemma." That there is *a* tension is a necessary correlate—indeed, a condition—of our living creatively in the world, and the tension itself can be creative. The special problem was rather in the *terms* in which the tension appeared—or, more precisely, the terms in which it might variously appear for particular individuals. For Winnicott, as we have seen, though the motility impulse itself is inborn, the character that the impulse takes for any particular individual depends on the conditions of its development. Winnicott began, then, to wonder whether the same is not true as well for the experience of the *tension between projection and exteriority*; whether, that is, the tension inherent in the idea of a creative engagement with a world of external objects also has an individual history that is variable.

A moment ago, I quoted Winnicott on the necessity for "gradual disillusionment." But on what terms does this disillusionment occur? It is common to describe the infant's encounter with the reality of the world in terms of frustration and the aggression to which it gives rise. That there is, indeed, "anger at frustration in such phases" can hardly be denied: "The Reality Principle," as Winnicott puts it succinctly enough, "is an insult" (1986, 40). But if external reality brings with it frustration, it can also bring pleasures. Must we, then, conclude that the very satisfaction at which the motility impulse aims—of "moving and meeting something," of pushing up against an otherness, and so on—depends on an experience of externality that grows just out of frustration? Does the very encounter that the motility impulse seeks develop only as an experience of insult? Must the recognition of externality come about wholly as an experience of imposition, an impingement of personal impulse? Or might it rather be the case that the recognition of externality, though it involves frustration and while in some less fortunate cases involves primarily the experience of imposition, can, in healthy development, come about in part *through* the infant's own impulse, as something that the infant does, and not merely something that is done to it?

Winnicott came to believe that the latter was indeed so. But he saw that to understand how it could be so required a revision to his account of early aggression. Winnicott had long believed that the aggression that was part of motility was "originally a part of appetite, or of some other form of instinctual love" (1939, 88), that which appears, for instance, in the aggression of the baby pressing itself against the breast, an aggression that is perhaps best captured, he suggested, by the word *greed* or *eagerness* (1939, 88, 1968b, 240). It is this form of aggression that manifests in the *pressing* quality of the motility impulse, in the physical pleasure of "moving and meeting something." And it is this form of aggression that, through the experience of pressing into another object, gives rise to an incipient experience of a Not-Me. Even *in utero*, "the foetal impulses bring about a discovery of environment … being the opposition that is met through movement," and with it "an early recognition of a Not-Me world, and an early, and precarious, establishment of the Me" (1950–1955, 216).[5] Winnicott never abandoned this view. But what he came to see is that if this aspect of aggression well described the early pleasures of physical movement, it was inadequate, taken alone, as an account of the complex pleasure of psychic motility in creatively encountering an external world. In the more distinctly psychic context, the natural tendency of appetitive aggression would be to close in on the world, to press into it and to encounter it as primarily a bundle of one's own projections. If the pleasure of motility consisted in its relation to an *external* world, a world with "its own autonomy and life" (1971d, 90), with which there could be a live relationship, there had to be, in addition to and alongside appetitive aggression, a force for separation.[6]

Winnicott's extraordinary 1969 paper, "The Use of an Object," is concerned with just this other force.[7] The subject of that paper is what

Winnicott will now call "the most difficult thing, perhaps, in human development": the capacity for "the subject's placing of the object outside the area of the subject's omnipotent control, that is, the subject's perception of the object as an external phenomenon ... [a] recognition of it as an entity in its own right," and not merely "as a projective entity" (1971d, 89). The development and exercise of that capacity requires a different form of aggression, and in "The Use of an Object," Winnicott refers to this form of aggression as *destruction*.[8] Whereas "in orthodox theory, the assumption is ... that aggression is reactive to the encounter with the reality principle" the aggression or "destructive drive" with which he is concerned in "The Use of an Object" is that which "*creates* the quality of externality." "It is generally understood that the reality principle involves the individual in anger and reactive destruction, but my thesis is that the destruction plays its part in making the reality, placing the object outside the self" (1971d, 93, 91). By "destruction," Winnicott does not mean the actual destruction, or even the intended destruction, of an external object, in the sense of wanting it no longer to exist. Such impulses at some point arise, generally linked with hate and anger, but that is not the impulse that is the focus of "The Use of an Object." The destruction with which Winnicott is concerned is rather that of what might be called relinquishment or repudiation.

For Winnicott, as we have already discussed, there is an incipient experience of a Not-Me that grows out of physical encounter, but this early experience is not the subject of "The Use of an Object." Winnicott situates the destruction with which he is concerned in that paper as arising at the point at which the object is already "in process of being found instead of placed by the subject in the world" (1971d, 91). There is, then, already a sense of internal and external that is grounded in bodily experience, but it is a psychically thin and tenuous one, complicated by the infant's desires, needs, fears, and fantasies. Early on, "internal" is synonymous with omnipotent and includes the capacity to protect; while what is outside is "wasteland" (1963a, 230). To allow an object to be truly "outside," to repudiate the object as part of the Me, is thus to risk its survival, placing it "outside the area of omnipotent control, that is, out in the world," in the wasteland of "liability not to survive" (1971d, 89, 93). From the perspective of the infant, this repudiation is destructive, though destruction is not the aim. There are, in fact, two aspects of this destruction. There is the destruction of removing protection, of allowing-to-be-destroyed. "[T]he experience of maximum destructiveness," as Winnicott puts it, is of the "object not protected" (1971c, 91); "put[ting] [the object] over there," "kicking" it out from the area of protection (1970a, 287). There is also (relatedly) the destruction of the tie *between* subject and object, destruction of the imperial claim over the object. "The central postulate in this thesis is that, whereas the subject does not destroy the subjective object (projection material), destruction turns up and becomes a central feature so far as the object is objectively perceived, has autonomy, and belongs to 'shared' reality" (1971d, 91). "It is important to note that it is not only that the subject destroys the object because the object is placed outside the area of omnipotent control. It is equally significant to state this the other way round and to say that it is the destruction of the object that places the object outside the area of the subject's omnipotent control. In these ways the object develops its own autonomy and life, and (if it survives) contributes-in to the subject, according to its own properties" (1971d, 90).

The capacity to repudiate or relinquish objects, to *put the object over there*, and test its survivability, Winnicott argues, can only develop slowly, through play and in the right supportive environment: for example, in the infant's play of throwing away an object that is brought back to be thrown again. Where such a capacity does not develop, there is, in the most extreme case, a failure to distinguish internal and external, and this we call psychotic. In the less extreme case, objects, while in one respect known to exist outside, are never quite allowed to be released. When conditions are good enough, the infant is able to learn slowly to repudiate objects without overwhelming anxiety. And as it does so, the infant is encouraged by the pleasure of the rewards, the primary pleasure being externality itself. "From this moment, or arising out of this phase, the object is in fantasy always being destroyed. This quality of 'always being destroyed' makes the reality of the surviving object felt as such, strengthens the feeling tone, and contributes to object constancy." "The subject may now have started to live a life in the world of objects" and to experience the pleasure of pressing up against a world that is not of its own making (1971d, 93, 90). As Clare Winnicott put it in an essay written after Donald's death: "Destroying of the object in unconscious fantasy is a cleansing process, which facilitates again and again the discovery of the object anew" (1989, 3).

This form of aggression is not that of appetite or greed,[9] which is part of the primitive, appetitive love impulse that, as I have suggested, has the quality of pressing into. It is rather an aggression, as I have said, of letting go or relinquishing. These are both, for Winnicott, aspects of aggression, and in one respect, they pull in opposing directions. But seen from the perspective of primitive motility they are two sides of "one thing" and "[t]his unity," which "turns up in the baby by natural maturational processes," is primary" (1969, 245). Each is born from, and is a necessary component of, that primary "impulsive gesture [that] reaches out" for "opposition," that finds pleasure in encountering it, and "that makes the infant need an external object, and not merely a satisfying object."

Yet, this pleasurable and vital relationship of internal and external is threatened from both sides. On the one side is the tendency toward solipsism, a tendency in all persons, and acute in those for whom the destructive drive has been especially inhibited. It is not uncommon to find "people … [who] may do work that is even of exceptional value and yet [who] may be schizoid or schizophrenic … because of a weak reality sense." Indeed, perhaps a "large proportion … of adults never achieve a reliable capacity for objectivity." On the other side and to "balance this one would have to state that there are others who are so firmly anchored in objectively perceived reality that they are ill in the opposite direction of being out of touch with the subjective world and with the creative approach to fact." On this side, then, is the danger of "compliance," of being taken over by the external world, of being "reliably objective," but "comparatively out of touch with [one's] own inner world's richness." From a clinical perspective, these two extremes appear in the expression of dissatisfaction by two kind of patients, those who "come to … psychotherapy because … they do not want to spend their lives irrevocably out of touch with the facts of life" and those who come "because they feel estranged from dream" (1950–1955, 208, 1971a, 66–67). Each of these represents a kind of aggressive failure; "compliance" is the consequence of an inhibition of appetite, "solipsism" of an inability of destruction.

Motility, Aggression, and Social Life

I have spent much of my allotted space here describing and drawing out what, to my mind, is a central motif in Winnicott's thinking. It has been necessary to devote this space because, despite the centrality of these ideas, Winnicott himself never synthesized them in a single work. Indeed, it may well be *because* they were so central to his thinking that he did not; for he was still struggling with these ideas, which he had been thinking about for over thirty years, up until his death in 1971. As I indicated at the outset, my ambition in this essay is not to offer a program. What I do want to do in the brief space I have left is to suggest in broad terms why and how these ideas are significant for political thought.

The most general and obvious reason *why* is that they tell us something quite important about human beings. All political thought relies on some conception or set of conceptions, implicit or explicit, of those beings for whom it is meant to apply—of what it means to live a human life or a worthy human life, of what sorts of things matters or ought to matter to such a life, and so on. This need not be a full-blown conception of human beings, and insofar as it is considered political, the focus will frequently be on the social aspects: on questions such as what we need and want from others, on how social institutions and social life are to be organized, and so forth. One way of asking the question of how the Winnicottian account that I have discussed might matter to our political thought is by asking, then, how that account might add to our approach to these questions.

I began my discussion of Winnicott by distinguishing the motility impulse from the classic psychoanalytic characterization of drives—or, as I put it, those drives which were once taken to be primary. Drives on this account (or of this sort) are characterized by a pressure or tension felt in some part (or parts) of the body, a pressure that seeks reduction or release through a particular aim and object. These drives, then, have something like a "subject"—that which the desire is a desire of (in one respect the particular part of the body that is the source, in another the whole person whose part of the body it is). They are experienced as a longing, and they seek an object that can satisfy it. It is a complex question, about which there is much disagreement within psychoanalytic thought, how these various aspects of drives get organized. But however it comes about, we can say, crudely, that what comes about is a subject constituted as an array of longings for particular kinds of relationship with a particular set of objects. Desire wraps itself around those objects (in such a way that we cannot decide whether to say that the source of the attraction is the desiring subject or the object) and is constituted in part by the idea of an object that will both fill the subject (eliminate absence) and empty the subject (relieve tension). Aggression (and the reality principle that it ushers in) is, in the standard view, a response to the frustration of an object (or more precisely the aim for which the object is desired) that is kept out of reach.

What attitude toward social life is suggested by this view? In asking this question, I am not asking about the historical influence of this psychoanalytic account. I am interested rather in the view of human beings that this account entails and of which, in some respect, it may be trying to make sense. One central view with which it is connected, I think, is the conception of social life as (to borrow Hegel's phrase) a system of needs. This does not have to imply a crude understanding of all needs and desires. The broad conception encompasses views of that sort—utilitarianism of the Benthamite sort, its consumerist varieties, and so on—but it is not limited to them. It includes as well, for example, the view that political justice is fundamentally concerned with the distribution of "primary goods," understood as goods that are desired whatever else is desired (Rawls 1971, 92). Even the desire for recognition, especially as it is understood as a desire for recognition of one's desires, can be understood in accordance with this conception. Many more such examples could be given.

At the outset, I said that Winnicott's account of motility is not a rejection of the classic view of drives, and nothing about his account (or my suggestions of what might follow from it) denies the importance of various sorts of needs and desires to human beings, or the significance of the myriad political questions about how the social order should treat these and their various demands for satisfaction. Winnicott's conception of motility does not replace these concerns, but rather adds a crucial dimension to our understanding of the constitution of the self.[10] The political question is of the implications of this for social life.

This is a large question to which our discussion here will point only broadly, in two general directions. The first of these proceeds from these associated ideas: that the self develops not only as a subject of desire (in the classical sense) but even more primordially as impulsive movement that seeks pleasure in finding opposition that it can push against; that at its origin aggression comes not from frustration with the failure of the world to relieve tension, but in the pleasure of tension with the world; that creativity does not begin in sublimation of unsatisfied drive aims (Freud) or reparation for the fantasied damage from aggression (Klein) (although these will be important sources), but is primary, taking an early form in the "impulsive gesture" and in the psychic reach that is connected with it, inventing the world that it discovers; that in all of this there is a primary need to "knock up against things," to find "objects that get in the way," to "enjoy going around looking for … opposition" (1950–1955, 216, 212, 1964b, 237); and that in this there is a kind of opposition that is not experienced as a frustration of desire, but as pleasurable and necessary.

Such ideas are not wholly absent from political thought. To the extent that they have found any serious reflection in *contemporary* discourse about social organization, they have been, I think, mostly on the (political) Right. From those quarters we could hear, not too long ago, an unabashed veneration, for example, of the virtue of war as renewing the body politic by expression of the natural need for antagonistic struggle. This is less common now, at least manifestly. A more common form of the celebration of aggression on the Right appears in the mythology of capitalism, especially of the Ayn Randian sort: capitalism as an arena for (or in some versions just the natural expression of) creativity and creative destruction, a form of life that gives free reign to the pleasures of risk-taking and healthy antagonism between strong individuals.

This is indeed mythological and at several levels. It ignores the fact that for most, modern capitalist society does not offer an arena for creativity, that the risks and antagonisms of everyday existence are experienced under conditions of survival, domination, and exploitation that are generally much more akin to what Winnicott would call "imposition"—a disruption of "being"—than a manifestation of "personal impulse." It is also mythological in a deeper sense of treating the abstract virtues of aggression as though they were identical with the particular institutions and practices of a particular capitalist form of organization (whatever that is taken to include), thus foreclosing not only the questions of *for whom* the particular organization of society offers these attractions, but of the particular character and quality they assume within the particular social forms in which they appear.

There is nonetheless an attraction to this myth and that itself deserves notice, particularly because of its appeal beyond those who materially benefit from it. It is sustained in part by the paucity of "actually existing" social forms that might offer alternative versions of the goods and pleasures of aggression, but also by the absence, outside of the purveyors of the myth, of much imaginative concern with aggression as a good. In our political–social discourse more broadly, we have tended to focus on aggression primarily as a danger to society that needs to be either suppressed, or deflected, or "vented" into harmless outlets such as sports. (The criticism of sports from some Left quarters has been just that it is not harmless enough.) Precious little thought—especially on the Left—has been given to the basic, aggressive (or, as I have discussed it here, motility-aggressive) needs of the human being.[11]

We are back at Winnicott's opening statement in "Aggression in Relation to Emotional Development": "If society is in danger, it is not because of man's aggressiveness but because of the repression of personal aggressiveness in individuals." Winnicott's own primary focus was on the repressions of childhood and the importance of a "facilitating environment" for allowing the proper development of the motility impulse. These are of undeniable importance, for what is at stake is the primary organization of the self from which flows the possibilities for encountering the world. But this can only be half the story. The capacity for exercising creative aggression depends both on the development of the capacity and on the conditions available for its exercise. These are related and neither is fixed. As important as is the early period, there is (at least for most), the potential for continued development of the capacity over the course of life.[12] And the question is not just of whether, or how much, but also of what sort. What are the avenues for creative aggression that social life might foster? What *forms* of aggression should we seek to cultivate? What are the material preconditions for these? What organization of social life is required for the cultivation of these forms of creative aggression in relation to others? These are deeply political questions. They do not admit of simple answers, and as with any questions of this sort concerning the organization of social life in ways quite different from what we have, we need to avoid the temptation (a kind of utopianism) to imagine that we can produce a blueprint. Nonetheless, these kinds of questions and the recognition of the needs that underlie them deserve much more of our attention that they have received.

The second direction that is worth pointing to is more difficult and yet if anything even more neglected—although in this case it is perhaps the Left that has given the bulk of whatever small attention has been paid. As we have discussed, it is part of Winnicott's insight into the motility impulse that its proper and healthy development requires not one but *two* forms of aggression: on the one side, the aggression associated with the primitive, appetitive impulse, aptly described in the language of *pressing-against*, and on the other side the destruction that is involved in *letting go* of objects. As for the former, so, too, the relinquishment of the subjective hold on objects—or more precisely the relinquishment of a *particular* subjective hold on objects, so as to re-find the object as external—is both a developmental achievement and a practice.[13] The developmental achievement, which is variable (failure ranging from the extreme of psychosis to degrees of more ordinary schizoid object relations) consists in the capacity for allowing objects to be encountered as external, as having an existence independent of the subject's mind. It is developmental in that its emergence, through its early exercise, can be traced to a particular time period and depends on the existence of facilitating conditions. The development of the capacity, however, does not guarantee its exercise or the robustness of its exercise. What is important about the achievement is what it makes possible, and as with other capacities (e.g., the capacity for empathy), the capacity to destroy in order to re-find and re-make the object is strengthened and enriched by its exercise and by practices that encourage it.

Winnicott offers an example of this kind of healthy destruction in "the art-lover" who "uses" "the picture" "in unconscious fantasy destroying it over and over again" (1965, 232). To "use" is Winnicott's term of art to refer to a relationship to an object whose externality is allowed. It is a good example. As it so happens, one such art-lover was living not too far from Winnicott when he wrote these very words, though (as far as I am aware) he was quite unknown to him. Here is how Richard Wollheim would later describe his own practice of encountering paintings:

> I evolved a way of looking at paintings which was massively time consuming and deeply rewarding. For I came to recognise that it often took the first hour or so in front of a painting for stray associations or motivated misperceptions to settle down, and it was only then, with the same amount of time or more to spend looking at it, that the picture could be relied upon to disclose itself as it was. (1987, 8)

Winnicott might rather say "to disclose itself in a new way," but we need not press too hard on the relation of invention and discovery. In Winnicott's terms, Wollheim's description is of the process of destroying the "old painting," and what emerges is the experience of encountering the object anew as a found object. Over time, that sense of discovering the object may give way to a new sense that the subject's perception of the object is a "misperception" or a projection, followed by another attempt to encounter the painting afresh "as it was."[14]

Especially during his last years, Winnicott took an increasing interest in the role of "culture" and cultural practices in mediating the relationship between "inner and outer reality" (see, e.g., 1951, 240, 1971b, 1971c) and the description of the "art-lover" is an example of this.[15] But while Winnicott himself tended to use the term "culture" in a more limited sense, referring to such things as art and religion, there is no reason to restrict the arena of destructive, "cleansing" practices to these. Treating the question of "culture" more broadly—in the sense of something like *Sittlichkeit*—Winnicott's work points generally to the vital importance within social life for practices of destruction or relinquishment, and raises, again, question concerning the kinds of such practices that are needed and the conditions of social life that could sustain them.

I came to the discussion of Winnicott's view of destruction/relinquishment as a counter-force to what I called for shorthand the appetitive (or "pressing-in") form of aggression. This was all part of describing the complexity of the motility impulse. But as different as appetitive aggression is from the classical representation of drives, what they share is an appropriative character: in the case of the latter, the impulse to obtain those objects that can satisfy desire (of whatever form and sort); in the case of the former, a kind of psychic appropriation of objects in the form of projection. In relation to each of these, the destructive drive is a counter-appropriative impulse. In the tension between projection and release, cathexis and decathexis, internal and external, possession and relinquishment, it is the "quality of 'always being destroyed'" that provides the "backcloth for love of a real object … an object outside the area of the subject's omnipotent control" (1971d, 94). With respect to objects of desire, it is the destructive aspect that "makes the reality of the surviving object felt as such," the "destructive element … that fixes the object and determines the need that is felt for [its] … actual presence … and survival." With respect to creative aggression, where there is a tension between the fact that we can only perceive the world as we perceive it and the fact that there is a world independent of our perceptions, it is the destructive impulse that works against the tendency for the creative urge to be sabotaged by its own productions, and that offers a possibility for re-encountering the world anew. In respect, then, to both of these forms of appropriation, practices of destruction are the condition for vital engagement and re-engagement with a world. This is not a new idea; it is one, for instance, that I believe is behind many of those ancient practices that we refer to under the name of *sacrifice*. But Winnicott offers us a new understanding of why it matters, and why it is essential that we attend now to the need for social practices that are destructive in these ways, and to the questions of the shape that those practices might take.

A central contribution of Winnicott's work to political thought, I am suggesting, is in taking us to these sorts of questions; not in setting out a program, but in setting out a path. In that spirit, I hope I may be forgiven for ending this discussion of Winnicott with the further suggestion that, at the place at which we have arrived and in the direction we are pointing, there is a joinder with the work of a very different kind of thinker, one with whom Winnicott has rarely been associated. Yet, let us remember that Nietzsche began his philosophical work precisely with the thought that the creative urge both seeks form and its destruction (Nietzsche, [1872] 1999); that for Nietzsche as well, though in a very different vein, the problem of the relationship between the "semblance" [*Schein*] that is needed for life and the semblance that tyrannizes life, was a central and abiding one. We cannot here explore the connections and the potential synergy between Winnicott's thought and Nietzsche's in this area. But it is appropriate to mention Nietzsche here because in his work we are constantly urged to see that this question, which is a question of "the fundamental concerns of life itself" (in Nietzsche's phrase) or "what life itself is about" (in Winnicott's) is a question of *civilization*, and therefore for us now a "question[] of politics" in the deepest sense (Nietzsche [1888] 2005). The question of politics is not Winnicott's primary focus. Yet in his contribution to our understanding of the question of the human we have much to learn when it is ours.

Notes

1. This is true, as well, of course, for Winnicott's own limited attempts to extend his ideas to political–social problems and that tend to raise (sometimes quite keenly) the questions that they purport to answer. For an example, see 1970c. All references are to Winnicott except where otherwise noted. Some passages in this chapter, particularly in the discussion of "the aggression of being" and "psychic motility and creativity" are taken from Elkins (2015).
2. He seems to have borrowed the term, as a translation of *motricité*, from a paper given the previous year by two French psychoanalysts (Marty et Fain 1955) given at the Conférence des Psychanalystes de Langues Romanes in Paris, in November 1954 and published in early 1955. Winnicott attended the conference and wrote a commentary on the Marty and Fain paper. The first of the talks that make up "Aggression in Relation to Emotional Development" was written in 1950, and in publishing this part of the consolidated paper, Winnicott marks his adoption of the term "motility" just by a footnote added in 1955 (1950–1955, 204). The third talk, written in November 1954, uses the term "motility" only once. It is

the second sub-paper, written in January 1955, in which Winnicott most frequently uses the term "motility," and even here one can easily get the sense that Winnicott had inserted that language into a paper partly already written. So there is a certain messiness to all of this, and in describing the consolidated paper, and Winnicott's thinking about this question generally (some of which preceded the 1950–1955 paper and some of it succeeded it), I shall feel free to use the term "motility" more consistently than he himself did.

3. I put it in this way to emphasize that what is being described is not all that may be identified with the "me," but with that which gives them the sense of genuine "ownness." "Ownness" here means aliveness, the feeling of real, being. "We now see that it is not instinctual satisfaction that makes a baby begin to be, to feel that life is real, to find life worth living. In fact, instinctual gratifications start off as part-functions and they become seductions unless based on a well-established capacity in the individual person for total experience, and for experience in the area of transitional phenomena. It is the self that must precede the self's use of instinct; the rider must ride the horse, not be run away with" (1971b, 98–99).
4. Winnicott describes this early experience in several places. As the citation makes evident, I have taken the liberty of combining two of these accounts.
5. As I have quoted earlier: "It will be understood that in practice these things develop gradually, and repeatedly come and go, and are achieved and lost" (1950–1955, 217).
6. While Winnicott had always opposed the biological basis of Freud's death drive, this development took him close to the logic of it as a psychic impulse. See Winnicott (1969).
7. The paper was delivered in 1968 and published the following year. It was revised for inclusion in Playing in Reality. References are to the revised version.
8. In earlier work, Winnicott had discussed the infant's destructive impulses. In "The Use of an Object," there is, however, a new significance given to the idea of destruction.
9. Though it may feed off it. For the sake of clarity, I leave aside here such complexities.
10. I am speaking here of motility-aggression as an impulse distinct from the classic form of drives. In actuality these often appear together and in some kind of relation.
11. The interest in recent years in "agonistic" politics is not, I think, an exception to this, but rather a symptom. This, I think, for the same general reason that Marx insisted that the modern Rousseauian idea of a political community of equals was not an antidote to the problem of modern man, but a deflection of it.

12. As Winnicott rightly puts it, there are "basic patterns...laid down in the process of emotional growth, and [those] near the beginning...have the greatest influence." At the same time, for "[m]ost people," who have not suffered the extremes of deprivation or imposition, there is "the opportunity for us to affect our own patterns" (1970c, 39–40).
13. In this sense, the negative of Freud's finding as re-finding (Freud 1905, 222).
14. Winnicott's use of the term "destruction" in his description of the "art-lover" may cover two ideas: the destruction of appropriation, which is closer to what I have referred to as appetitive aggression, and the destruction of separation. I do not think that Winnicott, who was still working on these ideas at his death, ever fully sorted out the terminological usage.
15. Winnicott, in my view, never finished working out the relationship between the destruction that is the subject of "The Use of an Object" and his ideas about transitional objects. The phrase that I have quoted is from "Transitional Objects and Transitional Phenomena" (1951) which was reprinted in his final collection of essays, Playing and Reality (Winnicott (1971d). There, Winnicott writes that "the task of reality-acceptance is never completed, that no human being is free from the strain of relating inner and outer reality, and that relief from this strain is provided by... arts, religion, etc.," which serves as an "intermediate area of experience," the direct descendent of the transitional object and of the child's play where the distinction between inner and outer, invention and discovery, apperception, and perception, is blurred (1951, 240). This account sits in an ambiguous relationship to the description of the art-lover, which seems to be used as an example of the life of fantasy that a recognition of externality makes possible.

References

Elkins, J. 2015. Motility, Aggression, and the Bodily I: An Interpretation of Winnicott. *Psychoanalytic Quarterly* 84: 943–973.

Freud, S. 1905. Three Essays on the Theory of Sexuality. In *The Standard Edition of the Complete Psychological Works of Sigmund Freud*, vol. 7 (1953), ed. James Strachey, 123–243. London: Hogarth Press.

Freud, S. 1933. New Introductory Lectures on Psycho-Analysis. In *The Standard Edition of the Complete Psychological Works of Sigmund Freud*, vol. 22 (1964), ed. James Strachey, 1–182. London: Hogarth Press.

Freud, S. 1938. An Outline of Psycho-Analysis. In *The Standard Edition of the Complete Psychological Works of Sigmund Freud*, vol. 23 (1964), ed. James Strachey, 139–207. London: Hogarth Press.

Marty, P., etM. Fain 1955. La Motricité dans la Relation d'objet. *Rev. française Psychanal.* XIX(1–2). Presses Universitaires de France.

Nietzsche, F. [1872] 1999. *The Birth of Tragedy*. Cambridge: Cambridge University Press.

Nietzsche, F. [1888] 2005. Why I Am So Clever.In *Ecce Homo. The Anti-Christ, Ecce Homo, Twilight of the Idols and Other Writings*, ed. Aaron Ridley, and Judith Norman. Cambridge: Cambridge University Press.

Nozick, R. 1974. *Anarchy, State, and Utopia*. New York: Basic Books.

Rawls, J. 1971. *A Theory of Justice*. Cambridge, MA: Harvard University Press.

Winnicott, D.W. 1939. Aggression. In *Deprivation and Delinquency (1990)*, ed. C. Winnicott, R. Shepherd, and M. Davis, 84–92. New York: Routledge.

———. 1948. Paediatrics and Psychiatry. In *Through Paediatrics to Psycho-Analysis (1975)*, 157–173. London: Hogarth.

Winnicott, D.W. 1949a. Birth Memories, Birth Trauma, and Anxiety. In *Through Paediatrics to Psycho-Analysis (1975)*, 174–193. London: Hogarth.

Winnicott, D.W. 1949b. Mind and Its Relation to the Psyche-soma. In *Through Paediatrics to Psycho-Analysis (1975)*, 243–254. London: Hogarth.

Winnicott, D.W. 1950–1955. Aggression in Relation to Emotional Development. In *Through Paediatrics to Psycho-Analysis (1975)*, 204–218. London: Hogarth.

Winnicott, D.W. 1951. Transitional Objects and Transitional Phenomena. In *Through Paediatrics to Psycho-Analysis (1975)*, 229–242. London: Hogarth.

———. 1952. Psychoses and Child Care. In *Through Paediatrics to Psycho-Analysis (1975)*, 219–228. London: Hogarth.

Winnicott, D.W. 1956. Primary Maternal Preoccupation. In *Through Paediatrics to Psycho-Analysis (1975)*, 300–305. London: Hogarth.

———. 1959. Nothing at the Centre. In *Psychoanalytic Explorations (1989)*, 49–52. London: Karnac.

Winnicott, D.W. 1960. Ego Distortion in Terms of True and False Self. In *The Maturational Processes and the Facilitating Environment (1965)*, 140–152. London: Hogarth.

Winnicott, D.W. 1963a. D.W.W.'s Dream Related to Reviewing Jung. In *Psycho-Analytic Explorations (1989)*, 228–230. London: Karnac.

Winnicott, D.W. 1963b. From Dependence Towards Independence in the Development of the Individual. In *The Maturational Processes and the Facilitating Environment (1965)*, 83–92. London: Hogarth.

———. 1964a. Further Thoughts on Babies as Persons. In *The Child, the Family, and the Outside World*, 85–92. Cambridge, MA: Perseus.

———. 1964b. Roots of Aggression. In *The Child, the Family, and the Outside World*, 232–238. Cambridge, MA: Perseus.

———. 1965. Notes Made on the Train, Part II. In *Psycho-Analytic Explorations (1989)*, ed. C. Winnicott, R. Shepherd, and M. Davis, 231–233. London: Karnac.

———. 1968a. Breast Feeding as Communication. In *Babies and Their Mothers (1987)*, ed. C. Winnicott, R. Shepherd, and M. Davis, 23–34. Reading, MA: Addison-Wesley.

Winnicott, D.W. 1968b. Comments on My Paper 'Use of an Object'. In *Psycho-Analytic Explorations (1989)*, ed.C. Winnicott, R. Shepherd, and M. Davis, 238–240. London: Karnac.

Winnicott, D.W. 1969. The Use of an Object in the Context of Moses and Monotheism. In *Psycho-Analytic Explorations (1989)*, ed. C. Winnicott, R. Shepherd, and M. Davis, 240–246. London: Karnac.

———. 1970a. Individuation. In *Psycho-Analytic Explorations (1989)*, 284–288. London: Karnac.

———. 1970b. Living Creatively. In *Home Is Where We Start From (1986)*, 39–54. New York: W.W. Norton.

———. 1970c. The Place of the Monarchy. In *Home Is Where We StartFrom (1986)*, 260–268. New York: W.W. Norton.

———. 1971a. Creativity and Its Origins. In *Playing and Reality*, 65–85. London: Tavistock.

———. 1971b. The Location of Cultural Experience (1967). In *Playing and Reality*, 95–103. London: Tavistock.

———. 1971c. The Place Where We Live. In *Playing and Reality*, 104-110. London: Tavistock.

———. 1971d. The Use of an Object and Relating through Identifications. In *Playing and Reality*, 86–94. London: Tavistock.

_____. 1971e. Transitional Objects and Transitional Phenomena. In *Playing and Reality*, 1–25. London: Tavistock.

———. 1986. *Home Is Where We Start From*. New York: W.W. Norton.

———. 1988. *Human Nature*. New York: Schocken Books.

Winnicott, C. 1989. D.W.W.: A Reflection. In *Psycho-Analytic Explorations*, ed. C. Winnicott, R. Shepherd, and M. Davis, 1–18. London: Karnac.

Wollheim, R. 1987. *Painting as an Art*. Princeton: Princeton University Press.

CHAPTER 3

The Isolation of the True Self and the Problem of Impingement: Implications of Winnicott's Theory for Social Connection and Political Engagement

David P. Levine

What does a psychoanalyst, whose primary focus was not only on the inner world but on the most private aspects of the inner world, have to tell us about the meaning and possibility of social connection and political process? Winnicott's preoccupation with private experience was intense even for an analyst. This much is clear from the centrality of ideas such as creativity, the capacity to be alone, and making contact with the self. All of these ideas involve a central proposition—that the capacity to enter into relationships with others depends on the ability to protect the self from relating.

In this essay, I explore the importance of not relating for political engagement. In doing so, I place special emphasis on the capacity of the individual to protect his or her original vitality or true self from damaging forms of relating as those develop in political processes and institutions.

D.P. Levine (✉)
University of Denver, Denver, CO, USA

M.H. Bowker, A. Buzby (eds.), *D.W. Winnicott and Political Theory*,
DOI 10.1057/978-1-137-57533-3_3

I link these damaging forms of relating in politics to the fantasy that the individual or the group has the ability to "create the world."

Subjectivity and Relating to Others

According to Winnicott (1962, 68), there is a "tendency in personality growth" that "can be discerned from the very beginning," which is the tendency to develop "a capacity to make relationships with objects in spite of the fact that in one sense, and an important sense, the individual is an isolated phenomenon and defends this isolation at all costs." If Winnicott has something to tell us about social connection, then it must involve this need to protect the self from relating. I will, therefore, begin with a brief summary of Winnicott's central theme, which is the importance of the isolation of the true self and the need to cope with the problem he refers to as "impingement."[1]

Isolation begins in what Winnicott terms the holding environment, which is the mother-infant unit and the infant's world at the outset of life. Winnicott makes it clear that, in considering the holding environment, we are not dealing with relating, or, in psychoanalytic language, object relating. According to Winnicott, in the holding environment there is no object relating because there is, on the side of the baby, no *capacity* for object relating. There is no capacity for object relating because there is no capacity to conceive, or form in the mind, an object. It can be said that the purpose of the holding environment is to facilitate the development in the child of this capacity to conceive an object and therefore enter into object relations.

Paradoxically, the holding environment facilitates the development of this capacity for relating by isolating what Winnicott refers to as the "true self" from object relations. The true self is the individual's center of psychic or emotional existence. Self-experience, which is so essential to relating, links our center of awareness, the "ego" as Freud terms it, with our center of vitality and emotional experience, the true self. Winnicott's claim is that relating depends on the capacity to isolate our center of existence from relating. How can we understand this seeming paradox? To answer this question, we need to focus our attention on what is essential about the holding environment, which is the matter of adaptation.

The main quality of the holding environment is that, in it, the world adapts to the child. Adaptation here refers not only, or primarily, to satisfaction of specific needs as they arise, though that is important, but to satisfaction of the child's need for emotional sustenance, especially in the form of responsiveness to expressions of emotional existence. Our emotions act as signals to us of meaning and significance. Indeed, our emotional existence is synonymous with our capacity to invest meaning in our world. When we have this capacity, we *exist* in a special sense of the term; but, more importantly, we experience our*selves* existing in this special sense, and we make an emotional investment in our own existence as a center of emotional experience. In the holding environment, the importance of adaptation is that it fosters in the child this capacity to invest significance in the self. This, in turn, makes it possible for us to feel emotionally alive and to act as a center of initiative.

When what we do is informed by our presence, doing is, in Winnicott's phrase, an expression of being (1986). Adaptation refers most importantly to responsiveness of the environment to the child's presence; it is the quality of a world that has no expectations other than that the child will exist and be present there. Failure to adapt means to impose a presence other than that of the infant or young child on its world.

The idea that we can treat presence as our starting point is by no means something to be taken for granted, especially in a psychoanalytic study. Typically, in psychoanalysis, the starting point is not presence, but instinctual endowment as that is expressed in what are usually referred to as "drives." To begin with this endowment tends to lead us in the direction of conceiving society as an aspect of our natural existence, something for which we are biologically programmed. Doing so, however consistent it may be with lines of argument going back to Freud, makes it difficult to understand something essential about society, which is the idea of a world that comes into existence as a result of the exercise of human subjectivity. Here, I will treat society as the locus of human subjectivity rather than as an expression of the species' natural imperatives.

Developmentally, the first moment of subjectivity is the expression of presence in the holding environment. Winnicott speaks of this in the language of illusion. The seamless adaptation of the environment to the child affirms the illusion that the child's need has the power to produce, or create, gratification. Adult subjectivity can be thought of, then, as "the retention throughout life of something that belongs properly to infant experience: the ability to create the world" (1986, 40).

What does it mean to create the world? To create means to produce presence out of absence, in this case to make the absent world appear. But, what is the "world" that we would claim the power to make appear for us? The "world" can be thought to consist of everything that is relevant to human existence: the place we exist and everything in that place. Put another way, the world is everything we experience or could experience, everything we conceive or could conceive, everything we have or could have. At the beginning, everything we have or could have is gratification. The power to create the world, then, is simply the power to cause gratification to happen.

For Winnicott, the infant's ability to create the world is the same thing as its ability to exist, which is to say: to be for self rather than for other. The mother's role is to constitute for the infant an adaptive world, a world whose existence provides proof of the child's creative power. The maturation process leads the child into a world he or she does not create, an already present world in which it is possible to seek gratification and be creative, a world where creativity is no longer a magic power to make gratification happen, but an active involvement of the individual in a complex external reality. As a result of the maturation process, a world emerges for us that we do not, indeed cannot, create, which is also a world of objects defined independently of our love and hate, need and its frustration.

According to Winnicott, adaptation to the child's presence begins as the exclusive quality of the child's environment, which subsequently moves in the direction of "de-adaptation." This de-adaptation results from "new developments" in the emerging individual that make it possible for the "mother" gradually to reassert "herself as an independent person" (1963, 239).[2] The factors responsible for disrupting the holding environment come from outside, but they also emerge internally, as the essential aspect in the infant's emotional development: the aspiration to exist as a subject in the world. But, this factor is not only present in the holding environment, for the child the holding environment is synonymous with it; it *is* that environment. So, we can think of the holding environment as the original form of the existence of subjectivity. It follows that, if subjectivity is the factor that disrupts the holding environment, that disruptive factor can be said to be internal to it.

On the side of the parent, subjectivity disrupts the holding environment because the parent's existence there is a form of nonexistence. Only by being absent from the holding environment can the parent enter into a space that is one of the parent's subjectivity and not of the child's. It is not only the parent's subjectivity, however, that disrupts the holding environment, but also that of the child, whose own subjectivity implies the need to exist outside. The reason for this will be clear if we bear in mind that the term "subjectivity" refers to existing as a creative center, and that to exist in this way it is necessary to create something. So, what we do must cause something to happen; our environment cannot be the seamless reality of satisfaction, but must also present us with a resistance we must overcome. The environment must become something outside us that responds to the expression of our existence; and it cannot respond if it is not (1) external in a way excluded by the terms of the holding environment, and (2) altered as a result of our assertion of presence. This whole notion of cause and effect, action and response, carries with it the implication of separation and division (on subjectivity and intentionality in infant development, see Trevarthen 1979).

We can say, therefore, that the holding environment embodies a contradiction: It is the original form of human subjectivity, yet it lacks an element required for the nascent person to exist as a subject, or creative center. To create something is to place it outside the sphere of the subject's control, especially the control implied in the idea of creating the world. So, the exercise of the capacity to create, by creating an object, limits our creative power. But to fail to create an object means we have no creative power, or, put another way, we cannot make our creative power real (see Levine 2016).

To be sure, viewed from outside, objects conceived in this way, most notably the mother, already exist, but for them to exist for the individual emerging out of the holding environment, they must be conceived, which is to say formed in the mind as internal objects. If objects cannot be conceived in the mind, they cannot exist for the individual, and they cannot be something to which the individual relates. Winnicott refers to this act of conception as "creating the externality" of things, which involves "the subject's placing of the object outside the area of the subject's omnipotent control," and leads to "the perception of the object as an external phenomenon" (1971, 89). The emphasis here is on the active nature of the process through which the subject does not simply come to recognize an external reality, but places the object there (see also Elkins, this volume).

But, for this act to be a continuation of, rather than the end to, subjectivity, it cannot simply mark the movement of the nascent person outside of the holding environment and into a world of objects over which he has no control, objects that are wholly and at all times simply given to him. Put another way, the nascent person cannot simply move from subjectivity in the holding environment to adaptation once outside. The urge to be a creative center must also take form in a world of the externality of things. To secure his existence in this sense, the individual creates an internal object world over which he exerts control, and through which he shapes his engagement with external things not exclusively on the basis of their givenness for him, but also on the basis of his power to conceive them. In other words, he must create a world of internal objects, and, then, negotiate a complex relationship with objects whose purpose is to secure his existence in a world that he has placed outside the sphere of his omnipotent control.

We can think of this process beginning with the creation of a world of internal or fantasy objects. Objects that, from outside the individual, we consider external, are here internal in the sense that they are shaped by fantasy relations with fantasy objects. External objects begin their existence *for the individual* as projections of internal, or fantasy, objects. Projection can be considered the most primitive form of an object relation, or, more accurately, a transitional form that makes objects part of a subjective world. The next step in the process of conceiving and relating to external objects is the creation of the externality of things to which I have already referred.

The transition to an engagement with external objects involves negotiating the complex relationship between internal and external that becomes necessary once the externality of things has become an issue. This is also a negotiation between the infantile illusion of omnipotence and the need to create something that holds its shape against the power of subjective control, whatever may be its source. This object that holds its own against the pressure of omnipotent control is what Winnicott refers to as a "thing in itself," or "an entity in its own right" (1971, 88–89).

Thought about in this way, the developing individual does not simply move out of the holding environment. Rather, in an important sense, he seeks to retain the state of being he experienced in the holding environment as a basis for the negotiation between internal and external to which I have just referred. Because the holding environment is not simply the *space* in which the child expresses subjectivity or presence of being, but is experienced as synonymous with subjectivity, the child cannot simply leave, or move out of, the holding environment, as doing so would mean leaving subjectivity behind. If the child is to maintain contact with his subjective being, he must retain a residue of the formative experience in which he was present and his existence was invested with emotional significance. To do this, the child creates an experience of the holding environment in its absence. This is the inner world kept separate from objects outside, in other words isolated from them. In Winnicott's language, through internalization of the holding environment, the child creates for himself an inner world that is conducive to making contact with the self.

The Consequences of Impingement

The creation of what Winnicott refers to as a "benign environment" of the inner world is the most important of the "new developments" Winnicott refers to as disruptive factors in the holding environment (1958). But, the inner world may or may not develop as a benign environment. If the loss of the seamless unity of parent and child (holding environment) is not a response to the gradual development of the inner world as a benign environment, but instead to the intrusion of object relating before the child is emotionally prepared to cope with it, then the inner world, rather than being positively invested with the emotions associated with the holding environment, can be negatively invested with anxiety and aggression associated with its absence. In this case, the internalization of the holding environment is impaired as is the process of de-adaptation.

While the forming (conceiving) of internal objects expresses the power of the subject to create his or her world, the world created in this way may not be a welcome place for subjectivity, which it is not if the fantasies engaging self and objects are a source of anxiety and aggression. Impingement is the term Winnicott uses to refer to the experience of objects that turns subjectivity against itself in this way. It is the demand that the child adapt to the needs of the parent who, rather than responding to the child, expects that the child will respond to him. In response to impingement, the child creates an inner world that is not a safe place to be. This is a world that, while created by the individual is, in an important sense, not his or her own.

Impingement is the attack on subjectivity through the imposition of a relationship (1952, 222, 1960, 47). In so far as impingement can be said to create an object relation for, or to impose an object relation on, the child, it can be said to be, for the child who experiences impingement, the first moment of social life. But, this is a social life of a special kind. It involves the creation in the individual of a link between relatedness and loss; and it also involves creation of a reality infused with a significant measure of anxiety and aggression associated with the predominance in the psyche of the experience of loss of the holding environment. For the child with a good-enough experience of the holding environment, loss is not so absolute or damaging because loss can be understood, to a significant degree, as the result of the child's internal development, or at least as consonant with it.

Winnicott introduces the idea of impingement as the intrusion of object relating into the holding environment. A more general usage, consistent with the spirit of the idea and relevant to our concerns with social processes and institutions, would be to treat impingement as an object relation the internalization of which undermines the isolation of the true self. Understood in this way, impingement is not restricted to an intrusion on the holding environment, but refers to any object relation whose intent is to disrupt contact with the self. While not inevitable, it is possible for there to develop in the individual an equation of object relating with impingement because relating, in his or her experience, has had as its primary purpose to undermine the isolation of the true self as experienced originally in the holding environment. In other words, the purpose of relating is to create, as a dominant reality of the inner world, the demand for adaptation and the suppression of creativity.

Coping with relating means managing the presence in the world of objects with their own needs, intents, or purposes. In other words, it means relating to subjectivity as an external object. What enables the emerging person to cope with a reality in which he is not the only subject is the capacity to maintain the possibility of contact with his core being. For this to be possible, the individual must create a place where he or she can be apart. Doing so is essential to establishing the individual's existence as a person and to entering into relations with, therefore recognizing the existence of, others. The inner world forms, then, as an aspect of the creation of external objects and of the necessity to relate to them. Put in the more advanced language of social connection, the formation of an inner world takes on meaning because entering into society depends on the possibility of withdrawing from society into a world held apart from it (see Levine 2011, 18–19). If we have no place to be in relation with ourselves, then our existence is inconsistent with relating to others in a way that respects their distinct subjectivities.

The transition out of the holding environment and into object relating does not happen all at once, but involves a growing experience of the mother not as the holding environment, but as an object, an experience that parallels the growing experience of the self as a separate subject, and in that sense also as an object for self and other. Because it does not all happen at once, but proceeds through stages, it is possible for the individual to find him or herself stuck in transition: no longer in the holding environment, but yet not quite able to engage with objects existing outside it. When this happens, a major goal of relating will become what I will refer to as the articulation of the holding environment as an object relation. The less fully we have internalized the holding environment as a benign environment of the inner world, the more powerful the urge to find or create it outside, in object relating. The articulation of the holding environment as an object relation can take shape as an impulse to form family-like groups or communities based on the hope to recreate the holding environment in relations with others.

I use the term "articulation" to emphasize the link between object relating and the use of language, even if only in a primitive form. Clearly, object relating depends, in part, on the development of cognitive capacities involved with use of language. But it also depends on the development of emotional capacities, also involved with use of language. And it is the latter with which I am concerned here. The important link between object relating and the use of language has to do first, of course, with communication. But it is not communication in the abstract that is required by object relating, but the formation of, or conceiving, an idea of an object, however primitive that idea might be.

There is, however, a contradiction built into this development, since the articulation of the holding environment as an object relation—the relation of mother to child—violates something fundamental both about the holding environment and about the nature of object relating. To make the holding environment dependent on object relating means that adaptation to an object replaces environmental adaptation to the child. This contradiction is of central importance in shaping social processes and social conflict, which can be organized around a search to find the holding environment in object relating, where it will never be found. Most notably in groups, members must adapt not only their wants, but also their very identities, to the group. For this adaptation to occur, the true self must be reduced or eliminated in its effect on doing and relating.

What represents the experience of the holding environment as an aspect of the inner world is the possibility for what Winnicott refers to as making contact with the self. If this is not possible because the inner world is formed to facilitate not creativity but adaptation, not presence but absence, then a search for the holding environment in the world of object relating substitutes for making contact with the self. The individual has no safe refuge from relating, and as a result cannot make relating an expression of subjective being, in other words, he or she cannot make relating the doing that expresses being.

Civility and Subjective Causation

In the holding environment, there is no relating, but only the development of the capacity for relating. Movement out of the holding environment is a movement into a world of relating, but, at first, all relating in this world is dominated by fantasy objects conceived internally as an expression of need, in other words everything "outside" is determined by the internal situation shaped by the experience of the holding environment. Subsequently, the developing capacity to create the externality of things enables the individual to form or conceive objects that are not subject to omnipotent control. These objects remain, however, emotionally invested; they are the source of, or obstacles to, gratification. At this point, the world is a world of object relations. For Winnicott, however, there is also a modality of relating beyond that of object relating. This is the modality Winnicott refers to in his discussion of the "false self" as that develops in the healthy individual. According to Winnicott, the false self "in health" is "represented by the whole organization of the polite and mannered attitude," or, what we might term civility (1960, 143). Winnicott links the formation of the false self "in health" to the capacity for gaining a "place in society."

The false self in health relates to others in a special way, one in which the center of emotional experience is not engaged. To achieve this disengagement, it is not enough simply to decide to do so; rather, a specific emotional capacity must be available. This capacity can be thought of as a special way of conceiving objects. It is essentially an aspect of the capacity to withdraw from (object) relating, and in this sense carries forward into mature forms of connection something originally characteristic of the holding environment: the isolation of the true self.

Typically in psychoanalysis the term "object" refers to an external subject experienced as a potential source of, or obstacle to, gratification. In a setting in which relations engage the false self, however, there must be a way to mentally appropriate objects that are not emotionally invested. These objects are subjects, but they are not related to in a personal way because they have been disinvested of those qualities that make objects suitable for a personal connection. Civility is the expression of our ability to accomplish this disinvestment. A society in which the ideal of civility applies does not engage the true self. Treated in this way, the term "society" does not refer to object relations writ large, nor is it the defining moment in the individual's existence. It is understood more narrowly as a system of interaction in which object relations are absent as is the defining quality of the individual's unique presence of being.

While Winnicott speaks of civility as if it is a small thing, a matter of having the appropriate "manners," this is not the case, and the failure of civility is really a symptom of a deeply rooted problem, which is the inability to conceive objects independently of their causal involvement in frustration and gratification. One implication of the articulation of the holding environment as an object relation is that it involves the construction of the "world" beyond the holding environment as a system of object relations, which, then, leads to an experience of the world as a place in which everything is imbued with subjectivity, or intent, and to the related conviction that whatever frustration we experience in life is the direct consequence of the harmful intent of individuals and groups having power over us. This conviction expresses our deep belief in a principle of subjective causation (Levine 2017). The principle of subjective causation governs what we do and how we relate when we are emotionally unable fully to recognize and accept the operation of laws and societal processes operating independently of the will of individuals and groups.

Impingement plays a primary role in blocking the movement into a world where causation can be objective in the sense that what happens to us is not inevitably the result of intent. Impingement blocks this movement by blocking or limiting the establishment of the benign environment of the inner world that enables us to find in ourselves the locus of responsibility for our states of mind. Unable to take responsibility ourselves, we search for it outside, seeking out individuals and groups to whom responsibility can be assigned with the resulting excessive dependence on object relations characteristic of a world governed by intent. This excessive dependence on others leads to the conviction that the world we live in is ruled by their intentions toward us and consequently leaves little room for the recognition of objective laws and processes that might be understood to shape our world.

We see the operation of the principle of subjective causation in politics when the frustrations people experience in their lives are attributed to individuals or groups in pursuit of their own gratification. When the logic of subjective causation dominates, the only explanation needed for our frustration is the evil intent of our enemies, and, when this situation develops, whatever norms of civility and reason exist are beside the point since, even were they accepted in principle, they could not be made the active factors in politics because of their inconsistency with convictions about the role of subjective causation, convictions that operate at the most basic levels of the psyche.

Consider in this connection, Molly Ball's description of the state of mind of supporters of Donald Trump, candidate to be the Republican nominee for President in 2016:

> I was with Trump in Alabama and Georgia last month, in the days after he caused an uproar by briefly declining to disavow the support offered to him by David Duke. When I asked his fans about it, they repeatedly brought up the Black Lives Matter movement, asserting that politicians should be pressed to denounce all race-based agitators, not just those representing white people. *Why are they allowed to do things that we're not allowed to do?* [...]
>
> Trump's supporters have told me that minorities commit crimes with impunity, that illegal immigrants get benefits at higher rates than Americans, that gays and Muslims are afforded special status by the government. They lament that Confederate symbols, and the people whose heritage they represent, are sidelined while diversity is celebrated. They don't understand why Democrats can campaign on overt appeals to the interests of blacks and women and Latinos, but Republicans are deemed offensive if they offer to represent the interests of whites and men. They hear, incessantly, on talk radio and the Internet, that they are under attack by the emboldened legions of minorities who, in the age of Obama, seek white domination and reparations and race war. (2016, *emphasis in original*)

What is important for our purposes about the resentment to which Ball draws our attention is not whether its object is in fact the source of the frustration felt by Trump's supporters, but how it mirrors the angry protests of those who denounce "white privilege" and understand their own frustration to result from the ability of others to have their needs met at their expense, how it constructs the world as a place where either attention is paid to us so that we "matter" or it is paid to others and we do not. In Winnicott's language, those engaged in this conflict are busy "collecting impingements" (Winnicott 1965, 150) as they build a case for making the attention paid to others the cause of their suffering. On neither side of this conflict are participants willing to entertain, or even able to tolerate, the idea that important things happen to us in our lives that no individual or group causes to happen.

If, rather than attempting to test the grievances of participants in struggles of this kind against reality, we consider for a moment the psychic meaning of those grievances, we can begin to understand the prominence of incivility and violence in political engagement. However, disconnected from reality the theories of causation held both implicitly and explicitly, those theories have significant psychic meaning in that they express powerful wish- and fear-invested fantasies. If we ignore psychic meaning, then, we miss what is essential in much political conflict.

We demonize our opponents as they have demonized us. We force others to play a role in our psychic dramas. The reality of psychic drama replaces the reality of an objective or external world. As a result, resolution is impossible and conflict intensifies with the attendant expressions of the violence already implicit in any construction of the world organized around the logic of subjective causation.

Modalities of Relating

We can summarize the modalities of relating in the following way:

The holding environment: The holding environment is not a relationship but the setting in which the capacity to relate develops. Defined by adaptation and the infantile illusion, the central tension of the holding environment is the dominance of limitless subjectivity in a form that prevents any realization of subjectivity in the creation of an object.

Internal object formation: Objects begin to take form in the mind. The characteristic mode of relating to objects is to experience them, via projection, as elements in fantasy life. The infantile illusion now requires control over objects. The externality of objects is experienced as their resistance to their roles in fantasy and must be overcome. The central tension is represented in the struggle against the externality of things. This means that the articulation of the holding environment (primitive subjectivity) as an object relation continues the original tension regarding the realization of creativity in the creation of a thing that endures against our subjective control.

Object relating: This is the modality involving the creation of the externality of things and the forming in the mind of a conception of a thing existing in its own right. External objects exist, but only as potential sources of, or obstacles to, gratification. The central tension is that objects are external, and it is recognized that their externality is what makes them potential sources of gratification, yet their only significance is determined by their connection to fantasies of gratification and deprivation.

Civility: This is the modality marked by the forming of the idea of an object whose significance is not determined by its role in gratification. What takes on significance in relating is not what is unique about the person, but universal qualities shared with others: the person as bearer of rights.

The modalities of relating represent moments in a development process all of which exist in adult mental life where the individual can experience forward and backward movement in service of the end of protecting subjectivity and the possibility that it can be made real in the world.

Impingement and the Fantasy of Political Community

Modalities of relating shape political institutions and processes consonant with their intrinsic logic and with the impulses stemming from the tensions inherent in them. One of the most important of these is the political process that expresses the impulse to articulate the holding environment as an object relation by finding a special object in connection to which it is believed that the qualities of the holding environment will become available to us. Among these qualities, the most important is the ability to create the world. The political process appears to be capable of creating a world, and, to the extent that this idea is ingrained in the collective psyche, primitive modes of relating become the basis for that process. Thus, the fantasy about the holding environment becomes a fantasy about politics, notwithstanding the contradiction inherent in the effort to articulate the holding environment as an object relation.

The fantasy of politics as providing the special object that can make our world so that it is well adapted to us conceives that object not only as a particular person, the leader of a political movement or institution, but also as a group or community. The idea of a political community continues the effort to conceive the holding environment as an object relation that is at the same time not a relationship with an object existing *in its own right*. The group or community is the special reality that both is and is not an object relation because, while it has separate persons in it, its creation subsumes those persons into a larger unity that overcomes the differences that make them objects one to another. The inherent contradiction in this act of creation indicates how it must inevitably fail, a failure marked by an endless process of forming the special object, which then comes apart due to its defining contradiction and must be formed once again.

The instability of systems built around the fantasy of political community indicates how a more mature form of politics depends on the ability of the polity to foster in its members a mode of relating more consistent with the presence in them of the ability to enter into relations whose purpose is not to retrieve the holding environment, but to keep the residue of the holding environment in the mind a reality isolated from social and political process. This alternative involves the struggle to conceive the purpose of politics as assuring the possibility of a society in which the norm of civility is well established as an aspect of psychic life.

Democratic process derives its importance from the way that, in it, the goal, rather than creating the world, is to protect individuals from the fantasized power to create the world and the damage the effort to exercise that power can do. Ideally, the world fostered by democratic process would be one defined by the capacity of those in it to renounce the primitive creative power, which is the magic power to make gratification happen. Renunciation of the primitive creative power then becomes the basis for creative living in Winnicott's sense of the term (1986). In other words, creativity—the doing that expresses being—becomes a way of living in the world rather than the act that creates the world. We can consider politics imbued with the end of establishing an environment conducive to creative living a progressive force in the sense that it facilitates the exercise of mature emotional capacities. By, contrast, politics driven by the wished-for ability to create the world is inherently a conservative force as it seeks to reinstate a primitive state of being.

The more powerful the fantasy of creating the world in the psychic organization of citizens, the less likely the political process will produce a secure environment for creative living and the more likely that process will be dominated by a struggle over who is able to exercise the power to create the world (for an example, see Levine 2017). When this happens, government is imagined to be the locus of a fantasized power, and, rather than protecting citizens from fantasy, it makes them more vulnerable to it. Then, the possibility increases that democratic process will consume itself in an increasingly aggressive struggle over whose fantasy will be made real, notwithstanding the impossibility of realizing any of the opposing fantasies.

Expressed in the language of the infantile illusion, the more powerful impingement in shaping individual psychology and social institutions, the more politics will be defined as a struggle over who controls the power to create the world. It is an important consequence of impingement that the individual never really gives up the infantile illusion and embraces the reality principle. This is because, while impingement means that the child loses the power to create the world, it also means that the parent has that power. So, the child who can become the parent, will gain the power he or she has lost.

Political struggle over who shapes political community becomes the struggle to secure the power of omnipotent control over external objects that was lost in childhood when those objects were first conceived, which is inevitably a struggle against the reality principle, and for the purpose of dismissing any limits the reality of other persons might place in the way of gratification. But, the other side of this is the inevitability within this system that others will be conceived as the obstacle to gratification, and more specifically, that their pursuit of gratification will be understood as the primary obstacle to our own.

Notes

1. It may be that the term "isolation" is not the best, especially if we are interested in application outside the clinical setting where a term such as "privacy" may have more suitable and accessible connotations. See Modell (1993) for a discussion of the private self and its complex relationship to relating.
2. In the contexts discussed in this chapter, Winnicott's use of the term "mother" is not gender-specific.

References

Ball, M. 2016. The Resentment Powering Trump. *The Atlantic*, March 15. http://www.theatlantic.com/politics/archive/2016/03/the-resentment-powering-trump/473775/. Accessed 15 March 2016.

Levine, D. 2011. *The Capacity for Ethical Conduct: Public and Private Worlds of the Self.* New York: Palgrave.

———. 2016. *Psychoanalytic Studies of Creativity, Greed, and Fine Art: Making Contact with the Self.* East Sussex: Routledge.

———. 2017. *Psychoanalysis, Society, and the Inner World.* New York: Routledge.

Modell, A. 1993. *The Private Self.* Cambridge, MA: Harvard University Press.

Trevarthen, C. 1979. Communication and Cooperation in Early Infancy: A Description of Primary Intersubjectivity. In *Before Speech: The Beginning of Interpersonal Communication*, ed. M. Bullowa. Cambridge: Cambridge University Press.

Winnicott, D.W. 1952. Psychoses and Child Care. In *Through Pediatrics to Psychoanalysis (1958)*. London: Karnac Books.

———. 1958. The Capacity to be Alone. In *The Maturational Processes and the Facilitating Environment: Studies in the Theory of Emotional Development (1965)*. Madison, CT: International Universities Press.

———. 1960. Ego Distortions in Terms of True and False Self. In *The Maturational Process and the Facilitating Environment (1965)*. Madison, CT: International Universities Press.

———. 1962. Providing for the Child in Health and in Crisis. In *The Maturational Processes and the Facilitating Environment: Studies in the Theory of Emotional Development (1965)*. Madison, CT: International Universities Press.

———. 1963. Psychiatric Disorder in Terms of Infantile Maturational Processes. In *The Maturational Process and the Facilitating Environment (1965)*. Madison, CT: International Universities Press.

———. 1965. *The Maturational Processes and the Facilitating Environment: Studies in the Theory of Emotional Development*. Madison, CT: International Universities Press.

———. 1971. *Playing and Reality*. East Sussex: Bruner-Routledge.

Winnicott, D.W. 1986. *Home Is Where We Start From: Essays of a Psychoanalyst*. Ed. C. Winnicott, R. Shepard, and M. Davis. New York: W.W. Norton.

CHAPTER 4

The Psychoanalytic Winnicott We Need Now: On the Way to a Real Ecological Thought

Melissa A. Orlie

Where We Start From

If one had to choose a single sentence to sum up what is distinctive about D.W. Winnicott's psychoanalytic thinking, "There is no such thing as a baby" would be one likely candidate. By Winnicott's own account, when he first offered the sentence to the British Psychoanalytic Society in the 1940s, "I said it rather excitedly and with heat....I was alarmed to hear myself utter these words" (1958, 99). Winnicott's excitement suggests a new joining up of thing and word. Such a reunion of primary and secondary process thinking accompanies the shift in perception and greater contact with reality Winnicott associates with feeling real and alive, and more free. Still, that paradigmatic sentence may seem an unpromising place to start with in using Winnicott for political theory. I think we need to go back to that start, though, if we are to hold in mind a psychoanalytic way of thinking which can access the political ecological capacities of attunement we so badly need now. Psychoanalytic thinking is the antidote to our contemporary parlance, which eradicates the psychic capacities of living forms.

M.A. Orlie (✉)
University of Illinois, Urbana-Champaign, Champaign, IL, USA

M.H. Bowker, A. Buzby (eds.), *D.W. Winnicott and Political Theory*,
DOI 10.1057/978-1-137-57533-3_4

"There is no such thing as a baby" is a tricky sentence, though. The sentence is more likely to be mistaken than to lead on to the greater complexity of understanding Winnicott is after when he challenges the biological internment of subjectivity. Winnicott's sentence suggests that there is no such thing as an individual, yet the difficulty of holding in mind the full implications of this insight are evident in the ubiquity of reference to "the mother" in use of his work. We misunderstand Winnicott if we take him to mean that subjectivity is the product of "the environment" or, worse still, the product of the subjectivity of "the mother." With any of these moves I assert that Winnicott ceases to be a psychoanalytic thinker.

At issue in different ways of taking up Winnicott is not so much a matter of personal failing, though, but the peculiar challenge of psyche–somatic self-responsibility as "appropriating or owning up to one's needs and impulses as one's own, impulses and desires we appear to be born with or that seem to have taken shape in interactions with parents during infancy" (Loewald 2000, 392). Ironically, among the primary manifestations of human psychic life is an inclination to disavow the reality of psychic capacity and thereby to imagine active subjects as passive objects, including children as the product of parents, and mind as the product of physical chemical laws (Nagel 2012). This endeavor has become remarkably comprehensive. If anything unites the natural and social sciences and the humanities today, it is befuddlement before the reality of singular inner life. An array of apparently antagonistic positions diminishes the importance of the personal dimensions of subjectivity, avoids the intimacies of self-experience, and excises the psychic capacities of all living forms. At times, it can seem as if psychoanalysis is alone in insisting upon the reality of having a mind to oneself (Bollas 1993, 228–237). However, there is psychic life wherever there is mind turning inward on the way to relating outwardly. There is psychic life, that is, when perception and intention are evaluative and interpretive, and thereby motivated and intentional, which is not to say conscious. It is a challenge for any human psyche–soma to hold with the complexity of having a mind to oneself, let alone meeting the complexity of other living forms. Although it has become common no longer to be bothered with taking in this singular reality of other minds, I hue closely to others' words here in acknowledgment that surrendering to "no-differentiation may be needed as a prelude to any new integration of me and not-me," and that truly receiving another's psychic capacities may be a needed prelude "in a re-emerging into a new division of the me-not-me, one in which there is more of the 'me' in the 'not-me', and more of the 'not-me' in the 'me'" (Milner 1987, 223).

Given what has become our contemporary parlance, it is not surprising how even our best psychoanalytic readings of Winnicott can slip into the more chimerical implications of his path-opening sentence. As if—in place of the idea that all is finally reducible to biological instinct—we are to consider it a great advance to find that everywhere we look there are mothers and each is reducible to her, to them. This may sound like a caricature. Yet I think Jacqueline Rose (2003) makes a compelling case for just how much work this fantasy idea of the mother does in psychoanalysis after Winnicott. The endless reiteration of the "imprint of her care on the being of the subject" risks turning "the mother" into a singular determinative cause (153), while the radical promise of psychoanalysis is to do away with the idea of one such truth or cause (151). So, even as psychoanalysis would affirm the power of unconscious processes, those efforts can feel "in a sense powerless in the face of this mother, her capacity to draw back everything to herself" (150).

If I follow Rose's argument, the tone of her commentary may suggest I will criticize Winnicott. However, my aim is to bring forth a more distinctly psychoanalytic Winnicott for whom primary process truths are elemental. For this Winnicott, facilitating care is provided by ways of experience with infants and children—and with earthly life more generally—that hold in abeyance the too rigid sense of subjects and objects which can characterize secondary process thinking. Good-enough stewarding of earthly life—like good-enough parenting—involves capacities to surrender to the boundless fluidity of experience and to apprehend the psychic life of living forms. Whatever we may think we know about ecology, materialism, or life, we are surrounded by evidence suggesting we have hardly recognized the complex challenges of psychic life, let alone aspired to meet them. No wonder. It seems to have taken Winnicott himself decades to find the right secondary process words and distinctions—specifically, his differentiating dreaming from fantasy, and object use from object relating—before he could more fully and fittingly put into words that insight of primary process thinking he found himself uttering, very much to his own surprise, from whence ever it came.

"The Mother"

There may be no psychoanalytic thinker more strongly aligned with a fantasy mother than Winnicott. Yet, in a paradox befitting him, Winnicott is a vital source for tapping into what Jacqueline Rose argues fixed ideas of the mother are motivated to cover over: "that there might be a world without boundaries where all founding distinctions are lost…a space too full, a space that will become our dream of the mother, but which is in fact a space with no single origin, and for which no one is accountable, where the divisions inside my own mind, and between me and the other, are unclear" (2003, 154–155). There are truths of primary process which fantasies of mothers and fathers occlude. Read through our common parlance, Winnicott furthers this occlusion. Read with keen attention to his psychoanalytic expression, Winnicott can facilitate our access to the good-enough world which incorporation of primary process truths can reveal.

Although Winnicott's path-opening sentence can be taken in many directions, there is tolerable damage done to complexity if we begin with the idea of two primary ways of taking up the idea of there being no such thing as a baby. At one end of a spectrum, we follow Winnicott by referring to "the mother" and "maternal care" as posing little problem. At another end of the spectrum, we follow Winnicott's own need to work more abstractly and cumbersomely, even as he so obviously seeks simplicity of expression. Winnicott must have good reason to opt for unusual formulations such as "facilitating environment" and "individual maturational potential" or "an environment-individual set-up, the entire set-up" (1958, 99). These formulations are too labored to be casual or accidental.

From one perspective, call it a psychological object relations perspective, even if there is no such thing as a baby, there surely does seem to be such a thing as a mother (Abram 2007; Greenberg and Mitchell 1983). Rose begins her paper "Of Knowledge and Mothers" by recounting the observation of one of her seminar students that contemporary psychoanalysis can yield the impression that, psychically speaking, there are only mothers in the world. Rose finds that the student has a point: "No amount of trying to stress the infinite plasticity of the unconscious, the fluidity, transferability, mobility of its objects quite worked" to unsettle this fixated idea of the mother (2003, 150). However, there is good reason for Winnicott to give greater attention to "the environment mother" (153). He thereby recovers a sense of what is done to the infant, and counters that absolute primacy which Freud and then Melanie Klein court granting instinctual infant projections. Although his pediatric and psychoanalytic practice availed him of plenty of instances of not good-enough parenting, Winnicott emphasizes the commonness of the "good-enough mother" and her "ordinary maternal devotion." At times, it can seem as if this mother makes all the difference. Christopher Bollas gives expression to the notion in this way: "Maternal care, then, is a knowing that is an act of love, and whether we have our right to a destiny or whether we are to have a fate will...depend on whether a mother can love her infant in a knowing way" (Rose 2003, 157, quoting Bollas). Rose rightly judges Bollas to be indulging a fantasy of the mother here. Such fantasy not only imposes mightily upon mothers, while evacuating their subjectivity, it also subjects a child to an imprisoning maternal omniscience (Rose 2003, 157; Benjamin 1988, 1995, 81–113).

Yet, unnerving as this all-knowing, over-mastering mother may be, mothers and former children alike may be all too ready to let our minds go there. Why? Because it enables us to look away from what arises beyond this fantasy—that complex intensity of experience which comes with having a mind to oneself.

Like Rose, I do not want to pursue the matter of better representation of the mother. The limits of knowledge as knowledge remain untouched by that approach (Rose 2003, 157). Rather, what is unconscious and opening out beyond this fantasy mother should be the principal concern of psychoanalytic thinking—not as an object of knowledge so much as a primary venue and vortex of experience. While Rose still seems to lean away from this crucible of experience as an unbearable abyss, Winnicott explicitly links capacity for "going on being" to experiences of "unintegration" and potential space of ecstasy. That is the Winnicott I seek here.

Primary Process

Before feminist and realist objections to Winnicott's apparently secure idea of the mother, kindred spirits among psychoanalysts worried that his too ready use of conventional idioms might distort his insights. Hans Loewald puts it this way: It is "unnecessarily misleading to speak," as Winnicott does, "of the infant's primary creativity as purely subjective," to speak of mental life in this domain as a matter of "illusion," or to rely too heavily on imagining distinct objects (mother) and subjects (infant) in the domain Freud designated "primary process." Perhaps, Loewald speculates, Winnicott simply wants for "a less traditional conceptualization" (2000, 472–473).

Nonetheless, Loewald senses affinities with Winnicott, especially those innovations which underscore Winnicott's role in the revaluation of primary process after Freud. Primary process is one among a number of areas, as Masud Khan writes in the 1970s, where "contemporary analytic thinking and clinical work...is different from the classical approach....Today it is possible to envisage psychic states that further and actualize self-experience through predominantly primary process functioning" (Khan 1983). So much has been written of the idealism or realism of Winnicott's ideas of the mother, yet in speaking of what is ordinary and of a "good-enough mother," he clearly wants to be heard as realist. Making contact with what is real, and feeling real and alive, are among Winnicott's chief associations with health, while he notoriously associates too much sanity and false order with what is ill. The Winnicott we need now is convinced that primary process somatic thinking lives on, and not only for ill as in psychosis, but also for health and meaningful life. To be sure, these moments in Winnicott's sayings and writings are emphasized only by some.

Consider Marion Milner, who opts to "take as her text" for one of her papers on Winnicott "something he once said to his students just before a lecture: 'What you get out of me, you will have to pick out of chaos'" (1987, 246). Like Khan, Milner knew Winnicott personally and, while acknowledging that Winnicott himself only rarely uses Freud's specific terminology, she still came to think of Winnicott's work as very much engaged with primary process. She also judges Winnicott to have been on very good terms with his own primary process—"it was an inner marriage to which there was very little impediment" (251). Milner joins Loewald and Khan in affirming primary process as vital to ego's synthetic integrating activity, where ego itself is understood as a process-structure, rather than operating primarily defensively, as Freud emphasizes (Loewald 2000, 3–32). Given this new meaning, Milner thinks that "the concept of primary process is implicit in all of [Winnicott's] work and integral to his idea of what it means to be healthy" (Milner 1987, 251).

Milner's own creative amendment of Freud's notions of primary and secondary process is a helpful place to start thinking here. Milner notes that there seem to be "two ways of being which differ according to whether one feels joined up, merged with what one looks at, or separate from it" (Milner 1987, 280). The structure of the world as perceived by the joined up "'depth mind' is totally ungraspable by the 'surface mind'," says Milner, "not because of repression of offensive content but because of its structure." Because of "its peculiar structure [depth mind] can achieve tasks of integration that are quite beyond the capacity of the conscious surface mind." It is depth mind or primary process which "enable one to accept paradox" (276).

Milner's own writings stress the role of various practices of attention in accessing primary process for living creatively. In addition to his preoccupation with abiding paradox, Winnicott offers "creative apperception" as a capacious term for our many ways of "deliberately relating ourselves to our perceiving" (250). Indeed, creative apperception is the heart of Winnicott's recommendations for the cultivation of good-enough facilitating care. Yet, the idea is relatively neglected when compared to reflections upon "the mother" as object. Perhaps this is because creative apperception arises only in "going on being." I follow Nietzsche in regarding such "becoming like a child again" as rarer than Winnicott seems to hope. Looking about at anxiety ridden children and destroyed land, we have even less reason to hope. At moments, Winnicott indicates he well knows creative health in living can be under cultural assault. I will return to this theme.

Winnicott says that "creativity belongs to being alive, that it belongs to the whole approach of a person (if not ill) to external reality" (Milner 1987, 281). Yet, when Milner considers his various examples, she finds it not immediately obvious what binds them all together: "Sometimes he seems to be talking about a way of looking at the world, sometimes about a way of doing something deliberately and sometimes about simply enjoying a bodily activity that just happens, such as, he says, enjoying breathing. Certainly, I did have to ask myself, in what sense are all these creative?" (281). The key shared dimension among these is the "undoing of the idea of a separation" (204) and settling into experiencing no-separation to access intimations of primary process thinking. Milner surmises that experience of unintegration and feeling joined up with the object—rooted in first experiencing of undifferentiation—may be a necessary phase in all creativity (280–281).

This idea of creativeness involves "lifting an image out of the stream of perception," yet finding "true self" in Winnicott's sense is also related to quality of awareness of one's own body. Milner finds that both associate with an intrinsic relationality of all matter:

> What is the relation of the sense of being, which Winnicott says must precede the finding of the self, to the awareness of one's own body? I think there is a hint about this when he speaks of the "summation or reverberation of experiences of relaxation in conditions of trust based on experience." For me this phrase stirs echoes throughout years of observation of how deliberate bodily relaxation brings with it, if one can wait for it, a reverberation from inside, something spreading in waves, something that brings an intense feeling of response from that bit of the outer world that is at the same time also oneself: one's own body. Here is what I think [Winnicott] means when he speaks of enjoying one's own breathing as an example of creativity. (Milner 1987, 250)

The aim of accessing primary process as edgeless mind (Reid 2015) is not to derogate or jettison conceptual mind, but to enrich it by sustaining and restoring access to the passional roots of conceptual mind. In a similar vein, Loewald writes, language "is a binding power. It ties together human beings and self and object world, and it binds abstract thought with the bodily concreteness and power of life. In the word primary and secondary process are reconciled" (Loewald 2000, 204). Or, primary and secondary process can be reconciled, if we can find the right words.

When Winnicott finds himself saying there is no such thing as a baby, he reveals his concern with the first dimensions of subjectivity. Or should we say the first domain of subjectivity? The problem with either of these choices, or any other, is that where, when, what, and who, do not apply. Primary process is not only primary because it arises first, before secondary process. As Loewald explains, "mental and memorial processes are primary if and insofar as they are *unitary*, single-minded,...undifferentiated...non-differentiating, unhampered...by laws of contradiction [or] causality," "distinctions and dichotomies do not hold sway," these "non-splitting" ways of mind "do not manifest or establish duality or multiplicity, no this and/or that, no before and after, no action as distinguished from its agent or its goal or its object" (2000, 167–168).

Winnicott is preoccupied with individual maturational potential "before unit status." Yet, to convey what it is like to be a person under such as yet undifferentiated conditions, before the idea of a separation has set in, poses difficulties of transposition and translation. The unfolding of infant subjectivity is dependent on the qualities of mindedness in facilitating environments. To the degree there is undifferentiated experience of me and not-me, to that degree experience is dependent, even absolutely so, upon facilitating environment. Winnicott is keen that we not confuse dependence on the qualities of the more developed psyche–soma of a facilitating environment with the idea that individual maturational potential is determined by those other minds. Winnicott stresses that dependence, even absolute dependence, does not mean determined—and yet Winnicott is often read to say just that, by a common parlance which cannot imagine psychic life. Even when facilitating care fails to meet the infant's spontaneous gesture, however, and adults intrude by substituting their own gesture in lieu of meeting the infant, the movement is "given sense by the compliance of the infant" (Winnicott 1965, 145), which is to say that the infant's own psychic life and "projections" are primary in construing experience (1965, 61).

Part of the trouble here is that secondary process thinking does not readily hold these insights. Winnicott would have us bear the conundrum—of dependence, even absolute dependence, without absolute determination—by cultivating mind formed up in holding with basic paradoxes which express primary process truths of unintegrated experiencing. There is a perspective available to mind for which the sense that there is a "separation which is not a separation" does not mean that subject and object are merged. Rather, the experience is of a state in which self and other "both are there, and the same and not the same" (Milner 1987, 290).

The experience of undifferentiation in infancy is not synonymous with union or merger. Union and merger express the idea of subject and object being joined up from a secondary process perspective, which already presupposes distinct entities. Sensory experience of infancy is such a global affair that there is contact with what is not me and, along with it, there is the possibility of feeling intruded upon as well as abandoned, indeed, almost certainly so. When Winnicott evokes infant experience "before the first object relationship," there is no suggestion that the experience of undifferentiation is either blissful union, or without any sense of objects, or no experience of me, albeit me not known to me as me. Think instead of no reliable experience of skin or ego as one's own, with their ways of keeping out or pushing away or holding on with awareness as mine, as under my control, for which I can be responsible (Ogden 1989). Which is to say that unlike the connotations of merger or union, reference to undifferentiation and unintegration do not deny the infant's experience of an "interpersonal world" (Stern 1998). Rather, undifferentiation is "the state before the child is able to distinguish between himself and the world in terms of actuality" (Milner 1987, 173).

To say that the infant's experience of me and not me is not yet oriented by actuality is not quite to say there is no self. How true self forms up from unintegrated experience can be understood through aggression as a basic assertion of appetite and motility reaching out to meet and shape what is met (Winnicott 1939). True self-experiencing likely never loses its relation to first experiences of undifferentiation, whether that goes well or poorly or, more often, somewhere in between. Winnicott writes:

> The True Self comes from the aliveness of the body tissues and the working of body-functions, including the heart's action and breathing. It is closely linked with the idea of the Primary Process, and is, at the beginning, essentially not reactive to external stimuli, but primary. There is but little point in

> formulating a True Self idea except for the purpose of trying to understand the False Self, because it does no more than collect together the details of the experience of aliveness. (Winnicott 1965, 148)

In this sense, the kernel of self is intrinsically not-self and "incommunicado." True self is not-self, and Winnicott insists that such paradox must be tolerated.

If infant subjectivity before unit status is not oriented by actuality, then what serves? Here, readers of Winnicott lean one way or another. Some imagine infant oriented by "the mother" and pick up exclusively on Winnicott's own language of dependence upon the mother's "ego-relatedness" and "ego-coverage." I find that it is easy then to lose the psychoanalytic quality of Winnicott's understanding. To be sure, we can hold any set of words in a psychoanalytic way—sensing the complex dynamism of what is real by imagining through a prism of interplay of secondary and primary process thinking. However, when words reveal no mindfulness of paradox, they are more susceptible to reductionism. Here we arrive at an irony, not a paradox: What Winnicott deems pathological—a "shell" reactive to environment intruding upon the "kernel" of infant subjectivity—is very close to an understanding of Winnicott to which we may succumb. We think we know infant mind as mother's object, and this is consistent with our habit of knowing beings and things only within our own mind as an object rather than as another incarnate psyche–soma.

We can draw another understanding of facilitating care from Winnicott for which individual maturational potential is held as it grows into experiencing true self, and on to living it from the inside out. Winnicott gives us a strong feel for this differentiation of qualities of facilitating care in "Anxiety Associated with Insecurity":

> With a good-enough technique the centre of gravity of being in the environment-individual set-up can afford to lodge in the centre, in the kernel rather than in the shell. The human being now developing an entity from the centre can become localized in the baby's body and so can begin to create an external world at the same time as acquiring a limiting membrane and an inside. According to this theory there was no external world at the beginning although we as observers could see an infant in an environment. How deceptive this can be is shown by the fact that often we think we see an infant when we learn through analysis at a later date that what we ought to have seen was an environment developing falsely into a human being, hiding within itself a potential individual. (1958, 99–100)

Winnicott highlights the distortion, indeed the full-blown misapprehension of what is real, that follows upon the intrusion of secondary process categories too soon. Only "we as observers" see an infant in an environment. Seeing things in this enclosed secondary process way—mindless of infant experience of "no external world"—is the very sort of imposition which has "an environment developing falsely into a human being, hiding within itself a potential individual."

Unknowing intrusion of secondary process thinking entombs individual maturational potential. The same dissociates us from the living reality of earthly life upon which we are dependent, even absolutely so.

What Is Psychoanalytic? Abiding Paradox

The advance in psychoanalytic understanding Winnicott seeks depends upon attuned attention turning inward then leading outward, including awareness of how words and ideas shape our perceptions. By rejoining secondary process thinking to its primary process roots, Winnicott bears witness to ways of enlivening experience of earthly life as good enough, including generating the sort of personalized meaning needed for life to feel worth living.

To find more fitting, less distorting words for what it is like whence we begin is where Winnicott starts. He differs with Freud and Klein about their neglect of what is neither under the control of an infant nor its responsibility. He also objects to their moralizing against what is the infant's own from the beginning, what Winnicott calls aggression, and Freud and Klein call death or destructive instinct. Winnicott thinks Freud and Klein peddle a secular version of original sin (Winnicott 1971, 94–95). While it is important to note the differences, for my purposes, what Winnicott shares with Freud and Klein is as important as where they differ. Winnicott's differences from Freud and Klein are only important here because they can be taken to mean that Winnicott asserts the importance of "the environment" against their less relational, instinct-driven understandings of psychic life (Greenberg and Mitchell 1983). Winnicott does want significantly to shift our frame, but not beyond psychoanalysis. Freud and Klein's thinking remains prone to entanglement in disputes between the intrapsychic and the intersubjective. Winnicott is among those who contribute to an emerging psychoanalytic thinking which points beyond our common parlance for which object and subject are opposed or conflated and, either way, thinking mind is lost. Scientific materialism and antireductionism are usually regarded as antagonists (Nagel 2012), yet they are underwritten by shared incomprehension of psychic capacity and the singularity of living form cultivated by these interpretive evaluative powers.

At bottom, Winnicott is a psychoanalytic thinker because of his conviction that human subjectivity is invariably intentional and constructive. There is mind from the start, though this primary psychic life of creative construing is a somatic form of thinking we still struggle to imagine. For a key set of psychoanalysts after Freud, instinct is "a psychic representative of organic needs and not an organic stimulus operating on the psyche" (Loewald 2000, 472–473). Freud wrestles with this possibility when he calls drive (*Trieb*) a "borderland concept," though he never escapes altogether thinking of drive in terms of cause–effect relationship of soma upon psyche. Yet, Winnicott is among those psychoanalysts after Freud for whom "soma and psyche—superficial appearances not withstanding—signify not two different items of reality but two different modes of experiencing or ordering reality" (Loewald 2000, 472–473). Primary and secondary process are distinctly minded ways we order experience. Psychoanalytic understanding works best beyond scientific materialist reductionism and idealism and, thinking through a "neutral monism" (Nagel 2012, 5), considers the key question whether a vehicle or venue is an integrative synthesizing force or a defensive, even dissociative, one. Most often it may be some admixture of mind as psychic capacities seeking elaboration while also shutting down (Ghent 1990).

Winnicott does not deny Kleinian phantasy nor the intra-psychic. However, he eventually does feel the need to distinguish dreaming from fantasy, convinced that fantasy serves neither dreaming nor living. Where fantasy dissociates, Winnicott finds that "dreaming experience" serves life by facilitating the elaborative experience of inner reality, as well as enabling imaginative entering into earthly life (Khan 1983; Milner 1987, 275–278; Winnicott 1971, 31). Dreaming uses imagination with discretion (1971, 48), is deliberate and delimited, while fantasy evokes feelings of omnipotence. Dreaming has poetry in it—"layer upon layer of meaning related to past, present and future, and to inner and outer, always fundamentally about [self]" (Winnicott 1971, 35). Dreaming serves life by bringing the dimensions of living form seeking what is real and alive into contact with those qualities inside and out (27).

What experience is actually like defies conceptual language. Yet, conceptual thought often retains the upper hand over experience simply by failing to track the distortions it un-self-knowingly produces. Psychoanalysis calls this domain what is unconscious. For his part, Winnicott uses the idea of paradox to address this conundrum of how to hold and handle the limits of what knowledge can know and say about experience. Paradox is intrinsic to experience and Winnicott's sense is that creative living requires bearing paradox. Indeed, abiding with it.

Invocations of paradox are so ubiquitous in contemporary political theory that we may have difficulty receiving the sharpness of the contradictory claims contained in psychoanalytic uses of paradox. For Winnicott, paradox can only be held in the going on being of psyche–soma. We do justice to paradoxical truths only if psyche–soma can surrender to experiencing the truth of positions that are, and will remain, conceptually irreconcilable. Yet not everyone can or will. One tact Winnicott takes with those who do not abide paradox is to use humor. For instance, he manages philosophical objection to the metaphysical implications of his words by calling the philosopher out of his armchair to join his patient on the floor (1971, 90). Still, humor, like any other maneuver to manage the "metaphysics of grammar," ultimately fails when those whom one would have receive the reference have no psyche–somatic familiarity with the experiencing evoked.

To see the vital role of acceptance of paradox, we need begin with Winnicott's observation that creative living occurs in a third, intermediate space, between inner psychic life and the actual world in which the individual lives, but to which both ultimately contribute. This transitional space is the area where playing first takes place, wherein creativity is rooted, and from which life is found to be worth living because both the world and self are felt to be real and lively. Feeling real, says Winnicott, "is more than existing; it is finding a way to exist as oneself, and relate to objects as oneself, and to have a self into which to retreat for relaxation" (1971, 117).

Acceptance of a series of paradoxes enable transitional experiencing to arise. The first paradox we need abide is that in play, as in cultural experience, the object is created, yet is there waiting to be created (1971, 89). To this basic paradox, Winnicott adds three others even more uncanny than the first. When it comes to matters of separating and union, we need be able to hold, first, that two objects can be both joined and separated at the same time; second, that "with human beings there can be no separation, only the threat of separation"; and third, that there is a manner of union which can become an infinite area of separation filled with play and cultural enjoyment and creativity (1971, 108). Paradoxes are allowed and sustained by a quality of attitude transitional phenomena require—to be perceived rather than conceived of, to be felt there rather than only experienced conceptually in the mind. One can accept paradox if one can bear to embody an attitude of "not knowing" (Winnicott 1971, 86–87, 102; Khan 1983).

By contrast, the drive to resolve paradox is generally accompanied by unremitting fantasy omnipotence. As Winnicott once so aptly put it, when one finds the world not good enough, one has a mind instead (Winnicott 1958, 247) such that self-enclosed experience of mind becomes our perception of the world in lieu of fuller psyche–somatic living: "It is part of one's manic defense to be unable to give full significance to inner reality" (Winnicott 1958, 129). When there is withdrawal from inner reality and its "psychological register" of emotional intensity (Loewald, 41), this turning away from inner reality leaves external relationships and interactions deprived as well (Winnicott 1958, 130) because "without further differentiation of the inner world, no further differentiation of the object world takes place" (Loewald 2000, 267).

Reflective affective work on psyche–soma is needed to rejoin primary to secondary process, not only for further differentiated development of inner reality, but also for the elaboration of more conscientious external worldly relations. For the purposes of such work, what are paradoxes for secondary process are abiding truths for primary process thinking.

Abiding Not Knowing

The psychoanalytic Winnicott we need now is the thinker who can help us understand how a schizoid condition can become accepted as a common culture (1965, 59; see Buzby, this volume) such that we may come to live as if minds (or brains) alone are real, dissociated from earthly bodies, and seemingly compelled to bring ecological catastrophe upon what would otherwise be a good-enough world. Not until Winnicott differentiates between object-relating and object use, however, does he truly flesh out the qualitative distinctions in facilitating care he seems to be working toward all along. Facilitating individual maturational potential depends upon the capacity to survive object use. It may turn out that the survival of earthly life depends upon the same.

We tend to take for granted that we are able to use objects, just as we may presume that all children can play and that all adults can experience and participate in a culture (see Mehdi, this volume). Yet, Winnicott calls it "one of the most difficult things in human development" acquiring this capacity to use objects playfully and creatively. To be able to use an object is not the same as relating to an object. Here, Winnicott challenges common usage. Ordinarily, we think of using as exploitative and relating as mutual and dialogical. However, on Winnicott's account, object use is more open to the other, for object relating habitually entails trading in one's internal projections of the object. The paradox of object relating and use is that "usage cannot be described except in terms of acceptance of the object's independent existence, its property of having been there all the time" (1971, 88). When there is object-relating in the absence of capacity to use objects and be so used, then fantasy (not dreaming) defines experience. When capacities for object use prevail, mutuality arises in a transitional space between self and other, where the independent existence of beings and things becomes sensually apprehended and acknowledged.

The declarations of independence of living forms arise in a paradoxical play of aggression and love, joy and destruction. True loving is destructive not only because our unconscious fantasies need be continually destroyed if we are to meet. Other living forms only become available for use—in contrast to merely fantasy relating—by withstanding the assertions of self required to meet them. Object use works with that basic appetite and movement Winnicott calls aggression. Living forms survive object use when a gap opens between fantasy projections and dreams of the object in which both may come to participate, or not. It seems such loving survival will be felt only when the object can bear an attitude of "not knowing" what will happen, and conveys some sense of that "not knowing" to the one who seeks to use them in hope of meeting what is real. If we can go on using an object it is because this object, or others, have survived the play of loving aggression needed for destroying our fantasy ideas. Such play in loving aggression defines good-enough object use.

Surviving love entails a taste for separation (Epstein 2005) because it can arise only in the presence of someone able to tolerate that love does not only mean meeting or cultivating dependency needs (Winnicott 1971, 108). Varieties of non-survival of an object include "retaliation, withdrawal, defensiveness in any of its forms, as overall change in attitude in the direction of suspiciousness or diminished receptivity, and finally, a kind of crumbling, in the sense of losing one's capacity to function adequately" in relationship (Ghent 1990, 123; Winnicott 1971, 91, 93). When love is experienced as genuinely allowing for movement from dependency to autonomy, the space of intermediate experiencing can become "an infinite area of separation, which the baby, child, adolescent, adult may creatively fill with playing, which in time becomes the enjoyment of the cultural heritage" (1971, 108). If this is a potential space of ecstasy, it includes a dreaded possibility: "It could be said that with human beings there can be no separation, only a threat of separation; and the threat is maximally or minimally traumatic according to the experience of the first separatings" (1971, 108). As usual, Winnicott leans toward ecstasy while nodding to trauma lurking near.

Although these passages are too rich to be certain about, I make the following suggestions informed by Winnicott's attending to truths of primary process. All that is, in fact, *is* all knotted together and going on being, whether we perceive and experience it as such or not (Orlie 2014). Which is to say that "the ecological thought" of primary undifferentiation emerged for Winnicott, Milner, and Loewald some time ago, and as experience of soma–psyche always located some place in particular (Winnicott 1971, 95–110). By contrast, our common parlance and prevailing ways of life, place mind nowhere in particular and even celebrate as much (Morton 2010, 1–58). These earlier thinkers had a degree of luxury we may not—finding a world still sufficiently formless to be experienced as good enough (Winnicott 1971, 34–35, 95–110). What makes earthly life good enough is the possibility of creative confluence of imagination and form—as when the infant's spontaneous gesture meets a suitable medium. By now, the logic of capital so forcefully patterns the world—turning every being and thing, person and place, into commodities for sale—that experience of formlessness is threatened with foreclosure. If access to non-patterned experience closes, lost with it are experiences of unintegration from which inner experience of a good-enough world can arise and dream its way outward and forward.

According to this psychoanalytic understanding, "trauma" is the idea of a separation in going on being, even as there can be no actual separation, but only the threat of separation. When there is the trauma of threat of separation, soma-psyche feels and knows only separation to be real. Long before he thought to differentiate fantasy and dreaming, Winnicott got that the dissociated mind of manic defense is a flight from inner reality to the external world: "Omnipotent control of reality implies fantasy about reality. The individual [when ill] gets to external reality through the omnipotent fantasies elaborated in an effort to get away from inner reality" (1958, 130). By degrees, we are all ill in this sense, and Winnicott acknowledges his own gradually deepening appreciation of inner reality and with fluctuations in that appreciation "related to depressive anxiety in oneself" (1958, 129). Manic defense is Winnicott's word for experience of secondary process dissociated from primary process thinking, psyche and soma undone, leaving only rudderless mind. Though there is no meeting *that* mind. One can discern the operation of manic defense only after the fact, when health is emerging, when "the fantasying is changing into imagination related to dream and reality" (1971, 27). When fantasy omnipotence reigns, however, there is no incarnate undoing of this idea of a separation.

There is the paradox and the rub: It is only the idea of a separation, not actual. Yet, it is no mere idea because how we think about a capacity affects how it works (Milner, 223, 217). Which is to say that when there is trauma in this sense, we still operate under the idea of a separation, without perceiving that we are doing so, and even when we think that we are not doing so, say when we've had "the ecological thought," or are "new materialists." Fantasy omnipotence cannot know itself until it begins to become otherwise, dreaming its way to health and surrendering to what is real.

Winnicott observes traces of the threat of separation in evidence of mortal terror as unthinkable, annihilating anxiety (1974). Still, the separation is in actuality only a threat because there is no separation, at least so long as there is not actual murder. However, at the start—and perpetually for primary process thinking—subjectivity is "not oriented by actuality" (Milner 1987, 173). So, even if separation remains only a threat rather than actual, for any soma–psyche the threat is hardly an empty one. Winnicott emphasizes the experience is not of frustration, but of anxiety about the prospect of annihilation which need be continually, even manically, kept at bay, perhaps because it has already happened.

A most likely consequence of traumatic threat of a separation—in contrast to that infinite space of separation where creativity can arise and carry through—is a tendency to have a mind, and only a mind, in lieu of fuller psyche–somatic experiencing of a good-enough world. Secondary process is untethered from primary process, minds shorn from psyche–soma are taken to be brains (and might as well be in vats, as in the infamous philosophical thought experiment). The likely repercussion of traumatic threats of a separation—when separation from earthly life feels more real than feeling joined up with it, is fantasy omnipotence so entrenched as not to be able to be destroyed. As a consequence, no true object use can ensue, no deeper feelings of being alive and real arise, nor that boundless attachment to earthly life which Nietzsche hopes will "compel and enchant us relentlessly until we have become its humble and enraptured lovers" (Nietzsche 2001). What is tragic is that such unloved minds may themselves tend to become unlovely, and so see and make the world unlovely too. Is there anywhere you look where this seems not to be so?

What remains promising is that a good-enough world is still here to be found, only waiting to be created. Winnicott and Milner explicitly evoke a potential space of ecstasy. Melanie Klein, notes Milner, "laid great stress on the fact that it is dread of the original object itself, as well as the loss of it, that leads to the search for a substitute." Milner avers, "there is also a word needed for the emotional experience of finding the substitute, and it is here that the word ecstasy may be useful" (1987, 87). If earthly life is a potential space of ordinary ecstasy, then how is this promise of a good-enough world found and created? What are the qualities of facilitating care that can make it real?

A Taste for Separation in Singularly Loving Earthly Life

Many of our ways which purport to be for well being relentlessly foist a shell upon the kernel of individual maturational potential—not only upon children, but upon all earthly life—until "an environment [is] developing falsely into a human being, hiding within itself a potential individual" (Winnicott 1958, 99–100). A whole new range of meanings of Winnicott's sentence come alive in the Anthropocene when humanity has formed itself into a geophysical force altering the planet for millennia. From Winnicott I draw another way of facilitating care, what for present purposes and borrowing a phrase from Leo Bersani, I will call an impersonal narcissism (Bersani and Phillips 2008). The potential space of the ordinary ecstasy of earthly life requires a taste for separation (Epstein 2005). The taste, if you will, is the primary narcissism, the separation is what is impersonal.

Both ways of facilitating care live within us, as does a full array of primary and secondary process thinking. Perhaps a story about a weed can help illustrate such interplay. There is an annual weed which has become native to some land which I aspire to steward. The thing is not invasive, but it is pervasive, because conditions are such as they are, including a history of disturbance. I dislike the weed, finding its proliferation somehow unbefitting the form for which I am entrusted to care. For a long time, my predominant way of relating to the weed was to survey it from atop a skid steer, decked out with a sizable brush mower. In that way, I surely took care of that weed. There are parts of the land, especially near the garden and orchard fence, where more intimate contact can arise because no machine can work. One day, I was on my knees along the fence. It was a late summer day—that time of year when if you encounter any sizable patch of woods or field, the death in the air is palpable, without the sprinkler systems and fertilizers in town yards and city parks which obscure nature unfolding in its own way, from the inside out. I forget exactly why I was on my knees—most likely going to war with my bare hands—when in the brilliant quiet of that day, I heard the massive, at once frenzied and methodical, hum of honeybees. After many years of regularly engaging in a sort of nonpurposive meditation, Milner describes, I've become receptive to such reverberations from without, even when atop the skid steer, but especially when not. This was one of those "sudden moments" both Winnicott and Milner discuss, "when one's whole perception of the world changes—changes that happen, sometimes apparently out of the blue, but sometimes as the result of a deliberate shift of attention, one that makes the whole world seem newly created" (Milner 1987, 249). That weed in particular appeared new to me on that late summer day, when hardly anything else is in bloom for those hungry roaming pollinators but that darn weed. In the years since, I now join in the ordinary ecstasy including that weed, on this patch of good-enough world, where honeybees are now otherwise so often ravaged.

Have I ceased to cut, hack, and brush mow that weed? Hardly. Letting be and doing nothing, as every gardener knows, is not facilitating care. However, what, when, and how I do anything to that weed, and much else, is deeply changed by that momentary experience. This is just one story, among many I can tell, about how what I am entrusted to care for teaches me everything.

Yet is that storied moment really such a big deal? Every gardener knows we call weed any plant taking its place where we would have it be otherwise. Yet how does thinking that, or even saying it, get us anywhere nearer where we need to be in finding and creating a good-enough world? Only if we get on our knees, or at least down on the floor (Winnicott 1971, 90).

All of which is to say that there is an interplay of our capacity to survive being used as an object and our own capacity for object use. Winnicott's use of the parent–infant frame to discuss object use can inhibit our sense of its broader implications. The decisive matter of what enables one to survive being used as an object may fall out of mind. To begin, we need capacity to undergo the destruction of our fantasy "objects," starting with seeing beings and things, not as objects, but as "interactions and relationships" (Loewald 2000, 262). We might even find ourselves receiving intimations of the mindedness of all the other animals, insects, spiders about us (Nagel 2012, 32), or what I prefer to call the psychic life of living forms. Even the most fixated fantasies can become unbound, even edgeless, if we give due attention to primary process amidst the lively intimations of psyche–soma. To continue, a differentiated yet still developing mind's capacity to surrender to the destruction of fantasy, and to enter into a dreaming relationship with earthly life, is facilitated by abiding paradox and bearing not knowing, and as these feel for psyche–soma at the mercy of earthly life.

It is no easy matter for psyche–soma to bear "feeling the feeling in the feeling" of being alive (Reid 2015). Given psychic capacities, each of us is neither helpless nor powerless before other beings and things, yet we are dependent and interdependent, and sometimes absolutely so, and not only at the beginning. If we can acknowledge how ordinary it is to dissociate this being at mercy with all the rest of matter, we may appreciate the need for some practice of nonpurposive attention to mitigate the drive of psyche–soma to flee inner reality and indulge more than fantasy destruction of external reality. Milner explains how from a simple nonpurposive attention may emerge "a feeling of change in one's whole body perception as well as a move towards a feeling of intense interest in the sheer 'thusness', the separate and unique identity" of another being or thing. Along with this focused apperceptive appreciation for the singularity of an object, Milner elaborates a broader deliberate relating to perception "that is concerned with the actual conaesthetic awareness of one's existence in space and time." With such broadened awareness, Milner finds there is "not the narcissistic impoverishment of one's relation to the external world that one might have expected, but an actual enrichment of it…[and]…a sense of well-being that is a different kind from that which results from lack of tension between the ego and the super-ego, as when feeling one has lived up to one's standards" (Milner 1987, 281–282).

Following along, consider how an impersonal narcissism may be an antidote for a relentlessly personal narcissism eviscerating both children and earthly life. If facilitating care is not to become arid and depersonalized, there need be some taproot to a primary narcissism in which love and aggression, appetite and assertion, are inevitably entangled. "Perhaps the so-called fully developed, mature ego," Loewald offers in an explicit challenge to Freud, "is not one that has become fixated at the presumably highest or latest stage of development, having left the others behind it, but is an ego that integrates its reality in such a way that the earlier and deeper levels of ego-reality integration remain alive as dynamic sources of higher organization....It would seem that the more alive people are (though not necessarily more stable), the broader their range of ego-reality levels is" (Loewald 2000, 20).

And yet, surrendering our fantasy-fixed objects seems as difficult for us when it comes to earthly life as it is for many parents when it comes to our children. The problem is different in each case, though mutually illuminating. In the case of children, fantasies of the personal tend to eclipse truths of impersonality. In the case of earthly life, fantasy ideas that confound the impersonal with the depersonalized cut at our capacity to attune to the myriad ways we are thoroughly joined up with earthly life. Good-enough stewarding of earthly life, like good- enough parenting, passes through primary process, folding in its truths, as vital dimensions of integrating psychic capacity. By no means must we think of the rebinding of primary to secondary process as getting lost down there, so to speak, as when there is psychosis or, more familiarly, descent into unremittingly personal narcissism. Good-enough parenting and stewarding of earthly life require a distinctly impersonal narcissism.

It is fitting to refer to a primary (process) narcissism, as Winnicott means the term (1965, 148), because good-enough facilitating care requires significant immersion in the singularity of psyche–somatic experience if one is to be responsive to singular needs and attuned to a particular child or landscape. In good-enough parenting or stewarding, one is "all there," accessing the invariably singular qualities of psyche–soma, inside and out. Singularity of psyche–soma is availed by live roots to experiences of primary undifferentiation and later unintegration, made mindfully emergent by virtue of creative apperception.

Yet, it is fitting also to speak of the impersonality of this narcissism, whether conducted toward children or land, because one holds in abeyance secondary process categories of social and self-preoccupation, in some cases, surrendering them altogether. One meets this reality through identifications to be sure, but they need have a strongly impersonal dimension—not to say depersonalized—if one is to be singularly there, rather than impervious, intruding, imposing secondary process concerns, and substituting personally narcissistic gesture for what the other's spontaneity requires. One is making empathic contact, yet with some significant curtailment of the vicissitudes of personal and social secondary process preoccupations.

When interactions and relationships are explicitly, even deeply, asymmetrical—as they are with children and land—the issue is not what one gets in the way of self-recognition or personal gratification, at least not as these matters are construed by secondary process. When it comes to good-enough parenting and stewarding, the defining concern is what is skillful to give and how. If this sounds like giving too much, Winnicott affords ways to understand that good-enough facilitating care cannot be given while betraying true self. Indeed, what makes the self feel real and alive is the only sure guide when it comes to discerning whether the particulars of care are good enough in any given moment. Of course, this is not to say that good-enough facilitating care may not leave one bone-tired, sometimes sliding from unknowing to unsure, even courting the limits of surviving love. Still, personally narcissistic gratification of the false self leans away from good-enough facilitating care. Why? Because lively experience of the intimations of our own primary aggression is the only reliable guide in surviving love. "Social activity cannot be satisfactory," Winnicott offers, "except it be based on a feeling of *personal* guilt in respect of aggression" (1958, 207), which is to say that one needs feelings of concern in respect to one's own appetite and assertion, in respect to one's own object use and being so used in turn. False self is at once too personal and too depersonalized, not singular psyche–soma going on being.

I see the "threat of a separation" enacted in many of our predominant ways. Yet, before bringing to mind "fracking" for natural gas, think of our fantasy ideas of mothers and fathers, and the way children are imagined to reflect upon us, especially when we recollect that how we think about a capacity affects how it works (Milner 1987, 223, 217). As all great wisdom traditions concur, our children are not our children, they belong to themselves and all of life. However much more so is this true of earthly life. Yet, as much as anything we think of as mine or me, parents may have difficulty seeing how unfamiliar our children actually are. Truly loving a child, like truly loving anything, requires that we first acknowledge the impersonality of what we always begin presuming is ours, so that we may come more fully to meet and truthfully love what actually is, not our fantasy of it (Orlie 2014). Funny as it is to say, we must begin using our children as objects if they are to have much hope in using us. Only then do we have any hope of apprehending their actual psychic capacities. The same goes for the rest of earthly life.

References

Abram, J. 2007. *The Language of Winnicott.* 2nd ed. London: Karnac.

Benjamin, J. 1988. *Bonds of Love.* New York: Pantheon.

———. 1995. *Like Subjects. Love Objects.* New Haven: Yale University Press.

Bersani, L., and A. Phillips. 2008. *Intimacies.* Chicago: University of Chicago Press.

Bollas, C. 1993. *Why Oedipus? Becoming a Character.* New York: Routledge.

Epstein, M. 2005. *Open to Desire.* New York: Avery.

Ghent, E. 1990. Masochism, Submission, Surrender—Masochism as a Perversion of Surrender. *Contemporary Psychoanalysis* 26: 108–136.

Greenberg, J., and S. Mitchell. 1983. *Object Relations in Psychoanalytic Theory.* Cambridge, MA: Harvard University Press.

Khan, M. 1983. *Hidden Selves.* London: Karnac.

Loewald, H.W. 2000. *The Essential Loewald: Collected Papers and Monographs.* Hagerstown, MD: University Publishing Group.

Milner, M. 1987. *The Suppressed Madness of Sane Men.* London: Routledge.

Morton, T. 2010. *The Ecological Thought.* Cambridge, MA: Harvard University Press.

Nagel, T. 2012. *Mind and Cosmos.* New York: Oxford University Press.

Nietzsche, F. 2001. *The Gay Science.* New York: Cambridge University Press.

Ogden, T.H. 1989. *The Primitive Edge of Experience.* Latham, MD: Aronson.

Orlie, M.A. 2014. For the Love of Earthly Life: Nietzsche and Winnicott Between Modernism and Naturalism. In *The Aesthetic Turn in Political Theory*, ed. N. Kompridis, 169–187. New York: Bloomsbury.

Reid, W.T. 2015. Personal communication, August 24.

Rose, J. 2003. *On Not Being Able to Sleep.* Princeton: Princeton University Press.

Stern, D. 1998. *The Interpersonal World of the Human Infant.* London: Karnac.

Winnicott, D.W. 1939. Aggression. In *The Child and the Outside World (1957)*, 167–175. London: Tavistock.

———. 1958. *Through Pediatrics to Psycho-Analysis.* London and New York: Tavistock and Basic Books.

———. 1965. *The Maturational Processes and the Facilitating Environment.* London: Hogarth.

———. 1971. *Playing and Reality.* New York: Routledge.

PART II

The Subject Faced with Deprivation and Disaster

CHAPTER 5

Playing 'Riot': Identity in Refuge—Absent Child Narratives in the 2013 Hindu–Muslim Riots in Muzaffarnagar, India

Zehra Mehdi

Nineteenth-century Persian Urdu poet, Mirza Ghalib, was a self-proclaimed atheist, whose poetic reference to Allah was at best a dialog with self. In the couplets 'Where there was nothing, there was Allah/When there will be Nothing, there will be Allah/Existing is what has erased me/ Had I not existed, would I be, me?,' his existential speculation about the self in conjunction with belief of the eternal presence of Allah also echoes the dread of the Muslim in India who is killed because he is Muslim. Allah becomes an adjective, whose omnipresence contrasts the finite identity of being Muslim. This erasure of existence in the face of an overarching presence of Allah has been the trajectory of all communal riots where individual lives are disregarded in the name of religion and people are killed in the name of God. While Ghalib's poetry psychoanalytically explores a nihilistic desire of self, it also presents the dilemma of Muslim identity in India, which meets its erasure in the annihilatory fantasy for the Other.

The unconscious Kleinian fantasy of obliterating the Other (Isaacs 1948, 75–76) is what binds the two communities—Hindus and Muslims—in

Z. Mehdi (✉)
Ambedkar University, Delhi, India

M.H. Bowker, A. Buzby (eds.), *D.W. Winnicott and Political Theory*,
DOI 10.1057/978-1-137-57533-3_5

India. Noted political psychologist Ashish Nandy (1987, 1990), in his study of Partition and communal riots that followed, wrote how Partition ruptured the syncretic culture of India where Hindus and Muslims lived *with* differences. While there would always be such fantasies, it was the event of Partition, rudimentarily conjectured on the basis of religion, which unleashed these fantasies at a scale that can at best be described as a 'psychotic break'—a loss of reality and an acting out of impulses. Almost all communal riots following 1947 pitted Hindus against Muslims in the name of supremacy of religion, unconsciously reacting to the 'unmourned loss of Partition reinvoked in all communal violence' (Nandy 2013, 65).

The communal riots at Muzaffarnagar, a district in Western Uttar Pradesh, were no different. The 2013 electoral campaign tacitly propagated the rhetoric of Muslims overpowering Hindus, and called for restoring 'Hindu Raj in Muzaffarnagar.' Hate speech fuelled by the party leaders instigated speculations of a love affair between a Hindu girl and a Muslim boy. It was projected as an attempt of the Muslims to appropriate India as an Islamic state (evoking the dread of Partition) by entrapping Hindu women in fallacies of love, popularly known as 'love jihad'. Muzaffarnagar was known for a syncretic culture, preserved in the face of the rampant communal riots during Partition, and this was torn apart in August 2013. Mobs of Jats (the predominant Hindu caste) set fire to houses of their Muslim neighbors, insidiously raped women, and dismembered Muslim men (Dixit 2013, 2014, 2015; Bhalla 2013). The Muslim community, though a significant minority, did not stage a resistance primarily due to the political clout that Jats had with the campaigning party. They only resistance was their attempt to survive. Several men and women managed to escape through the sugarcane fields clutching their children, but did not emerge alive. They were chased by Jats cheering 'Clean India of Muslims,' who ravaged the fields with swords raping and killing primarily women while men managed to escape with children. Most relief camps had a larger population of children in comparison to men and a scanty number of women. These children were the ones who had been orphaned, had witnessed the riot, and had somehow escaped while their families perished. Where does this riot-witnessing child feature in the Hindu–Muslim narrative of *Othering*? How does he/she understand what he/she saw? And, more significantly, how does one engage with his/her expression of the riot?

In the words of Adam Phillips (1998, 23), 'language is the beast in the nursery,' such that the child is expected to do the things others do or do them the way they do. To listen to a child talk one needs to allow the child to speak its language, which D.W. Winnicott expounded as *playing*. While allowing children to play, one needs to understand how they are not just representing their psychic reality, but also creatively negotiating the paradox between inside and outside, and, in this context, historical othering and victimization. The chapter makes an attempt to talk to the child as it allows the child to play and makes sense of their playing while keeping in mind the context of the play: *the riot itself*. It also outlines how this playing, when located in the historical discourse of Muslim identity in India, reveals something that has been perpetually absent: *the experience of being Muslim in India*. It is not only what a Muslim experiences being a Muslim but rather what possibly underlies the unconscious mechanisms at work that manifests this experience. It goes on to conclude how playing serves as a refuge to the identity of the child, by allowing it to play and hence be alive!

Locale of the Environment: The Relief Camp at Kandhla, Muzaffarnagar

The communal violence that sparked on August 13, 2013, across several villages in Muzaffarnagar between Jats and Muslims led to a massacre of Muslims. Some escaped to reach Kandhla, a neighboring district less affected by the riot (Mody 2014). Lisarh was among the five villages that recorded maximum deaths of Muslims, with the village being entirely wiped of its Muslim population. It was also a village where maximum houses of Muslims were burned. It was ironic since the Muslims belonged to a community whose primary occupation was brick making, and almost all the Jat houses were constructed by largely their Muslim neighbors. These displaced Muslims had now come together to build a new at Kandhla, a relief camp that suffered grossly from government neglect. Hosting the largest number of displaced Muslims from Lisarh, it provided few amenities. Even the compensation, which was sanctioned by the state government, was withdrawn citing reasons of documentation.

Kandhla is a few miles away from Lisarh in the Muzaffarnagar district. Survivors from Lisarh arrived over a period of five months, having spent weeks hiding in sugarcane fields. Though people appeared in spurts from the 50-acre sugarcane field surrounding the camp, and over several months it housed more than 25 families, or about 80 people, most of whom were children under ten (Mody 2014). These were the children who had lost their families or parts of it to the pogrom, and had escaped in groups through the sugarcane field to reach the camp. Having lost their families, they were taken care of by young men as the camp had a scarce population of women. It was rumored that most of the women from the district of Lisarh (maximum number housed in this camp) had been raped and in most cases immolated (Dixit 2013, 2014, 2015). Older women from Kandhla volunteered to care for the children at the camp, and would feed and bathe them, leaving them in care of men at the camp during the nights. Most of the children had witnessed deaths of their parents, and several of them had seen their fathers being dismembered and mothers being raped while they hid in the sugarcane fields.

My research on Muslim identity took me to Kandhla five months after the communal riot (January 2014). Although my initial research frame warranted narratives of adolescents who had witnessed the riots, I found myself intuitively drawn to the children at camp. Following are extracts of my field notes from research:

> There was a huge muddy patch where the soaked mud stood as if fresh every time I entered the camp. It reminded me how an intense cold wave had gripped north India, making the otherwise receding winters in Muzaffarnagar wet and damp. Several young mothers with children less than a few weeks or a few months old lost their newborns to the relentless winter chill and in six months, the Kandhla relief camp had already seen deaths of 12 newborn babies. Several life stories of men and women came my way, never as a narrative, but as a series of broken dialogues developed over several months of visits to the camp. I was aware of the 'silence,' which was looming in accounts of the riot (Visvanathan 2013) where the mainstream coverage of the riot documented by a government who was speculated to have instigated them remained exceedingly political. I chose to collect narratives from the relief camp of adolescents as I was developing a larger psychoanalytic narrative of being Muslim in India. Even as life stories unfolded, poignant and reflective I found myself unable to engage with the narratives of adolescents. I was able to listen to their experiences and empathize with them but something was missing. I was anticipating a theme and it kept emerging across narratives and I began to speculate my exploration of the unconscious which felt confirming and complaint. I kept wondering what was I doing as a psychoanalytic researcher—how was my work analytic?

Winnicott in his works in the 1960s states how psychoanalytic work can only truly happen when there is something that is unknown. Adam Phillips writes how, according to Winnicott, the role of a psychotherapist is where there is the unconscious and only when we are truly in the 'grip of something unknowable we begin to understand something which is tentative and barely knowable' (Horne and Lanyado 2012, xxi). This 'not knowing' was most acutely felt in my observation of the children roaming around in the camp, largely left on their own. They collected themselves near the sugarcane fields and engaged themselves in rigorous activities. Most of them ran around in circles while others chased puppies in the camp. Undaunted by the enormity of their loss and the helplessness of their circumstance, the children of the relief camp piqued my interest. I experienced two distinct emotions: anger and amazement. I was angry at them for being unaffected by the tragedy that had befallen them. But I was equally amazed at their ability to not be locked in it. None of the academic material that I read about children in communal violence (Priya 2012; Bhadra 2012; Apfel and Simon 2000; Apfel and Simon 1996; Garbarino and Kostelny 1996; Apfel and Simon 1991) cited children in camps who were able to play. They had narratives of how children were traumatized and deeply disturbed speaking about the violence, borrowing language from adults (Das 1990) to speak about the riot. Children of Muzaffarnagar did speak about the riot, but in a Winnicottian language: They played.

As I sat to observe them over weeks, I did not know what they were doing or how they were doing it. I knew it was something I did not understand, and a psychoanalytic engagement was the only means through which I could hear what the children of Muzaffarnagar had to say: I had to let them play. So in some ways this chapter is pithily about their play, my observation of their play, and the analysis 'in between.'

Play in the Relief Camp: 'The Sugarcane Escape' and 'The Loyal Swine'

Using Winnicott's idea on psychoanalytic research (Winnicott 1965) one can conjecture that play lies between the poetic truth and scientific enquiry, between the poet's epiphany and the scientist's sustained engagement. In psychoanalytic research, one gains accesses to possible meaning through a revelation what Winnicott (1967) would call surprise. For it to emerge as an interpretation, however, the observation needs to be endured through time and patience. It is then that it emerges as a 're-searched' plausibility of the unconscious. Explaining further the significance of time in psychoanalytic research, Honey Oberio Vahali writes in 'From the Researchers

Notebook' (2003, 23–28) that what looks like a simple observation at the outset becomes a spectrum of unconscious communication over time and includes the researcher as a part of the field, rendering their observation to carry potent moments of analysis. Interested in what engaged the children at the camp and guided by psychoanalytic value (Frosh 1991; Young 1994)—to use psychoanalytic sensibility to understand the riots—I sat at the edge of the sugarcane field to observe their play. During several hours of sitting silently, awaiting some semblance of knowing, I found myself gripped with a sense of an odd energy where something crucial was happening among the children. After sustained observation it emerged as a pulsating engagement between children, games that I call 'Loyal Swine' and 'Sugarcane Escape.' I describe them and present an analysis of these games as idioms of Winnicottian playing.

The Loyal Swine

A sickly, starved puppy ran around the relief camp. A bunch of little children ran behind it, trailing and cuddling, almost cradling it in their laps. Taking turns to caress it, they reached the side of the camp that adjoined the sugarcane fields, separated by sewer drain. All the dirt and waste of the camp flowed through it. Standing on top of the sewer, they dropped the puppy into it and roared with laughter. As the puppy struggled to find its balance and tried to run, they stepped down into the sewer themselves and ran after, catching him again to throw him in. It was interesting how every time it was dropped in the muddy waste, the hapless puppy was exclaimed to be a *soor* (a pig). After a while, one could see the puppy was tired and unable to run or even stand up after being thrown. This worried the boys, who picked it up and once again placed it in their laps cradling it. They would take turns to walk with it throughout the camp and one could sense them talking to the puppy. The puppy that was cared for throughout the day was dropped yet again in the drain toward the evening, and the entire routine was repeated until he was picked up and caressed during the night again to be dropped in the drain in the morning.

These five-year-old children displayed the perplexity of the riot etched in their nascent psyches as they struggled to comprehend it. They echo a scene in Deepa Mehta's (1998) cinematic version of Bapsi Sidhwa's *Ice Candy Man, 1947-Earth*. In a scene, the eight-year old Lenny, a Parsi girl disabled by polio, watches a Muslim man being ripped apart as vehicles to which his limbs were tied move in opposite directions. Later, she enacts the same with her doll when she pulls it from one end while her cousin pulls from the other. After it is ripped open, she mends the ripped parts with a safety pin. Her mother is perplexed about her ripping the doll and then mending it. She asks the governess: 'Is my little Lenny trying to understand this madness?' 'I don't know Madam ji ... maybe she is mending it,' she replies.

The Loyal Swine can be best understood as act of mending what remains torn, not just in their syncretic village population but also in their minds. A 'generalist' (Erikson 1966, 152) in nationality, ethnicity, religion, or political ideology, the child finds a reservoir to externalize its unintegrated bad and good self and object images (Volkan 1988, 1997, 1999). In the utilization of this reservoir, he no longer remains a generalist, and avoids feeling the tension of object relations. This utilization, however, does not come through experiences that the child might have had on its own. It is brought into the awareness of the child where the other community is identified as this reservoir (Paul Williams 2010, 195–196) and where the unintegrated 'bad' self/object images can be externalized. The child thereby enters the adult discourse of 'self verses them' which is essentially historical and predates his/her own experience. Volkan (2000) illustrates this idea using the example of pig in the tense political relations between Greeks and Turks in Cyprus. The pig, reared by the Greek as a pet and considered dirty by the Moslem Turk, becomes the reservoir of the externalized 'bad' self and object images such that the Moslem child is discouraged from playing with it, even if he/she might want to. The child unconsciously finds a suitable container for its aggressive tendencies and renders the pig contaminated and forgoes its desire to love it.

An Identity in Refuge

The play with the puppy at the camp illustrates a similar story of the child entering into the world of historical discourse, and shows a psyche assimilating the assault in the name of religious and political identity in the riot. *Soor* is the local dialect for the pig. It is proscribed in Islam, and was a frequent target of abuse for Muslims rampant in the riot. Mobs storming the village and circling the sugarcane field deprecated Muslims as pigs, vowing to dismember them and throw their parts to Pakistan. The dog, on the other hand, was a favorite animal in the village, and almost every Hindu family had a dog to call its own. When the children throw the puppy, they are not only externalizing the badness onto the collective reservoir of the Hindu. They are also identifying with their own expatriation as Muslims in the village. Their familial loyalty is denigrated as they descend from being dogs to being pigs. When thrown in the accumulated muck of the drain, a metaphor for existing history of Partition, Muslims are not only dislodged of their allegiance, but in being called pigs they are banished in their own identity, as the pig is denounced by Muslims as well (*Khabeesh ka bacha* [son of a pig] was a popular abuse in pre-Partition India in Muslim communities). A puppy being referred to as a pig is not just a metaphor of betrayal that the Muslims feel at the hands of the Hindus—who in their assault threw them out of the village. It also leads a Muslim child to see his/her own Muslim identity in the piglet: contaminated and dirty. Erik Erikson's negative identity (1963) and Frantz Fanon's 'blackness' (1952) are the best examples of projective identification in the sociohistorical realm, where self has been prismed through the way one has been 'looked at' by the opposing community (Frosh 1989; Rustin 1999; Elliot 1994). The child is thereby unable to arrive at a capacity for object relating where he sees himself disempowered and ostracized as a Muslim, and acts that out in the play. Loyal Swine, besides being a telling tale of an identity in refuge, intricately captures the impact of the riot on the psyche of the child.

A Delinquent Hope of Finding the Mother

The act of little children throwing the puppy in the drain and erupting in laughter can be conjured as an act of delinquency, an expected consequence of witnessing unfathomable violence at an early age. However, Winnicott's conceptions of delinquency are most useful to understand the five-year-olds as architects of this play. In his famous talk on *Delinquency as a Sign of Hope* (1960), he says it's important to understand that the child displaying the tendency toward delinquency is enacting a state of deprivation. Unlike privation the child is not acting out an environmental absence, but a state of deprivation where once 'things went well and then they did not go well enough' (1986, 92–93). The riot was a 'change in the environment happened which the child was not old enough to understand' (1986, 91). Throwing of the puppy is the antisocial drive that takes the child back to the moment where the deprivation occurred—where they felt the onslaught of the riot. Things were seemingly fine prior to the riot, however the advent of the riot produces unthinkable anxiety in the little child who does not and perhaps cannot understand it. He copes by being unaffected by it in the initial months. After a while, there is an urge to go back to the moment of deprivation, back to the state where the child first felt overwhelmed by anxiety, the scene of the riot itself. It is here that Loyal Swine is recreation understood as an attempt to undo the acute vulnerability evoked within the child by the riot. Only when the child is able to make sense of the riot can he begin to undo the anxiety and begin assimilating the trauma.

In this moment of getting back—throwing of the puppy—one can read hope. 'There is some beginning of hope as the child unconsciously gets back' (1986, 92) to the incidence of the riot. This hope is the unconscious desire of the child to be able to take someone who will listen back to the moment of deprivation or to the phase in which deprivation became consolidated into an inescapable reality (1986, 98). The hope is that the boys playing will be able to reexperience in relation to the therapeutic capacity (created by the sustained presence of the/my observation) the intense suffering that followed immediately as the reaction to deprivation. As they go back to the intense feeling of suffering of the fateful riot, there follows a memory of before the riot where the child has reached back either to the lost capacity of objects or the lost capacity of framework (1986, 99) and this is manifested through their caressing of the harassed puppy. However, as their actions become cyclic and throwing and caressing conjoin to form a pattern of compulsive action, one knows that hope remains fractured in these children. Despite their ability to express consistent affection for the puppy over weeks they never stop throwing the puppy and keep referring it as a pig. What do their repetitive actions connote?

Winnicott writes in his (1963) paper on 'Concern' that the mother serves two functions for the infant: that of an environment called environment-mother and that of an object called object-mother (74). The idea of the mother begins through the process of continuity where she is experienced as the environment before she is experienced as an object (Bollas 2011, 2). As an environment, the mother enables the creative use of the world and of creative use of objects. A discontinuity in the environment would leave the child bereft of creativity, plunging him into an intolerable state of confusion and terror, which is something that happened in the riot. Their playing fosters hope as the child unconsciously caught in the compulsive act of throwing the puppy tries to creatively find the mother through playing. This finding is of creating the mother as an environment instead of an object. Playing thereby becomes hopeful as the child exhibits his/her capacity to create rather than find an object (1963, 93). This capacity to create can be further understood as the capacity of the child to be alone. For five months these children were compliant and easy to handle, but after five months they began consistently exhibiting their routine with the puppy. It is of significance to note that this playing began upon my visits to the camp. Once my presence was ascertained with its consistency and permanence they were able to be alone in my presence (Winnicott 1958, 29) and find their environment-mother in my psychoanalytic observation of their play.

Fractured Concern in Muslim Guilt

It is of some usefulness to also understand how the actions of throwing the puppy and of caressing it are contained in this 'creative environment' of playing. It can be done through engaging with their capacity for concern. Winnicott differentiates between concern and guilt, and it is useful to understand if the caressing of the puppy comes as a reaction to the guilt of throwing it or as genuine concern. The sense of guilt originates out of 'anxiety mixed with a special quality—the conflict between love and hate' (Winnicott 1963, 72). Concern, on the other hand, functions as a healthy sense of guilt, which requires the ability to integrate further by tolerating ambivalence and accepting responsibility without foreclosing, deadening, cauterizing, or, most significantly, splitting. In the play, the child expresses being torn between love and hate—predominant split emotions experienced as Muslims in the camp. Even as the child joins the externalizing of the Muslim and hates it by throwing, it also expresses love for the injured, abused, and harassed Muslim through caressing and embracing. Even as the child attempts to go back to the moment of assault in the riot through the act of abusing the puppy, it remains unable to completely return to hope in expressing love for it. It is here that the Loyal Swine, the pig, finds the guilt of the Muslim in the experience of the riot and still awaits it to become concern. As Muslims in the camp oscillate between being hated and wanting to experience love, they are left with guilt of being Muslims. They are being seen as the disloyal puppy, conjectured as a traitor and cast outside its own identity of a loyal friend and rendered a swine.

While little children in Loyal Swine narrate the pernicious consequence of the riot onto their psyche, the older ones (seven to ten years) recount their witnessing of the pandemonium of the riot. It marks their entry into the psychic world of Muslim identity with its political and historical relations. I have named this play Sugarcane Escape.

The Sugarcane Escape

Seven- to ten-year-old boys were running one after the other. Initially, it seemed random, but soon it was clear that the groups were made contingent on speed. Those who ran faster comprised one group, and those who did not composed the other. It was interesting since there were no formal divisions between them, and often while chasing they would ask each other who was being chased. Often the number of children *to be chased* declined and several of them were found chasing one person. The way the person could outrun the group was to run toward the sugarcane field. That was the outer limit, and if a child managed to reach it, he/she did not have to be a part of the running anymore and could take rest. However, this run toward the sugarcane field was conditioned. While running they had to pick up something that belonged to them and run. That could be anything from pieces of rags, which were strewn across their makeshift tents, to the younger children who were playing nearby. In some cases, older girls were grabbed by the arm and forced to run as well. They joined in almost seamlessly and let the boys lead. As the boys dodged their pursuers before making a run for the sugarcane fields, some of the children who had been chasing would stop to sling mud at them. They had to undergo the mudslinging as the running children cheered '*jalla* ... *jalla*' (burnt ... burnt).

What was most interesting that none of the children really ever entered the sugarcane field even when ahead of the chase. The children would slow their speed, drop what they were carrying, or get busy washing away the mud from their face, and often would stop few feet from what would constitute their final escape. They would get caught by the ones chasing, and would be taken to the sugarcane field by the entire group who would stand at the edge and hurl abuses at them. While listening to the abuses, the child, now *caught*, would stand silently pressing his knees against one another and it looked as if he was pressing something between his legs. He was then pulled back into the group after an exchange of embraces where he soon joined others and started chasing someone else. It was amazing how almost all the boys in the group were able to assay this role effectively, and no one ever picked a fight. Through a collection of child narratives, it was revealed that it was a play that the children had devised in the camp itself, and was not something they played back in their villages. Different aspects to the play were additions that were brought by each new child who entered the camp from the sugarcane fields. If the addition was not agreeable to the other children, it was not assimilated into the *play*. Only parts that were mutually agreed upon were retained.

The Sugarcane Escape can be understood as an enactment of the riot most of the children witnessed. The inability to differentiate between groups and its members in the play represented the homogeneousness of Muzaffarnagar, which was its hallmark until the riot. The riot had come as a shock to most who never saw communities defining themselves through religion and had remained unaffected even during the divisive communal violence of 1947. The play of children reflected the confusion of not knowing who was on whose side—perhaps confusion about the existence of sides themselves. The crude difference that emerged was on the basis of strength; those children who ran fast occupied one side and those who did not took the other. This primary difference signified the (im)balance of the riot where Jats outnumbered the Muslims. As they chased their Muslim neighbors, they were met with no resistance from the Muslim mobs who fled toward the sugarcane field. It is no wonder that the final escape was the sugarcane field for the child and to survive the chase one had to run toward it. As their houses were doused with fire, several Muslims attempted to flee, grasping whatever belongings they could lay their hands on. In fact, several of them could not make it to the 'sugarcane escape' because they were unable to leave the premises of their houses and perished with them. Most escape attempts were made by men who struggled to get their families out. In re-creating the final run, the children solemnly demonstrate the loss of their families. The mudslinging represents the literal attack on Muslims. While they were escaping, there were burnt logs of woods thrown at them from the streets by Jats, and several women and children were severely injured. They fell behind succumbing to their assault. The ones who survived had to dash in the mud to douse the fire and survived with scars. Most of these children had survived such attacks personally, and hence their play became an unconscious means of recreating their wounds and sharing their scars.

Besides play being a technique through which one 'gains insight into the unconscious processes' (Klein 1955, 122), it is both a process of doing (Winnicott 1971, 14) and of pleasure (1989, 278). According to Winnicott 'play' was neither a matter of inner psychic reality nor a matter of external reality (1967, 368). It was both inner and outer meeting at an 'in-between space.' Winnicott describes it as the transitional phenomena, 'the intermediate area of experience … between primary creative activity and projection of what has already been introjected, between primary unawareness of indebtedness and the acknowledgement of indebtedness' (1971, 2).

This 'in-between-ness' of Winnicottian playing allows for the understanding of the Sugarcane Escape as a space created to reverse the emasculation which was brought upon Muslims in the riots as well as their struggles in their identity of victimhood.

Finding the Father in (In)Destructible Environments

The suddenness of the riots caught Muslims by surprise, and they offered no resistance and fled toward the sugarcane field in huge numbers. This led to their being denounced as cowards not just by the Hindus, but also by Muslims in neighboring districts. Even the women who came from Kandhla to take care of the children during the day chided their masculinity for blemishing Islam through their impotency in fleeing. Children in Sugarcane Escape represent the visual execution of the emasculation of Muslims, and reverse it by identifying with the perpetrator: the Jat. It is evinced in the squirming body and pressing legs of the child who stands listening to the shouts flung at him after being caught in his attempt to reach the sugarcane field. This impact carries connotations of historical violence where killing of Muslim men was unfolded through stripping of their lower bodies to ascertain their identity as Muslims by the circumcised penis. Women and female children could hoodwink assaults by doing away with the burqa, but Muslim men and boys did not have this choice. Muzaffarnagar was different since the ones killing knew their Muslim neighbors. Ripping the pants, even of little boys, then acquired a different meaning than discerning identity. It was a deliberate act of humiliation where the pants, or *salwars*, of Muslim male members were sliced with swords as they ran for their lives. The insistent abuse in the play gave space to the fury of the Muslim, which was absent in the riot to come into existence. The rage of the Muslim evoked by being humiliated was expressed by acting out the castration experience onto the other. Across several observations, I thought they were embodying the Hindu as they castrated the Muslim in their rage: a fragment from the riot. However, over months it emerged that through playing the children were able to provide for each other something which was not provided by the framework of the riot: an expression of aggressiveness.

This aggressiveness in seven- to ten-year-old boys is most difficult to address, however crucial to exhibit. Aggressive tendencies are difficult to address since they carry a certain omnipotence as a manifestation of the child's destructive impulses. While a delinquent child seeks return to an environment, the mother who can restore the deprived state of the child's fantasy, the aggressive child seeks the father who can tolerate his destructive impulse. According to Winnicott, the child 'can explore crude destructive activities related to movement in general, and also more specifically express destruction that has to do with the fantasy that accumulates round the hate' (1963, 94) as he knows that his environment will survive it through the father. For Winnicott, the father is the indestructible environment that allows the child to do a very complex thing—integrate his destructive impulses with his loving ones and organize his life constructively in order not to feel too bad about the real destructiveness that goes on in his mind. Along with the mother, he provides for an environment that is not destroyed by the anger of the child and thereby becomes safe for the child itself. These impulses are contained in the idea of social security (1944, 114–115) by the union of parents who together offer the child an environment which has rules and limits that he/she abides by and which he/she can trust: rules that will control them and trust that will take care of them. However, in the scenario of the riot, the cohesion of the environment crumbled crudely. While the younger children display their psychological need to re-create the mother, the older children portray the need for the father in their rule-bound aggressive play. In the absence of a sense of control of one's surroundings in the riot, the destructive impulses of the child ran amok. Unable to find a suitable outlet for it they recreate the scene of the riot and express their destructive impulses.

It was not the violence of the riot that caused the greatest terror among the children. It was the absence of the family that caused this dread. Their families would have been able to lend them a sense of dependence and continuity ensuring their survival. The absence of it fractured the capacity of the child to tolerate his own destructive impulses, and further created a state of despair, where witnessing the death of parents intensified helplessness and perpetuated terror. Winnicott's conception of disintegration explains this terror. It is the failure of holding and the absence of the maternal ego support in absolute dependence where acute experience cannot be gathered within the ego (1958, 150). It leaves the child plagued by the intensity of the impulse where he is unable to assimilate it. Some assimilation comes through their playing where they are able to regress, act out, be destructive and yet do not fall apart. Winnicott would call this a means of a creating an environment that the child can trust through continuous play where these children 'unintegrate.' Mirroring the scenario of the riot where they were both spectators and protagonists, the children do more in moving from regressive tendencies to ego capacities and its evinced through the way they add to the play aspects that demonstrate not just their creativity but through their creativity their ability to enter the discourse of Muslim identity in its discursive aspect.

Playing Riot: The Muslim Experience

The discursive aspect is etched in the deliberate attempt of the child being chased to get caught. This can be explained by understanding how after being made the visual spectacle of humiliation the child is embraced three times and brought back into the group seamlessly.

I believe that it is here that Winnicottian playing happened. It is in playing that the children are able to create an intermediate space between the historical truth of the riot—Muslims been driven out through the sugarcane field—and narrative truth (Spence 1982) of victimization as a Muslim. It chronicles the experience of Muslims festering through riots, which lies between being evicted and not being able to return to the village as a Muslim. The play creates the experience of the Muslim where despite being abused he is welcomed in the village as a Muslim. It is evinced in embracing the abused child three times which is a social salutation exchanged among Muslim men both within and across communities, characteristic for Muslims in India. It narrates the unconscious desire of Muslims who despite their humiliation are not abandoned rather are accepted as they are back into the community. It was interesting how this intermediate space in the play carried the unconscious associations of the community as well. Several months later, I began collecting narratives of Muslim men who had evaded speaking to me. They echoed a sense of 'loss of masculinity' in saving their lives rather than putting up a defense. They further expressed trepidation about returning to their village with the dignity of being Muslim hoping not to be discriminated against. What these men in the relief camp discussed urgently 11 months after the riot was already unconsciously expressed by the children through their playing. The abuse 'created' at the edge of the sugarcane and not found in the field itself connotes how the play uses the boundary to accommodate two stifled experiences of Muslims, of being unable to retaliate as Muslims and being able to return back as Muslims.

By playing the child is able to have a place for the Muslim to exist which was neither created by the Hindu who exiled the Muslim into the sugarcane field nor could be found by the Muslim who remained lost to the sugarcane field and forever cast as different. The play allows the Muslim to return, undo hurt and reimagine integration in the community. It thereby goes beyond the realms of history of violence and the experience of victimization. The experience of being a Muslim in India is located in this play, this in-betweenness which is not locked in blame for the Hindus or in one's own helplessness as a Muslim. Playing thereby becomes the means of experiencing between inner and external life.

How does the riot survive within the children of the camp? It survives in them through playing as an experience which puts the Muslim experience of the riot in between its historical trajectory of being Muslim and a subjective narrative of the same. Through playing the child is able to create an in-between space where the feelings of betrayal, abuse, externalization, and guilt as a Muslim can coexist with the feeling of wanting to be a part of the community. It is therefore not play carrying rudiments of the riot which narrate the Muslim experience, but rather it is this in-between space which the child creates by 'playing riot'—playing to create an experience of the riot where the Muslim father is sought and the Muslim mother is created by the Muslim child.

Winnicottian Experience at Kandhla: Finding the Muslim Experience

Winnicott finds playing to be precarious. He writes about how 'the thing about playing is the precariousness of the interplay between personal psychic reality and the actual control of objects' (1967, 47), but goes on to compare this precariousness with magic which arises in intimacy and is sustained through reliability. I wish to add another dimension to this magical precariousness of playing: ***not knowing***. But then where does the access to not knowing lie? How does one know not knowing?

It is a presumption that the unconscious can be known and a myth that the psychoanalyst can know. Freud states that it is the task of the analyst to make out what has been forgotten from the traces of what is left behind, or, more correctly, to construct it (1937, 258). Even as he constructs from the rudiments of the patients psyche, the analyst primarily only 'makes out' and does not know. Thomas Ogden writes that, 'the utter unpredictability and power of the unconscious can be felt but never known' (2007, 18). It is crucial for analysis that the analyst does not know and can tolerate not knowing. But where does this not knowing lead us, and how it is useful in comprehending the unconscious—the task at hand? Philips lends a potential answer. According to him, the analyst and the patient pursue a creative dialog where neither the analyst nor the patient know, or can know, but consistently endeavor knowing. He calls it 'the Winnicottian experience' (Kuhn 2013). For him, Winnicott in his work was able to access those aspects of the unconscious, which lacked form and shape because he 0premised engagement with the unconscious through a relationship instead of interpretation. This relationship creates an experience as means to access the unconscious through playing, which in Winnicottian conceptions of the psyche is the fundamental capacity for healthy living. While for Freud, a healthy individual was able to love and work, for Winnicott he should also be able to play, to be able to exist in the in-between spaces of not knowing and wanting to know, of experience.

Negotiating between what felt unreal in the reality of the riot, my several visits to the camp over months accrued what Robert Langs (1977, 34) would call 'subjective aspects of a analytic setting,' which assisted me to enter 'an evenly suspended attention' (Freud 1912, 28) sustained through a duration of eleven months. As a researcher in search of the Muslim question, I found myself in analytic capacity of being a psychoanalytic psychotherapist in the relief camp. What transpired between us can be best described as the Winnicottian experience. We both shared the reality of being Muslim in India not knowing what it meant. This is what brought us together, possibly as a research dyad (Vahali 2003, 27) existing in the potential space of analytic experience where we both endeavored to know what it meant to be Muslim in India. This attempt at knowing was facilitated in the 'in-between space,' which we allowed to emerge between us spontaneously. This spontaneity led the playing be unselfconscious and also lend itself unwittingly to my analysis of it. It is the Winnicottian experience that created a relationship between the children and me where we both participated through our unconscious. I was able to access the precariousness, articulate and give some shape and form to their playing as they creatively found what was missing in the discourse on Muslim Identity in India.

Identity of Experience

Unfairly held responsible (Mayaram 1997) for the Partition of India with their presence as a constant reminder of what was taken away in the Partition (Ward 2011), Muslims in India are lost children to India's Partition. They bear the stigma of the past, are suspected for Pan-Islamist leanings with their loyalty questioned time and again (Jefforelot and

Gayner 2012, 14). They find themselves in arguments and debates on identity where historians, sociologists, and political scientists who defend them by illustrating the historical compulsion and the political motivation of perceiving Muslims as the 'Other.' Psychoanalysts use conceptions of 'villain hunger' (Akhtar 2005) and necessary other (Kakar 1996) to explain the Othering of Muslim in India. Religious and political violence such as the Hindu–Muslim riots often carry the proclamation of 'identity.' Irrespective of personal allegiance to religion, ones political identity becomes like Lacan's Gaze—the way one is looked at by the other.

However what is crucially missed is the experience of Muslims in India. This 'experience' is difficult to define and further impossible to describe. It is embedded in the realm of what Winnicott would render as 'culture' (1967, 99). He identifies culture to be space where history and its subjective reading come together and demonstrate the interplay between separation and union (1967, 100). It becomes difficult to read culture as only history or only having personal meaning. It is best expressed as a potential state of 'experiencing.' A study of this culture in the context of the 'experience' of Muslims in India is awaited. Such a study can only be possible through the praxis of psychoanalysis and politics primarily because the unknown and the unknowable must constitute the realm of experience. It is through this unknowing that depths of unconscious and its links with conscious political identity be explored.

Children at the relief camp contribute to this missing aspect in their playing: *The experience of being a Muslim in India*. This experience of being Muslim lends refuge to the identity of being Muslim through the cultural idiom of playing. Playing in its ability to create a cultural experience of the Muslim becomes the refuge where the community seeks its identity and unconsciously pursues its experience.

Keeping the Child Alive: Playing

As we end the discussion on how playing becomes the psychological means to create an in-between space where experience can be 'found,' it is also of use to understand how playing was important for the child and what it did for them.

Clare Britton Winnicott writes in *Children Who Cannot Play* (1945) about how coming to terms with reality is extremely difficult for a child tormented by destructive impulses who has no means to channelize them (1945, 117). Finding no security and reassurance, he feels unable to manage life and eventually get cuts off from the real world. Clare Winnicott recognizes the role of acknowledging and understanding the objective reality of children's losses and trauma to help them achieve the goal of successful maturation (Kanter 2004). With children coming from states of violence and assault where loses are insurmountable, the goal of any psychoanalytic interaction is to keep the child alive. By alive, Clare Winnicott means to maintain their capacity to feel: 'If there are no feelings, there is no life; there is merely an existence' (1964b, 12). Children coming from painful experiences clamp down their feelings because to feel is to get in touch with the isolation, the vulnerability and the aggression within all of which overwhelms the child. Such a child loses a sense of the past and thereby loses a sense of present and future as well. Though he may come across as a functioning child and caretakers may feel that he 'sees them as loving people, the truth remains that the child doesn't see them at all' (Winnicott and Winnicott 1944). This means that the presence of people does nothing to the child's inner world from which he has withdrawn. The child develops a False-self (Winnicott 1960), which helps him survive in the objective world by severely compromising or, in states of brutal violence, impairing his capacity of being spontaneous. This spontaneity is what gives rise to playing. Playing is what keeps the child alive (see Orlie, this volume).

Winnicott writes how playing is the continuous evidence of creativity, which means aliveness (1942, 144). Creating is the means by which the child separates form the mother. Winnicott (1971) states that the child uses the space between itself and the mother to be creative and to create its own relation with the external world. This creativity is expressed best through playing. When the child is able to create, he is able to not only vent his aggressive and conflicting impulses he is also able to forge links with the outside world of objective reality. These links helps to process inner reality as well and access what remains unconscious in both.

The children of Muzaffarnagar relief camp are unique because of their ability to create—their ability to play. They not only recreate the trauma of the riot they witnessed, but are also able to create an in-between space of finding their experience of the riot. They are able to create an intermediate space in their playing where paradox can exist (see LeJeune, this volume). The person who assaults and the one who is assaulted can both be Muslims. Despite inflicting with castrating and humiliation, the Muslim is welcomed back into the community with grace and warmth. A puppy can be called a pig and can be caressed and cared for after being purposefully injured and abused. In this unquestioned, unchallenged space they are able to find many experiences; that of escaping a chase only to be caught, inviting humiliation in order to be accepted, and inflicting injury only to await concern to merge with guilt. But the most creative find of these children goes beyond their finding space for the Muslim experience in the riot. It is their finding of themselves as children: creative, alive, and playing.

Conclusion

My work with children from Muzaffarnagar attempts to create a potential space where the objective reality of my being the researcher and the subjective reality of my quest for understanding the unconscious persuasions of Muslim identity both come together, and I can find playing happening among children in the relief camp. What built over several visits and eleven months of observation is a Winnicottian experience we both sustain, not knowing what it meant to be Muslim, yet joining unconsciously to find possible answers. Loyal Swine and Sugarcane Escape emerge as possible answers where through playing these children are work out the hate and aggression came their way as Muslims in the camp and create a potential space where one finds their experience of the riot—something that has evaded the question of identity in historical and political discourses. Playing also works as a gateway to the unconscious (Winnicott 1942, 146) and both the plays unfold different aspects of children's unconscious. Sugarcane Escape reveals the search of the older child for the father in his aggressiveness. The young child reveals in Loyal Swine an attempt to create the environment that can provide the continuity of the mother, where through delinquent actions he is able to both go back to the moment of trauma and struggles to undo it.

Who is the child in the relief camp at Kandhla? Is he the child who has lost his parents, home, and community, and recreates them in his play? Is he the child who unconsciously finds the experience as a Muslim in his creation of the play? Is he the child who finds the absent or creates the lost? Most crucially, is he the Muslim who is struggling to find himself, or he is the child who is hiding waiting to be found? Potential spaces were created between historical realities and subjective narratives such that several identities could find their refuge in them: that of a child and that of a Muslim. While playing created the cultural experience of being Muslim in India, it also became the refuge for child primarily because of his ability to keep the child alive-feeling! Ghalib's couplets echo the dilemma of Muslims whose political identity has been erased, and it is the child in the relief camp who found the Muslim in play and kept it alive in playing.

References

1947 Earth. 1998. *Film*. Directed by D. Mehta. Bollywood.

Akhtar, S. 2005. Hindu-Muslim Relations in India: Past, Present and Future. In *Freud Along the Ganges*, 91–137. New York: Other Press.

Apfel, R.J., and B. Simon. 1996. *Minefields in Their Hearts: The Mental Health of Children of War and Communal Violence*. New Haven: Yale University Press.

———. 2000. Mitigating Discontents with Children in War: An Ongoing Psychoanalytic Inquiry. In *Cultures Under Siege: Collective Violence and Trauma*, ed. A.C. Robben, and M.M. Suarez-Orosco, 102–130. Cambridge: Cambridge University Press.

Bhadra, S. 2012. Psychosocial Support for Children Affected by Communal Violence in Gujrat, India. *International Journal of Applied Psychoanalytic Studies* 9(3): 212–232.

Bhalla, N. 2013. Fear Stalks Displaced Muslims After Muzaffarnagar Riots. ReutersIndia.http://inreuters.com/article/muzzafarnagar-riots-muslims-displaced-fe-idINDEE9810CA20130919

Bollas, C. 2011. *The Christopher Bollas Reader*. London: Routledge.

Das, V. 1990. *Mirrors of Violence: Communities, Riots and Survivors in South Asia*. Delhi: Oxford University Press.

Dixit, N. 2013. Thread Bared. *Outlook*. http://www.outlookindia.com/article/thread-bared/288907

Dixit, N. 2014. Shadow Lines. *Outlook*. http://www.outlookindia.com/article/shadow-lines/291494

Dixit, N. 2015. The Law Is Under Trial Here. *Outlook*. http://www.outlookindia.com/article/the-law-is-under-trial-here/293296

Elliot, A. 1994. *Psychoanalytic Theory*. Oxford, UK: Blackwell.

Erikson, E. 1963. *Childhood and Society*. New York: Norton.

———. 1966. The Concept of Identity in Race Relations: Notes and Queries. *Daedalus* 95(1): 145–171.

———. 1968. *Identity, Youth, and Crisis*. New York: W. W. Norton.

Fanon, F. 1952. *Black Skins White Masks: Experiences of a Black Man in a White World*. New York: Grove Press.

Freud, S. 1937. Constructions in Analysis. In *The Complete Standard Edition of the Complete Psychological Works of Sigmund Freud 23*, ed. J. Strachey, 258–259. London: Hogarth.

Freud, S. 1912. The Dynamics of Transference. In *The Complete Standard Edition of the Complete Psychological Works of Sigmund Freud 23*, ed. J. Strachey, 167–173. London: Hogarth.
Frosh, S. 1989. *Psychoanalysis and Psychology*. New York: NYU Press.
———. 1991. *Identity Crisis: Modernity, Psychoanalysis and Self.* New York: Routledge.
Garbarino, J., and K. Kostelny. 1996. The Effects of Political Violence on Palestinian Children's Behavior Problems: A Risk Accumulation Model. *Child Development* 67(1): 33.
Horne, A., and M. Lanyado. 2012. *Winnicott's Children: Independent Psychoanalytic Approaches with Children and Adolescents.* London and New York: Routledge.
Issac, S. 1948. The Nature and Function of Fantasy. *International Journal of Psychoanalysis* 29: 73–97.
Jaffrelot, Christopher, and Laurent Gayer. 2012. *Muslims in Indian Cities: Trajectories of Marginalization.* New Delhi: Harper Collins India.
Kuhn, A. 2013. *Little Madness: Winnicott, Transitional Phenomena and Cultural Experience.* New York: Palgrave.
Kakar, S. 1996. *Colors of Violence: Cultural Identities, Religion and Conflict.* Chicago: University of Chicago Press.
Kanter, J. 2004. *Face to Face with Children: The Life and Work of Clare Winnicott.* London: Karnac.
Klein, M. 1955. The Psychoanalytic Play Technique: Its history and Its Significance. In *New Directions in Psycho-Analysis. The Significance of Infant Conflict in the Pattern of Adult Behavior*, ed. P. Heinemann, and R.E. Money-Kyrle, 3–22. London: Tavistock.
Langs, R. 1977. *The Therapeutic Interaction.* New York: Jason Aronson.
Mayaram, S. 1997. *Resisting Regimes: Myth, Memory and Making of Muslim Identity.* Delhi: Oxford University Press.
Mody, A. 2014. A Separation. *Caravan.* http://www.caravanmagazine.in/reportage/separation
Nandy, A. 1987. *Traditions, Tyranny and Utopias.* Delhi: Oxford University Press.
———. 1990. *Science, Hegemony and Violence.* Tokyo: United Nations University Press.
———. 2013. *Regimes of Narcissism, Regimes of Despair.* Delhi: Oxford University Press.
Not Allowed to Cry: Excerpts for Discussion From Jerusalem Children-In War Conference. 1991. *Film.* Directed by R.J. Apfel and B. Simon. Cambridge, MA: Intersection Video Producers.
Ogden, T. 2007. *The Art of Psychoanalysis: Dreaming Undreamt Dreams and Interrupted Cries.* New York: Taylor and Francis.

Phillips, A. 1998. *Beast in the Nursery: On Curiosity and Other Appetites*. New York: Pantheon.

Priya, K.R. 2012. Trauma Reactions, Suffering, and Healing Among Riot-Affected Internally Displaced Children of Gujarat, India: A Qualitative Inquiry. *Qualitative Research in Psychology* 9(3): 189–209. doi:10.1080/14780887.2010.500353.

Rustin, M. 1999. Conclusions: A New Culture of Warfare. In *Welfare and Culture in Europe: Towards a New Paradigm in Social Policy*, ed. P. Chamberlayne, A. Cooper, R. Freeman, and M. Rustin, 275–281. London: Jessica Kingsley Publishers.

Spence, P.D. 1982. *Narrative Truth and Historical Truth: Meaning and Interpretation in Psychoanalysis*. New York, London: W.W. Norton and Company.

Vahali, H.O. 2003. From a Researcher's Notebook: Scattered Thoughts on Research and Researching. *Psychological Studies* 48(3): 21–29.

Visvanathan, S. 2013. The Silence of Muzaffarnagar. *Asian Age*. http://www.sacw.net/article7102.html

Volkan, V. 1988. *The Need to Have Enemies and Allies*. Northvale, NJ: Jason Aronson.

———. 1997. *Bloodlines: From Ethnic Pride to Ethnic Terrorism*. New York: Farrar, Straus and Giroux.

Volkan, V. 1999. Large Group Identity: International Relations and Psychoanalysis. Lecture, "Deutsche Psychoanalytische Gesellschaft e.V. (DGP) Meeting" Gasteig Cultural Center, Rosenheimer Platz.

Volkan, V. 2000. Vamik D. Volkan. http://www.vamikvolkan.com/Animals-As-Large-Group-Symbols.php

Ward, B. 2011. *Riot Politics: Hindu Muslim Violence and the Indian State*. London: Hurst.

Williams, P. 2010. *The Psychoanalytic Therapy of Severe Disturbance*. London: Karnac.

Winnicott, D.W. 1964a. Ego Distortion in Terms of True Self and False Self (1960). In *The Maturational Process and Facilitating Environment: Studies in Theories of Emotional Development (1958)*, 140–152. London: Hogarth.

———. 1964b. The Capacity to be Alone (1958). In *The Maturational Process and Facilitating Environment: Studies in Theories of Emotional Development*, 28–35. London: Hogarth.

———. 1964c. The Development of the Capacity for Concern (1963). In *The Maturational Process and Facilitating Environment: Studies in Theories of Emotional Development (1958)*, 73–82. London: Hogarth Press.

———. 1964d. Why Children Play (1942). In *The Child, the Family, and the Outside World*, 143–146. Harmondsworth: Penguin Books.

———. 1965. The Theory of Parent Infant Relationship (1960). In *The Maturational Process and Facilitating Environment: Studies in Theories of Emotional Development (1958)*, 33–57. London: Hogarth.

———. 1971. *Playing and Reality*. London: Tavistock.

———. 1984. The Antisocial Tendency. In *Deprivation and Delinquency*, ed. C. Winnicott, R. Shepherd, and M. Davis, 120–131. London: Tavistock.

———. 1986. Delinquency as a Sign of Hope. In *Home Is Where We Start From: Essays by a Psychoanalyst*, ed. C. Winnicott, R. Shepheard, and M. Davis, 90–100. New York: W.W. Norton.

———. 1989. Absence and Presence of Guilt Illustrated in Two Patients. In *Psycho-Analytic Explorations*, ed. C. Winnicott, R. Shepheard, and M. Davis, 272–283. Cambridge, MA: Harvard University Press.

Winnicott, C. 2004a. Children Who Can Not Play (1945). In *Face to Face with Children: The Life and Work of Clare Winnicott*, ed. J. Kanter, 112–121. London: Karnac.

———. 2004b. Communicating with Children- I (1964). In *Face to Face with Children*, 184–197. London: Karnac.

Winnicott, D.W., and C. Winnicott. 1957. The Problem of Homeless Children (1944). In *Children and the Outside World: Studies in Developing Relationships*, 98–116. London: Tavistock.

Young, R.M. 1994. *Mental Space*. London: Process Press.

CHAPTER 6

Safety in Danger and Privacy in Privation: Ambivalent Fantasies of Natural States Invoked in Reaction to Loss

Matthew H. Bowker

This chapter analyzes experiences of deprivation and fantasies of privation, particularly as they are expressed in the liberal, contractarian heuristic of the state of nature. While not categorically distinct from Edenic and Arcadian (i.e., "Golden Age") fantasies known since antiquity, or from popular idealizations of what is "natural," the state of nature offers up a fantasy in which we can clearly see otherwise obscure ambivalences and psychological dynamics that hold powerful influence over the discourses, ideologies, and behaviors of modern and contemporary individuals and groups.

In what follows, I argue that fantasies of states of nature are counterproductive to the extent that they are addressed to (real and fantasized) experiences of deprivation. I hope to show that the fantasy of returning to something like a psychic state of nature, where what is real is the absence and not the presence of selves, is both common and unfortunate. While such a claim may seem surprising at first, perhaps it ought not, given our obvious popular fascination with apocalypse, atrocities, and other disasters that destroy others or institutions that represent depriving objects, just as they depict a state of extreme privation as a state of moral "safety" or innocence.

M.H. Bowker (✉)
Medaille College, Buffalo, NY, USA

M.H. Bowker, A. Buzby (eds.), *D.W. Winnicott and Political Theory*,
DOI 10.1057/978-1-137-57533-3_6

Privation and Deprivation

It is most helpful to begin with a distinction that is simple enough, yet crucial to the line of argument that follows: the distinction between privation and deprivation. "Privation" is a term I will use to describe lack; "deprivation," loss. If we accept this manner of speaking, "deprivation" will mean that there was once something—such as adequate care, order, or a nurturing person or environment—but then that something was removed, taken away. For the deprived child, "*things went well enough and then they did not go well enough*" (Winnicott 1986, 91, *emphasis in original*). "Privation," on the other hand, will be reserved for absences or deficiencies that precede the individual's *coming into being* or that coincide with it. At the earliest stages of life, pervasive privations and "environmental disturbances distorting the emotional development of a baby" may lead to psychotic illness or to other severe "distortions of reality testing" in no small part because they are "with" the individual from the beginning (92). That is, from the perspective of the experiencer, privation is a *timeless* condition, whereas deprivation is a change, perhaps even a change marked by a singular event.

If deprivation implies a change, it also involves the individual in a process. In deprivation "a change has occurred which altered the whole life of the child," and this has happened at an age when the child is "old enough to know about things" (Winnicott 1986, 91). The world of the child is upturned and the child suffers "unthinkable anxiety." In response to this anxiety, she radically reconceives her orientation to herself and others, adapting to what she perceives to be a new order based on control. A compliant child, now living "in a fairly neutral state, complying because there is nothing else that the child is strong enough to do" (1986, 92), identifies with the new order in order to feel safe, although her freedom *to be safely* is precisely what has been lost.

A depriving home environment is "unsafe" for a child in several respects: It is unsafe for the child to be herself, unsafe to experience or display aggression, unsafe even to be aware of the loss of freedom and all it implies. The environment is no longer "indestructible," as it must be, and therefore the home, and the other people in it, seems unable to survive the child's (fantasized) aggressive and destructive attacks, attacks that are healthy and necessary if she is to establish and ultimately relate to the world as something external, outside of herself (Winnicott 1971, 86–94). Fantasized destruction of the object takes the object out of the child's inner world and places it outside, where, perhaps paradoxically, it can be found again. This destruction, then, is not hateful or angry, but an important part of the process of beginning to relate to others not as subjective objects but as beings in their own right, beings who can be loved precisely because they can survive being separated from the child (and therefore the child, too, can survive their separation).

If the environment or important people in it are perceived to be incapable of "surviving" the child involved in this process, it is equally true that the child cannot survive herself or her own destructiveness, so she places herself under strict control (1986, 94). This strict control means not merely obedient behavior, but an internal restriction on play, creativity, and the aggression and fantasized destructiveness that accompany these. We might say that when something in the child's environment goes *out of control*, and the child finds it necessary to *take control*, she finds a way to "survive" but loses contact with her innermost, developing self. Holding her aggression "inside," she "becomes tense, over-controlled, and serious. There naturally follows a degree of inhibition of all impulses, and so of creativity" (Winnicott 1990, 94).

Nevertheless, even after months or years of living in a compliant and self-controlled state, Winnicott surmises, the child may discover a glimmer of "hope," an intuition of the possibility of "get[ting] back behind the deprivation moment or condition." To find hope is to become aware of "the urge to get back behind the moment of deprivation and to undo the fear of the *unthinkable anxiety or confusion that resulted before the neutral state became organized*" (1986, 92, *emphasis in original*). The child finds hope and terror concurrently, and this intense emotional experience, Winnicott argues, is often expressed in delinquent or antisocial behavior, in which, for instance, he steals or breaks a physical object.

The child is not seeking, of course, to steal or break a particular physical object for its own sake, but is hoping to rediscover a less controlled, more free, and more "destructive" way of experiencing objects in general, a way that has been lost since the moment of deprivation. In what may be a single instant, the child experiences hope, reencounters the terror of deprivation, rediscovers aggression and destructiveness, and enacts—in however misguided a way—a vital aspect of himself by committing a "compulsive" act (1986, 93), one that is "dangerous" in the sense that it may provoke both external and internal (guilt) forms of punishment.

This is a typical "process" of childhood deprivation, as Winnicott sees it. By contrast, let us take one of Winnicott's examples of privation: a child who suffers from insufficient oxygen, presumably since birth or even before. We might say, although Winnicott does not put it like this, that what is missing for this child is missing too early for it to be missed. This too-earliness, this missing of missing, Winnicott seems to mix up with the physical nature of the child's privation—which is by no means the only sort of privation with which we should be concerned—a mix-up that may reflect Winnicott's belief that the effects of privation are more obdurate than those of deprivation.

The child who suffers a limited supply of oxygen, although he may ultimately survive and grow up, will never say to himself, "I miss oxygen," nor will he "go around hoping to convince someone that if there had been enough oxygen, things would have been alright" (1986, 92). But the deprived child may well miss what has been lost, by remembering, imagining, or fantasizing about it. This is an important matter.

The child who suffers privation, who misses missing, who "lacks" rather than "loses," does so because his privation—whether it began *in utero*, at birth, or in the earliest months of life—preceded his psychic being. The child who suffers privation may, for any number of reasons, including parental anxiety and smothering forms of care, never find it "safe" to destroy loved objects in fantasy, but neither will he be suddenly forced to renounce that activity in order to take control of himself. Since "privation," according to our usage, signifies the absence of an antecedent condition by which one might compare one's state of lack, privation *cannot* be experienced as loss. Indeed, depending upon what exactly one means by "experience"—a question that is far more complex than most contemporary psychoanalytic thinkers permit, to their detriment (see Bowker 2016)—it is arguable that privation may not be psychically "experienced" at all.

Perhaps this seeming invulnerability to the experience of loss, this missing of missing, is what makes the sufferer of privation in some sense special, and what makes the experience of privation ambivalently terrible and enviable, an ambivalence expressed in any number of common sayings, such as "Ignorance is bliss" and "You don't know what you're missing." Privation, like a formative object-relationship, is at first unthinkable because we are rather deeply "inside" it, which is to say, it is "inside" us. To paraphrase Alice Miller: Privation is the "air we [don't] breathe" (1997).

I must admit that the distinction proposed here between privation and deprivation does not hold up etymologically—although it hardly needs to—since both "privation" and "deprivation" derive from the same Latin root, *prīvo*, which means (1) to take away or rob, (2) to free or deliver, (3) to be separate from the public or state, and (4) to be peculiar to the individual (Leverett 1874; Lewis and Short 1879). But although the shared root of the two terms cannot ground our case for differentiation, this consideration of etymology offers us an insight even more valuable: *Prīvo* gives us not just the terms "privation" and "deprivation," but also "privacy," "privy," "proper," and even "privilege."

The nearly contrary meanings contained in the terms "privacy" and "privation" reflect the possibility of a relationship between individual growth and flourishing, on one hand, and impoverishment and debilitation on the other. What appears to be at stake, then, is likely more complex than mere absences, be they absences of oxygen or of loving contact. It might be easier to work this out if the English language had an adjectival form of "privation." Although we might like to, we cannot say that the child lacking oxygen is "prived." In French, it is possible to speak of conditions and persons *privés* and *déprivés*. And, just as in Spanish (*privar* and *deprivar*) and in Italian (*privare* and *deprivare*), the terms are all but synonymous. If, in Italian, one may be *privo di vita* (lifeless), but also have a *vita privata* (private life), and if, in French, one may have a *vie privée* (a private life), but also be *privé de vie privée* (deprived of private life), we may come closer to appreciating the ambivalent connections between privation and privacy, separation and isolation, freedom and lack.

Let us consider this more deeply. An unfortunately common yet radically disruptive developmental experience is that of being impinged upon by parents or others such that one is *privé de vie privée* (deprived of private life). Of course, having a "private life" does not imply a "privation" of the self. Quite the opposite: Having a private life is necessary if one is to have a self. As Thomas Merton wisely notes, without private, interior lives, we would be "merely submerged in a mass of impersonal human beings pushed around by automatic forces," having "lost [our] true humanity, [our] integrity, [our] ability to love, [our] capacity for self-determination" (1958, 13).

*De*privation of privacy threatens the very core of our selves, even if it does so by leaving us feeling helplessly alone. Take, for instance, Job's excruciating deprivations at the hand of Yahweh (see Bowker 2011, 2016), with which none of his friends, or even his wife, could genuinely empathize. Of course, Job's deprivations also marked Job off as peculiar or singular, as they ultimately earned him a rare audience with God. We must consider the possibility that, although deprivation seems to threaten all that is private and unique about the self, it also seems to offer the individual a privileged or unique position vis-à-vis the group or community. Giorgio Agamben's use of the Latin term, *sacer*, meaning sacred and profane, is a well-known illustration of this dynamic (1998). If we are not careful—and I will argue that we are not—we may come to idealize deprivation because it seems to make us special, forgetting that the price of this specialness is our private selves and private lives. This danger forms a part of the thesis of this chapter, to which I return shortly.

Before I do, it seems important to acknowledge—although without the time to give it a fair hearing—the idea of "lack" as it appears in the work of Jacques Lacan and his followers (see also Žižek 2002). Lacan's conception of lack, *le manque*, seems to defy the distinction urged here between privation and deprivation, lacking and losing, likely because, for Lacan, coming into being entails both privation and deprivation. That is, privation and deprivation are indivisible since *being*, itself, is constituted by lack. The greatest *manque*, for Lacan, is the *manque à être* [literally: lack of being'], which Lacan translates as the "want to be." The *manque à être* both precedes and determines the subject (1988). The subject discovers it, or it uncovers the subject, because "it" is already there. Johnston calls it a "primordial Ur-privation of a *nihilnegativum*" (2015). Perhaps less mysteriously, it is akin to the accountant's discovery of a *manque à gagner* (loss of earnings), in that the *manque à être* is "not a sum that previously existed and disappeared: it's a sum that was never registered. Similarly, the subject's being is not something that existed and was then lost in the course of development, but rather that which the subject never had and yet strives for" (Focchi 2005).

At an experiential level, to say that "a subject becomes a subject by striving for a subjectivity that he has never had" borders on nonsense. What is worse, this formulation elides the distinction between privation and deprivation and, at least in one sense, essentializes lack/loss. Persistently fashionable anti-subjective discourses with lack or loss at their root—whether influenced by Lacan or not—rely on a vision of a similarly *essentially* deprived subject, even though they simultaneously eschew "essentializations" of other sorts. I discuss the implications of such discourses in more detail in the concluding section of this chapter.

For now, I submit that both a distinction between privation and deprivation *and* a cognizance of the ambivalences at their core are needed if we are to understand the fascination with and, often, the idealization of experiences of privation. Privation may be imagined to grant access to something private and unknowable to others. It may, therefore, be thought to make "peculiar" or unique those who are "privileged" enough to suffer it. If the person who suffers privation cannot recall an antecedent condition with which to contrast his experience, it is also true that the *de*prived person *can* recall a condition of adequacy, but *cannot* recall an experience of privation. That is, the *de*prived person can only imagine privation *through* the experience of deprivation, which is to say, to mix up memories of sufficiency, privacy, and even privilege with her experience of loss.

Put in slightly different terms, privation and deprivation are, in an experiential sense, mutually exclusive. Straining the powers of memory and imagination, the psychic experience of deprivation relies on fantasy to resolve its attendant anxieties. Indeed, the fantasy-component of the experience of deprivation *is* the fantasy of privation, the fantasy of an experience without antecedent conditions of adequacy that also leans heavily on the ambivalent associations between privation and privacy, peculiarity, and privilege, these latter three being concomitants of self-presence and the kind of vitality and freedom known (or imaginatively remembered) before the moment of deprivation. This hypothesis and its implications are the real subject of this chapter, and their complexities appear with particular clarity in the well-known construct of the state of nature, to which we now turn.

The State of Nature

The idea of a state of nature, a human condition preceding organized society and government, may be found in the texts of Judaic, Dharmic, Islamic, and Christian religions, in the classical thought of Plato and Hesiod, in contemporary theories of justice advanced by John Rawls and David Gauthier, in the psycho-historical imagination of Sigmund Freud, in the apocalyptic visions of dozens of postmoderns such as Maurice Blanchot, Jean Baudrillard, and many others (see also Jay 1993), and in popular representations of catastrophic events that eliminate law and political order, leaving survivors to contend with warring groups and, sometimes, monsters. But its distinctively modern expression, like its connection to the ideal of natural freedom, is found in the works of Hugo Grotius, Thomas Hobbes, Samuel von Pufendorf, John Locke, and Jean-Jacques Rousseau.

The state of nature has seen its share of criticism, from Carole Pateman's influential critique with respect to the status of women (1988), to Charles Mills' similar critique with respect to race (1997). But the best-known critique of the state of nature has been voiced for centuries: that the realities of human dependence seem to have no bearing upon contractarians' view of human subjects "as originally isolated and self-enclosed," asocial, disembedded, and abstract (see Gerson 2004, 777).

This critique has been advanced by a number of contemporary theorists such as Annette Baier (1994), Seyla Benhabib (1987), Christine DiStefano (1983), Virginia Held (1993), and Martha Nussbaum (2000), as well as earlier critics like Mary Astell (1704) and Mary Wollstonecraft ([1792] 2004). In response to Hobbes' famous analogy in *De Cive* that we may "consider men as if but even now sprung out of the earth, and suddenly, like mushrooms, come to full maturity, without all kind of engagement with each other" (1972, 205), Astell writes sarcastically: "How I lament my Stars that it was not my good Fortune to live in those Happy Days when Men spring up like so many Mushrooms or *Terrae Filii*, without Mother or Father or any sort of dependency" (Achinstein 2007, 22).

While such critiques are, in one sense, undeniable, in another sense they miss the mark, for they do not fully appreciate the fantastical quality of the state of nature, which includes the ambivalent wish for privation and privacy. It is true, of course, that proponents of the state of nature vacillate between casting it as mere fantasy and as prehistorical reality. States of nature are presented as heuristic devices or thought-experiments to assess the legitimacy of government. But although all serious state-of-nature theorists (except Locke) admit the historical unreality of the state of nature, this admission is often obscured in elaborations (and critiques) of the construct.[1] Hobbes, for instance, plainly states that "there was never such a time, nor condition of warre" as his state of nature suggests, but then reminds the reader that "there are many places, where [people] live so now," such as "the savage people in many places of America … [who] have no government at all" (1985, 187).

Similarly, Rousseau famously opens his second *Discourse* by "putting aside all the facts, for they have no bearing on the question" of the origins of inequality (1987, 18). The state of nature is a state "which no longer exists, which perhaps never existed, which probably never will exist, and yet about which it is necessary to have accurate notions in order to judge properly our own present state" (1987, 34). This would be clear enough, were it not that Rousseau simultaneously proclaims: "O man … listen:

here is your history, as I have thought to read it, not in the books of your fellow men, who are liars, but in nature, who never lies .... The times about which I am going to speak are quite remote: how much you have changed from what you were! (1987, 19, *emphasis added*).

Locke takes special care to obscure the unreality of the state of nature from the beginning. Citing one of his favorite authorities, the "judicious [Richard] Hooker," Locke affirms the historical validity of the transition from "living single and solely by ourselves" to a civil state: "Forasmuch as we are not by ourselves sufficient to furnish ourselves with competent store of things, needful for such a life as our nature doth desire ... as living single and solely by ourselves, we are naturally induced to seek communion and fellowship with others: this was the cause of men's uniting themselves at first in politic societies" (1980, 13). When addressing the "mighty objection" that men cannot be found in the state of nature in the world, Locke replies, "since all princes and rulers ... all through the world, are in a state of nature, it is plain the world never was, nor ever will be, without numbers of men in that state." Indeed, "all men are naturally in that state, and remain so, till by their own consents they make themselves members of some politic society" (13–14).[2]

Thus, while ambivalently denying and hinting at its historical reality, state-of-nature theorists suggest its continued presence—even its immanence—in contemporary persons, societies, and "states of mind." "Natural is not the opposite of social or civil," C.B. Macpherson notes, "the natural condition of mankind is within man now, not set apart in some distant time or place" (1971, 74). The ambivalence about the historical status of the state, combined with its transposition into a psychic state carried forth into the contemporary world, demonstrates the powerful connections between imaginative accounts of "natural" humanity and wishful (even magical) thinking in contemporary human experience, to be discussed forthwith.

"Born Free"

Perhaps the most remarkable wish, or fantasy, expressed in the state of nature is found in the famous opening line of Rousseau's *Social Contract*: "Man is born free, and everywhere he is in chains" (*L'homme est né libre, et partout il est dans les fers*). Most of us are familiar with this Romantic notion, just as Rousseau was not particularly concerned to explain it to his audience: They already *knew* what it meant, since the attribution of a natal freedom to the creatures living in the state of nature is hardly unique to Rousseau. While our originary freedom was, and still is, taken for granted, Rousseau did not even feel the need to explain "how … this change [took] place," about which he confesses: "I have no idea."

But if, as Rousseau and others acknowledge, the state of nature is an ahistorical contrivance, then what does it mean to say that "man is born free"? To be "born free," must we assert the historical reality of the state of nature and, with it, a (pre)historical "original state" that "differ[s] so greatly" from the state of civilization (1987, 80)? This condition would seem to degrade, if not demolish, the basic presuppositions of social contract theory. Alternatively, may we consider ourselves "born free" even while acknowledging the fictional aspect of the state of nature? If so, may we be "born free" because it is possible for us to imagine ourselves having been "born free" in a state of nature? And if this is the line of argument state-of-nature theorists intended, *can* we, in fact, imagine ourselves as such? Two problems arise immediately in light of such a suggestion: (1) It may not be possible for us to imagine ourselves in a state of nature, for reasons outlined below, and (2) Even if we could, our actual freedom would seem to depend upon our capacity to imagine ourselves as having once possessed an original freedom, making our freedom not only precarious but magically derived, such that we are "born free" (or "born [again] free") simply by wishing it were so.

Perhaps we are to understand the claim that we are "born free" at an ontogenetic or individual level. If so, we might ask what someone like Winnicott—or any object relations theorist, or, indeed, any psychoanalytic thinker—would make of the assertion that the human infant is "born free." On one hand, if we apply almost any definition of the word "freedom" to this formulation, we may find it prima facie absurd. Human infants are born to extreme dependence and vulnerability; their biological and emotional needs keep them "in chains" (*dans les fers*), as it were. A human infant, seen objectively would be, in Rousseau's own language, utterly "enslaved," since the infant's needs make him utterly "incapable of doing without another" (1987, 59).

In the state of nature we are presented with grown adults who have (magically) grown without care or nurture. While it is true that in the state of nature "there is no such thing as a baby" (1992, 99), it is for very different reasons than Winnicott had in mind. On the other hand, it is true that many infants enjoy an early *experience* we might call "free." The experience of "primary narcissism," as Freud would call it, includes illusions of total freedom and omnipotent control over the infant, objects, and the environment, which are, at this stage, not yet differentiated. In fact, primary narcissism, the "libidinal complement to the egoism of the instinct of self-preservation" (1914, 74), comes fairly close to the psychic condition of the human being depicted in most states of nature, particularly Rousseau's: a childlike creature with an adult body, living "in himself" (1987, 81), happily gratifying his own desires, but (unknowingly) lacking company, culture, and the potential for maturation.

> Wandering in the forests, without industry, without speech, without dwelling, without war, without relationships, with no need for his fellow men, and correspondingly with no desire to do them harm ... savage man ... had only the sentiments and enlightenment appropriate to that state .... If by chance he made some discovery, he was all the less able to communicate it to others because he did not even know his own children. Art perished with its inventor. There was neither education nor progress; generations were multiplied to no purpose. Since each one always began from the same point, centuries went by with all the crudeness of the first ages; the species was already old, and man remained ever a child. (1987, 57)

Of course, the infant who experiences something of this freedom is not aware that the experience has been provided by an attuned and generous caregiver. As far as she knows, her wishes magically create and destroy. Freud thus links the state of primary narcissism to the propensity for magical thinking and to the "omnipotence of thought" (1938, 873–874): the belief that wishing alters reality, that wishing makes things so. The wish to be "born free" is likewise related to a kind of magical thinking, both in its form (by presupposing an original freedom without evidence or reason) and in its content (because the wish is that reimagining the individual's original relationship with the world will create an actual change).

Indeed, the "remarkable change" involved in the process of transforming natural beings into citizens (Rousseau 1987, 150) is not entirely unlike the first stages of the "process" of adapting to deprivation outlined in the first section of this chapter. Both involve movements from freedom to (self-)control: Indeed, what is offered to each "associate" in Rousseau's formula of the general will is not markedly different from the safety and power offered to the child who identifies with the new, depriving framework of control. Rousseau's formula relies on what Louis Althusser calls a "sleight of hand" and a "play on words" (1972, 130), whereby in "giving himself to all each person gives himself to no one," for "obedience to the law one has prescribed for oneself is liberty" (Rousseau 1987, 148–151).

Whereas the compliant child seizes upon the "hope" (one that contains a substantial element of fantasy) of getting "back behind the deprivation moment" and so of undoing the past, Rousseau's formula fuses control and hope together, such that "the total alienation of each associate, together with all of his rights" (1987, 148) and the experiences of freedom and omnipotence are one and the same. The child seeks a return to a place where his private self may be expressed "freely," while Rousseau seeks to eliminate all traces of the private self by imposing a civil self-deprivation that is equivalent to the natural self-privation imagined in the state of nature, calling this condition "freedom."

Imagining the Self and Its Absence

The state of nature presents us with a picture of ungoverned, unnurtured, and largely unrelated human beings, to be sure. But it also offers us a vision of human beings without selves. The distinction between the human being and the self amounts to more than hair-splitting. Consider, for instance, the longstanding liberal–communitarian debate, represented in part by figures like John Rawls, Michael Sandel, Charles Taylor, and Alasdair MacIntyre. A prominent—perhaps *the* prominent—point of contention is how to regard the political self or subject, whether it is possible to abstract the self from its commitments and community, and whether it is desirable, even in theory, to do so.

Human beings cannot develop the capacities of selfhood without the interventions of civil society and its institutions, especially those of the family. At the same time, human beings do not become selves in nonproblematic alignment with the traditions and norms established by families, groups, or communities, which is to say: Group identities and community traditions do not necessarily encourage the healthy development of selves. Human beings live and have always lived in groups, but this mere fact does not mean that *being in a group* lies at the center of what it means to *be a self*. Rather, the self depends upon families, groups, and even polities that facilitate its capacities to withdraw from and resist their own pull, as well as to meaningfully participate in them when desired. Selves do not develop in isolation, but they do depend upon early experiences of isolation (of a sort) within a context of care and attunement (see Levine, this volume).

Because the state of nature presents us with a narrative of *originary* human experience, an experience of being human without selfhood, the fantasy of the state of nature is one of lack—and not *loss*—of self. This gets a bit tricky. If we, as adults, reared in families living in contemporary civil society, try to imagine ourselves in a state of nature—be it Hobbes' state of nature or Rawls' original position (1971)—we may find that we cannot, that it is impossible to call upon the self to imagine its own absence. More likely, we will find that, although we are asked to imagine ourselves in a state of privation, we can imagine only *de*privation, a loss of everything and everyone, our attachments, our meanings and purposes, our identities, our families.

The idea of a state of nature asks us to imagine ourselves subjected to extreme privation, yet without the knowledge of privation or its opposite. Just as the child who has suffered privation cannot recall an antecedent condition wherein he did *not* suffer privation, we have difficulty imaginatively traversing this boundary in the other direction. How can we imagine ourselves without parental care, relationships, ethnicities, goals, memories, communities, experiences? We cannot imagine our*selves* in such a condition because this condition is not a condition of selfhood at all.

Winnicott hints at this difficulty when he suggests that "we cannot so easily identify ourselves with men and women [of the distant past] who so identified themselves with the community and with nature and with unexplained phenomena such as the rising and setting of the sun, thunderbolts and earthquakes" (1971, 70). Even Rousseau acknowledges how "unrecognizable" the early, 'natural' being is to the civilized person in arguing that each step of scientific progress removes us further from our comprehension of "the most important knowledge of all," which is the knowledge of our origins (1987, 33). But it is precisely the "unknown" and "unidentifiable" quality of human beings in the state of nature that permits deeper levels of fantasy and identification to function. That is, the human being in a state of nature cannot conceive of himself existing in an alternative condition. Since he is not a self, he cannot conceptually abstract himself from his current state. Theoretically, we who are selves can imagine ourselves in almost any condition, but when we try to imagine ourselves lacking (but *not* having lost) everything, including our very selves, we fail, and this failure gives us a glimpse, albeit a rather obscure one, of the free and thoughtless being we are after.

Perhaps more importantly, even if we fail to appreciatively imagine the impossible state of privation that the "natural" being lives in, we do undertake an imaginative experience of deprivation when we try. That is, in trying to imagine the state of nature, all we can do is to imagine a total deprivation of our selves, one that throws into question the very purpose of existing. In his incisive discussion of Rawls' original position, Fred Alford writes (1991, 9), "a self shorn of its interests, ends, talents, goals, and relationships with others, even if it could be imagined, is a self that seems hardly worth protecting." That is, while my argument runs perpendicular to Alford's, we might say that the imagined loss implied by the state of nature is so great—tantamount to self-annihilation—that what is left over is deemed worthless, "hardly worth protecting." Of course, we would not assess the situation in this way had we not imagined the privation (or lack) suggested by the state of nature as *de*privation (or loss), since newborns, or even soon-to-be-born babies, although lacking "interests, ends, talents, goals, and relationships," are not "shorn" of anything and are very much "worth protecting."

Of course, we are tempted to conclude that our selves are not "worth protecting" particularly if our private, isolated, vital cores—what Winnicott called our "secret" or "incommunicado" parts of self—have been violated (1965, 187). If Winnicott is right, the most private part of the individual must be isolated and protected from contact and communication with others. This private or sacred core develops in the context of parental care—and therefore does not belong to the human being in the state of nature who is more of a species-member than a self—but it is crucial to recognize that the specific form this kind of care takes is very near to a benevolent privation which could be imagined to obtain in natural states.

If we can keep in mind the ambivalent nature of privation as lack and privacy, we may see that fantasies of privation may represent the wish for the erasure of the possibility of ever having established a real, vital self. Were this wish to come true, it would seem preferable to the experience of deprivation, because in deprivation one knows and recalls the loss as well as its antecedent condition of adequacy: "Better," as they say, "not to know what one is missing." Clinically speaking, the idea of (and the wish for) self-privation may arise frequently in defense against a real or threatened loss of self, that is, in self-destructive behavior or even in statements such as "All is already lost" or "I had nothing to lose."

While it sounds bizarre, a part of the child *must be* neglected, abandoned, left absolutely alone. Indeed, it is perhaps the most important part of parental care that the infant be protected from the parent's own impulses to know, reach, or discover every part of the child. Rather, a part of the child must be let be, un-"mothered," so that the infant's fragile and developing self is not subjected to premature contact with objects that alter or intrude upon it.

Since many forms of deprivation occasion a loss of what is most private in the child—a vital core which gives the self a feeling of reality—it is perhaps not surprising that experiences of deprivation would lead us to fantasies of privation, fantasies containing ambivalent and even confused wishes for austere isolation and absolute privacy. Experiences of deprivation, real or imagined, if linked with fantasies of privation, will call upon imaginations of states of being that cannot quite be imagined, yet whose very unfathomability permits their ambivalences to remain unrecognized and unconscious. At the same time, fantasies of privation contain the wish for privacy, the wish for a kind of care that protects (by leaving alone) the most private part of the self.

Such fantasies express both the desire never to have had a self to lose, *and* the wish to recover or recreate a self out of the experience of loss, a wish to have had the inalienable privacy that would have helped secure a sense of self in the first place. To be sure, as it is expressed in states of nature, in apocalyptic visions, and even in severe depressive episodes, the fantasy goes to extremes, as fantasies will do, throwing the baby out with the bathwater, so to speak. In grasping at extreme privacy, we find abject isolation, but the wishes never to have had a self to lose and (simultaneously) to have a kernel of self, free and untouched, un-parented and unrelated, even if locked up within itself and subjected to constant war or conflict, is more appealing than the threat or reality of losing something so important that it makes the self "hardly worth protecting."

Safeties and Dangers

The political theoretical traditions of which social contract theorizing forms a central part begin with the (sometimes implicit) assertion that something vital has been lost in civil society, in being bound to others by law, custom, and political authority. The individual must, to a considerable extent, adapt, comply, and obey. If we assume that the typically modern preoccupation with legitimizing or "making right" this obedience, adaptation, and compliance, so as to keep it consistent with declarations of essential and inalienable individual rights, has only to do with politics, we miss the bigger picture. It would be nothing new to suggest that the need to redefine adaptation and compliance as if they were rooted in "contracts" that respected the interests of the individual reflects the desire to control the terms of the self's engagement with others in the world, and perhaps even to avoid the narcissistic injury associated with living in a shared, social world (see also Alford 2005). Depending upon what we mean by "control," or, even how much "control" we intend, this desire may reflect a healthy need to express and realize the self in the world, or it may express a regressive demand that objects forfeit their externality and be reconceived according to the roles and attributions assigned to them in the individual's subjective experience and fantasy.

We have seen how the state of nature fantasy seems to combine ambivalent wishes for privacy and privation into a complex and perhaps unimaginable condition where, even as our physical lives and perhaps our property are in danger, the absence of law and sovereignty offers protection from loss and impingement. In this light, Hobbes' brutal vision of the state of nature is not so different from Rousseau's idyllic depiction. Two sides of the same coin, Hobbes' vision expresses both the liberty of personal authority and the terror at the loss of control implied by the absence of sovereignty, just as Rousseau's vision underscores both the freedom from coercion by others and the emptiness of a life without purpose, attachment, relationship, and culture.

Sovereignty, in such cases, may be interpreted as a metaphor for fantasized omnipotence, and not only the power to impress upon the world one's will, but the power to defend what is sacred and private in the self from others. Thus, if it were not already apparent, we are dealing here with different sorts of "danger," and different kinds of "safety." There is a safety in what Winnicott calls the "cavalier" attitude toward objects that permits of their "use," where "use" means the object's survival of fantasized destruction and where "survival" means that objects do not change or retaliate against the self (1971, 90–93). Since the child "destroys" (in fantasy) to make objects external, and makes objects external to relate her internal and external worlds, we may say that in order for the child to come alive in a robust sense, it must be safe for the child to be dangerous.

Something of this psychic or environmental safety may even (or especially) be found in fantasized "condition[s] of Warre of every one against every one; in which … there is nothing he can make use of, that may not be a help unto him, in preserving his life against his enemyes … [and in which] … every man has a Right to everything: even to one another's body" (Hobbes 1985, 190). The human being in Hobbes' state of nature lives in great physical danger, but is free to do what he will: to use, to exploit, to damage, to kill. Of course, the other human beings he may kill (in this fantasy) may not physically survive, but, being unattached to them, their physical survival is of little importance. What is important is that Nature "survives." The environment, as "dangerous" as it is, "survives" because, while natural law operates in various forms throughout many variations on the state of nature, Nature is, for lack of a better phrase, a "safe space." Nature does not retaliate against human beings for acts of aggression, as a parent, a court of law, or even a guilty conscience might. Although the law of nature "forbids" a human being in the state of nature from destroying his own life, this prohibition is not a matter of right and wrong. Indeed, in the state of nature, "nothing can be Unjust. The notions of Right and Wrong, Justice and Unjust have there no place" (Hobbes 1985, 188). This moral and psychological "indestructibility" of Nature is a feature of states of nature perhaps too often overlooked.

Considered in this light, the invocation of the state of nature in the project of renegotiating or reassessing the social contract is quite similar to the effort of the deprived child to undo his deprivation via "antisocial" acts—indeed, one might even argue that the imagination of a state of nature is the ultimate (fantasized) antisocial act. "Hope" inaugurates this undoing process: the hope of getting "back behind the deprivation moment." Like the imagination of the state of nature, the compulsive theft or breaking of an object is an imaginary breaking of the child's "social contract," an effort to "take back" her aggression and to "give back" to the environment its "indestructibility," carried out with the hope that an earlier, "safer" world will survive or be resuscitated.

The imagination of the state of nature relates to the "antisocial" acts of stealing candy or smashing vases by "taking back" and "breaking down" objects that symbolize the framework of control held responsible for withering the self, particularly its most private and sacred parts. This attempt to redefine relationships to objects is coincidental with the breaking down of the depriving "social contract" in force in the depriving home or society. The child, like the state-of-nature theorist, reaches back "to the lost security of the [early] framework ... in which spontaneity was safe, even if it involved aggressive impulses" (1986, 98).

In *Rethinking the Politics of Absurdity* (2014), I argued that antisubjective discourses, desubjectifying conditions, and apocalyptic, disaster-oriented fantasies served the psychic interests of individuals seeking regressive experiences of innocence. I might have done more there to explain the relationship I am alluding to now between innocence and a form of safety, which is not difficult to understand. To use more Kleinian language, what weighs on our psyches is guilt and fear concerning our own hate and destructiveness: For Klein, "the central conflict in human experience ... is between love and hate, between the caring preservation and the malicious destruction of others" (Greenberg and Mitchell 1983, 142). But if the world is already destroyed, or if its destruction is imagined to be inevitable, then one need not feel guilt about annihilating hatred or rage. Of course, this is so only because one finds oneself in a world where there is nothing good to harm: the freedom of desolation.

Of course, Winnicott takes issue with Klein's approach to hate, nowhere more famously than in his explicit denial of the presence of anger in the destructiveness mobilized in efforts to use objects (1971, 93). But Winnicott also acknowledges that, in deprived environments, Klein's vision may be applicable in that aggression is *not* available for "use," nor does it operate primarily as fantasy, but, rather, turns genuinely dangerous and destructive (Winnicott 1986, 80–100, 1990, 84–99). In good enough environments, we can use aggression in positive ways, discovering objects and differences, protecting ourselves, and forging relationships with others that permit of separateness. But in the context of deprivation, children, and later adults, must return to infantile fantasies of "magical control" and the "magical destruction of all objects" where the world is only made "safe" by holding on to the illusory power to destroy it in "the blink of an eye" (1990, 97–99).

Trauma, the "Natural" Self, and the Good

Several years ago, I interviewed a young woman who told me about a gruesome experience of having been kidnapped and held in captivity, alone, for four days, in a small room, until she was eventually rescued by the police (Bowker 2014).[3] A 14-year-old girl at the time, Maria's experience of captivity was traumatic and terrifying. "I screamed so much I forgot my talking voice," she recalled. And "by the third or fourth day, I really didn't know who I was. I was afraid of how I behaved. I was full of rage." In the years following her abduction, Maria experienced uncertainty, anxiety, paranoia, difficulty performing in school, and a feeling that she was involved in a daily struggle to "figure out what was going on." "I'm not normally a person who yells and screams," she explained, "but I behaved in the most odd manner and, for months after, [I] behaved strangely."

In spite of all this, Maria referred to her experience of captivity as her "natural state," presumably because she was alone in a bare room, with no one explicitly (i.e., physically or sexually) violating her. Her involuntary confinement was undoubtedly a form of violence, but she did not experience it in precisely this way. In fact, the link between her confinement and what she called her "natural state" was what troubled her the most. Maria wondered why she was so afraid to confront her "natural state." "Why didn't I feel safe there?," she asked, almost angrily. "Should I have really been afraid of myself that much?"

Of course, there is nothing "natural" about a child being held in captivity against her will; and Maria may have feared any number of things other than "herself" during those awful four days. Maria's attempt to comprehend her experience as "natural," like the desire she expressed in the interview to "thank" her captors and to "buy them dinner," seemed intended to transform a horrific experience into a learning experience. Maria reported that she now saw her captors as her most valuable "teachers," because they showed her "the most crucial purpose and thing in my life," which is "to understand me."

In striving to transform a horrific experience into a positive one, Maria relied on the concept of a "natural state," perhaps even one informed by state-of-nature theorists and their powerful impact upon modern and postmodern thought. Her association of deprivation with "nature" permitted her to indulge (after the fact) in a fantasy of privation, whereby she reimagined her captivity and loss as a natural and "safe" condition in which contact with herself was not only possible but unavoidable. This fantasy is, in my view, of greater importance for Maria's interpretation of her own experience than what some may see as a need to identify with her aggressors (Freud 1993).

Maria's effort to "take" something from her experience was not merely a defense, nor a denial of mourning the pain she had suffered. It *was* those things, but it was more as well. If we may say her fantasy contained an "error"—an odd way of speaking since, of course, fantasies contain factual errors; that is their point—the error here lay in the assumption that Maria's self was to be found inside a panicked child locked up in a room. It is this same "error" I have sought to bring into relief above, an error at the heart of state-of-nature fantasies and, perhaps, of all originary and apocalyptic fantasies: that in being subjected to deprivation, one becomes "free" to return to a "natural state," a condition of "original" privation that protects against self-loss and a condition of "original" privacy that makes genuine self-contact and self-experience possible.

Maria's self-chastisement for her fear and anger—"I should not have been so afraid"—along with her desire to "thank" her captors suggests more than an internalization of guilt or a desire to make reparations for her own violent fantasies. It signals, more importantly, an attempt to transform a depriving environment into a holding environment by the magical means of re-description and reimagination. In Maria's fantasy, her captors became her teachers and caregivers, affording her the privacy/privation she needed in order to make contact with herself, while, in reality, she was so terrified, so violated, and so "full of rage" that even well after the event she "did not know who she was."

Although we may consciously acknowledge the fiction of the state of nature, semi-consciously or unconsciously the fiction has come to be accepted as reality. This reality has been used to frame and comprehend countless modern and contemporary moral and political projects: the constitutions of liberal states; ideas and ideologies concerning the legitimate scope and function of governments (see also Curtis 2010); and the tenets of contemporary moral philosophies. The state of nature is a "dangerous" idea if it encourages us to respond to the experience of deprivation, as Maria did, by fantasizing about privation and privacy. I have sought to argue not that fantasies of states of nature are dangerous in themselves, but that in the face of deprivation we may turn to them unwittingly, with unfortunate results. Instead of acknowledging and working through the losses implied by deprivation, and instead of mobilizing energy to repair them in the present or to prevent them in the future, we wish and hope to "get back behind the deprivation moment." This wish and this hope are perhaps understandable for deprived children but are dangerously immature for adults living in a civil society.

We may remark that in those civic environments where state-of-nature fantasies hold the greatest sway, efforts to protect citizens from privation and deprivation are often less comprehensive and less successful. As Alford notes, this may be the case because, instead of "design[ing] their accounts so as to help men and women become more autonomous and free," state-of-nature theorists and their intellectual progeny set out about "convincing them that they already are" (1994, 7). When freedom is construed as "original" and when deprivation is imagined to return us to a "natural state," then in place of a lucid awareness of the ambivalent push and pull of privacy and privation we are likely to find unrealistic idealizations of suffering. Consider how such a perspective might help explain the vast indifference, in countries like the United States, to issues of inequality, poverty, and deprivation. If an ailing, elderly, disabled, or unemployed person, for instance, is unconsciously envied for not having to adapt to the order of the office or the control of the factory—that is, for having "private time" and for being "left alone"—then the office- or factory-worker will have little sympathy for such a person in spite of his situation.[4]

What is dangerous about the idea of the state of nature and the fantasy of privation it inspires is that they offer the wrong kind of safety: not the kind of safety that permits of spontaneity, creativity, or even "useful" destructiveness, but the kind of safety that protects us from thoughtfully examining the ambivalences and attractions of privacy and privation. Surely it is not a thoughtful recognition of these ambivalences that informs today's celebrations of the death of the subject, traumatic ruptures, and other "open wounds" of the self. These are conceived to be channels through which the Other, or others, may enter to depose the self's "sovereign subjectivity."

Judith Butler, for instance, offers an influential account of the value of grief as that which keeps open our "wounds" of loss, wounds whose agony reminds us of "the thrall in which our relations with others hold us" and the degree to which the self is (and ought to be) "given over to the Other in ways that [we] cannot fully predict or control" (2004, 23, 46). What is thought to be gained from this preoccupation with and preservation of loss, and from "remaining exposed to its unbearability," is the renunciation of the self's capacity to hold a piece of itself apart, in private. Instead, if one develops "a point of identification with suffering itself" (30), the Other overtakes one's innermost space, alienating oneself from oneself. And this deprivation of that which is most private, the very core of the self, leads to a sense of "foreignness to myself," which, Butler writes, "is, paradoxically, the source of my ethical connection with others" (46).

On the contrary, object-relations theory, and Winnicott in particular, would argue that those who have not been deprived of the capacity to make contact with what is private and hidden in themselves are *more* likely to relate to others ethically, as separate and external objects. What is more, the wounded and deprived individual lives with tremendous pain and anxiety as a result of too-early impingement, and is more likely to feel the need to assert subjective control (i.e., aggressive or domineering "sovereign subjectivity") over others to simulate a feeling of reality that is lacking internally (see also Levine, this volume).

The ethical idealization of the destruction of the subject—and, more specifically, the destruction of the self's potential for solitude and privacy—is equally apparent in academic valorizations of trauma, where the traumatized person is imbued with the terrible privilege of bearing a "literal" truth inside her, a truth *so literal*, in fact, that she *cannot bear it*. It is this literal "truth of traumatic experience," writes Cathy Caruth, "that forms the center of its pathology or symptoms." Trauma and posttraumatic symptoms are therefore "not a pathology … of falsehood or displacement of meaning, but of history itself," for the traumatized "carry an impossible history within them, or they become themselves the symptom of a history that they cannot entirely possess" (1995, 5).

Let us imagine, for a moment, what such an assertion really means. What is "true," on this line of thought, is not what is found inside the self, in private, but the opposite: What is true and real is what has penetrated the psyche–soma without the self's permission or foreknowledge, what has overtaken the individual such that she herself becomes a "symptom," a receptacle for something absolute, external, and incomprehensible to her. If we look carefully at the "truths" putatively offered by traumatic experience, we shall find that they regularly boil down to one: the "truth" of the inevitable destruction of the self (see Bowker 2016). This is the "truth" that tells us that we are all—and must all be—traumatized, that we inhabit "a catastrophic age" (Caruth 1995, 11) where "history" is "the history of trauma" (Caruth 1996, 60), where we must read "history as holocaust" (Felman 1992, 95) because "history is precisely the way we are implicated in each other's traumas" (Caruth 1996, 24).

On this line of thought, our collective experiences of trauma, suffering, and deprivation are the very substance of our human experience, and, thus, "must move beyond isolation and be shared with participants willing to engage in the victim's torment" (Nossery and Hubbell 2013, 11). They must be spread and shared even if doing so transmits "not the normalizing knowledge of the horror but the horror itself" (W.B. Michaels quoted in Leys 2000, 268), and even if this transfusion of horror makes each recipient a "participant and co-owner of the traumatic event … partially experience[ing] trauma in himself … com[ing] to feel the bewilderment, injury, confusion, dread and conflicts that the trauma victim feels (Laub 1992, 57–58).

The underlying fantasy here is that the extreme deprivation known as "trauma" will provide a "link" between individuals that will serve us better than possessing selves. That is, transmitting deprivation and trauma means collectively losing our selves. And, according to this variation on the fantasy of privation I have tried to highlight here, by "listen[ing] through the departures we have all taken from ourselves" (Caruth 1995, 11), we may return to something not unlike a psychic state of nature, where what is real is the absence, and not the presence, of selves.

I hope to have shown that there is more than "catastrophizing" at work when individuals and groups, when confronted with (actual or imagined) deprivation, respond in what would seem to be self-defeating ways, by heaping austerity upon deficiency, and by valorizing lack in the face of loss. If, when faced with the dangerous realities of deprivation, we refer ourselves to fantasies of privation, we ought not be surprised when our personal and political narratives evince fascination with atrocity and disaster, when they express powerful impulses to destroy others or institutions that threaten to deprive us of our putatively original or "natural" freedoms, or when they offer ideological support for aggression or destruction in the name of "safety" or innocence, or, what amounts to the same, in the name of returning to a state of (moral) goodness and (political) greatness.

Notes

1. They should deny the historical reality of the state of nature, given all (currently) available anthropological evidence (see, e.g., Gamble 1999; Leakey and Lewin 1978).
2. This claim is not unique to Locke. Hobbes would agree (1985, 187–188), and Kant would follow a similar line of thought as well.
3. I have changed the name and identifying characteristics of this respondent to an interview protocol conducted from 2008 to 2012 (see Bowker 2014).
4. While well beyond the scope of this chapter, it would be worthwhile to examine narratives and criticisms of welfare programs, welfare reform, "welfare mothers," and the like with an eye to this dynamic.

References

Achinstein, S. 2007. Mary Astell, Religion, and Feminism: Texts in Motion. In *Mary Astell: Reason, Gender, and Faith*, ed. W. Kolbrenner, and M. Michelson, 17–30. Burlington, VT: Ashgate.

Agamben, G. 1998. *Homo Sacer: Sovereign Power and Bare Life*. Trans. D. Heller-Roazen Stanford, CA: Stanford University Press.

Alford, C.F. 1991. *The Self in Social Theory: A Psychoanalytic Account of Its Construction in Plato, Hobbes, Locke, Rawls, and Rousseau*. New Haven, CT: Yale University Press.

———. 1994. *Group Psychology and Political Theory.* New Haven, CT: Yale University Press.

———. 2005. *Rethinking Freedom: Why Freedom Has Lost Its Meaning and What Can Be Done to Save It.* New York: Palgrave Macmillan.

Althusser, L. 1972. *Politics and History: Montesquieu, Rousseau, Hegel, and Marx.* Trans. B. Brewster. London: NLB.

Astell, M. 1704. *Moderation, Truly Stated: Or a Review of a Late Pamphlet Entituled Moderation, a Vertue.* London.

Baier, A. 1994. *Moral Prejudices: Essays on Ethics.* Cambridge, MA: Harvard University Press.

Benhabib, S. 1987. The Generalized and the Concrete Other: The Kohlberg–Gilligan Controversy and Feminist Theory. In *Feminism as Critique: Essays on the Politics of Gender in Late Capitalist Societies*, ed. S. Benhabib, and D. Cornell, 77–95. Minneapolis, MN: University of Minnesota Press.

Bowker, M.H. 2011. The Meaning of Absurd Protest: *The Book of Job*, Albert Camus, and C. Fred Alford's *After the Holocaust. Journal of Psycho-Social Studies* 5(1): 163–183.

———. 2014. *Rethinking the Politics of Absurdity: Albert Camus, Postmodernity, and the Survival of Innocence.* New York: Routledge.

———. 2016. *Ideologies of Experience: Trauma, Failure, Deprivation, and the Abandonment of the Self.* New York: Routledge.

Butler, J. 2004. *Precarious Life: The Powers of Mourning and Violence.* London: Verso.

Caruth, C. (ed). 1995. *Trauma: Explorations in Memory.* Baltimore, MD: Johns Hopkins University Press.

———. (ed). 1996. *Unclaimed Experience: Trauma, Narrative, and History.* Baltimore, MD: Johns Hopkins University Press.

Curtis, C. 2010. *Postapocalyptic Fiction and the Social Contract: "We'll Not Go Home Again."* Lanham, MD: Rowman and Littlefield.

DiStefano, C. 1983. Masculinity as Ideology in Political Theory: Hobbesian Man Considered. *Women's Studies International Forum* 6(6): 633–644.

Felman, S. 1992. "Camus' The Plague, or a Monument to Witnessing." In *Testimony: Crises of Witnessing in Literature, Psychoanalysis, and History.* ed. S. Felman and D. Laub. New York: Taylor and Francis

Focchi, M. 2005. The Indiscrete Language and the Unrepeatable. *The Symptom* 6. http://www.lacan.com/symptom6_articles/focchi1.html. Accessed 10 March 2016.

Freud, S. 1914. On Narcissism. In *The Standard Edition of the Complete Psychological Works of Sigmund Freud* ed. and trans. J. Strachey, vol. XIV, 67–102. London: Hogarth.

Freud, S. 1938. "Totem and Taboo: Resemblances Between the Mental Lives of Savages and Neurotics." In *The Basic Writings of Sigmund Freud.* Trans and ed. A.A. Brill, 807–930. New York: Random House.

Freud, A. 1993. *The Ego and Mechanisms of Defense*. Rev. ed. London: Karnac Books.

Gamble, C. 1999. *The Palaeolithic Societies of Europe*. Cambridge: Cambridge University Press.

Gerson, G. 2004. Object Relations Psychoanalysis as Political Theory. *Political Psychology* 25(5): 769–794.

Greenberg, J., and S. Mitchell. 1983. *Object Relations in Psychoanalytic Theory*. Cambridge, MA: Harvard University Press.

Held, V. 1993. *Feminist Morality: Transforming Culture, Society, and Politics*. Chicago: University of Chicago Press.

Hobbes, T. 1972. *Thomas Hobbes' De Homine and De Cive*. Ed. B. Gert. New York: Anchor Books.

———. 1985. *Leviathan, or The Matter, Forme, and Power of a Common-Wealth Ecclesiasticall and Civill*. Ed. C.B. Macpherson, Penguin Classics ed. London: Penguin.

Jay, M. 1993. *Force Fields: Between Intellectual History and Cultural Critique*. New York: Routledge.

Johnston, A. 2015. Lacking Causes: Privative Causality from Locke and Kant to Lacan and Deacon. *Speculations* 6: 19–60.

Lacan, J. 1988. *The Seminar of Jacques Lacan, II*. Trans. S. Tomaselli and Ed. J.A. Miller. Cambridge: Cambridge University Press.

Laub, D. 1992. "Bearing Witness, or the Vicissitudes of Listening." In *Testimony: Crises of Witnessing in Literature, Psychoanalysis, and History*, edited by S. Felman and D. Laub, 57–74. New York: Taylor and Francis.

Leakey, R., and R. Lewin. 1978. *People of the Lake: Mankind and Its Beginnings*. New York: Avon Books.

Leverett, F.P. 1874. *A New and Copious Lexicon of the Latin Language*. Philadelphia, PA: J.P. Lippincott & Co.

Lewis, C.T., and C. Short. 1879. *A Latin Dictionary*. Oxford: Clarendon Press.

Leys, R. 2000. *Trauma: A Genealogy*. Chicago: University of Chicago Press.

Locke, J. 1980. *Second Treatise of Government*. Ed. C.B. Macpherson. Indianapolis, IN: Hackett.

Macpherson, C.B. 1971. The Social Bearing of Locke's Political Theory. In *Life, Liberty and Property: Essays on Locke's Political Ideas*, ed. G. Schochet, 60–85. Belmont, CA: Wadsworth.

Merton, T. 1958. *Thoughts in Solitude*. New York: Farrar, Straus and Giroux.

Miller, A. 1997. *The Drama of the Gifted Child: The Search for the True Self*. Rev. ed. Trans. R. Ward. New York: Basic Books.

Mills, C. 1997. *The Racial Contract*. Ithaca and London: Cornell University Press.

Nossery, N., and A. Hubbell 2013. "Introduction." In *The Unspeakable: Representations of Trauma in Francophone Literature and Art*, edited by N. Nossery and A. Hubbell, 1–20. Cambridge: Cambridge Scholars.

Nussbaum, M. 2000. *Women and Human Development: The Capabilities Approach*. Cambridge: Cambridge University Press.

Pateman, C. 1988. *The Sexual Contract*. Stanford, CA: Stanford University Press.

Rawls, J. 1971. *A Theory of Justice*. Cambridge, MA: Harvard University Press.

Rousseau, J.-J. 1987. *The Basic Political Writings*. Ed. and Trans. D. Cress. Indianapolis, IN: Hackett.

Winnicott, D.W. 1965. *The Maturational Processes and the Facilitating Environment: Studies in the Theory of Emotional Development*. Ed. M. Khan. London: Hogarth and the Institute of Psycho-Analysis.

———. 1971. *Playing and Reality*. London: Routledge.

———. 1986. *Home Is Where We Start from: Essays by a Psychoanalyst*. Ed. C. Winnicott, R. Shepard, and M. Davis. New York: W.W. Norton.

———. 1990. *Deprivation and Delinquency*. Ed. C. Winnicott, R. Shepherd, and M. Davis. London and New York: Routledge.

———. 1992. *Through Paediatrics to Psycho-Analysis: Collected Papers*. Ed. M. Khan. New York: Brunner-Routledge.

Wollstonecraft, M. [1792] 2004. *A Vindication of the Rights of Woman*. Ed. M. Brody. New York: Penguin.

Žižek, S. 2002. *Did Somebody Say Totalitarianism: Five Interventions in the (Mis) Use of a Notion*. London: Verso.

CHAPTER 7

"Out Like a Lion": *Melancholia* with Euripides and Winnicott

Bonnie Honig

In this chapter, I enlist D.W. Winnicott to develop a new reading of Lars von Trier's *Melancholia* in which I interpret von Trier's film alongside Euripides' *Bacchae*. Where Freud had *Oedipus Tyrannos*, Lacan *Antigone*, and Melanie Klein the *Oresteia*, though she ought to have claimed *Medea*, to Winnicott, surely, belongs the *Bacchae*.[1] With Winnicott's help, the *Bacchae* is opened to a new reading, different from the standard ones (see Wohl 2005). These usually focus on a conflict, whether between a disrespected, angry god (Dionysus) and a stubborn King (Pentheus); or between a king and the unruly or liberated women he would like to domesticate; or between a son and his wild mother who, failing to recognize him, (un)wittingly kills and horrifically dismembers him (Pentheus and Agave). The focus here is different: it is on a young king's quest for authenticity out of the ruins of compliance.

A modified version of this chapter appeared in *Theory and Event* 18(2) (2015) and appears in *Politics, Theory, and Film: Critical Encounters with Lars von Trier*, edited by Bonnie Honig and Lori Marso (Oxford University Press, 2016). I am grateful to Matt Bowker for his generosity as a reader and editor of this essay.

B. Honig (✉)
Chesler-Mallow Senior Research Fellow, Pembroke Center, 2016–17 Nancy Duke Lewis Professor, Modern Culture and Media (MCM) and Political Science, Brown University, Providence, RI, USA

M.H. Bowker, A. Buzby (eds.), *D.W. Winnicott and Political Theory*,
DOI 10.1057/978-1-137-57533-3_7

This is where Winnicott, with his work on adolescence, will take us, though he never discussed Euripides' play.[2] And adolescence, we shall see, provides a fitting angle on von Trier's film, which is reopened for critical examination when we switch our focus from the ostensibly main characters, the sisters Justine and Claire, to the young boy, Leo.

Winnicott's work invites a reconsideration of the *Bacchae* whose depiction of Pentheus' horrific dismemberment can be seen as a way of working through the adolescent craving for, and horror of, disintegration—a necessary step to integration in the (post)adolescent stage. The mother's later reassembly of her son's dismembered body for burial can also be seen as part of this process, in which the "good-enough mother" helps her son break out of his false, sovereign self and integrate his several parts into a "unit," as Winnicott says, bordered by a "membrane" that is permeable, but not formless (1971, 143, 1964, 87, 96; Winnicott et al. 1987, 11).[3] This approach to Euripides' tragedy transforms what is usually seen as filicide into a kind of Winnicottian act of compassionate care. What dies, on this parable-like reading of the play, and is then buried is not Pentheus but his false self, his carapace of sovereignty. One detail that might underwrite such a reading is the fact that his mother mistakes him for a lion—the icon of sovereignty—suggesting she meant to kill not him but his sovereignty or his office, that is to say, the social role or investiture that maims him (Knox 1952).

Treating *Melancholia* as a reception of Euripides does not mean von Trier intended to rewrite the *Bacchae* as *Melancholia*, nor does it even assume he is familiar with the ancient play, though, as we shall see, there are numerous uncanny overlaps between the play and his film. But it does suggest that the 2011 film reworks—consciously or otherwise—some of the ancient tragedy's themes and that attending to that reworking may illuminate both the play and the film. *Melancholia*, too, is about adolescence and sovereignty, disintegration, and integration. This becomes apparent if we attend not just to the two lead characters, Justine and Claire, the sisters for whom the two main parts of the film are named and on whom most critics focus. Focusing on the young boy, Leo, enables a new interpretation of the film in which the catastrophe of planetary destruction can be seen to represent what Winnicott describes colorfully as the world-ending experience of adolescence. As he says to parents of adolescents: "You sowed a baby and you reaped a bomb" (1971, 145). In von Trier's film, Leo's aunt, Justine, seems to worship the foreign planet and to beckon to it. With Winnicott's help, we may think of its explosive impact as the sound of Leo's adolescence, making itself heard, with her help and support. On this reading, the posttraumatic situation then presents Leo, his mother, and his aunt with the task of collecting him not, like Pentheus, for burial, but for life. We may hazard the same even for Pentheus, in fact, whose false and dismembered sovereign self is first re-collected by his grandfather, Cadmus, progenitor of the line of kings, but then buried as a re-membered body by his mother.

Alongside the adolescents looking to find themselves, the women featured in both the *Bacchae* and *Melancholia* refuse their assigned social roles. In both, a maternal figure who is under some rogue spell, whether of a foreign god or a godlike planet, abandons work (at the loom or in advertising) and family (husbands and children are left behind), is threatened or lured to return, and refuses. In Euripides' play, Agave abandons her work and her son to go gamboling in the fields of Cithaeron, though the king repeatedly calls her and the other women to return to their looms. "I'll either sell them as slaves or have them work the looms" says Pentheus (2014, 513–514). At Justine's wedding, her boss, an advertising executive who is there as a guest, hounds her and has brought along an underling to do the same for the express purpose of getting one last tag line from Justine before she goes away on her honeymoon. In response, she—Agave-like—tears him apart, verbally, exposing him so painfully (to the whites of his ribs we might say, thinking of poor Pentheus) that the boss, Jack, smashes a plate, gets in his car, and leaves in a rage of humiliation.[4]

Both Euripides' and von Trier's tales of destruction contrast unpalatable adulthood with a young boy/man whose plight is his difficulty in breaking out of his assigned role. The boy/man rebels against maternal/paternal expectations, meets with maternal resistance but also care, and makes a fantastic bid for what Winnicott called "BEing." This adolescent maturation requires that the youth abandon his infantile omnipotence, and the sovereigntist fantasies in which, later in life, such omnipotence finds shelter, meaning, and justification. This requires that he take the risk of world destruction (or what feels like that). "How shall the adolescent boy or girl deal with the new power to destroy and even to kill, a power which did not complicate feelings of hatred at the toddler age?" Winnicott asks. "It is like putting *new wine into old bottles.*"

The pacing of the opening scenes of *Melancholia*, languorous and slow, point to the tempo of adolescence, which Winnicott calls the "doldrums" and warns must not be avoided or averted. Adolescence needs to resist the pulls to move, preternaturally, forward or backward in time or development. The rushed imposition of sovereignty *and* the delaying of maturation by insistent infantilization are both refusals to *be* in the transitional state. Winnicott says: "Triumph belongs to this attainment of maturity by growth process. Triumph does not belong to the false maturity based on a facile impersonation of an adult. Terrible facts are locked up in this statement" (1971, 147). Pentheus' story is a story of such "terrible facts." So is Leo's.

The Other Calamity: Manhood, or "I'm the King of the Castle"

Those who see von Trier's film as a story of the end of the world tend to treat Justine, the main character who suffers from melancholia and is drawn to the rogue planet, also named "Melancholia," as a way for von Trier (who himself suffers from melancholia) to explore something a therapist once said to him: that melancholics are better than anyone at handling catastrophe. They are more prepared for it and less invested in denying it than others might be.

But there is another calamity in the film, one faced by Leo, the boy on the brink of adolescence who is looking for a way to assert him*self* while his mother clings to him, and his father dwarfs him. As the catastrophic collision nears, Leo plays with his visionary aunt, Justine. They build a "magic cave," a structure that provides Leo with an ideal family to replace his actual one. In the closing shot of the film, Leo sits in the magic cave with his mother, Claire, and her sister, Justine, and the three *hold* hands.

This by contrast with one of the movie's opening shots, that of the two sisters and the boy, standing parallel on the estate lawn about ten feet apart from each other.

Absent from both iterations of this nuclear family is Leo's father, John: a man so wealthy his golf course has 19 holes, and so used to being in control that he commits suicide to avoid the catastrophe of planetary collision (and perhaps also to avoid confronting his own errors; he had disparaged those who thought the collision was coming when scientists said it would not). This is John's way of coping with what Winnicott calls "the immense shock of the loss of omnipotence" which normally happens at the "very earliest stages" of development, but can recur throughout a life (1971, 95). Like so many of von Trier's limited men, John is not up to the challenges he faces. He dies alone in a stable. It is not a bad death, but it is not a good one, either. John's suicide may be mistakable for stoicism; but he is no Cato. John's is a liberal death: voluntarist, unconnected, and devoid of ritual. Claire provides a bit of a rite, dutifully, perhaps caringly, covering her husband's body with straw, though they are all of them about to die "unwept, unmourned," as Antigone says of Polynices under Creon's edict).

The two women in the magic cave with Leo, his aunt and his mother, Justine and Claire, have had their differences about how to confront the end. Like her husband, Claire has her own methods of avoidance: she had hoped to commit suicide with Leo but John has used the pills she bought for that purpose. Now, she hopes to anesthetize herself in a different way: she wants to greet the end of the world with a soirée. She asks Justine to meet her for a glass of wine on the terrace. "I want us to be together when it happens .... Help me. Justine. I want it to be nice .... We could have a glass of wine .... Will you do it, Sis?" Justine responds: "Do you want to hear what I think of your plan? I think it's a piece of shit! You want it to be nice? Why don't we do it in the fuckin' toilet?" This is Justine's nonconformism; niceness does not tempt her.

Justine, by contrast with Claire, does not seek to absent herself from the catastrophic situation. She will see it through, with Leo. She heeds Winnicott's admonition to the philosopher to "*come out of his chair and sit on the floor with his patient*" (1971, 120). She joins Leo to build a structure. They play. They gather wood and carve it to build the "magic cave." She holds Leo's hand, guiding the knife, and then steps back as he gains confidence and assumes responsibility. He now knows what he is doing. This mentoring contrasts with the boy's experience with his father, whose telescope—enormous and phallic—dwarfs Leo's homemade apparatus and accentuates the difference between them.[5]

Melancholia famously depicts the end of the world. But the film supports the idea that it is also about the less obvious catastrophe of Leo's adolescence. At the beginning of the film, which seems to presage the end, amidst the signs and portents of world destruction presented in a somewhat random, confusing, and terrifying way, we see Claire holding her son in her arms, sinking into the softened ground as she seems to try to hasten somewhere to save him. There is something awkward in the image. Leo is too big to be held in this way. This may speak to the hugeness of the catastrophe; or the hugeness of the catastrophe may *be* that he is held in this infantilizing way by his mother. (Recall *The Bacchae*: "You will be carried home ... held in your mother's arms," Dionysus says ominously to Pentheus [965–970].) The vision changes as the film unfolds. It gets better and it gets worse. In the second half of the film, Leo is similarly carried, but the ground does not sink. Then, as they await the unavoidable catastrophe, Claire sits on the terrace with her son, clutching him even more closely, as he sleeps like a swaddled baby, in her lap. In the end, though, Leo leaves his mother's body and sits holding hands with her and his aunt in the little wooden structure he and his aunt have built (Fig. 7.1). The house of sticks unites the three who earlier stood apart. What has made that transformation possible?

To answer the question, it is useful to return to the film's opening sequence, that chaotic assemblage of film references, unnatural and unnarrated still and moving images. Most of the film's interpreters find this opening sequence confusing (see Elsaesser 2016). Although it seems to presage the coming catastrophe, not everything in it comes to pass. It is called "Prologue," but what if we interpret (a bit of) it as Leo's dream? There are reasons (the tempo, the prophecy, the anxiety) to do so. And we would thus be naming a third perspective to go with the other two parts of the film, named respectively for Justine and Claire, in which each one faces her own personal challenge: Justine has to negotiate the inauthenticating demands of heteronormalcy (the wedding) and Claire the existential demands of finitude (the end of the world). Neither one is cut out for what she must face. Leo has his challenge, too, and it has implications for the other two. He has to negotiate a new relationship with a mother who still (like all mothers) carries him like a baby. For this, he will use, or invent, his aunt.

Held in an infantilizing way by his mother in the opening sequence, Leo dreams a way out. He turns to Justine, his Aunt, and symbolic mother (figure). She knows how to play—a Winnicottian requirement (see Winnicott 1964)—and she will enable or inspire him to make the cut.

Fig. 7.1 Together, at the end

With Justine's help and encouragement, Leo will move from the parental holdings of his infancy—the paternal holdings (investment, wealth, symbolized by the golf course green) of John, the father, and the maternal (infantilizing) holding of Claire—to a holding *environment*: the magic cave. These holding environment activities counterbalance the holdings of capitalism and maternalism that keep us in what Winnicott called the "shop window faces" that reflect back but do not take us or others in, just like the shiny new things advertised in such windows. Pleasing the father or the mother (the latter, a big issue for Winnicott himself), in conformity with social expectations, we want what we are told is desirable, regardless of whether it supports our flourishing.

Claire, her great care for her melancholic sister notwithstanding, seems the sort of mother figure Winnicott had in mind when he warned: "If the mother's face is unresponsive, then a mirror is a thing to be looked at but not to be looked into." That is to say, the mirroring that *integrates* the child and makes him real, the gift that transitions him to adulthood, cannot happen here. (To be fair, it may well be that Claire is a "good enough mother," that Leo needs both her, as she is, and her sister. After all, the "good enough" mother is of necessity also the bad enough mother, the one who fails the child enough to open up the possibility of autonomy: "What happens if the mother is able to start on a graduated failure of adaptation from a position of adapting fully?" Winnicott asks. Only good things, is the implication.) Sometimes, the glass' reflection is treated in more positive terms by Winnicott, as when he discusses Francis Bacon's use of glass over his paintings so as to meld the viewer with the subject portrayed. When the viewers see their own reflection in the glass, they are superimposed on the painting (Winnicott 1971, 126, 152–154).

It is even possible, given this is a von Trier film (and mine, thus far, a Winnicottian reading!), that the disappearance of the father and the pacification of the mother are no accident, as it were. Leo's parents may well be killed off, at least in fantasy, by their child, who handles his knife rather thoughtfully in the image above (Fig. 7.2). "If, in the fantasy of early growth, there is contained *death*, then at adolescence there is contained *murder*," Winnicott observes, describing the "life-and-death struggle" of adolescence (1971, 196, 123).

The film's final, fantasized "family" breaks the Oedipal family structure as well as the sentimental mother–child dyad. We see a nuclear family made up of two sisters and a son/nephew. In a way perhaps more Kleinian than Winnicottian (see Klein 2013), Leo has split the mother in two. In

Fig. 7.2 Making the cut: Leo's emergent autonomy

Leo's dream, the mother who carries and holds him like a baby when he is far too big for it is the mother who will not permit entry into adulthood. This is her role-assigned task: "If the child is to become adult, then this move is achieved over the dead body of an adult," Winnicott observes. Lest he be mistaken, Winnicott adds parenthetically: "I must take it for granted that the reader knows that I am referring to unconscious fantasy, the material that underlies playing" (1971, 195–196). The Prologue/dream telegraphs Leo's anxiety and informs the cure: from being held to holding environment, from infantilizing mother to playful aunt, Leo in fantasy sets his mother aside (a process in which Aunts are especially useful), and devises the magic of the magic cave. His solution is Justine. His solution is to steal her from his mother, her sister, her double.

This is one of two options listed by Winnicott: stealing or miming. "Stealing belongs to the male element in boys and girls. The question arises: what corresponds to this in terms of the female element in boys and girls? The answer can be that in respect of this element the individual *usurps the mother's position and her seat or garments*, in this way deriving desirability and seductiveness stolen from the mother" (1971, 114). In the *Bacchae*, Pentheus mimes. "How do I look in my getup? Don't I move like [Aunt] Ino? Or like my mother Agave?" says Pentheus in drag (925–926).[6] In *Melancholia*, Leo steals. He calls his Aunt "Steelbreaker," or perhaps it is "Steal-breaker." Is this because he *steals* her? From his mother? And because in so doing he *breaks* the Oedipal contract? (Do these possibilities seem like a stretch? They may be. But no one else has a clue what this nickname might mean!)

In Justine, Leo finds or fantasizes the midwife of his rebirth. She absorbs the risk (melancholia) and rises to the challenge of Leo's transition when she joins him to keep the promise of the "magic cave." There, the two mother-figures will come back together and hold Leo by the hands. "Somehow I see myself in both of the sisters. You can also, if you choose, see them as one person, two sides of the same person," notes von Trier (Carlsen 2011). Perhaps this is one of the magics of the magic cave: its capacity to reunite the mother split by the transitioning son.

In psychological terms, the various feared catastrophes—the end of the world, dismemberment, the fiery earthquaked destruction of the palace—may be allies in a broader struggle for authenticity and against sovereign subjectivity. The end of the world may be awful (the world is all we have, and for sovereign individuals like John it feels pretty good) or hopeful (this world is ALL we have? For the Justines of the world, and so many others less privileged, that is a betrayal). That world-endingness—the collapse of our palaces, big and small—may be what we want above all to avoid; but it may be what we need to risk in order to act in solidarity with others on behalf of new forms of life more authentic, more empowered, less compliant, and less oppressive than those we live by now.[7]

In von Trier's reception of the *Bacchae*, the sisters welcome Leo and hold his hands, by contrast with the sisters who, in Euripides' *Bacchae*, tear the King limb from limb. When Pentheus turns (in)to his aunt(s), miming Agave's sister Ino in a dress, no aunt is available for him to use as Leo uses Justine. Pentheus cannot successfully split his mother into controlling mother versus caregiving aunts, as Leo does, perhaps because Agave and her sisters are united in dance and bacchanalia, or perhaps because their unity is also political, even regicidal, as we shall now see. Together, these two acts of sorority, hospitable (in *Melancholia*) and inhospitable (in the *Bacchae*), lay out the way things might go once we attenuate sovereign subjectivity and violate normative expectations of compliance and orderliness whether by leaving our looms (as the women do, in the *Bacchae*), or by way of the postadolescent cross-dressing or the preadolescent maturation for which no one in our heteronormative social order is ever ready.

I suggested at the outset that Agave's effort to suture Pentheus together for burial might be seen as an act of compassionate care in support of her son's effort to move toward a more authentic existence, away from the falsenesses of sovereign investiture. I now turn to look at the play in detail, and will argue that her acts exceed both filicide and filiphilia. Her son is a king and we do well, therefore, to assess Agave's actions in the context of the shocking regicide at the play's center. Regicide may serve as an allegory for a psychological process, as indeed Winnicott suggests when he comments on the children's rhyme: "I'm the King of the castle," but regicide may also point more insistently to a politics. Able only to kill a king but never kingship, regicide points beyond the world-endingness of psychic life to the never-endingness of political life.[8]

The King's Three Bodies

My reading of *Melancholia* is supported by the idea that von Trier can be identified with Leo, and not only—as virtually all the film's viewers assume—with Justine. One warrant for the proposed pairing is to note that we have here two leonine-named boys: Lars/Leo. So, let us turn to the other leonine boy, Pentheus, the one whose mother in fact mistakes him for a lion, a Leo. "I seem to see two suns," says Pentheus, in the *Bacchae* (Vellacott 1973, 224). Von Trier's Leo seems to see two suns too. One of those suns is a rogue planet that will soon collide with the earth and destroy it. Thus, it is as disturbing a sight for him as it seems to have been for Pentheus.

In the *Bacchae*, Dionysus destroys his cousin Pentheus' kingdom in retaliation for Pentheus' rejection of Dionysus and also for the rejection by Agave and her sisters, years earlier, of Dionysus' mother, their sister, Semele. Semele, a stigmatized, single, pregnant woman, claimed Zeus was the father of her not yet born infant. The sisters disputed Semele's claim and demanded she prove it by calling Zeus to come to her. Calling on Zeus is a perilous act, however, and indeed Semele died as a result, a victim of sororicide. The sisters have instrumentalized Zeus to their purpose. (They commit another sororicide later, a sororicide-by-proxy, when they act in concert to murder Pentheus.) Zeus takes the fetus into a womb of his own and later births the baby. The baby will grow up to be Dionysus, the new wine-god. Dionysus repays the harms to himself and his mother by bewitching Agave and her sisters and all the women of Thebes into a Bacchic frenzy with catastrophic consequences for the kingdom.

Now of course, psychoanalytically speaking, and democratically speaking, too, consequences that are catastrophic for the "kingdom" are not necessarily a bad thing. Pentheus' palace is destroyed by an earthquake—"Pentheus' palace is falling, crumbling in pieces!," the Chorus reports (Vellacott 1973, 211)—and his stables are leveled by fire; earthquake and fire being the fifth century versions of von Trier's twenty-first century catastrophe: planetary collision. "Now he's dazed and helpless with exhaustion," reports Dionysus, who makes all this happen, of the once omnipotent king (213). But the earthquake and fire are not just bad news. Attenuating Pentheus' sovereign subjectivity, they offer him up for a possible posttraumatic reorganization, which begins with cross-dressing (suggested by Dionysus, so the King can spy undetected on the women Bacchants) and ends with dismemberment, *both* of which the once well-ordered subject-king may be said to have craved.

That is, the dismemberment need not be seen as a moral judgment against his cross-dressing, or as retribution for his sovereign rejection of Dionysus. Both the cross-dressing and the dismemberment can be seen as Dionysian efforts to attenuate a too rigid or dispassionate Apollonian subjectivity. From a Winnicottian perspective, the fact that Pentheus is maimed and not just thwarted is how we know Pentheus was in quest of being. "The male element does while the female element (in males and females) is. Here would come in those males in Greek myth who try to be at one with the supreme goddess. It seems that frustration belongs to satisfaction-seeking [i.e., doing]. To the experience of being belongs something else, not frustration, but *maiming*" (1971, 81, *emphasis added*).

Unlike Leo, Pentheus needs disintegration, not integration. Pentheus is, after all, a king, formed by royal investiture and maimed by it, too. Was Pentheus rushed in to office, unready? Perhaps so. His grandfather and the former King of Thebes, is still alive and well, but has stepped aside. When Dionysus arrives in Thebes, he reactivates buried anxieties about pasts not justly dealt with and a future hurried into at some cost.

Most readers of the *Bacchae* treat the murder of Pentheus as an awful mistake, planned by Dionysus who sets Pentheus up, and performed unwittingly by the women who worship Dionysus. Agave and her sisters mean to kill a lion, but it is Pentheus they kill. He calls to his mother, begging for his life, but in her frenzy she cannot hear him and in the delight of the sacred hunt she and her sisters tear the young man limb from limb. "He heard what must have been his last scream," reports the messenger, conveying the horror of the scene (1132). When it is all over, Agave carries Pentheus' head home, thinking it is that of an animal, and proud to show her trophy: she wants it hung in the palace to mark her hunting prowess. This is the standard reading, anyway (see, e.g., Euben 2011, 73). Another reading opens up, however, if we recall that these sisters have killed before and if we ask: Which comes first, the animalization or the killing?

The Messenger reports how Pentheus sat high in a tree, enjoying for a moment his sovereign capacity to see the women in their worship without being seen by them. Then, "out of the sky a voice—Dionysus, I suppose," says the Messenger, "pealed forth: Women, here is *the man* who made a mock of you, And me, and of my holy rites" (Vellacott 1973, 231). Agave then calls the Maenads to "catch this climbing *beast*," and so perhaps the animalization begins at this moment, but there is still no word yet of a *lion*.[9] Not until after Pentheus is dead, does the messenger refer to the animal. For the first time we hear of a lion when he describes Agave carrying home the head of her kill, "thinking it" he says, "the head of a young mountain lion" (Vellacott 1973, 223). Even when Agave tells her own version of what happened, she says that she and her sisters brought down a "beast," then caught their "prey." She only mentions a lion cub when she refers in the present moment to the severed head in her hands as she announces her own return to Thebes.

That Agave refers to Pentheus' remains as a lion *cub* might suggest he was thwarted in his transition to adulthood or perhaps that his mother has now reclaimed him as her child. But that she refers to him as a *lion* cub surely points in a different direction. She did not kill him *because* he was a lion. He was not one yet. But having killed him, he has now become one for her. Why? Is she now focused on his investiture? The lion is the sign of his office, the icon of (his) sovereignty. In *The Beast and Sovereign* (2009, 129), Jacques Derrida recalls Machiavelli's argument that the Prince is both lion (strength, honesty) and fox (canny, dissembling). Notably, in the *Bacchae*, which Derrida does not discuss, these traits are divided between the two rivals: Pentheus is lion (possessed of brazen, open power), and Dionysus is fox (dissembling, crafty, conniving). One implication, of course, is that neither can rule alone. This may underlie the Chorus' invitation to Dionysus, the fox, to "come, and appear to us … like a lion snorting flame from your nostrils!" though many other creatures (bull, snake) are mentioned as well. Following Machiavelli, we might say that sovereignty requires a balance or a partnership between lion and fox. But that balance will not come in the *Bacchae*, hence the tragic ending. In any case, the key, as Derrida notes, is not how lion and fox differ, but what they have in common. That is, the issue is not the lack of balance between them but, rather, that both lion and fox, like sovereignty itself, are outside the law. That lawlessness or liminality testifies to the power of the sovereign who, as such, can become beast. *The lion is the king of the jungle*. And the lion is also, as it were, *the jungle of the king*; it is the icon that marks the sovereign's prerogative to reach outside of law to the state of nature—the law of the jungle, which is no-law—to govern the kingdom.

Derrida in his book cites Kantorowicz's *The King's Two Bodies* (1997), but we might do better to think in terms of the king's *three* bodies. The first two are Kantorowicz's: the mortal-material-natural human body that singularizes the king, and the divine right-immortal-symbolic body that secures the office of kingship, an institution with a line of succession that exceeds any one king. But there is also the third body, the animal body of the sovereign, who is variously cast in the history of political thought as lion, fox, or leviathan. With that third beastly body, it is worth noting, we complete Hannah Arendt's triptych of the human condition, as well, in which we all have three bodies. All of us—and not just the king—experience immortality (in the domain of Action called the *vitae activa*), mortality (as *homo faber* in the domain of Work, one of whose contributions to political life is the work of law-making), and perishability (living as *animal laborans* in the domain of Labor) (1998). Notably, Arendt connects animality to Labor, and not to sovereignty. In so doing, she counters the idea that the animal body is as such a site of great brute power (sovereignty) by positing it as a site of vulnerability (perishability). This is worth recalling in this context because it helps us see how, in the *Bacchae*, the animality of Pentheus as lion, the king's third body, does not stand just for Pentheus' investiture as sovereign power holder; it also stands for his vulnerability to being undone. What we see with Arendt's help is that once the door to the state of nature is opened, anything can happen. In the state of nature, hunter can become prey; sovereignty can be challenged; and even a king can be hunted down like a lion. In the state of nature, we are—whatever else we are—animal laborans, as Hobbes would agree: deprived of letters, arts and culture, we are subject to the needs of mere life (see also Bowker, this volume).

If the filicide in the *Bacchae* is also regicide, could this play about Pentheus' murder also be a political parable, in which the king, as king, is shown to be vulnerable to sororal action in concert? Returning to Hannah Arendt's terms, we may say that Pentheus sought to confine the women to Labor, as mothers, and to Work, as loomers. But they resist confinement and claim Action as their domain, too. The concertedness of their action is key for such an Arendtian reading. The women first respond individually to Dionysus' call to violence. They throw rocks and tree limbs up at Pentheus, on his perch, but to no avail. It is only when they encircle the tree as a group that they succeed in bringing him down.

Regicide is not easy. The sisters have to do it over and over. Or, perhaps better, it takes place in three acts: first, by collective murder, then, second, by dispersing the king's body in pieces so widely they cannot all be found, and finally, third, by reattaching Pentheus' head to his dead body for burial. That work of burial is also multifaceted. Agave may just love her son and want to bury him whole, as I suggested above. Second, approached in a psychological context, this may be an act of Winnicottian care. But, third, approached politically, something else may also be going on. We know Agave is no stranger to the idea that things left out on a field may produce an odd crop. Recall that Agave is the daughter of Cadmus, founder of Thebes. Cadmus sowed the teeth of a slain dragon to reap a crop of new men. Did he sow a baby and reap a bomb? These men, born of the earth, are born fighting each other to the death until only five remain. One of these five is Echion, who will go on to marry Agave and father Pentheus. Who would know better than Cadmus and Agave that a regicide that ends with bones and body parts strewn in a field may turn out to be no regicide at all? No wonder Cadmus went out of his way to collect Pentheus, finding, as he puts it, "all I could" and doing his best to reassemble "this gory jigsaw" (1299, 1221).

When Agave insists on Pentheus' identity as a lion, might this indicate that she wants to kill not just this one boy-king, but kingship as such? If so, her desire is undone when Cadmus breaks the Dionysian spell by re-impressing her into the roles she left behind: "When you were married, whose house did you go to then?," he asks. Agave responds: "You gave me to Echion, of the sown race, they said." Next, Cadmus asks: "Echion had a son born to him. Who was he?," to which Agave responds: "Pentheus. His father lay with me; I bore a son." "Yes," says Cadmus, "and whose head is it that you are holding in your arms?" (Vellacott 1973, 237–238). Agave will now see that the head she holds belongs to Pentheus and she will grieve accordingly. Martha Nussbaum says this series of questions returns Agave to the real world of moral reasoning (1990). But, in my view, something else has (also) happened to Agave. Cadmus has repatriated her to patriarchy. She is no longer a bacchant. She is once again daughter, wife, mother: she belongs to father, husband, son.

Taking her through these steps, slowly, as they talk, Cadmus does not necessarily return her to herself. It is not clear who she is. What is clear, though, is that he recasts her regicide as filicide, secures it as only one and not the other. Are Agave and her sisters brought down by the awful realization of what they did? Killing their son/nephew? Or are they brought down by Cadmus' recasting of what they did, by his conversion of their political crime of regicide into the unpolitical crime of filicide?

Still, in spite of Cadmus, the regicide remains; or it might. When Agave (now out from under Dionysus' hypnotic spell, but is she under Cadmus' now, instead?) sews the head of Pentheus onto the body for burial, there is no way to tell whether Agave's work, is, to borrow Eve Sedgwick's distinction, reparative or paranoid. Is Agave collecting the son? Or killing the king (again)? It may be undecidable. Perhaps we do best to call her action para-reparative. Para- in the sense that is *like* the reparative (mistakable for mother-care) and *para-reparative, as in: reparative with a touch of the paranoid.* Seeking a new form of community, knowing the old sovereign forms always return, Agave goes to work. She returns to her sewing, the sort of woman's work once mandated by Pentheus, the King. Thus, Agave yields to her boss, in a way Justine never does, but it is an ironic submission, an intensification of the sovereign demand: Resistance. Sewing the head back on to the body, Agave buries the office, not just the man. She mortalizes the immortal king by joining Pentheus' two bodies, the mortal *and* immortal, immanent and transcendent, the head and the crown, the body and the head.[10] She will bury *all* of him.

Conclusion

Treating *Melancholia* as a reception of the *Bacchae* generates a reading of *Melancholia* that offers insights into both Euripides' play and von Trier's film. The film shares the ancient drama's interest in women's worship, but (at least on the reading developed here) it amplifies the dimensions of the play that have to do with youth, masculinity, and maturation, while downplaying the more overtly political dimensions that have to do not only with these but also with sovereignty, violence, and rebellion. Does this mean von Trier emphasizes the psychological at the expense of the political? Perhaps. Von Trier's film does replace the woman's community with a single woman, a communal Bacchanalian dance with solitary acts of sexual license, a foreign god with a rogue planet. But politics are not totally displaced. It is important that his treatment of Justine in *Melancholia* rejects any merely psychological treatment of her condition, almost as if rebutting Winnicott who seems to have someone like Justine in mind when he says: "Should an adult make claims on us for our acceptance of the objectivity of his subjective phenomena, we discern or diagnose madness" (1971, 4, 18). This may be. But Winnicott points, further, to the bit of madness always lurking in *any* such claims, which amount to acts of Kantian judgment, which themselves involve soliciting others to accept our judgments as compelling for them. And, in any case, Justine, in her unyielding commitment to her "subjective phenomena," is redeemed by von Trier, who depicts those subjective phenomena of hers as—in the end—undeniably objective. Has she brought us around? If we enter into her madness does it cease to be madness? Or was it never that, in the first place?

Then there are the resonances between Dionysus and the planet Melancholia. Indeed, on some readings, the rogue planet in von Trier's film comes rather close to *being* a foreign god. It is surely not unfair to say that Justine worships Melancholia when she runs off to the wild, like Agave, to bathe naked in its lunar light and to straddle a young man on the grass, leaving her groom behind. "Our women go creeping off, this way and that to lonely places and give themselves to lecherous men," says Pentheus, reporting what he has heard of the Bacchae who, as Dionysus tells him, worship "chiefly by night" because "darkness promotes religious awe" (Vellacott 1972, 198). The report given in the *Bacchae* by the Herdsman also resonates with von Trier's depiction of Justine: In "the high pastures," the herdsman says, he saw women who "all lay relaxed and quietly sleeping. Some rested on beds, of pine-needles, others had pillows of oak-leaves" (215) (Fig. 7.3).

It is as if, with his depiction of Justine, von Trier wants to undo the work of Cadmus, to take Agave out of the house of Echion, not restore her to it; to send her back to the fields of Cithaeron with her sister(s) and her son. In his favor, we may say that if the price of that undoing is the end of the world as we know it—or regicide—von Trier is willing to pay

Fig. 7.3 "Our women go creeping off, this way and that to lonely places .... Some rested on beds, of pine-needles, others had pillows of oak-leaves"

the price. Indeed Justine's isolation in von Trier's version of the story may not displace politics so much as comment on the current situation of political displacement, in which those who see the limitations of neoliberal life's promises and dangers are so often isolated and pathologized, forced to pay the price of world-endingness (see Honig 2016). What we learn from the *Bacchae* is that regicide is not easy and it is never over. As we also know, from Foucault (1977), regicide needs to be performed again and again (see also Huffer 2015). Beheading the king may kill the king but sovereignty remains; it may seek out new bottles, but the old wine remains potent.

Although there are moments in Winnicott where he seems to see this, where he prizes the kind of conflict necessary for parties to move forward together, and criticizes the niceness that stands in the way of authenticity, there are others where he seems to me to give way to niceness, to fall for its lure (1971, 196, 202–203).[11] This von Trier does not do. Perhaps one way of capturing their difference is to say that von Trier is the more tragic of the two. Certainly, niceness is his target; it does not ever seem to be something he falls for and it is what he satirizes throughout his film archive (just like Dionysus, that other director accused of misogyny).

Postlude

A regicide-centered reading of the *Bacchae* may seem to work against the idea of pairing the ancient tragedy with von Trier's recent film. After all, if von Trier's film has a politics, that politics on the reading offered here is feminist, not regicidal. But it may be better to say its feminism is regicidal, as instanced in *Melancholia* by John's command to Justine that she be happy on her wedding day (see Fazlalizadeh 2013; Bever 2013). This is a sovereign command to which she does not yield. Later, when she *is* happy, it is in her fashion, and it is not at John's command, and this is the beginning of the end of him and his world. Similarly, when Agave later does return to her women's work (to sewing, if not looming) it is only after Pentheus is dead and not at his command; and this is the end of him and his world.

Melancholia as I read it here has the happier ending, but it takes a pairing with a Greek tragedy for this to emerge. Reaping a bomb (the explosion at the end of the film), we know we have sowed a baby: that is, a natal human who will *not* simply reproduce the world as we know it. Perhaps because Leo has no royal responsibilities and because he has or invents an aunt who knows how to help him (dis- and re-) integrate himself (or else he has the imaginative powers to fantasize her), he finds the way out that eludes Pentheus. And since we know the world as we know it to be—whatever else it is—also a false and unjust place with which we have made terrible compromises, this knowledge is comforting. Perhaps that comfort, subtly delivered but there, and not the critics' complaints about von Trier's depiction of misogyny, privilege, and nihilism, is the severest criticism of all that can be made of *Melancholia*. It also helps to explain why some people (including the film critic for *The Village Voice*) reported feeling inexplicably euphoric after seeing the film (Hoberman 2011). The end of the world can be a liberation. And it can leave us feeling *fine*.[12]

Notes

1. Every school of psychoanalysis, that is, can be said to have its own tragedy.
2. Pentheus' name means grief.
3. Winnicott on "The Ordinary Devoted Mother": "All the bits and pieces of activity and sensation which go to form what we come to know as this particular baby begin to come together at times so there are moments of integration in which the baby is a unit although of course a highly dependent one" (Winnicott et al. 1987, 11). See also Winnicott (1965) on the mother's role in "collecting" and "gathering" the baby together. The mother provides a "framework" for "the process of integration" of "the infant's feelings of activity and violence" (1971, 143, 1964, 87, 96). Thus, Winnicott leads us away from Wohl's great reading, which emphasizes "polymorphous dispersions instead of integration and structure." If our readings remain parallel without intersection, it is because for me what is pivotal is Agave's reattachment of Pentheus' head to his body, an action which, I argue below, is partly reparative. Wohl (2005, 150) stays focused on the *sparagmos* (tearing apart, dismemberment) that turns Pentheus from a human into a body-without-organs.
4. In the Robertson translation, it is said that "his ribs were clawed down to the white" (1136).
5. Leo is made available for his experience with his aunt by the loss of his father. John was said by Claire, Leo's mother, to have gone into the village on Abraham, the horse. In fact, John committed suicide, but Claire is keeping that a secret. Soon after, however, Leo spies Abraham on the estate lawn and seems to take in the meaning of it. His father is gone and his mother has lied to him. Leo is now available for Justine.

6. Dionysus in the scene acts as director, adjusting his actor's costume, instructing him how to pose.
7. Taken as psychological catastrophe, one interpretative problem is eased. If the world ends with the film, then, as London's critics once said about Herman Melville's *Moby-Dick*: who has survived to tell the story? *Moby-Dick* was first published in London without the last chapter and seemed to end, therefore, with the destruction of everyone on board the Pequod, leaving critics to wonder how Ishmael could be telling the story. On this problem in *Melancholia*, see Szendy (2015). On my reading, Leo survives the catastrophe of adolescence. Or he *might*, anyway. What happens next, after his fears are (un)realized, is outside the scope of the film.
8. These could also be reversed, of course and we could speak of the never-endingness of psychic life and the world-endingness of political life.
9. Earlier, in Murray's translation, though not in the Greek, a disguised Dionysus refers to the lion as his prey: "Damsels, the lion walketh to the net!" The Robertson translation is different: "He swims very fast, women, into my net," figuring the king as fish (the fisher king? *Roi-pêcheur/pécheur*, the king whose sovereignty is prosthetic, castrated) (see Murray 1915, 52; Robertson 2014, 44).
10. As I noted above, it is uncertain whether Agave just gathers her son together or sews his head back on. The possibility that she reattaches his head, sewing rather than looming, as it were, is one way to fill the text's lacuna. As Robin Robertson puts it (2014, 72), "there is a lacuna in the original text. Agave may have joined her son's head to the rest of his body."
11. To Winnicott may belong the *Bacchae*, but at bottom he is nonetheless not a tragic thinker. (Thanks to Amanda Anderson on this point.) Writing for parents who—he hopes—can occupy the therapeutic role and provide adolescents questing for autonomy with the kinds of confrontation they need, providing limits without demanding compliance, he says: "Let the young alter society and teach grown-ups how to see the world afresh; but, where there is the challenge of the growing boy or girl, there let an adult meet the challenge. And it will not necessarily be nice. In the unconscious fantasy these are matters of life and death [at stake] … freedom to have ideas and act on impulse." Neither yielding nor dominating, the good-enough Winnicottian parent simply survives. This does not mean, however, "they may not themselves grow" in the process. The confrontations can have a welcome impact. What is wanted, that is, is neither too much clash, nor too little. What is really wanted is a certain "richness" in the confrontation, for those in the clash to BE there (1971, 196, 202–203). What is really wanted, for want of a better word, is agonism. Elsewhere, though, Winnicott reassures a society shocked by its adolescents' counterculture, saying that when the youths grow up they will mature into defenders of the culture the

society worries is currently threatened by them. This reassurance seems to me to be a false note in what is otherwise a healthy commitment to agonism in parenting. Of course, it may be tactical. Winnicott's aim is to stop the pathologization and criminalization of adolescence. That such practices are, in our own day, aimed even at kindergartners, and fall disproportionately on minority children, would surely shock and appall him.

12. "It's the end of the world as we know it (and I feel fine)." The chorus of the song by R.E.M. leaps to mind. So does its opening Euripidean line: "That's great, it starts with an earthquake."

References

Arendt, H. 1998. *The Human Condition*. Chicago: University of Chicago Press.

Bever, L. 2013. Tatyana Fazlalizadeh on Street Harassment: 'Stop Telling Women to Smile'—Video Interview, August 7. http://www.theguardian.com/commentisfree/video/2013/aug/07/stop-telling-women-to-smile-tatyana-fazlalizadeh

Carlsen, P.J. 2011. The Only Redeeming Factor Is the World Ending. Film, May 4. http://www.dfi.dk/Service/English/News-and-publications/FILM-Magazine/Artikler-fra-tidsskriftet-FILM/72/The-Only-Redeeming-Factor-is-the-World-Ending.aspx

Derrida, J. 2009. *The Beast & the Sovereign*. Chicago: University of Chicago Press.

Elsaesser, T. 2016. Black Suns and a Bright Planet: Lars von Trier's *Melancholia* as Thought Experiment. In *Politics, Theory, and Film: Critical Encounters with Lars von Trier*, ed. B. Honig, and L. Marso. Oxford and New York: Oxford University Press.

Euben, J.P. 2011. What Good Is Innocence? In *In Search of Goodness*, ed. R.W. Grant. Chicago: University of Chicago Press.

Euripides. 1915. *The Bacchae*. Trans. G. Murray. New York: Longmans, Green.

———. 1972. *The Bacchae, and Other Plays*. Rev. ed. Trans. P. Vellacott. Harmondsworth: Penguin.

———. 1973. *Medea and Other Plays*. Trans. P. Vellacott. London: Penguin.

———. 1990. *The Bacchae of Euripides: A New Version*. 1st ed. Trans. C.K. Williams. New York: Noonday Press.

———. 2013. *Euripides V: Bacchae, Iphigenia in Aulis, The Cyclops, Rhesus*. Trans. W. Arrowsmith, C.R. Walker, and R. Lattimore. Chicago, IL: University of Chicago Press.

———. 2014. *The Bacchae*. Trans. R. Robertson. New York: Vintage Classics.

Fazlalizadeh, Tatyana. 2013. Stop Telling Women to Smile. http://www.stoptellingwomentosmile.com

Foucault, M. 1977. *Discipline and Punish: The Birth of the Prison*. 1st American ed. Trans. A. Sheridan. New York: Pantheon Books.

Hoberman, J. 2011. Cannes 2011: Lars Von Trier's Melancholia. Wow. *Voice Film*, November 9. http://www.villagevoice.com/2011-11-09/film/not-with-a-whimper-but-a-bang-the-end-times-of-melancholia

———. 2016. Title. In *Politics, Theory, and Film: Critical Encounters with Lars von Trier*, ed. B. Honig, and L. Marso. Oxford and New York: Oxford University Press.

Honig, B., and L. Marso (ed). 2016. *Politics, Theory, and Film: Critical Encounters with Lars von Trier*. Oxford and New York: Oxford University Press.

Huffer, L. 2015. The Untimely Speech of the GIP Counter-Archive. In *Active Intolerance: Michel Foucault, the Prisons Information Group, and the Future of Abolition*, ed. A. Dilts, and P. Zurn. London: Palgrave.

Kantorowicz, E.H. 1997. *The King's Two Bodies: A Study in Mediaeval Political Theology*. Princeton, NJ: Princeton University Press.

Klein, M. 2013. Notes on Some Schizoid Mechanisms. In *Projective Identification: The Fate of a Concept*, ed. E. Spillius, and E. O'Shaughnessy. New York: Routledge.

Knox, B. 1952. The Lion in the House. *Classical Philology* 47(1): 17–25.

Nussbaum, M. 1990. Introduction. In *The Bacchae of Euripides: A New Version*. Trans. C.K. Williams. New York: Noonday Press.

Szendy, P. 2015. *Apocalypse-Cinema: 2012 and Other Ends of the World*. New York: Fordham University Press.

———. 1964. *The Child, the Family, and the Outside World*. Harmondsworth: Penguin Books.

Winnicott, D.W. 1965. Family and Individual Development. New York: Basic Books

———. 1971. *Playing and Reality*. New York: Basic Books.

Winnicott, D.W., C. Winnicott, R. Shepherd, and M. Davis. 1987. *Babies and Their Mothers*. Reading, MA: Addison-Wesley.

Wohl, V. 2005. Beyond Sexual Difference: Becoming-Woman in Euripides' *Bacchae*. In *The Soul of Tragedy: Essays on Athenian Drama*, ed. V. Pedrick, and S.M. Oberhelman. Chicago: University of Chicago Press.

CHAPTER 8

Forgiveness and Transitional Experience

C. Fred Alford

Forgiveness is a political, religious, and psychoanalytic concept. Its most well-known employment in political theory is undoubtedly by Hannah Arendt. Though her concept is creative, I believe that she misunderstands the nature of forgiveness. Winnicott can help set us straight.

Arendt sees forgiveness as a willed act that allows people to live together in a political society. Winnicott reminds us that forgiveness is not just an act of will, but an act that comes from deep changes within the self, changes that cannot always be commanded. Additionally, Winnicott reminds us that forgiveness is an intimate act, one that is not readily subordinated to political purposes. Seen from this perspective, it often makes more sense for people to discover ways other than forgiveness if they must or choose to live with those who have offended. This is the case not only in political matters, but personal ones as well.

Because forgiveness is an intimate act, it can take place only between persons, and among friends and family. A community is the largest setting in which forgiveness is possible, or at least the type of forgiveness with which Winnicott is concerned. Forgiveness is not a cosmopolitan virtue, or at least it cannot be practiced in the cosmopolis. Arendt believes forgiveness can be practiced in the polis; the Athenian polis (or city-state) is

C.F. Alford (✉)
University of Maryland, College Park, MD, USA

M.H. Bowker, A. Buzby (eds.), *D.W. Winnicott and Political Theory*,
DOI 10.1057/978-1-137-57533-3_8

her ideal. As long as the polis remains a community this is probably so, but Arendt's concept of forgiveness remains far from that of Winnicott. One might argue that their views are incommensurable: one talking about politics, the other about intimate relationships. I think their views are incompatible, as discussed below, and that Winnicott's is superior.

Arendt

Arendt argues that only forgiveness allows us to be free to act, for we live in a world in which political action reverberates with unforeseen consequences. "Forgiving serves to undo the deeds of the past." Without being released from the consequences of our acts, our capacity to act would, as it were, be confined to one single deed from which we could never recover; we would remain the victims of its consequences forever, like the sorcerer's apprentice who lacked the magic to break the spell. Without forgiveness, the burden of acting in history would be too great.

Forgiveness allows us to begin the world anew, and in that respect forgiveness is a font of creativity, one of the few reactions that shares with action the capacity to surprise. Forgiveness intervenes in the tragic nature of existence and action: that we are bound to harm others no matter what we do, and no matter what our intentions. Forgiveness makes "it possible for life to go on by constantly releasing men from what they have done knowingly" (Arendt 1958, 237, 240).

In arguing for the centrality of forgiveness, Arendt reads the Greek Testament tendentiously, arguing that in the gospels the duty to forgive "does not apply to the extremity of crime and willed evil .... Crime and willed evil are rare, even rarer perhaps than good deeds; according to Jesus, they will be taken care of by God in the Last Judgment, which plays no role whatsoever in life on earth" (Arendt 1958, 239–240).

In an odd way, Arendt has caused the concept of forgiveness to vanish. The harm inflicted in everyday life by virtue of what it means to act in error, what she calls "trespass," is automatically forgiven. Or, at least she sets no conditions, such as having acted with prudence and thoughtfulness. Conversely, not only acts of hatred and evil, but crime, are lifted out of the domain of human forgiveness altogether. To be sure, Arendt does not render acts of hatred, evil, and crime beyond human punishment. Just human forgiveness. In so doing, she neuters the concept.

Much of life takes place between the unavoidable trespasses of everyday life and murder. Yet, about this in-between land Arendt has nothing to say.

Why Arendt treats forgiveness as she does is unclear. Part of the answer seems to be her desire to save the concept for special duty, as it were, in the realm of political action. Another part of the answer seems to be her desire to keep the realm of action free from the complex personal relationships required for forgiveness. She might have done so by rendering forgiveness a private, or even social, relationship, but she does not. She brings forgiveness into politics, but only by creating a world to which it does not apply, except within the narrow confines of a concept of everyday trespass, designed to liberate action from the limits of infinite responsibility (see LeJeune, this volume).

And yet perhaps this is not the whole story. The psychoanalyst Hanna Segal writes that creativity is impossible in the absence of mourning: "It is only when the loss has been acknowledged and mourning experienced that re-creation can take place" (1952, 199). Segal's view supports Arendt's, in so far as Arendt suggests that forgiveness is itself a form of creativity, allowing the world, or at least a piece of it, to begin anew. Forgiveness breaks old molds, old patterns, surprising offender and victim alike. On the other hand, Segal understands, in a way that Arendt does not, that forgiveness is no easy matter. Real forgiveness for serious offenses is the outcome of an act of mourning, a process which takes time and hard labor, the work of grief. It is, in any case, hardly as easy as Arendt suggests. Forgiveness is in large measure the work of mourning.

What Is Forgiveness?

It is only in recent years that psychoanalysts have turned their attention to forgiveness. The most acute among them are properly suspicious of forgiveness.[1] Smith (2008) puts it this way:

> The adhesiveness of [the concept of forgiveness] may be because the work of accepting the reality of the traumas we have suffered—and which we have caused others to suffer—is so difficult and so fraught with failure that we embrace the promise that forgiveness will heal our pain, rage, and guilt. The leap of forgiveness is a solution that has become part of our psychic lives.

The alternative to the leap of forgiveness is the slow work of mourning our losses, complicated by the fact that the loss is often not only of a person, but of a world: one that was once secure enough to relax and just be in, one that was once good enough to want to live in. Coming to terms with such losses is subtle and complex work, in large measure because for some of the most catastrophic losses there is no one to forgive.

Most serious people who write about forgiveness (those for whom forgiveness is not merely a form of therapy on the cheap), secular and sacred alike, pay a great deal of attention to the question of *who* deserves forgiveness. The answer is almost always some version of the one who repents, demonstrating his or her repentance by changing his or her ways. This is expressed in the steps of repentance laid down in the twelfth century CE by Moses Maimonides (1983). This is my loose, contemporary interpretation of the criteria for forgiveness:

1. The offender acknowledges his or her offense in such a way as to demonstrate an understanding of why the offense was so hurtful.
2. The offender expresses remorse and regret to the victim, as well as to those close to the victim. Expressions of remorse and regret to the victim's family are especially important when the victim is no longer in a position to acknowledge remorse (e.g., when the victim is dead, whether or not he or she has been killed by the offender).
3. The offender makes compensation when possible and relevant. The compensation must be directed to the victim and victim's family. Compensation to substitutes, such as acts of contrition aimed as the poor and destitute, are appropriate, but only if the victim and his or her family agree with the substitute, or if the victim and family are unavailable or unreceptive.
4. The offender lives differently in the future, demonstrating that he or she is a changed person. A drunk driver who killed someone might give up drinking and join Alcoholics Anonymous, for example. For some interpreters of the Hebrew Bible, this is the step that validates all the others. Sometimes this is referred to as *teshuvahgemurah*, or complete repentance. Repentance is complete when opportunities to reoffend present themselves, and the offender refrains from doing so.

An interesting question is raised by the first requirement, acknowledging the offense. Griswold (2007, 51, 188–189) argues that in expressing regret, the offender should be able to demonstrate that he or she understands the damage done by his or her acts, as well as that he or she is no longer the sort of person who would commit such acts. Paul Ricoeur makes a similar demand, albeit more abstractly, when he states: "One must know how to tell one's own story as seen by others. That is to say, to let myself be narrated by the other .... This is difficult. Yet that is how notions such as forgiveness, loss and reconciliation are, it seems to me, related. They have a kind of common ground."[2]

Most secular accounts of forgiveness stress the value of viewing repentance as a step-by-step process, each party participating in making the other better. Griswold and Robert Roberts are exemplary. I draw from the psychoanalyst D.W. Winnicott, to make a somewhat different argument. Forgiveness need not involve this particular relationship with the offender. Instead, it is about a different relationship with the world, out of which forgiveness may happen. Forgiveness remains a relationship, but a more complex relationship, one not quite so dependent on the offender.

Robert Roberts (1995, 289) has about the sharpest statement of the aims and achievement of forgiveness: "Forgiveness is virtuous because one's anger is given up without abandoning correct judgment about the severity of the offense and the culpability of the offender." Forgiveness is not denial, not even of the fact that the offender's act caused outrage and hatred. Forgiveness rediscovers the human value of the person and the relationship behind the often righteous anger that devalues the person who has done wrong. Such anger, it turns out, is often rewarding to the victim and by no means easy to abandon, especially when this anger has solidified into the satisfactions of hate (Hampton 1988). This is one reason Winnicott turns out to be such a useful guide, telling us how we might let go of righteous anger. Or rather, how to live in the world so that righteous anger and hatred lose their value, indeed their meaning and purpose.

Among those writing in both religious and philosophical traditions, from Maimonides to Griswold and Ricoeur, repentance is the sign that forgiveness is deserved. In both traditions, repentance is not a goal in itself. Repentance allows the parties to return to the status of being fellow humans together in a shared world. This requires, as Roberts (1995, 295–295) states, that the offender possess a sense of self as both member of a community and individual actor, one who can accept and bear the responsibility of doing wrong.

> Forgivingness and the practice of forgiveness are at home in an ethic of community or friendship, one underlain by a sense of belonging to one another. But they [forgivingness and forgiveness] require that there be a

> strong differentiation of individuals as well, so that the one can bear responsibility for offending the other, and the other can choose to forgive. (290)

In *Before Forgiveness: The Origins of a Moral Idea*, David Konstan (2010) argues that this sense of individuality was largely absent before the eighteenth and nineteenth centuries, even as it made sporadic appearances centuries earlier, as in the work of Maimonides.

Interesting about Winnicott's account is its more subtle depiction of individuality, especially in what he calls transitional space, where the usual distinction between self and other does not apply, lest the creativity, freedom, and security found there be lost. It is from this space that forgiveness happens. Roberts' and Konstan's straightforward distinctions between self and other are insufficiently complex to capture what is happening in this space, a claim that applies to almost all who write about forgiveness.

Wholeness and Holding

Wholeness does not have a very good reputation these days, particularly when it is expressed as a metanarrative—that is, a grand narrative purporting to explain all that we experience. Metanarratives need not be told out loud; they may be implicit in the culture, such as the belief in progress through reason (Lyotard 1984). The trouble with metanarratives is their tendency to drive underground or erase all that does not fit the big story.

Winnicott's way of thinking about transitional space and transitional relationships allows us to think about wholeness in new terms, ones too fluid to make a good metanarrative. Winnicott's terms are not only especially suited for the concept of forgiveness. They have consequences for the concept, leading to the surprisingly fruitful result of rendering forgiveness less personal, less dependent on the offender and his or her remorse, while not allowing the concept to become a mere means to self-healing. It would be an exaggeration to say that for Winnicott, forgiveness happens when we no longer have a compelling need to forgive. Nonetheless, the exaggeration would betray a truth.

Consider what Winnicott calls transitional space (1971, 1–25). Transitional space is first experienced when the child is held by its mother or other caretaker. If the "mother" is in tune with her child, which means that she neither crushes the child with her anxiety, nor drops the child with her distraction and mental absence, the child does not have to even think: "I feel held."

Instead, the child is free to be, which means free to begin to explore his or her environment, free to begin to experience him- or herself as unique and yet connected to another. The capacity to think of oneself as both unique yet connected serves the individual his or her whole life long, making it possible to live in a community without feeling like a drone.

Seen from this perspective, wholeness need not be that imperialistic state that leads to the search for dominion, resulting in the exclusion of all that does not fit. Wholeness need not be about the elimination or homogenization of otherness. On the contrary, it is the absence of experiences of holding that lead to the intolerance of otherness, difference, and ambiguity. Why? Because in the absence of an experience of holding (originally the holding by parents, later by loved ones, communities, and even ideas and ideals), one tries to create its simulacrum, a wholeness that never was, a wholeness in which there is no otherness—that is, no tolerance of otherness. Totalitarianism is the great and terrible example of what holding in the absence of community looks like. George Orwell's *Nineteen Eighty-Four* is the great literary representation of holding transformed into crushing conformity.

One reason the intellectual representation of wholeness leads to intolerance is because it is a creation of the mind, a mind that has had to take over the function of holding, which means it can never let reality just be (Winnicott 1992, 245–248). The parallel between failed human holding of the child, in which the child must use its mind to hold itself together, and intellectual holding, which has no place for otherness and difference, is not merely coincidental. In both, the mind is doing the work of stringently ordering and categorizing the flow of experience, rather than letting it be—that is, rather than letting oneself experience the world in its rich diversity.

Winnicott refers to experiences of separation, experiences of individuation and loss, in terms of the "I AM" moment, a raw moment in which, "the new individual feels infinitely exposed. Only if someone has her arms around the infant at this time can the I AM moment be endured, or rather, perhaps, risked" (Winnicott 1965b, 155). For adults, cultural forms such as religion can take on this holding function, containing the individual so that he or she does not feel infinitely exposed when confronted with a world not made for the human being. For the fundamental claim of religion, in defiance of Albert Camus's (1955, 21, 28–30) definition of absurdity, is that the universe is not mindless of us, that we have a place here.

Forgiveness Without Repentance?

Sometimes hate and resentment seem as though they are the only secure things to hold onto in all the world, the only things we can control. When one is in a transitional relationship to the world, then one need not hold on so tightly. Forgiveness is easier as letting go becomes easier: We can let go of our hatred without fear of disintegrating or endlessly falling.

The ability to remain within a transitional relationship, a transitional space, is not just about the ability to avoid grasping onto rage and resentment, hatred and contempt. It is also about avoiding (or rather, not needing) the purity that obsession and ritual seek. In transitional space, there is no purity to be found, and no need to find it. The search for purity is another version of the quest for wholeness. One finds this quest in surprising places, such as Jacques Derrida's claim that true forgiveness can only forgive the unforgivable (2001, 39).

> Must one not maintain that an act of forgiveness worthy of its name, if there ever is such a thing, must forgive the unforgivable, and without condition? And that such unconditionality is also inscribed, like its contrary, namely the condition of repentance, in "our" heritage? Even if this radical purity can seem excessive, hyperbolic, mad? Because if I say, as I think, that forgiveness is mad, and that it must remain a madness of the impossible, this is certainly not to exclude or disqualify it.

In contrast to the radical or unconditional purity model of forgiveness, Derrida posits "ordinary forgiveness," which is based on the model of economic exchange: "You are in my debt; I forgive your debt." Derrida attributes such a view to Hannah Arendt, an attribution that seems simplistic. Whatever is wrong with Arendt's view of forgiveness, it is not primarily this. Derrida's search for the purity of forgiveness, unsullied by the spirit of exchange, is the opposite of a transitional relationship to the world.

Jews, many Christians, and most serious thinkers on the subject, such as Griswold, and Ricoeur, insist that forgiveness be bound to repentance. One does not forgive an offender who has not asked sincerely, and shown signs of repentance, signs that demonstrate an understanding of the hurt caused by the offender's act. Conversely, much that is wrong with the theory and practice of forgiveness today has to do with people granting forgiveness in the absence of its being properly asked for, as though forgiveness were therapy for the victim. We forgive, according to Smedes (1984, 12–13), "for our own sakes," in order to "heal ourselves" of hurt and hate. But perhaps it is not as simple as yes or no: "Don't forgive unless sincerely asked." Another possibility is suggested by Winnicott. We forgive not when the other has performed the proper ritualized steps of repentance, and not in order to heal or empower ourselves, but when we have reached that transitional space where we no longer need to hold onto our anger, our hatred, and our hurt.

Forgiveness in Transitional Space

Forgiveness is something that happens to us at a certain point almost as a byproduct of living in the world in a certain way. In other words, the repentance of the other may not be all that important, but not for the reason suggested by Smedes and others: to regain one's sense of power. Rather, forgiveness just happens when one is in a certain transitional state. It is not a matter of *realizing* that that anger and hatred are no longer central to our lives. Cognitive and emotional insight is not as important as the state of one's being.

Transitional experience is an internal process within the individual. Transitional experience is not about either/or, but about being in a place in which many possibilities exist, so that one can come to imagine oneself as an inhabitant of ever larger worlds. Where does this transitional state come from? From someone having had his or her arms around us during the "I AM" moments that impose themselves on adults, such as the death of a spouse, or child, or the transgression that is experienced as unbearable and unforgivable.

While transitional experience is intrapsychic, Winnicott was keenly aware that the distinction between internal and external, private and social, becomes problematic under transitional experience. Indeed, this is the point. And yet one must be careful not to simplify Winnicott here. In transitional experience the boundaries of the self expand to include parts of the external world. If this expansion does not occur, then culture could never become a living experience that can hold us when we are faced with the trauma of everyday life, from illness to old age, to death, to all the other heartaches that confront us, such as the death of a spouse. On the other hand, Winnicott remained committed to the idea that a portion of the self must remain incommunicado, hidden deep inside, so that the self need not be devoted to its protection. When it is, the self cannot use the culture because he or she is too busy protecting himself or herself from the intrusions of culture into the self.

While transitional experience is an internal process, it is conceptualized by Winnicott as a relationship in which at least one of the parties is unaware of the relationship, or rather, finds it unnecessary to be constantly aware. One might call this lack of awareness "security." Transitional experience may take place in a variety of settings, from "mother's" lap to the concert hall to a regular encounter with the community volunteer who brings the homebound man or woman a hot meal. Otherwise expressed, the "I AM" moment that allows us to feel separate is enabled only by the holding that keeps this separateness within bounds. "Within bounds" means that the experience of separateness does not devolve into feelings of disintegration, chaos, and endless falling. This holding may be individual, as in a mother's or lover's arms, or communal, such as a sense of confidence that there is some place I can go if I become hungry, sick, or terrified. It is from this perspective that one may speak of being in a transitional relationship to the world, even if transitional experience remains strictly intrapsychic.

Though community is no replacement for the loving care and concern shown by individuals, loving care and concern are much more likely to be forthcoming in a coherent community. This is the key point, and no single point stands out more clearly in Kai Erikson's (1976, 1994) study of manmade disasters. Destroy the community, and you make it much more difficult for individuals in these communities to care for each other. Communities hold the people who hold each other when things go wrong.

Forgiveness is supposed to be about a relationship. In Judaism, forgiveness is primarily a two-way relationship: human to human, when the offense is one human against another; human to God, when the offense involves an offense against God, such as those declared in the first four Commandments. Emmanuel Levinas (1990, 20) takes this position to an extreme, arguing that not even God can forgive a crime committed by one man against another. Only the victim can do that. "No one, not even God, can … pardon the crime that man commits against man …. The world in which pardon is all-powerful becomes inhuman."

In Christianity, the relationship is primarily between man or woman and God, though Jesus was clear that mending your relationship with your brother took precedence to making a sacrifice to God (Matthew 5: 23–24; Mark 11:25). An object relations approach in psychoanalysis, of which Winnicott is exemplary, must make a similar claim: Forgiveness is about the relationship between the offender and the victim. Conversely, most of the troubling and unsatisfactory accounts of forgiveness make it "all about me and how I can live with myself without corroding my spirit with hatred." Important, perhaps, but it is not about forgiveness.

Winnicott's view suggests that forgiveness happens when the victim comes to abandon hatred, rage and resentment, a consequence of his or her having come to reside in transitional space. The offender becomes less important. The other's offense is no longer the center of the victim's world. This too is an object relational (i.e., interpersonal) perspective on forgiveness. Only now the "person" in question is not just, or even primarily the offender, but the relationship between the victim and the larger community in which he or she lives, the holding community, one that begins with family, and includes as many people, practices, artifacts, and ideas as the victim can imaginatively allow to populate his or her world.

In "Forgiveness as a Process of Change in Individual Psychotherapy," Malcolm and Greenberg compare forgiving clients with unforgiving ones. At issue were serious offenses such as the sexual abuse of a student by his teacher. Though they draw from a few cases, their conclusion is that resolution without forgiveness does not prevent a person from overcoming trauma and getting on with his or her life. The difference is "that when forgiveness is not offered, anger is not followed by an expression of sadness, fear, or vulnerability (which are highly attachment-related emotions that indicate an action tendency toward comfort and/or moving closer)" (2000, 198). In other words, forgiveness is how we move closer to the other person, toward whom we feel both attachment and betrayal. Those who did not forgive tended not to have considered forgiveness as an option. Rather, they achieved resolution by moving away from the offender, and toward deeper involvement in other relationships within the community.

Forgiveness seeks closeness to the offender, often the reparation and restoration of actual relationships. Non-forgiveness seeks to regain a sense of one's lost place in, and value to, the community. Actual relationships are no less important; less important is only the relationship to the offender. Both strategies have their place, depending on the extent of the harm, but also on the previous relationship to the offender, as well as the willingness of the offender to repent. One problem with forgiveness today is the tendency to confuse these two goals, using forgiveness to seek power instead of reunion, either with the offender or the holding community.

Winnicott reveals that achieving a transitional position from which forgiveness happens does not, and should not, mean that forgiveness must happen, or even should happen. Transitional space is its own reward.

While genuine forgiveness is easier to grant from this space, whether it will be should depend on the values of the victim, as well as the circumstances, such as those studied by more traditional approaches to forgiveness. These include the willingness of the offender to act with repentance, as well as the desire of the victim for a restored relationship, which will depend, in good measure, on the previous relationship. Winnicott reveals sources of forgiveness deeper than the rituals of forgiveness, sources upon which the rituals depend, sources of experience that lead to or are the experience of transitional space.

Forgiveness, Hope, and a Good-Enough World

Hope is an important, and infrequently commented upon, aspect of Winnicott's work. Hope is most clearly seen, says Winnicott, in antisocial behavior, and even wickedness. (Winnicott is thinking of the wickedness of the child and early adolescent, not the cold, hate-filled wickedness of the adult terrorist or killer.) Antisocial behavior and wickedness reflect an inability to symbolize distress; the need to act it out instead. These acts remain a sign of hope, for they signify that the offender has not given up on the possibility that he or she can communicate his or her despair to someone who can crack the code and understand. Hope is locked up in wickedness, while hopelessness is marked by compliance and false socialization (Winnicott 1965a, 103–104; Abram 1996, 42). Hope is the not-yet-forsaken belief that a person can find someone to hold him while he faces that "I AM" moment. Hope that he will not be dropped again as he was once before, at a time before he was able to stand on his own.

Hope as it is expressed in forgiveness is not just the hope that an individual is worth forgiving, that he or she will not betray one's trust again. Forgiveness expresses the hope that the world itself is worth taking a chance on, that the world of family, friends, culture, and community can hold us from cradle to grave, the alpha and omega of holding. Hope trusts that this world is a good-enough place in which to live and die. Forgiveness bridges the gap in trust in the world, much as adult forms of holding, such as culture and religion, do. Only whereas culture and religion bridge this gap with stories that tell us that we belong here, forgiveness bridges the gap by saying that even though I may be victimized by particular human relationships, the world is a good-enough place to be. Forgiveness overcomes that strictly human absurdity, the unnecessary or "surplus absurdity," it might be called, created by hatred, greed, and lack of caring.

For the world to be trustworthy requires that the world be worthy of trust, and under certain conditions, this may not be true. Worthy of trust does not mean "good." It simply means good enough to live in, good enough so that one does not constantly have to be on guard, good enough to sometimes just be. Today this hope is possible in large parts of the world; in larger parts it is probably not. Which is which is likely more difficult to determine than one might first imagine. It is not as simple as drawing boundaries on a map. Some "traditional" societies (depending upon the pressures they are under) are likely easier places to just be than many "modern" societies.

Psychological boundaries also need to be taken into account. The world can seem worthy of trust one day, unworthy the next, depending on intervening experiences. Trauma can change everything in an instant, and change it forever. Trauma can transform a trustworthy world into a world with no place to stand, and no place to just be. Whether the world can ever again become a safe-enough place to be depends both on the extent of the trauma and the resources available to the traumatized. Narrative resources are important. So too are those wordless holding resources that so often go unnoticed, such as the way a secure community finds a place for the traumatized one to be, long before he or she is capable of putting words to his or her experience. Actually, this is not quite right. A secure community provides a holding environment secure enough for the traumatized one to sometimes not be, and so find respite from the terrible burden of self-holding.

Earlier, Smith was quoted as saying that the adhesiveness of forgiveness had to do with the terrible persistence of trauma and its resistance to therapy. The temptation to be avoided is substituting forgiveness for the long, slow work of mourning. Smith's is a good critique of popular forgiveness, but it is not the only psychoanalytic critique. Almost as common is the argument that even the sincerely held wish to forgive, even forgiveness given, cannot overcome the aggression and anger that remain.

> However much we reify it as an entity, what we call forgiveness is part of an ongoing dynamic process that involves continuing input from aggressive … wishes …. It is precisely this aggressive component that tends to be avoided when the concept of forgiveness is featured too prominently in the [psychoanalytic] work. (Smith 2008)

For Smith, as for many psychoanalysts, it is the aggression still felt against the forgiven one that needs to be worked through, and cannot be when forgiveness is given too readily, when forgiveness is seen as a solution, rather than as one possible outcome of therapy.

Seen from the perspective of Winnicott, the problem is both similar and different. Above all it is more poignant. Many people, including those who want to offer forgiveness, will never find themselves in transitional space, where they can just be. It is a state, perhaps more than any other, that cannot be willed. Though he is not referring to transitional space, Thomas Moore, psychotherapist and contemporary American spiritual writer puts it well when he says: "Forgiveness comes in its own time. Forgiveness comes from some other place. We can create the conditions under which we hope it will appear. We may feel good that it has appeared. But we can't control the whole thing" (qtd. in Doblmeier 2007).

We must, I think, recognize as legitimate two types of forgiveness. One is willed, and ideally stems from a conscious recognition that the offender has made atonement and demonstrated a continuing commitment to self-transformation. The four steps of Maimonides are exemplary. The term "willed" refers, of course, not to the willfulness of caprice, but the will expressed by developed character.

The second type of forgiveness is less thoughtful, more conducive to the soul of forgiveness—that is the mental and emotional state from which forgiveness is most freely given, that state that has been called transitional space. Of this second type of forgiveness, all we may ask is that it remembers that forgiveness is also a normative ideal, holding the forgiven to proper standards of conduct.

A certain level of trauma and hurt is going to make only willed forgiveness possible if there is to be any forgiveness at all. Furthermore, there is no reason to think that willed forgiveness will one day make transitional forgiveness possible. On the contrary, the work of willed forgiveness will make transitional forgiveness less likely; but it was probably unlikely all along. This does not mean that the wounded person cannot genuinely forgive. Forgiveness has different dimensions, different meanings. Some meanings are antithetical to any true understanding of forgiveness, such as, "I forgive you in order to feel better about myself," or "I forgive you in order to feel empowered." However, other meanings of forgiveness remain intact, such as, "I forgive you because you have revealed through your words and deeds that you understand why your acts hurt, feel remorse for having done them, and are trying to change your life."

Nevertheless, a certain experience of forgiveness, the experience implicit in a Winnicottian understanding of forgiveness, will remain unavailable to those still deeply wounded by the acts that have victimized them. This is the sad way of the world, and the best thing to be done is to acknowledge it, while appreciating how important social holding, what Erikson calls community, is in fostering not just relief from trauma, but the possibility of a particular type of forgiveness. Not forgiveness more genuine than any other, but possibly more satisfying. Or rather, the result of a more satisfying experience of life. At the same time, one must recognize the limits of social holding. For many, not forgiveness, not transitional space, but the lessening of trauma over time in a community of others who can offer social, economic and moral support seems the most reasonable goal, and one often within reach.

Conclusion

A Winnicottian view of forgiveness does not contradict Arendt on the importance of forgiveness in making a decent politics possible. Nevertheless, the forgiveness that Winnicott allows us to talk about is the forgiveness of the interperson, denizen of transitional space. One might regard the lack of political relevance of Winnicott as unfortunate. I regard it as essential, for forgiveness is not just about how we get on with life. It is about how we avoid using hatred and rage as something we can hold onto in a world in which nothing else seems certain and everything hurts. The personal is the political, as students and feminists of the 1960s taught us. So too is the interpersonal, including the interperson.

Arendt is well known for her devaluation of what she calls "the social," the space between the private and public. Hanna Pitkin calls it "the blob" (1998). For Arendt (1958), the social represents all that is wrong with mass society: a private sphere without privacy, a public sphere without politics. The space occupied by the interperson is more difficult to define once it moves beyond family and friends. Community is not a synonym, but it seems the only public place the interperson could flourish, and with it true forgiveness.

The term "community" has been banalized in recent years, as in "the business community." Community is not an interest group. It is a place where face-to-face relationships are still possible. While the community may share an external goal, the value of the community for its own sake, for the relationships it makes possible, must remain central. Or, as I argued in the introduction, forgiveness is not a cosmopolitan virtue, but a local one.

Notes

1. In addition to Akhtar (2002), Frommer (2005), Siassi (2004), and Smith (2008), there is at least one special edition of a psychoanalytic journal devoted to forgiveness, Psychoanalytic Inquiry 29 (5) (2009).
2. "Memory, History, Forgiveness: A Dialogue between Paul Ricoeur and Sorin Antohi," at www.janushead.org/8-1/Ricoeur.pdf (n.d.). Ricoeur's essay on forgiveness is a long epilogue to his Memory, History, Forgetting (2004).

References

Abram, J. 1996. *The Language of Winnicott.* Northvale, NJ: Jason Aronson.

Akhtar, S. 2002. Forgiveness: Origins, Dynamics, Psychopathology and Technical Relevance. *Psychoanalytic Quarterly* 71: 175–212.

Arendt, H. 1958. *The Human Condition.* Chicago: University of Chicago Press.

Camus, A. 1955. *The Myth of Sisyphus and Other Essays.* Trans. J. O'Brien. New York: Vintage Books.

Derrida, J. 2001. *On Cosmopolitanism and Forgiveness.* Trans. M. Dooley and M. Hughes. London: Routledge.

Doblmeier, M. 2007. *The Power of Forgiveness. Documentary Film.* Alexandria, VA: Journey Films.

Erikson, K. 1976. *Everything in Its Path: Destruction of Community in the Buffalo Creek Flood.* New York: Simon and Schuster.

———. 1994. *A New Species of Trouble: The Human Experience of Modern Disasters.* New York: W.W. Norton.

Frommer, M.S. 2005. Thinking Relationally About Forgiveness. *Psychoanalytic Dialogues* 15: 33–45.

Griswold, C. 2007. *Forgiveness: A Philosophical Exploration.* Cambridge: Cambridge University Press.

Hampton, J. 1988. Forgiveness, Resentment and Hatred. In *Forgiveness and Mercy*, ed. J. Murphy, and J. Hampton, 35–87. Cambridge: Cambridge University Press.

Konstan, D. 2010. *Before Forgiveness: The Origins of a Moral Idea.* New York: Cambridge University Press.

Levinas, E. 1990. *Difficult Freedom: Essays on Judaism.* Trans. S. Hand. Baltimore, MD: Johns Hopkins University Press.

Lyotard, J.-F. 1984. *The Postmodern Condition: A Report on Knowledge.* Trans. G. Bennington and B. Massumi. Minneapolis: University of Minnesota Press.

Maimonides, M. 1983. *The Book of Knowledge: From the Mishneh Torah of Maimonides.* Trans. H.M. Russell and J. Weinberg. New York: KTAV Publishing

House. www.torahlab.org/download/rambam_sourcesheet.pdf. Accessed 19 February 2016.

Malcolm, W., and L. Greenberg. 2000. Forgiveness as a Process of Change in Individual Psychotherapy. In *Forgiveness: Theory, Research, and Practice*, ed. M. McCullough, K. Pargament, and C. Thoresen, 179–202. New York: Guilford Press.

Pitkin, H. 1998. *The Attack of the Blob: Hannah Arendt's Concept of the Social.* Chicago: University of Chicago Press.

Ricoeur, P. n.d. Memory, History, Forgiveness: A Dialogue between Paul Ricoeur and Sorin Antohi. www.janushead.org/8-1/Ricoeur.pdf. Accessed 19 February 2016.

Ricoeur, P. 2004. *Memory, History, Forgetting.* Trans. K. Blamey and D. Pellauer. Chicago: University of Chicago Press.

Roberts, R.C. 1995. Forgivingness. *American Philosophical Quarterly* 32(4): 289–306.

Segal, H. 1952. A Psycho-Analytical Approach to Aesthetics. *International Journal of Psycho-Analysis* 33: 196–207.

Siassi, S. 2004. Transcending Bitterness and Early Paternal Loss Through Mourning and Forgiveness. *Psychoanalytic Quarterly* 73: 915–937.

Smedes, L. 1984. *Forgive and Forget: Healing the Hurts We Don't Deserve.* New York: Harper and Row.

Smith, H.F. 2008. Leaps of Faith: Is Forgiveness a Useful Concept? *International Journal of Psychoanalysis* 89: 919–936. www.onlinelibrary.wiley.com/doi/10.1111/j.1745-8315.2008.00082.x/full. Accessed 19 February 2016.

Winnicott, D.W. 1965a. Morals and Education. In *The Maturational Processes and the Facilitating Environment*, ed. M. Khan, 93–107. Madison, CT: International Universities Press.

———. 1965b. *The Family and Individual Development.* London: Tavistock.

———. 1971. Transitional Objects and Transitional Phenomena. In *Playing and Reality*, 1–25. New York: Routledge.

———. 1992. Mind and Its Relation to the Psyche-Soma. In *Through Paediatrics to Psycho-Analysis*, 243–254. London: Karnac.

PART III

Revitalizing the Subject of Political Theory

CHAPTER 9

In Transition, But to Where?: Winnicott, Integration, and Democratic Associations

David W. McIvor

Of all the concepts to spring from the fulsome mind of D.W. Winnicott, his idea of the transitional object is perhaps the most famous. Transitional objects provide the necessary bridge between self and not-self—between inner world and outer reality—while offering a defense against the anxiety of this crossing. However, readers of Winnicott often overlook the larger scene in which these objects appear. Transitional objects are *transitional*—they cannot serve as permanent sources of comfort, but are means of cultivating a capacity for negotiating the ambivalences and complexities of our internal and external worlds. As one of Winnicott's analysands put it, "the rug might be very comfortable, but reality is more important than comfort and *no* rug can therefore be more important than a rug" (1971, 34). We need to move beyond the transitional object, then, and this is especially true when we use Winnicott to think about *political* objects and *their* complex terrain.

Over the past decade, democratic theory has been becoming increasingly concerned with what we might call "the rug under our feet"—the social, material, cultural, and ecological environments that facilitate, or *fail* to facilitate, democratic subjectivities and commitments (Honneth

D.W. McIvor (✉)
Colorado State University, Fort Collins, CO, USA

M.H. Bowker, A. Buzby (eds.), *D.W. Winnicott and Political Theory*,
DOI 10.1057/978-1-137-57533-3_9

2014; Levine 2013; Butler 2015). For many democratic theorists, the ground-level conditions for democratic affects and action have been severely compromised in the opening years of the twenty-first century (Brown 2015; Urbinati 2014; Wolin 2008). As such, we are increasingly confronted with urgent questions about whether the word democracy can even apply to current social configurations (Winters and Page 2009; Winters 2012; Barker 2013). The question becomes this: how can citizens cultivate democratic consciousness—let alone robust practices of self-determination—if the cultural and social conditions for this consciousness are rapidly eroding?

Perhaps because of this sense of creeping democratic pathologies, psychoanalytic vocabularies and frameworks have become increasingly popular in political theory (Alford 2006, 2013; Luxon 2013; Dean 2013; Shulman 2011; Edelman 2004; Honig 2001; Honneth 1997), even if some warn against the tendency for psychoanalytic approaches to collapse the structural into the psychological (Luxon 2016). Within this psychoanalytic turn, the work of Winnicott stands out as particularly well suited to the task of theorizing the facilitating conditions—or what Winnicott called, in the context of his own analytic practice, the "holding environment"—of democratic development. Axel Honneth, for instance, has argued that Winnicott's account of interpersonal development testifies to the modes of social recognition underlying the realization of autonomy and social justice (1997). More recently, Honneth has theorized the facilitating environment necessary for modern practices of social freedom, the "social life praxis" of democratic *Sittlichkeit* that must shape the everyday lives of democratic citizens if the self-professed values of liberal democracy are to be more fully realized (2014).

In a different vein, Bonnie Honig has repeatedly turned to Winnicott to theorize the appropriate conditions for agonistic democracy (2001, 2013, 2015). For Honig, neoliberal norms of efficiency and cost-effectiveness threaten the existence of democratic transitional objects, which enable individuals to cross the terrain between omnipotent fantasies of self-sufficiency and a mature understanding of interdependency. Honig's work consciously analogizes Winnicott's observations about childhood development to citizens' need for public things. Just as transitional objects offer developing children experiences of magical comfort, so too do public objects provide a means of the affective political attachments or "enchantment" necessary for democratic subjectivity.

Yet, neither Honneth's nor Honig's approach goes far enough with Winnicott. Therefore, in this paper, I move beyond a theory of democratic transitional objects or *Sittlichkeit* to consider what Winnicott saw as the developmental trajectory of the holding environment. Beyond transitional objects of civic attachment, citizens need the space and capacity for negotiating conflict and disagreement. These capacities can be best approached through Winnicott's concept of "integration." Integration is both an achievement *and* a process, a realized capacity that is by nature fragile and fluid. Winnicott's concept of integration has inherent sociopolitical content, but this content has to be teased out of the analytic space in which the idea was originally articulated. Winnicott pointed to larger, social scenes of holding, but he did not study their possibilities or think concretely about democratic facilitating environments beyond the "good enough" household. Here I argue that the difficult work of (democratic) integration is reflected in what Paul Lichterman calls "reflexive" associations. Winnicott provides a novel lens into these associations. For Winnicott, constructive work and spontaneous action were essential aspects of integration, but the latter is only possible if the frustrations and antagonisms that accompany this work are simultaneously articulated and worked through. Democratic associations (and selves) therefore need conflict *and* cooperation, antagonism *and* mutualistic collaboration, in order to facilitate integration. By contrast, standard forms of civic volunteerism do little to develop citizens' capacities for constructive and spontaneous action and, in turn, feed patterns of what Winnicott called "false" selfhood, in which individuals avoid conflict in the name of a "polite and mannered attitude" toward others (1965, 142).

My argument proceeds as follows. In the first section, I review the Winnicottian turn within recent democratic theory, as represented here by Honneth and Honig. In the second section, I entertain counterarguments against this turn by theorists concerned less with reparative democratic labors than with significant radical ruptures from the liberal democratic imaginary. These theorists argue in various ways that the failure of our political holding environment is better viewed as an *opportunity* to forsake democratic fetishes. Against these theorists, I argue that the traumatic knowledge of democracy's failure is, paradoxically, only possible because of successful holding experiences. I then turn directly to the work of Winnicott, arguing that democratic theorists need to move beyond his emphasis on the holding environment and focus on the capacities made possible by this environment. These capacities are reflected in Winnicott's idea of integration and the associated concepts of cross-identification and concern. Integrated personalities arise not merely because of patient and supportive facilitating environments, but through environments that deal adequately with the frustrations and antagonisms of our internal and external worlds. Bringing this back, analogously, to democratic theory, in the final section I argue that citizens are best "integrated" in this double-sided way by work within reflexive associations, which enable and facilitate the expression of frustration, fear, vulnerability, and anger at the same time as they provide outlets for creative and constructive civic action. Winnicott did not fully explore integration's *political* conditions, but once we do so I believe that this concept can be understood as a vital aspect of democratic theory and praxis in our present age of democratic disenchantment. This argument therefore has significant implications how we think about the promises and practice of democratic association, public deliberation, and other forms of public work.

The Winnicottian Turn in Contemporary Political Theory

Prominent democratic theorists have turned to Winnicott repeatedly in order to think about the conditions for democratic freedom in an era of crisis and disenchantment. Yet, these theorists have not sufficiently put Winnicott's ideas to work for democratic theory and practice. Axel Honneth and Bonnie Honig, from different perspectives and critical traditions and for different reasons, have done the most to bring Winnicott into contemporary democratic theory. For Honneth, object-relations approaches formed an essential aspect of the turn within critical theory toward questions of just recognition in the context of late modern democratic societies. Object relations presented Honneth with a theory of intersubjective development that could orient and buttress a social theory of justice rooted in what Honneth called the struggle for recognition (1997). For Honneth, just as interpersonal development requires facilitation through successive interaction partners, social development can only occur through patterns of mutual recognition in which subjective intentions are given social space and standing (2014, 123). As he puts it, the "reality of freedom" is made possible by the acceptance of "mutually complementary role activities" through which social subjects recognize each other's aims and status (Ibid., 127). Winnicott's emphasis on the vagaries of interpersonal development within a facilitating or "holding environment," then, help constitute the ground floor and basic logic of Honneth's larger social theory. The object relations tradition, moreover, offered a theoretically valuable language of pathology and health absent the metaphysical pretensions and rigid teleology of the Hegelian tradition to which Honneth has also shown allegiance.

Honneth's work betrays what could be termed a Winnicottian *faith in the actual*. Although pathological formations are possible, healthy development is immanent to actual social conditions. Principles of justice and autonomy are already at work in the various social spheres of contemporary democratic life, even if these spheres are stalked by misdevelopments that threaten their normative potential. For Honneth, freedom has become the inescapable normative horizon for contemporary societies, a horizon that cannot be transcended even if it also can never be fully reached.[1] In turn, this horizon of freedom *holds* social actors, who reflexively view their lives, projects, and social interactions by light of this norm. However, to say that the ideal of autonomy is immanent to the various spheres of social life is not to imply that it is self-actualizing. For Honneth, the routines, role obligations, and customs of ethical life—what Hegel called *Sittlichkeit*—must constellate in a particular way in order to facilitate interpersonal, social, and political freedom. Autonomy depends upon the health of everyday norms and expectations in the lifeworld. Just as, for Winnicott, the good enough environment facilitates certain developmental possibilities, for Honneth the (good-enough?) spheres of action in contemporary societies—ranging from evolving norms of friendship and intimacy to those operating in the workplaces and consumer marketplaces of late capitalism to the values of democratic participation and will-formation—carry an implicit normative and developmental force.

However, despite the immanence of autonomy to actual social institutions and practices, various pathologies limn the spaces of social freedom. For instance, Honneth regards accelerating processes of flexibilization and individualization within social and interpersonal spheres as destabilizing the conditions for mutual recognition. In the economic sphere, moreover, Honneth finds almost a complete absence of "normative facticity" (2014, 175). The capitalist marketplace is less a sphere of social freedom than the heart of its perversion. Yet despite this fact, Honneth believes that norms and practices enabling individual freedom can be identified even in market relations. Therefore, the pathologies that shape contemporary life should be approached as rationally explicable deviations from an available—if currently distorted—developmental norm.

For Honneth, one of the sources of deviation is the seeming paradox that self-determination requires the acceptance of social role obligations. Arguing against dominant understandings of freedom as negative liberty, Honneth states that "we only experience an increase of freedom if we accept complementary role obligations that ensure the durability of practices that guarantee freedom … the other does not represent a limitation on my individual freedom, but its condition" (2014, 140). In the political sphere, for instance, the reciprocal role taking of speaker and listener are the means by which citizens "can clarify and realize their own political intentions in an unforced manner" (2014, 269). Discursive mechanisms across a variety of social spheres help to preserve awareness of mutual responsibilities and enable what Honneth calls cooperative individualism (2014, 175). Cooperative individualism represents the integration of the overlapping obligations, expectations, and social roles of democratic *Sittlichkeit*, and thereby serves as a telos of social freedom. However, Honneth admits that the political integration of citizens is precarious, in part because the mechanisms of integration are uncertain and in part because of the pathology of political "disenchantment," which alienates citizens from the political sphere and from practices of communicative will-formation (2014, 325).

For Bonnie Honig, on the other hand, civic disenchantment is merely one aspect of the "long crisis for democracy" in the twenty-first century, a crisis that has enveloped much of democratic theory in the "trope of catastrophe" (2015, 624). Amidst the concurrent crises of recent years—from "9/11 to neoliberalization … climate change to the carceral society"—Honig has focused on the plight of "public things": public schools, hospitals, parks, and so on (2015, 624). Just as Honneth roots his recognition-centric theory of social freedom in Winnicottian assumptions, Honig also turns to Winnicott in order to theorize democratic citizens' dependency on public things. For Honig, norms of efficiency and cost-effectiveness threaten the existence of these democratic transitional objects, which enable individuals to cross the terrain between omnipotent fantasies of self-sufficiency and a mature understanding of interdependency. In making this argument Honig consciously analogizes Winnicott's observations about childhood development to citizens' need for public things ranging from mundane objects such as public thoroughfares and payphones, to more expressive objects such as public schools and telecommunication infrastructure. Just as transitional objects offer developing children experiences of magical comfort, so too do public objects provide a means of the affective attachments or enchantment necessary for agonistic democracy. In this vein, Honig quotes Tocqueville, who argued, "the art of pursuing in common the objects of common desires [is democracy's] highest perfection" (2015, 624). Insofar as public objects are under pressure, democracy itself is threatened. As Honig puts it, "in health, democracy is rooted in common love and contestation of public things" (2013, 59).

Public things and desires are under pressure in part because dominant social discourses view them as inefficient and therefore unnecessary. Market-infused political *logoi* interpret public things in terms of "childish" dependency, as things that "we ... are supposed to outgrow and eventually leave behind" (2015, 624). Government services can be outsourced, and public functions can be privatized, because their purpose is seen as separable from their location or ownership structure. Yet, it is precisely their location in public that makes these objects important for democratic enchantment. Disregard for these objects, moreover, betrays a short-sighted assurance that they are no longer necessary. Yet, as payphones proved during Superstorm Sandy in 2012—when "smart" phones became useless after the storm wiped out 25 % of nearby cell towers—sometimes disregarded public things return to haunt those who have neglected them (Cohen 2012; Honig 2013).

Following the logic of Winnicott's theories of transitional objects, Honig argues that the threat to public things—not only parks, payphones, and airwaves but transportation networks, prisons, and energy projects—is not only socially shortsighted, but catastrophic. Here Honig follows Adam Phillips, who has argued that each psychoanalytic theorist has organized his or her theory around a "core catastrophe" (1988, 149). For Winnicott, the central catastrophe of human life was not castration or the triumph of the death drive (as it was for Freud and Klein, respectively), but the "failure of the holding environment" (1988, 149). The failure of a facilitating environment forces the subject to rely on its own (insufficient) resources for the work of maturation and development. Being dropped completely before the capacity for self-development arises marks a catastrophic "intrusion" upon and "annihilation" of what Winnicott calls the "core" or "True Self" (1988, 149). In turn, it leads to the overdevelopment of the "false, compliant self," which adapts and perversely attaches itself to the meager offerings of its surrounding environment (1988, 149–150). While for Winnicott there is *always* a split between true and false selves, the nature of this split and the extent to which communication across the divide is possible mark the difference between a healthy, integrated personality and a stultified, uncreative form of life (1965, 140–152).

For Honig, then, democratic citizens need public things—not just because their smart phones may stop working, but also because they need objects that move them from adaptation to agency. Yet, at various points Honig's conscious analogy between public things and transitional objects begins to break down. Transitional objects, according to Winnicott, inevitably dissipate and lose meaning; the comfort and reassurance they provide is essential, but eventually these objects are "relegated to limbo" and even if they are "not forgotten" they are also "not mourned" (1982, 7). Transitional objects are also never contested; they exist within "a neutral area of experience which will not be challenged" (1982, 17). Public things, however, are *constantly* contested—in fact, Honig finds the contestation over them to be part of their value, because it demonstrates that democracy involves agonism more than consensus. Lastly, public things require tending in ways that magical comfort objects do not. Or, as Honig puts it, "the difference [between Winnicott's objects and democracy's objects] … is that in a democracy … these things … may become ruins. They may decay if untended" (2013, 65).

The right Winnicottian concept for exploring democratic development and health, then, is not the transitional object so much as the larger, ongoing scene of the holding environment. Honig acknowledges as much when she argues that "it is not fundamentally about [public things] … it is also about how we think about [public things] … in what sort of holding environment we experience them … with what sorts of words we take them up or they, us" (2013, 68). Yet, there is a need to go even further than this. For Winnicott, holding *itself* has a purpose. The holding environment, in good enough circumstances, facilitates capacities for maturity and health that constellate under Winnicott's concept of "integration." Integration is both a process and an outcome, a mode of interaction that is also an *achievement*—albeit a fragile and precarious achievement, susceptible to rupture and always open to further development. Honig comes close to acknowledging the importance of this larger purpose when she notes that, if we are going to counter narratives that public things are either childish or fetishistic objects, we "may need to think about other ways to depict democratic maturation" (2015, 625). Yet, this insight remains undeveloped, a lack that I address below. Beyond a theory of democratic transitional objects, and beyond repairing the cracks in a democratic facilitating environment, we need theoretical and practical attention to the civic capacities, skills, and subjectivities that this environment can—in health—cultivate.

Embrace the Trauma: The Upside of Democracy's Failed Holding Environment

According to both Honneth and Honig, there are visible cracks in democracy's holding environment, understood both in terms of disregard for public objects of civic enchantment and pathologies within concrete ethical life. Yet, some contemporary theorists argue that these cracks should be *exploited*, in order to call out the false promises of liberal democracy. In this light, the solicitous attention to democracy's facilitating conditions amounts to little more than what Lauren Berlant has called "cruel optimism," which she defines as a "desire [for] something that is actually an obstacle to your flourishing" (2011, 2). Cruel optimism resembles an addiction, a structure of desire that imprisons the subject in a fruitless pursuit. The cruelty lies in the fact that the pursued object can *never* fulfill the subject's actual desires, but the subject imagines that if they just try a little harder, or find novel ways to approach the object, that they will achieve the long-awaited goal (2011, 2). As Berlant deploys it, cruel optimism reflects a sense of social impasse. Amidst deep dissatisfaction or disenchantment with present configurations of political economy, the seemingly reasonable solution on offer—*more democracy*; *better democracy*—is itself part of the problem.

For Berlant, efforts to patch up the holes in democratic *Sittlichkeit* forsake a greater political opportunity to envisage and bring about forms of sociality that are inherently less alienating or frustrating. Instead of accepting the endless tasks of repairing democratic objects and tending to democracy's facilitating environment why not utilize the theoretical and practical resources at our disposal to face up to the consequences of rejecting and transcending liberal democracy's illusory promises? Generalized feelings of democratic disenchantment might then be viewed less as symptoms of distress than as opportunities to alter dominant systems of political and social life.

For Jodi Dean, the key to mobilizing political disenchantment and discontent is to understand and maintain the distinction between democratic "drive" and the "desire" for actual equality (2012). Democratic drive reflects "our stuckness in a circuit"—a ceding of our desire for the realization of our goal (66). A will toward substantive equality is splintered and supplanted by democratic objects and practices. Similarly, Slavoj Žižek sees liberal democratic pieties about disenchantment in terms of "confusion between lack and loss" (2002, 37). Whereas theorists such as Honneth see threats to democratic *Sittlichkeit* in terms of regrettable (yet potentially reversible) misdevelopments, such perceptions merely serve to paper over the constitutive lack at the heart of democratic arrangements—a lack that, if listened to, might put us into closer contact with the real of our desire.

In a similar vein, Lee Edelman has argued that the encompassing hegemony of political desire forestalls actual social transformation by insidiously locking us into an order of production and reproduction. The heteronormativity of "reproductive futurism"—or the "social order of the child"—lives in denial of the radiating costs of its productivity and (to ward off an awareness of these costs) structurally excludes the possibility of "queer resistance" (2004, 3). Queerness, for Edelman, is the unacknowledged (and unacknowledgeable) trauma of the social order of futurism, and for that very reason it is the means by which we might reject the oppressive order surrounding us. The proper ethico-political response is not to repair the cracks in the social order, but to embrace queerness as the traumatic kernel that can explode the order as such.

Since queerness occupies the "place of the social order's death drive," Edelman argues that we can use its inarticulable surplus in order to "withdraw our allegiance [to] a form of reality based on the Ponzi scheme of reproductive futurism" (4). As an insistent form of negativity, queerness can rupture the foundational faith of society by testifying to the (traumatic) truth concealed by its symbolic order—namely, that "nothing, and certainly not what we call the 'good', can ever have any assurance at all …" (4). Queerness becomes a practice of the death drive that ruptures faith in the reproduction of the present, dragging us beyond the narrow bounds of identity as constructed under the objects and ideals of liberal democracy.

For Berlant, Dean, Žižek, and Edelman, then, the proper response to the catastrophe of a failed democratic holding environment is to embrace the trauma. Forsaking a nostalgic attachment to objects and norms that have never been effectively liberating is a necessary step toward a significant rupture. As opposed to the reassurance and continuity of a democratic facilitating environment—represented by Honig's public things or by Honneth's layered *Sittlichkeit*—the traumatic truth of "cleavage," "desire," or "queerness" emphasizes instead the ethical urgency of rupture or failure. Embracing the trauma of contemporary democracy reflects a kind of ethico-political knowledge that the means and mechanisms of reassurance are little more than fantasies, which ultimately infantilize our politics while endlessly deferring our deepest desires for equality.

However, what these theorists collectively fail to recognize is that the ethico-political knowledge of trauma—the fact that holding can and will fail, with potentially catastrophic results—is itself only possible from within a horizon of stabilized futurity. In other words, if to embrace the traumatic propulsions of desire or queerness amounts to a tragic knowledge of the inherent limitations of the symbolic order, then what accounts for the *achievement* of this insight or understanding? Who is capable of it and where are they located, if not within a symbolic order or actual social space? There is a kind of bad faith on display when theorists of traumatic rupture attempt to convey the essential traumatic kernel of the symbolic order from within the symbolic order itself.

As Fred Alford has argued, trauma *does* represent a kind of ethical knowledge. Trauma "takes away our confidence in the existence of a stable, ordered, and meaningful existence" (2013, 10). And this, Alford maintains, is part of trauma's ethical "truth":

> [T]his truth is always the same: that not just the order and stability of my world, but the very existence of the ideas of order and stability are mythic, a ratty human veil to hide the dark insight ... [quoting Iris Murdoch's novel, *The Time of the Angels*] 'there is only power and the marvel of power; there is only chance and the terror of chance'. (11)

Yet unlike Edelman or Berlant, Alford acknowledges that access to the ethical truth of trauma itself requires a supportive context. As he puts it, "the ability to experience the world in this way requires the support of others" (8). In fact, Alford argues that the ethical knowledge of trauma is only available from within a Winnicottian holding community, and "if one has let you down" or is otherwise unavailable, then you must "create one to hold you" (8). The construction of new holding communities is uncertain and precarious, but only a community of others who offer social and moral support can facilitate the acceptance of trauma's tragic lesson. For this reason, Alford argues that providing a holding environment is society's "most basic responsibility" (202).

This detour through theories of trauma and rupture adds an important wrinkle to an account of democratic holding. The possibility, if not the inevitability, of being "dropped," means that there is a duality to democratic attachment that must be acknowledged and worked through. Frustration and discontent with the object and its failures is, for Winnicott, part of mature object relations—a need, we might say, to recognize misrecognition (McIvor 2015). Therefore, facilitating environments need to provide not only supportive recognition and stabilizing objects, but also space for the acknowledgement of the dislocative traumas and mundane discontent that limn all significant attachments—including political attachments. In other words, to deal with democracy's ambivalences, we have to think about facilitating environments through which our capacities for acknowledging traumatic failures and pursuing ideal promises could be codeveloped. To this end, I now turn back to the work of Winnicott.

Holding and the Capacity for Integration

Winnicott's concept of integration has a kind of double impossibility built into it. The first impossibility is that integration—alternately described as "health," "maturity," or "wholeness"—is never fully realized or achieved. Integration's second impossibility, however (somewhat paradoxically), *is its aim*. Winnicott argues that "independence" is the telos of integration, but at the same time "there is no such thing as independence" (1986, 21). Although the individual, in health, may come to "*feel* free and independent, as much as makes for happiness and for a sense of having a personal identity," at the same time this feeling is blurred by a variety of "cross-identifications" that traverse "the sharp line between the me and the not-me" (1982, 188). Integration is an ineluctable movement toward something that does not exist; it is a *feeling* of independence alongside a capacity for cross-identification that enables the simultaneous acknowledgement of interdependency.

Theorists of democratic "holding" and transitional phenomena have as yet not explored Winnicott's idea of integration as the capacity that results from successful, good enough facilitation. This is both unfortunate and somewhat surprising because for Winnicott the capacity for integration and modes of democratic sociality and governance are deeply intertwined. In fact for Winnicott the very meaning of democracy is that a society "has a quality that is allied to the quality of individual maturity" (1982, 240). If integration marks the ability of an individual to advance toward independence while acknowledging interdependency, then democracy—as a "socially mature ... way of life"—marks the possibility of "identification with social groupings and with society, without too great a loss of personal spontaneity" (1986, 187). Winnicott even implies that integration is in fact *impossible* without the appearance of a democratic facilitating environment. As he puts it, "the abstractions of politics and economics and philosophy and culture [are] ... the culmination of natural growing processes" (187). The democratic *psyche* is dependent on the democratic polis—and vice versa—and their mutual (impossible) culmination is an achieved capacity for integration.

It is in this light that we might understand Winnicott's efforts at public outreach—his famous BBC broadcasts and his many speeches at professional societies and associations. In making psychoanalytic insights accessible and available to a broad audience, Winnicott implied that the public sphere could be not merely a site of collective will-formation but of subject- or self-formation as well. Nevertheless, these implications remained just that; Winnicott failed to think about democratic facilitation beyond the role played by the "ordinary, good home" (1986, 259). However, if autonomy is never fully separable from dependency—in fact if autonomy is a kind of healthy illusion made possible by a particular *mode* of dependency—then society necessarily continues (while modulating) the holding of its members initiated at birth.

To develop this line of thinking, theorists might focus more on the possibility of containing or holding spaces in political life (Luxon 2016, 153). Yet, again, holding operates as a standard for psychological and social facilitation only because it leads, in health, toward integration. Integration, therefore, is the crux of a Winnicottian democratic theory. Integration is a wide and sometimes fuzzy concept, but at root it consists of two central capacities: for "cross-identification" and "concern." Integration as a mode of "going on being," moreover, persists through a simultaneous expression of destructive and creative feelings (1982, 204)—which depends upon how such feelings are taken up by those around us. Each of these aspects of integration must be spelled out, then, if we are to understand the potential reach of and prerequisites for the democratic politics of holding.

Hannah Arendt argued that the thinking and judgment necessary for the protection of the world of appearances required capacities for traveling and spectatorship (1978). For Winnicott, these capacities are captured by his concept of "cross-identification," which involves "standing in the other person's shoes, and allowing the converse" (1986, 118). An adequate holding environment (including the space of analysis) facilitates an ever-increasing range of cross-identifications, compiling and composing an ever more complete "world" within the self (1982, 244). As Winnicott puts it, "when healthy persons come together they each contribute a whole world, because each brings a whole person" (244). Once again, if independence is the *telos* immanent to holding, the healthy realization of this autonomy involves a capacity for understanding how it is inevitably situated in relations and crosscurrents of interdependency. On this basis can individuals "get on with life and living, attempting to interweave with society in such a way that there is a cross-contribution"—moving, as it were, from overcompliance to shared agency (1986, 188).

Delusional cross-identifications are, of course, a perpetual possibility. They result when individuals locate the unpleasant aspects of the self in an external object, rather than maintaining contact with the full depth of the self and with ambivalent, whole others. For this reason, healthy cross-identifications arise simultaneously with the development of a capacity for "concern." Concern "refers to the fact that the individual *cares*, or *minds*, and both feels and accepts responsibility" (1965, 73). Responsibility here means a willingness to accept internal ambivalence, to bridge between the compliant and false selves, and to understand the ways in which internal and external worlds overlap and interact. Once again, concern arises from a combination of native capacities and a facilitating environment. The reliable, attentive, and mirroring presence of others enables the individual to contain the anxiety that results from ambivalence, which in turn deepens and enriches the self and makes possible both concern and mature cross-identifications (75).

Cross-identifications facilitate modes of cooperative individualism consistent with democratic maturity. In health, the ability to connect a whole world with whole others enables the individual to overcome what Winnicott—quoting James Baldwin—calls the "sin of unawareness" (1986, 119). Unawareness stems from projective identification through which the dark and difficult pieces of our experience are expelled because the self is too fragile to bear them. Unawareness is mitigated by the capacity for concern. As Winnicott puts it,

> [t]he easy way out for the individual is for him to see the unpleasant parts of himself only when these appear in others. The difficult way is for him to see that all the greed, aggression, and deceit in the world might have been his

> responsibility, even if in point of fact it is not. The same is true for the State as for the individual. (1986, 212)

Although Winnicott only mentions Baldwin once (and only then in passing), there is a striking overlap between Winnicott's and Baldwin's definitions of integration. As Baldwin wrote in *The Fire Next Time*, "if the word *integration* means anything, this is what it means: that we, with love, shall force our brothers to *see themselves as they are*, to *cease fleeing from reality* and begin to change it" (1963, 10). Moreover, Baldwin saw the interpersonal labors of integration as connected to the sociopolitical task of addressing living legacies of racial violence and disrespect—and vice versa. As Baldwin puts it, any change "in the state" requires an "absolutely unthinkable revision of the American identity," which begins with the acknowledgment that "all of us are much more devious and mysterious than we think we are" (Standley and Pratt 1989, 180, 165).

For Winnicott, too, integration implies the self's acceptance of its deviousness, or the fact that even "the life of a *healthy* individual is characterized by fears, conflicting feelings, doubts [and] frustrations" (1986, 27). Successful cross-identifications little resemble frictionless episodes of togetherness. Rather, they enable the individual to "get the full expression of [their] hate" instead of splitting hatred off and projecting it onto another individual or group (1982, 171). Integration is a developmental watershed insofar as it marks the newly formed capacity to tolerate destructive impulses. In "very early loving," individuals "cannot tolerate the destructive aim" (1986, 84). Destructive tendencies can be tolerated only if the individual "has evidence of a constructive aim already at hand of which he or she can be reminded" and if they are capable of taking up this aim or responding to it (84). In so many words, the construction of a shared world enables the integration of destructive with creative elements, which in turn "gives elbow room for the experience of concern" (87).

Winnicott's point here is somewhat obscure. Effectively he is positing that the self can only gain access to its full depth and deviousness if disappointment and aggression can be directed at the object of attachment, *and if* the other survives this aggression and emerges as a whole object on the other side. Individuals need to collaborate, we might say, in their destructiveness; in fact it is the *promise* of collaboration that enables this destructiveness to be integrated into the self rather than split off and lost. Or, as Winnicott puts it, "constructive and creative experiences ... [make] it possible for the child to get to the experience of her destructiveness"

(1965, 81). The combination of destructiveness and creativity in integration is satisfying—because it enables contact with a whole self and between whole selves—but it is also deeply *unsatisfying*—because it obliterates the fantasy of autonomy *without* dependence. In other words it shatters one of our earliest and most reliable defenses: omnipotence. However, the destruction of this fantasy of absolute separation is paradoxically what makes independence possible (see Elkins, this volume). "Freedom"—to use Winnicott's term—contains "little bodily gratification" and it "puts a strain on the individual's whole personality" (1986, 212). Yet, freedom implies a flexibility within the organization of defenses allowing for the "toleration of antagonism without denial of the fact of antagonism"—the awareness, in effect, of the traumatic failure of our social holding environment achieved through the simultaneous recognition of its success (214).

We may seem miles from democratic praxis at this point, but if Winnicott is correct then there is no bright line between the work of integration at the interpersonal level and the social level. Yet, where Winnicott falls short is in the description of the kinds of social interactions and political practices that might facilitate integration. If the measure and means of political health is the number of integrated individuals in a given society, for Winnicott the ordinary good household is the only real space of political education. The most valuable support for democratic tendencies is, as he puts it "organized non interference with the ordinary good mother-infant relationship, and with the ordinary good home" (1982, 241). Yet, by the logic of his theory there is no good reason to reduce the work of integration to early, intimate relationships, since the process of integration is endless and the boundaries of the facilitating environment are ultimately unknowable. Therefore, it is worth exploring the full range of the politics of holding, including not only public transitional objects and the norms, expectations, and institutions of democratic *Sittlichkeit*, but also the styles of civic interaction that enable cross-identification, concern, and collaborative interaction.

The Democratic Politics of Holding

Winnicott's concept of integration—understood as the developed yet fragile capacity for cross-identification and concern—has immanent sociopolitical content. Yet, the task still remains of identifying the practical means by which integration can be cultivated—that is, the kinds of holding environments suitable for this work. As Axel Honneth argues in *Freedom's*

Right, one potential response to political disenchantment involves the "bundl[ing of] the public power of organizations, social movements and civil associations in order to put coordinated and massive pressure on the parliamentary legislature" (2014, 326). Enduring relationships cultivated within associational life can create an opportunity for broad-scale civic agency that exceeds (but does not replace) the operations of formal institutions. Historically, however, practices of political "bundling" depended upon sources of solidarity that were provided by a "common background culture," which is steadily dissipating (327). Amidst unavoidable social complexity and pluralism, then, democratic integration requires the creation of civic relationships that can simultaneously address concrete social problems while bridging across social divisions, and that do so *from within* advancing cultures and customs of withdrawal.

This may sound suspiciously like a plea for social capital (Putnam 1993, 2000). Yet, social capital is an insufficient concept for understanding civic associations and social capacity. As Paul Lichterman has argued, social capital turns a "qualitative ... argument about meaningful, dynamic relationships into a quantifiable argument about the density of groups, individual acts, attitudes and behaviors" (2006, 531). To understand the democratic promise of civic associations, then, requires the study of the various styles of group relations—and this will, I argue, bring us directly back to Winnicott. Group styles are built-up patterns of interaction rooted in shared understandings and expectations about "how to be a good member in a group setting" (539). Group style, then, is less a *what* than a *how*, a way of *going on being* that either cultivates or curtails social capacity, which Lichterman defines as "people's ability to work together organizing public relationships" (535). This work, when it is most successful, forges relationships that bridge social divisions and differences.

Groups that successfully reach outward to build crosscutting relationships display certain styles of interaction. In particular, group-building groups develop norms and practices of what Lichterman calls "social reflexivity" (2005). Groups are socially reflexive when "they talk reflectively, self-critically, about their relations with the wider social context—the people, groups, or institutions they see on their horizon. A group can practice social reflexivity when its customs *welcome reflective talk about its concrete relationships in the wider social world*" (15). Communication *about* the communicative interactions that create social relationships matters greatly for the strength of those relationships (see Chalwell, this volume).

Civic bridge building, importantly, does not hinge on the sharing of common values or cultural frameworks. It depends instead on styles and customs of interaction, and whether these allow for and encourage open communication about group boundaries, goals, and concrete relationships in the wider social world. What matters is the ability to practice a group style of "partnership," which requires "paying attention to other groups [and] becoming a more pro-active member of the larger civic world" (2006, 553). Practices of partnership increase social capacity by "connect[ing] responsibility inside the group with responsibility to a variety of outside actors" (Ibid., 554). The scaling up and out of responsibility resembles what Winnicott saw as the capacity for concern, which similarly depends upon an acknowledgment of interdependency amidst difference. Difference, of course, is crucial, because responsibility can be a cover for omnipotence if the other is not seen as (at least partially) *other*. To imagine that one can anticipate the other's needs without communication marks the refusal of cross-identification. Cross-identification, by contrast, implies the ability to accept and "live through relationships that do go a bit bad, when [one does] become a bit angry and a bit disillusioned and somehow everyone survives" (1982, 173).

Among the groups studied by Lichterman, one in particular stood out for its partnership style. What set this group—which he refers to as "Park Cluster" apart from other, similar groups was its ability to be flexible and critical about itself, its goals, the goals and orientations of others, and the social spaces in which it found itself and to which it ultimately traveled:

> Park Cluster was a flexible group .... [T]he Cluster wondered what Park residents themselves thought about the proposed neighborhood school that had seemed like such a good idea at the outset. They mulled over the biweekly free meals that had seemed at the start like an unquestionably nice thing for the neighborhood. They became more and more uneasy about talking about the good of the neighborhood without neighbors at the table. It became increasingly urgent to figure out how they could work with Charmaine, the neighborhood center director, instead of bypassing her. Fitfully, the Cluster *changed* as a group. They transformed their own style of togetherness as they cultivated new relationships beyond the group. (2005, 256)

As the above example makes clear, a group style of reflexivity and partnership is not easy to practice. It inevitably leads to disappointment and self-doubt; it can be painful and embarrassing, as ideas and practices that seemed unquestionably beneficent take on a new light through engagements with those who had not been represented in their initial envisioning. Social reflexivity requires a comfort with uncertainty, ambiguity, and frustration. In fact, as Lichterman's study shows, it is *certainty* that threatens civic bridge building, whereas perplexity can facilitate it (2005, 256–257). Once again the concepts and categories of Winnicott seem a natural ally for this framework. Flexible, reflexive groups both imply and serve to cultivate a capacity for integration—their members are comfortable with ambivalence and uncertainty, tolerant of and even appreciative of difference, and less anxious about a lack of certain boundaries for the self and the group than they are about the damages that such boundaries can do. Bridge building groups seem to find ways to face down their own imperfections and to work through the complexities attendant to social interaction.

On the other hand is the group style associated with what Lichterman calls "plug-in volunteering" (2006, 541). Plug-in volunteering embodies a "modular, limited style of civic engagement" (542). The emphasis is on concrete actions, reliable patterns of interaction, and low-anxiety forms of engagement. As an example Lichterman describes a program he studied called "Fun Evenings," which was designed as a safe, fun-filled space for "at-risk" youth. The script of interaction for this program was set by its organizer, and deviations from the script were heavily policed. While volunteers got some practice with "creating brief, impersonal relationships," they "did not cultivate any broader, more collectively responsible meanings" of social interconnection (541). Volunteers were ignorant of basic facts of the program—where the participating kids were coming from, or what they thought about the event—in part because they were never asked to assume "ownership" of the program (545). Instead the emphasis was on "being good volunteers, working to keep kids busy and safe, carrying off wary watchfulness and cordial distance. Neither the structure of volunteer recruitment nor the meetings that shaped volunteering opened much space for sociability" (544).

Plug-in volunteering spaces are self-consciously spaces of compliance rather than agency or creative seeing. In this respect, for whatever civic benefits they may provide they are insufficient facilitating environments for integration, due largely to their rigid scripts and intentionally low expectations. The point is not, of course, that we can do *without* cultural scripts, which accompany every group style. The point is that if the script does not allow for or encourage creative deviations—for surprising cross-identifications and practices of concern—then the result is stultifying.

Similarly, for Winnicott the choice is not *between* a false, compliant self and a true self—the choice is about how the false self will *relate* to the true self, how the need for accommodation and compliance will be integrated with the capacity for creativity and spontaneity. The argument I am making here is that this is a compelling standard not merely for individual health but for civic associations and perhaps the democratic polity as a whole.

To move beyond typical scripts of civic engagement is to actively invite painful and uncomfortable conversations (Lichterman 2009, 856). Unfortunately, voluntary associations often police against difficult (or "controversial") subjects of conversation, rarely interrogate the boundaries of the group, and avoid disagreements that are seen as threatening to the "obvious" goods they are providing (Eliasoph 2011). The result is a stunted and self-limited form of civic participation; organizers focus on purely benign acts at the expense of more difficult conversations—for instance encouraging volunteers to collect cans of food rather than pondering the broader sources of hunger or homelessness, or actually developing spaces for cross-identification *with* the hungry or homeless (87). It is hard to develop customs of social reflexivity when questions that might inspire reflection are seen as threatening to the social setting in which they are asked. By contrast, spaces of democratic holding would be suffused with contestation *and* reassurance, antagonism *and* collaboration. Such spaces make room for unpredictable actions, not because they are radically open but because they are suffused with a group style that invites creative exploration amidst dissatisfaction, disagreement, and conflict. Lichterman uses the example of participatory budgeting forums in Brazil, where some participants have turned the hearings into spaces for civic engagement that greatly exceeded the intended agenda (2009, 863). Elsewhere I argue that the recent rise of grassroots-organized "Truth and Reconciliation Commissions" provide potential spaces for democratic exploration, in part because these spaces hold together contrary voices, commitments, and scripts (McIvor 2016; Zamalin, this volume). Integrated selves both need these contrary forces and are capable of tolerating them. Although this may seem unrealistic, that is precisely the point. As Lichterman puts it, "changing institutionalized relationships is not realistic. But that is just what community development advocates and activists try to do, occasionally with some success" (2009, 857).

Civic associations might increase their power and reach if their members read more Winnicott. Common experiences of burnout and frustration might, in the light of a theory of integration, be less a sign of unavoidable failure than an occasion for attentive listening and cross-identification. Collaboration across social divisions and differences could be seen less as a hazard than as an occasion for creative seeing and organization. Antagonism could be viewed not a threat of schism and separation but as a reflection of the ambivalence attached even to our cherished ideals and objects. Civic and political associations, even, might be viewed less as instrumental means of developing social capital and more as the necessary and logical extension of our nurturing environment. Within these spaces and through these interactions citizens can develop modes of cooperative individualism that could erode the harder and more pathological edges of disenchantment, while remaining sensitive to the inherent difficulties and disappointments of democratic life.

Note

1. As Honneth puts it, "[n]o social ethic and no social critique seems capable of transcending the horizon opened up two centuries ago by linking the conception of justice to the idea of autonomy." In fact, even postmodern attempts to challenge the idea of autonomy ultimately represented, according to Honneth, "a more deep-seated variety of the modern idea of freedom" (2014, 16).

References

Alford, C.F. 2006. *Psychology and the Natural Law of Reparation*. New York: Cambridge University Press.

———. 2013. *Trauma and Forgiveness: Consequences and Community*. New York and Cambridge: Cambridge University Press.

Arendt, H. 1978. *The Life of the Mind*. New York: Harcourt.

Baldwin, J. 1963. The Fire Next Time. New York: Dial Press.

Barker, D.W.M. 2013. Oligarchy or Elite Democracy: Aristotle and Modern Representative Government. *New Political Science* 35(4): 547–566.

Berlant, L. 2011. *Cruel Optimism*. Durham, NC: Duke University Press.

Brown, W. 2015. *Undoing the Demos: Neoliberalism's Stealth Revolution*. Brooklyn, NY: Zone Books.

Butler, J. 2015. *Notes Towards a Performative Theory of Assembly*. Cambridge, MA: Harvard University Press.

Cohen, B. 2012. After Sandy, Wired New Yorkers Get Reconnected With Pay Phones. *The Wall Street Journal*, October 31.

Dean, J. 2013. *The Communist Horizon*. London: Verso.

Edelman, L. 2004. *No Future: Queer Theory and the Death Drive*. Durham, NC: Duke University Press.
Eliasoph, N. 2011. *Making Volunteers: Civic Life After Welfare's End*. Princeton, NJ: Princeton University Press.
Honig, B. 2001. *Democracy and the Foreigner*. Princeton, NJ: Princeton University Press.
———. 2013. The Politics of Public Things: Neoliberalism and the Routine of Privatization. *NoFo* 10: 59–76.
———. 2015. Public Things: Jonathan Lear's Radical Hope, Lars von Trier's Melancholia, and the Democratic Need. *Political Research Quarterly* 68(3): 623–636.
Honneth, A. 1997. *The Struggle for Recognition: The Moral Grammar of Social Conflicts*. Cambridge, MA: MIT Press.
———. 2014. *Freedom's Right*. New York: Columbia University Press.
Levine, P. 2013. *We Are the Ones We Have Been Waiting For*. Oxford: Oxford University Press.
Lichterman, P. 2005. *Elusive Togetherness: Church Groups Trying to Bridge America's Divisions*. Princeton, NJ: Princeton University Press.
———. 2006. Social Capital or Group Style? Rescuing Tocqueville's Insights on Civic Engagement. *Theory and Society* 35(5–6): 529–563.
———. 2009. Social Capacity and the Styles of Group Life: Some Inconvenient Wellsprings of Democracy. *American Behavioral Scientist* 52(6): 846–866.
Luxon, N. 2013. *Crisis of Authority: Politics, Truth, and Truth-Telling in Freud and Foucault*. Cambridge: Cambridge University Press.
———. 2016. Beyond Mourning and Melancholia: Nostalgia, Anger and the Challenges of Political Action. *Contemporary Political Theory* 15: 139–159.
McIvor, D.W. 2015. The Cunning of Recognition: Melanie Klein and Contemporary Critical Theory. *Contemporary Political Theory*. doi: 10.20157/cpt.2015.47
———. 2016. *Mourning in America: Race and the Politics of Loss*. Ithaca, NY: Cornell University Press.
Phillips, A. 1988. *Winnicott*. Cambridge, MA: Harvard University Press.
Putnam, R.D. 1993. *Making Democracy Work: Civic Traditions in Modern Italy*. Princeton, NJ: Princeton University Press.
Shulman, G. 2011. Acknowledgement and Disavowal as an Idiom for Theorizing Politics. *Theory & Event* 14: 1.
Standley, F.L., and L.H. Pratt. 1989. *Conversations with James Baldwin*. Jackson: University Press of Mississippi.
Urbinati, N. 2014. *Democracy Disfigured: Opinion, Truth, and the People*. Cambridge, MA: Harvard University Press.
Winnicott, D.W. 1965. *The Maturational Processes and the Facilitating Environment*. Madison, CT: International Universities Press.
Winnicott, D.W. 1971. Playing and Reality. London: Tavistock Publications.

———. 1982. *Playing and Reality*. London: Routledge.
———. 1986. *Home Is Where We Start From: Essays by a Psychoanalyst*. New York: W.W. Norton & Company.
Winters, J.A. 2012. *Oligarchy*. Cambridge: Cambridge University Press.
Winters, J.A., and B.I. Page. 2009. Oligarchy in the United States. *Perspectives on Politics* 7(4): 731–751.
Wolin, S. 2008. *Democracy Incorporated: Managed Democracy and the Specter of Inverted Totalitarianism*. Princeton, NJ: Princeton University Press.

CHAPTER 10

Vanquishing the False Self: Winnicott, Critical Theory, and the Restoration of the Spontaneous Gesture

Amy Buzby

Critical theory contests that political theory, at its best, operates through a compassionate identification with the real subjects suffering under the often unjust systems it holds up to critique. Without this vitalizing linkage, even the sharpest analysis risks becoming an abstract intellectual exercise divorced from constructive praxis. Critical theory retains its power in the present, indeed, because it insists on speaking to and through a vigorous empathy, because critical theorists refuse to either give up on the hope of emancipation or accept the pain produced by advanced industrial capitalism; in other words, critical theory leaves the reader with a simultaneous sense of guilt for being a compliant part of a corrosive order and a renewed sense of responsibility to join the struggle for a mode of living worthy of free, fully developed, and autonomous human beings. Critical theory, therefore, stalwartly refuses to make any concessions to or excuses for what Adorno would term the full constellation of domination, the interconnections among the multitude injustices around the world that support and benefit hegemonic powers, and divests the reader of any excuses she might

A. Buzby (✉)
Arkansas State University, Jonesboro, AR, USA

M.H. Bowker, A. Buzby (eds.), *D.W. Winnicott and Political Theory*,
DOI 10.1057/978-1-137-57533-3_10

produce for tolerating those outrages in turn (Adorno 2007). Despite its strength at the level of critique and solidarity, however, I will contend that critical theory has generally faced immense difficulties in translating its ruthless exposition of both a rotten world *and* its identification of the internal damage that world does to the subject into effective action. It thus fails to translate its incisiveness into the kind of compassionate, constructive potency that it identifies such a desperate need for in the present.

There is no need, however, to abandon the hope that the as yet unrealized promise latent in human history will be redeemed. In previous works, I have argued that by returning to the psychoanalytic roots of critical theory, which Max Horkheimer called "one of the *Bildungsmachte* [foundation stones] without which our own philosophy would not be what it is," critical theory can begin to pursue more effective modes of engagement, both in the external realm of society and the internal one of the subject (Whitebook 1996, 1). In this chapter, I will focus on the work of one psychoanalyst, D.W. Winnicott, as particularly valuable to this project, and utilize his work to suggest new avenues and alternatives for critical theory as we find it today. I will contend that Winnicott's theoretical *and practical* focus on developing what he called the "true self," the authentic self as agent, and shattering the "false self," a defensive formation meant to fend off an overwhelming world, is an essential resource for critical theorists looking to restore subjectivity, autonomy, and spontaneity today. Because these aims are integral to making use of the insights of the Frankfurt School, I conclude that Winnicott is not only an important ally for critical theorists, one who richly deserves further engagement but also provides practical resources that critical theory can and must adopt to retain its utility.

Moving Beyond Critique: Critical Theory's Problems in Practice

Critical theory is damning and totalizing in its rejection of modernity. Although, as thinkers in the Marxist tradition, the members of the Frankfurt School saw the undeniable promise incumbent in the significant advances modern societies have made, they never ceased to recognize that these innovations can only come to serve human ends if they are unmoored from reified systems in which power is linked firmly to the lifeless ends of capital, even as it is atomized by globalization. As Adorno claimed, in other words, because "wrong life cannot be lived rightly," the total transformation of our way of living is necessary to unleash the potential for a better way of living, a capacity human hands have already built, but that docile, conformist modern man cannot recognize as such (Adorno 2005, 39).

Critical theorists have pursued many divergent means of translating the rejection of this failing world into the construction of one capable of unleashing humanity's long-stymied potential to be truly, wholly free and self-governing. As Stephen Eric Bronner has claimed, however, the goal always remains in no small part to render impossible the lives of those cowardly, and all too common, modern subjects who might "preserve their existence by denying their subjectivity" (Bronner 1994, 84). In this section of the paper, I will take three important exemplars of the Frankfurt School—Marcuse, Horkheimer, and Adorno—and I will explore the solutions they attempted to broach through their works. My central contention in this section is that these methods cannot take us very far. Because these thinkers were concerned with remaining true to their critiques, and given that they were skeptical of psychoanalysis as an ally in practice (although for different reasons), each was precluded from developing truly salutary alternatives (see Buzby 2014).

Marcuse

Herbert Marcuse was perhaps the most militant member of the Frankfurt School, in both the sweeping invective of his criticism, which held up the central tenet that "[d]omination is the internal logic of the development of civilization," and in his commitment to real-world activism, especially the New Left (Marcuse 1970, 11). Because he recognized that what modernity terms freedom is becoming synonymous with domination, he also saw that, in Orwellian fashion, the contemporary individual is thus induced to love the very forces that immiserate him. As such, internal and external life is rendered one-dimensional, and the project of civilization takes on a totalitarian character. One-dimensionality, which snuffs out the "very disposition, the organs, for the alternative: freedom without domination," grinds both subjectivity and the potential for progress in history into dust (Marcuse 1971, 17). The goal of restoring the potential of the individual and shared life worlds, of creating "man with the good conscience to make life an end-in-itself," is thus central to Marcuse's political project of resistance (Marcuse 1974, xiv).

The Marcuse who confronted that one-dimensional world, however, was left by definition with no starting point: one-dimensionality presents neither depth nor opening, only an eternity of placid surface. For Marcuse, the only escape from the *eutopos* of modernity is through the strategic deployment of utopian alternatives. To explode domination through utopian means, Marcuse urges his reader to make "the Great Refusal," the total rejection of contemporary ideologies, character structures and practices (Marcuse 1971, 14). The only means Marcuse provides to this end, however, are those of regression. Arguing that society imposes surplus repression, beyond what is necessary for constructive civilization, on the individual, Marcuse (1974) urges that individuals regress toward the unbounded psychological states of infancy. Only mature, unflinching individuals, developed enough to see and reject this world in its inhumanity, and strong enough to build the new, however, are useful in achieving his aims. In responding to a similar concern, Marcuse admitted: "That is the circle in which we are placed, and I do not know how to get out of it" (Marcuse 1970, 80). To realize the world, Marcuse so badly wanted to develop out of the failed state he so thoroughly condemned, we must find some alternative mechanism for building depth where none exists. In short, we must help the sober individuals capable of making use of utopia mature into citizenship.

Horkheimer

Max Horkheimer was not only the architect of the Frankfurt School, he also, in many ways, provided the moral core of critical theory: obdurate compassion. It is not enough, in other words, to critique injustice. Materialist political theory, valuable in that, "It frees of illusions, unmasks reality and explains what happens," must always be linked to the humans who deserve better (Horkheimer 1978, 94). The central problem in Horkheimer's political theory is best defined, in other words, in the epochal *Dialectic of Enlightenment*, where Horkheimer shared, along with Adorno, his concern for those who might follow Odysseus, and, "for the sake of his own self, calls himself Nobody" (Adorno and Horkheimer 2007, 53). The lack of subjectivity and the attendant loss of the sense of responsibility for social outcomes felt by the true, self-governing citizen, indeed, haunts Horkheimer's work. Without selfhood, in short, we lose the ability to empathize with the hurting other, or to feel any culpability for the social, economic and political sources of his pain. If "[m]en relate to each other, yet they do no see each other," democracy is thus fundamentally impossible (Horkheimer 1978, 17). Because the harms done to the masses stemmed from "the convergence of the positive elements on the absurdly small number of the free," economic and political privilege (as many others have recognized), are sufficient to induce those with real power to defend the extant, abusive system with any means, however cruel, necessary (Horkheimer 1978, 74). The central problem, therefore, Horkheimer diagnoses is that everyone, however exalted or degraded, is mutilated by the present system, and still the worse, the loss of subjectivity—the cruelest defense of all—makes us blind to and morally disengaged from even this basic truth.

Horkheimer recognized that to solve this problem, a new selfhood and mode of relating to others was necessary. The withered faculty of compassion must be brought to bear on the individual, to mobilize him to work to end the suffering he shares with those others, as Horkheimer claims: "I know of only one kind of gust that can open the windows of the house wider: shared suffering" (Horkheimer 1978, 18). Critical theory, to spark this conversation, cannot rely on mere critique. It must tap directly into the real emotional world obfuscated by reification and the forces supporting hegemony, and animate the internal world of the subject: Horkheimer, indeed, contests "[e]verything therefore depends on creating the free subject that consciously shapes social life" (Horkheimer 1978, 51). The problem here is that given the sweeping nature of the collapse Horkheimer himself diagnosed, wherein the subject is said to not exist, to be nobody and to be absolutely blinded to reality, it is utterly unclear how critical theory can even begin to move the subject to *feel* her suffering, much less to the confidence, clarity and concern necessary to *share* it.

The later Horkheimer, perhaps because of this central impasse in his works, seems to have fallen into a pessimism that arguably even led him to retreat, as the neoconservatives did, at least partly to a conservative standpoint. To take one narrow example, Horkheimer rejected support for the New Left, and even went so far as to speculate that many of the things that movement was aligned against, including the Vietnam War, might actually be worthy of his support (see Stirk 1992). Instead of doing the compassionate and ego-constructive work he urged on his reader as a young man, therefore, Horkheimer lost at least much of his analytical power by complying with the needs and demands of power. As such, the reader inspired by the young Horkheimer must look elsewhere for the methods that might do his critique justice.

Adorno

Theodor Adorno, perhaps more than any other critical theorist, struggled with the seeming futility of engendering meaningful resistance to a system that is overawing in the deployment of reactionary force. Like Horkheimer, he insisted that conscience and compassion are necessary to resist these forces, but he also saw that "an aroused conscience is not enough if it does not stimulate a systematic search for an answer" (Adorno 1993, v). Because Adorno felt that the modern subject is not just flattened, but made militantly reactionary (he would claim, for example, of the compliant mass man that "[h]is love of people as they are stems from his hatred of what they might be"), critical theory demands the creation of intellectuals capable of standing apart, but able to work together in full solidarity as the expose and resist all that blocks free alternatives (Adorno 2005, 25).

Once again, it is unclear where such activists might emerge, nor what would induce them to continue in such thankless work, given the nightmare critical theory diagnoses. Adorno turned to aesthetics for much of his resistance, which is perhaps unsurprising given the entanglement of what he and Horkheimer termed "the culture industry" in accelerating the modern subject's internal collapse. Art allows the individual to feel and grow, and can hold within itself both criticism and fresh alternatives. Art also helps to establish the boundaries between the self and the external world, and thus healthfully reorients the individual to his limits so that he might recognize his strengths. Adorno thus remained focused on reclaiming the nonidentity between subject and object in his later works, and thereby seems to see liberation *only* as "the unique and reflective experience of subjectivity" (Bronner 1994, 34). It requires more than subjectivity to fight an abusive system, it demands an individual able to reach out to and construct the new with and for others. It is thus that we must reach beyond Adorno, and critical theory generally speaking, to seek the Frankfurt School's ends. With that, I turn to D.W. Winnicott for answers.

Finding the True Self: Critical Theory, False Self-Formations, and the Problem of "The Muddle"

D.W. Winnicott eschewed the rigid orthodoxy that became the hallmark of mid-century psychoanalysis in both thought and practice. As an innovator content to *be present in his work as himself*, because he knew it was only as an authentic and compassionate agent that he could actually reach out effectively to the suffering individuals he treated and discussed, Winnicott gradually built a unique practice grounded in vibrant selfhood, playfulness, and an unwavering emphasis on spontaneous—yet responsible—engagement in the moment. Because these qualities are absolutely integral to developing functional solutions to the problems critical theory correctly diagnosed, this very cursory survey of Winnicott alone recommends him to our attention.

In this section, I will briefly present two of Winnicott's key contributions to psychoanalytic theory and practice, the idea of the true versus the false self and his discussion of what he called "the muddle," the overwhelming complexities and demands placed upon us by both our inner and outer worlds. I will argue that in the elucidation and use of these categories, Winnicott proved himself to have both the incisive criticism and the kind of compassionate commitment to genuinely struggling others that provide the backbone of critical theory. I contend, therefore, that Winnicott is true to the spirit of critical theory, and therefore can be utilized by critical theorists without losing the radical character and value of their criticism. I will turn to the use of Winnicott in the next section.

True and False Self Formations

For Winnicott, the overarching aim of psychoanalysis as a mode of intervention was the support and development of the true self. His psychoanalysis starts with the recognition that although maturation to autonomy is necessary, it is an achievement that many fail to make, or in his own words, "the infant may be assumed to be sound in body and *potentially* sound in mind; and what I want to discuss is the meaning of this potentiality" (Winnicott 1989, 4–5). For Winnicott, therefore, the chief concern is identifying and supporting the maturational conditions that lead to human health, a state he defined as being "emotionally mature according to the age at the moment" and as requiring an ever-expanding capacity for "responsibility for environment" (Winnicott 1988, 12). As such, I will first briefly discuss Winnicott's explanation of satisfactory psychological development before turning to the problem of the false self.

In proper maturation into true selfhood, we move from the unintegration of the infant (the unbounded state Sigmund Freud would call "infantile omnipotence") to integration. Because the infant begins as an entity with only the raw potential for integrated self, maturation begins as a question of the quality of the external environment on the level of supporting emerging selfhood. Natural growth, Winnicott argues, thus can only occur where parents and home "are good enough" (Winnicott 1989, 5). He does not demand perfect provision, but instead expects parents to adapt to the infant's needs during the early stages of life (wherein the child is doubly dependent on others for the satiation of both physical and emotional needs) such that the child can cease worrying about external concerns, and with that trust intact, begin to recognize and express burgeoning inner life. Winnicott identified these "good enough" environments, which need never be perfect and are within the grasp of ordinary families, as ones where the child's basic needs are met and he thereby feels "held" by the external world. Beyond meeting physical needs, holding environments must set the early groundwork for ego-relatedness with others, introduce the child gradually to the broader world at appropriate moments and reflect the child back at herself, so that she may begin to feel real, "a whole person related to whole persons" (Winnicott 1989, 14, 1990a, 100–112). As a real participant in the world, one capable of the complex and analytical work of reality testing, the subject can begin to reinvent the world she finds in subjective terms, invest it with personal meaning and energy (Winnicott 1989, 95–102).

Gradually, as dependence wanes and the child is more able to care for herself, the maintenance of this holding environment allows for a further shift from the dependence of childhood to the independence of mature, creative adulthood. This does not mean that the subject has escaped what Winnicott often called the struggles of living, or that development, which he viewed as "normally painful and punctuated by conflict" is ever a smooth process (Winnicott 1988, 28). Eventually, in full integration, however, the subject can contain and *use* these frustrations, along with hate and aggression, and come to take "full responsibility for *all* feelings and ideas that belong to being alive … it is a failure of integration when we need to find the things we disapprove of outside ourselves" (Winnicott 1990b, 82). In this state, the individual has become an actualized microcosm of the human potential inherent in the process of history, and can therefore contribute to society in constructive ways. As such, the subject has reached the true self, which expresses itself through the spontaneous gesture (Rodman 2003, 169). Even in this creative, relational and confident position, however, there is something fundamentally incommunicable, and the core of the true self remains an isolate that is protected from an overwhelming reality through defenses sufficiently flexible to allow ongoing, playful interaction with the world (Tuber 2008, 40).

In other words, if the individual is not given sufficient recognition and support as a real individual, first by Mother and then by broader world, to feel confident in being truly himself, the true self can be lost. Because "*the early stages are never truly abandoned*," and regression is always possible, this loss is a constant threat (Winnicott 1988, 158). Some restriction of spontaneity, moreover, is always necessary to maintain good social order, starting from the expectation that the infant comply with his caretaker's basic needs and running through adult social obligations like courtesy, but where the individual has succeeded in "[setting] up a 'human' internal strictness," she can maintain "self-control without too great a loss of that spontaneity which alone makes life worth living" (Winnicott 1989, 16). Through mature self-governance internally, the individual can continue to hazard the extension of the spontaneous gesture to the outside world. Were the world comprised of such people, Winnicott posits, democracy and a free and fair society would be easy to maintain. Integration, after all, directly produces a sense that the "environment is something to which the individual contributes and for which the individual man or woman takes responsibility" (Winnicott 1988, 152). Maturation thus produces democracy at the individual level, allowing us remain creative and critical in our citizenship while enduring the frustrations that are inevitable in productive group life.

The false self, on the other hand, is dangerously tenable, a lifeless mask of compliance aiming to satisfy powers that have shown only the capacity to let the subject down and use him as means to their own ends. In false selfhood, some trauma or environmental failure has led to a "breaking of the continuity of the line of the individual's existence" (Winnicott 1990b, 22). This breach of the holding environment threatens the subject with disintegration, the loss of previously attained identity and maturity, because a subject "in this position feels infinitely dropped" (Winnicott 1989, 108). Not only is this process of disintegration painful, a keenly felt and likely unendurable loss, but it also undermines the very conditions on which further engagement with an externality that must be invested with trust to be explored is possible. As such, these distortions make "impossible a normal or healthy growth at any later stage," as Winnicott firmly believed that "[t]he whole process of development must be carried through, each gap or jump in development is a distortion, and a hurry here or a delay there each leaves a scar" (Winnicott 1988, 38, 29). The true self, the subject's most precious accomplishment and quintessential core, must be protected from these overwhelming threats. The false self, in short, is the most successful defense against a world which fails the subject by treating him without sufficiently caring provision or by refusing him status as ethical agent and equal. It hides the true self away, especially from the subject, who is left feeling unreal and powerless before external authorities. The false self thereby deadens our capacity for care and concern makes the work of living authentically, much less compassionately, prima facie impossible (Winnicott 1990a, 90).

The false self is thus a clear, palpable problem for any democracy, one with which critical theory is intimately familiar. As a false self, one can only impersonate the citizen, but can so with alarming success because the center of the false self is compliance and passivity. Only the true self can have real membership in society, however, as the healthy are not only capable of self-rule, but also of identification with ever broader social circles, eventually reaching cosmopolitanism, without losing identity or spontaneity (Winnicott 1990a, 163). There is nothing real, however, about the false self, which must seek what Freud called "palliative measures" to conceal the evidence of his unhappy state and thus maintain the defense (Freud 1961, 23). Commonly, therefore, the false self will seek out authorities to which they can submit, and Winnicott claims that the tendency to seek out dictatorship in all spheres of life is the nearly inevitable result (Winnicott 1990b, 125). Unfortunately, Winnicott also argued that strong democracies must conform to their healthy members, who are in turn taxed with the burden of carrying the remainder. It is perhaps for this reason, that Winnicott also frequently warned that neither democracy nor maturity could be imposed: mature individuals are the very stock that necessarily comprises democracy (Winnicott 1989, 31, 67). Where the false self flourishes, we can expect to find democracy in name only, at best (see McIvor, this volume). Concerned as it is with any force that undermines the full realization of democracy and freedom, critical theory must therefore support all social processes that lead toward the achievement of true self by as many as possible. After a brief cautionary note, I will pick up with Winnicott's methods, so that critical theory may begin this work.

Navigating the Muddle

Out of Winnicott's developmental story emerge many problems familiar to critical theorists, above all the demand for autonomy and maturity. Where Winnicott differs from critical theory, however, is that he reminds us gently that living is the work of navigating these tangles, not of somehow straightforwardly solving them. If history is the struggle of humanity to gradually actualize its own potential, no easy answers can be found because we are constantly pushing, at least at our best, against the very limits of our capacities, and using the full measure of our abilities. In his biography of Winnicott, F. Robert Rodman associated Winnicott's "extraordinary capacity for reaching ways to restore hope," precisely with his understanding "that there are limits to the fulfillment of hope .... This, in a way, is the fullest expression of living: to come to the end of one's powers" (Rodman 2003, 244). Such a life will move history forward and create the new in every passing moment. True Selfhood, therefore, is marked by the ability to tolerate uncertainties, internal and external, and still remain productively engaged with self and world.

Critical theory, if it is to support the subject in reaching true selfhood, must tolerate this muddle, and must reject the positivist delusion that materialism can solve all of our confusions and difficulties. Winnicott's discussion of adolescence is useful in illustrating this attitude. Teenagers necessarily redefine self, and it is during this period that many accomplishments toward true self must be made. Because Winnicott saw maturation as an aggressive act, wherein we mark off definitively something that is *me* and *mine*, teenagers will be particularly engaged in challenging the external world and those within it. Winnicott insists, however, that we avoid the temptation to solve the problem of adolescence from the outside, urging instead that we meet the challenge and "include this as a permanent feature and to tolerate it, to go to meet it, but not to try to cure it. The question is: has our society the health to do this?" (Winnicott 1990a, 131). Each teen, in short, must work through adolescence, or the process will be fruitless. Critical theory, to learn from this example, must seek to set provocative conditions that prime the reader to work through the systemic problems it identifies, without seeking to impose solutions and limits on those who would join in constructive activism.

Rebuilding Spontaneity and Growth: Using Winnicott Psychoanalysis to Restore the Subject for Critical Theory

Winnicott's own methods for transcending the muddle and developing the true self centered on the use of play and the spontaneous gesture to restore subjectivity, agency and autonomy to the ailing other. Through these means, the defensive false self was induced to drop its guard and allow glimmers of the real, fragile subject to finally shine through. Using tactics like the famous squiggle game, wherein the patient would be allowed to finish a randomly drawn pattern from Winnicott into a finished product of their own design, the subject was finally able to reflect on self and world in relation to a genuinely supportive other. Development and maturation through and into the capacity to play, therefore, emerges as the core of Winnicott's means to restore the subject's ability and desire to build a life worth living in ways meaningful to the self in relation to the world, an end also urgently recognized by critical theorists.

In this section, I will explore Winnicott's methods, highlighting elements useful to contemporary critical theory. I will argue that, having identified similar problems to critical theory (although, admittedly, from a different standpoint and with divergent intentions), Winnicott approached the constellation of domination from the internal front of the psyche, not the external realm of politics and culture. By so doing, he built the subject necessary to resist the external trends problematized by his thinking. I will further relate these insights to those of critical theory, and conclude that they are aligned in purpose and means.

Play as Model

Play is the model on which Winnicott grounded his clinical practice, the beating heart of his theory and the bridge that allowed him to fuse the two into a rich and unique mode of praxis. Play is critical not only because it is a forum for spontaneous gestures, but also because it facilitates growth, communication, an inner reality rich enough to support reality testing, self-healing and the bridging of creative impulses to the work of living. Play has all of these fruitful capacities because it creates an intermediate space between inside and outside, one that begins as "*the area that is allowed the infant between primary creativity and objective perception based on reality-testing*" (Winnicott 1991, 15). This fusion of the private and the public allows the private to be safe while the external world is reached out to imaginatively and constructively. The preconditions of play are thus rooted in the maintenance of a trustworthy environment, one that allows for the unfolding of true self, and one that must therefore be carried over into the clinical space of psychoanalytic practice (see Mehdi, this volume).

Because the analytic space is defined by holding, play will become the work of psychoanalysis only after regression has undone the hitch caused by the original traumatic break in the subject's development. After that difficult process is sated, the work of maturation can resume, and play is thus integral as a developmental process. Gradually, the subject will become able to *use* play, because, "based as it is on the acceptance of symbols, [it] has infinite possibility in it," and through play one can "experience whatever is to be found in his or her personal *inner psychic reality*, which is the basis of the growing sense of identity" (Winnicott 1990a, 83). The work of play allows the subject to explain the world—inner and outer—in personally meaningful terms for the first time, and thus create his own life. In health, the subject is able to be creative because the subject finally exists, and the world becomes a vibrant space of human possibility. The healthy subject must maintain a playful attitude throughout life, not just as a means to spontaneity, but also as a way of avoiding the artificial, boring and deadening mask of compliance that our present unhealthy and intolerant society would slip on the unaware. If we are to make a potent impact on the world, as the man who claimed "My job is definitely to be myself" so richly knew, we can only do it as authentically, bravely ourselves (Winnicott 1990b, 55).

Clinical Methods

Winnicott's clinical work is an invaluable example of how theory and technique are both best understood through their fusion in praxis, and speaks to the power of professionalism that refuses to disengage from humanity. The central goal of Winnicott's praxis was to recreate the holding environment that failed, so that the subject could be met "*at the exact place that the individual reports failure*," and finally have the needed experience of "*[r]eliability meeting dependence*" (Winnicott 1989, 81, 1990b, 113). This requires the analyst to treat the subject in a fully individual way, based on a growing relationship of openness and trust, and not through the imposition of unfeeling theory or unbending clinical rules. As the holding environment finally proves "good enough," the analyst is able to lead the patient to develop her own "care-cure," which Winnicott sharply distinguishes from "remedy-cure" (Winnicott 1990b, 119–120). "Remedy-cure," wherein the doctor holds and provides a magical answer from outside, is something fiercely desired by the passive, docile false self. The effectiveness of the analysis turns on smashing this false self, and rebuilding the critical faculties the patient needs to move forward authentically, including care for self and world. Play is thus critical to providing the space for this new growth, and Winnicott's analysis is therefore rooted in the praxis of "*two people playing together*," such that the spontaneous gesture can finally be dared, and the subject can be affirmed through having that gesture recognized and held (Winnicott 1991, 51).

Play is not our only means toward integration, a process of regression and self-discovery is needed before maturation is possible and play can be useful. For this work to succeed, the analyst must be available for use by the patient, as the holding environment failed to be in the past. This process begins with mirroring, in which the calm professionalism of the analyst, along with his ability to respond to the spontaneous gesture, reflects the subject reality back to her, whether it is flattering or not (Winnicott 1991, 160). The use of the analyst continues through the subject's dependence on the holding environment provided in the analysis, through the analyst's indefatigable provision of care. Above all, however, the analyst must tolerate the "testing" of this environment, which is essential to the establishment of trust. The analyst must, in other words, survive the hate and anger of the subject, which must be integrated and made usable by the true self, if the analysis is to succeed. Especially given the frustrations stemming from the unreal existence of the false self, an almost superhuman compassion is necessary for the analyst to endure this use.

Hope, first held by the analyst, and then gradually extended to the subject through the relationship of playful mutuality, is thus the lifeblood of the analysis. This is not a blithe optimism, however, but rather the grounded belief of the dialectical materialist in the potential for human progress. It is, indeed, worth noting that the false self is in some ways the product of hope and integrity. Given time and the right conditions, the subject can recover and integrate, because the defense was driven from the start precisely by the valuation of selfhood. The false self, in other words, is a fundamental recognition and rejection of suffering, and, as Winnicott claimed, "[w]here there is suffering, there help can be given" (Winnicott 1990a, 223). Only unflinching compassion could find hope here, in the deepest roots of pain. For Winnicott, indeed, the psychoanalytic practitioner should be focused on doing as little as possible, allowing the subject maximum elbow room to organize and reveal himself as "an expression of I AM, I am alive, I am myself" (Winnicott 1991, 76). This "I AM" moment is the start of true selfhood, and from there everything is possible.

Communication, cognizant of the distortions stemming from the unconscious, is thus another key element of the analysis as it winds toward its conclusion. This communication, which is unlikely to be exclusively verbal, cannot be rushed and *must* be offered by the subject. For Winnicott, indeed, the right interpretation is meaningless, if not counterproductive, if the analyst imposes it: the subject needs to use the analytic situation to work through his own muddle, and to interpret himself (Tuber 2008, 10, 109). The analysis thus turns on being with one's patients and not talking at them. With the prospect of domination by the analyst removed, open discourse and freedom of thought are possible. The gentle encouragement of the analyst prods the subject to pick up these pre-political tools and recognize the citizenship and autonomy they enable as a moral responsibility owed to self and world.

Throughout, Winnicott served his patients not only as a paragon of professionalism and hope, but also as a model of the fully integrated, creatively engaged true self in action. It is also important that Winnicott models precisely the kind of authority that supports self-rule: one that wanes as the subject grows in autonomy and strength. As such, the analysis is a collaboration of the realized humanity of the analyst with the subject's growing reality. As such, Winnicott was absolutely dedicated to being authentically present *as himself,* with his real emotions engaged, not as an ideologue or dogmatist that might don the socially convenient mask of the false self. This flexible, personal commitment to *creating a better world through helping the other realize autonomy* is his greatest strength. Critical theory, weak at precisely this point, would do well to further theorize Winnicott's example.

Social Applications

There is, indeed, much to be done with Winnicott in social application. Both critical theory and Winnicott see most of our present difficulties as rooted in our increasing monadism, which destroys the play and relationality essential to acting spontaneously and growing (Winnicott 1989, 46). Monadism is also a condition of fundamental boredom, which stultifies us into docility, and makes the path of conformity seem like a vibrant one. Given critical theory's concerns about human isolation and one-dimensionality, moreover, fewer families will be likely to prove adequate at holding, and in addition to this collapse, hegemony will increase in pressuring individuals toward a false self formation. The urgency of this situation is a large part of why critical theory and Winnicott still matter: we must use both to navigate our present muddle without losing self and sanity.

Winnicott was as forceful as any member of the Frankfurt School in insisting that freedom terrifies and exhausts us, *especially because we need it for a satisfactory individual and shared existence.* Winnicott is useful to critical theory, indeed, because he allows us to access that inner dimension, the intimate sphere in which the absence of freedom is most keenly felt, and invest each individual directly in rebuilding self and world. Given his conviction that the world "cannot be better than the individuals who compose it," his firm recommendation to critical theory would be to build modes of praxis that open the subject's defenses up for reflection, such that they can be made more flexible and livable, elsewise, "[t]he unhappy will try to destroy happiness. Those who are caught up in the prison of the rigidity of their own defenses will try to destroy freedom" (Winnicott 1990b, 221, 237). As critical theorists, we must meet this challenge, and produce work that is available for use by those who would seek to work through personal and shared suffering.

Everything we do, especially in praxis, must thus capture play, creativity and spontaneity, or it contributes to the reification of the inner and outer world of real human beings that matter. The reader should be able to understand that a real human is speaking and growing in the work as they encounter critical theory, an authentic being driven by genuine concern for the other and spirited on through a hope that can be shared and practically used. Any rigidity or dogmatic purity in our work can only encourage the false self, which seeks masters who demand compliance and craves rigidity because it has no originality or agency (Winnicott 1990b, 68–69). This would be a calamity, a disastrous betrayal of the aims of critical theory. Without attention to the ego-relatedness and mutual growth demanded by the constructive solidarity critical theory seeks, indeed, we can never reach the inner foundations of the systemic problems the Frankfurt School so ably diagnosed.

Conclusion

Many have fought and died, in their own ways, to redeem the promise of a free human world. It cannot be enough to man the barricades, however, when the internal world is left unmediated. This is where Winnicott has immense value for critical theory: his work is particularly useful in building the subject that would resist, such that the provocations made through the sharp criticisms of those who follow the Frankfurt School can fall on able and eager ears. We must resist modernity, in other words, simultaneously on both the internal and external fronts, or we are doomed to fail. We cannot do this alone: it absolutely requires the collaboration of many true Selves working toward a better world for themselves, together.

It is impossible to read Winnicott's work without feeling the electric surge of being alive with one's own ideas, which is the truest sign of his mastery of praxis. His works, in turn, shine with creativity, innovation and fearlessness, and one can still feel Winnicott reaching out spontaneously through the page to the reader. Even here, Winnicott manages to convey the reciprocity and relationality we need so badly in the suffering present. It is my hope that other critical theorists will hear me now, in light of this need, and seek out Winnicott on their own terms.

References

Adorno, T. 1993. *The Authoritarian Personality.* New York: W.W. Norton and Company.

———. 2005. *Minima Moralia.* New York: Verso.

———. 2007. *Negative Dialectics.* New York: The Continuum International Publishing Group.

Adorno, T., and M. Horkheimer. 2007. *Dialectic of Enlightenment: Cultural Memory in the Present.* Palo Alto, CA: Stanford University Press.

Bronner, S.E. 1994. *Of Critical Theory and Its Theorists.* Cambridge: Blackwell.

Buzby, A. 2014. *Subterranean Politics and Freud's Legacy: Critical Theory and Society.* New York: Palgrave.

Freud, S. 1961. *Civilization and Its Discontents.* New York: W.W. Norton.

Horkheimer, M. 1978. *Dawn and Decline.* New York: Seabury Press.

Marcuse, H. 1970. *Five Lectures: Psychoanalysis, Politics and Utopia.* Boston, MA: Beacon Press.

———. 1971. *An Essay on Liberation.* Boston, MA: Beacon Press.

———. 1974. *Eros and Civilization: A Philosophical Inquiry into Freud.* Boston, MA: Beacon Press.

Rodman, F.R. 2003. *Winnicott: Life and Work.* Cambridge: Da Capo Press.

Stirk, P.M.R. 1992. *Max Horkheimer: A New Interpretation.* Hemel Hempstead: Harvester Wheatsheaf.

Tuber, S. 2008. *Attachment, Play, and Authenticity: A Winnicott Primer.* Lanham, MD: Jason Aronson.

Whitebook, J. 1996. *Perversion and Utopia: A Study in Psychoanalysis and Critical Theory.* Cambridge: MIT Press.

Winnicott, D.W. 1988. *Human Nature.* London: Free Association Books.

———. 1989. *The Family and Individual Development.* New York: Routledge.

———. 1990a. *Deprivation and Delinquency*. New York: Routledge.
———. 1990b. *Home Is Where We Start From: Essays by a Psychoanalyst*. New York: W.W. Norton and Company.
———. 1991. *Playing and Reality*. New York: Routledge.

CHAPTER 11

Adults in the Playground: Winnicott and Arendt on Politics and Playfulness

John LeJeune

Politics and the Paradox of Adulthood

This essay examines three questions. First, how does D.W. Winnicott's research into psychoanalysis and cognitive development inform our understanding of democratic politics? Second, what role do politics and political action play in Winnicott's theory of human flourishing and what is Winnicott's analytical assessment of political action and democratic participation? Third and most generally, how does engagement with political theory enrich our understanding of Winnicott and the significance of his work?

These questions are inspired by the centrality of *play* and *creativity* in Winnicott's account of healthy childhood development and the wholesome life of socially integrated adults. Winnicott describes play as virtually synonymous with "creative activity and the search for the self," and argues that "on the basis of playing is built the whole of man's experiential existence" (2005, 71, 86). Playing is not attached to any particular activity, but is a mode of "apperception as opposed to perception," a way of "seeing everything afresh all the time" (1986, 41). The scope of play encompasses

J. LeJeune (✉)
Department of History and Political Science, Georgia Southwestern State University, Americus, GA, USA

M.H. Bowker, A. Buzby (eds.), *D.W. Winnicott and Political Theory*, DOI 10.1057/978-1-137-57533-3_11 an endless variety of contexts and activities, ranging from artistic, cultural, and work-related enterprises, to sexuality, the old-fashioned vacation, to even mopping a floor or looking at a tree (see Winnicott 1986, 39–54). Indeed, "everything we do can be done creatively" (1986, 48), and "in playing, and perhaps only in playing, the child or adult is free to be creative" (2005, 71) in a manner that nurtures a genuine sense of self (see Mehdi, this volume).

Play is both psychologically healthy for adults and wonderfully amorphous. Yet curiously, Winnicott throughout his writings privileges one adult *playground* over others—namely the field of *cultural experience*, which links individuals in a healthy society and finds its roots in healthy childhood development. "There is a direct development," Winnicott writes, "from transitional phenomena to playing, and from playing to shared playing, and from this to cultural experiences" (2005, 69). Cultural experience starts "*in the potential space between a child and the mother when experience has produced in the child a high degree of confidence in the mother*, that she will not fail to be there if suddenly needed," and this healthy beginning "leads on to the whole area of man's inheritance, including the arts, the myths of history, the slow march of philosophical thought and the mysteries of mathematics, and of group management and of religion" (1986, 36, emphasis in original). Cultural experience is where adults as an integrated social unit share objects of meaning and play. If in early playing "the child … invests chosen external phenomena with dream meaning and feeling" (2005, 69) and this meaning becomes real when the mother recognizes it, then in cultural experience citizens and neighbors also invest meaning in shared symbolic objects, and this meaning is reflected (even when contested) by others. But to affirm this is to beget more questions: what do "transitional objects" and "potential space" mean in the context of culture? Who or what replaces the mother, and in what ways do cultural objects function as transitional objects? If adults do need a playground, what makes "cultural experience" the preeminent playground for adults?

Winnicott's statements on culture become especially interesting when contrasted with his less sanguine remarks on the role of playfulness in politics. In a speech delivered at the peak of the 1968 student protests (just two months removed from the French May Days), for example, Winnicott said it was "exciting that adolescence has become vocal and active, but the adolescent striving that makes itself felt over the whole world today needs to be met, needs to be given reality by an act of confrontation" (2005, 202). Winnicott did not criticize the student protestors. Indeed, in one sense he celebrated them, for "[i]t is salutary to remember that the present student unrest and its manifest expression may be in part a product of the attitude we are proud to have attained towards baby care, and child care" (2005, 202–203). But he sternly distanced their playfulness and creativity from responsible politics: "Let the young alter society and teach grown-ups how to see the world afresh; but where there is a challenge of the growing boy or girl, there let the adult meet the challenge. And it will not necessarily be nice. In the unconscious fantasy these are matters of life and death" (2005, 203).

The contrast between Winnicott's uninhibited embrace of playful cultural experience and his reluctance to treat politics as a space of play and creativity offers an opportunity to examine the role of political participation in a fulfilling human life. The problem is salient not only in the history of political thought, where republican and democratic theorists have long championed direct political participation as the highest form of freedom and public happiness (while others of course have disagreed)—but in analytic theory as well. For, as Ryan LaMothe (2014, 291) has written, "there is a correlation between political realities and patient-analyst interaction and goals." In other words, just as a therapist's political views or conclusions might inadvertently draw the patient into a position of unhappy compliance, so too can the stuff of politics—political equality or inequality, ideological conformity or genuine freedom of thought—decisively effect the balance of free personality development and unhappy compliance in a society at large.

In what follows, then, I seek to better understand the problem of "adults in the playground" in Winnicott's work and the normative distance he establishes between cultural experience and political action in this regard. To deepen this project, I engage Winnicott's work with that of political theorist Hannah Arendt. Recent scholarship (Honig 2013; LaMothe 2014) has recognized important connections between Winnicott's and Arendt's work, and Arendt is important for our purposes for two reasons: First, Arendt like Winnicott gives pride of place in her normative political theory to a mode of playful and spontaneous being-in-the world which renders available the most profound form of human happiness—what she calls "public happiness." At the same time, however, Arendt differs from Winnicott by locating this profound creative activity squarely in the realm of politics, rather than the field of cultural experience. What explains this divergence? Second, I will argue that the question of *play* and its location in Winnicott's and Arendt's respective philosophies of the best life—one in cultural experience, the other in political action—translate directly into radically different philosophies of education.

Winnicott's Theory of Play

We begin by considering what Winnicott means by *play* and how it contributes to a healthy and happy life. In Winnicott's work *play* is action entwined with *creativity*—"an experience, always a creative experience ... in the space-time continuum, a basic form of living" (2005, 67). And "in playing, and perhaps only in playing, the child or adult is free to be creative" (2005, 71). The notion of creativity leaves much to the imagination: "I am hoping that the reader will accept a general reference to creativity," says Winnicott, "keeping it to the meaning that refers to a colouring of the whole attitude to external reality" (2005, 87). And while *play* and *creativity* assume an extremely broad scope, Winnicott divides all lived experience into two polarized states of being, namely the creative and uncreative: "It is the creative apperception more than anything else that makes the individual feel that life is worth living," he writes, and the "two alternatives of living creatively or uncreatively can be very sharply contrasted" (2005, 87–88).

It is perhaps easier to understand living uncreatively than its opposite. It is to experience "a relationship to external reality which is one of compliance" (2005, 87)—to act (or not) out of fear or compulsion. In contrast, *play* is open and precarious, an "immensely exciting ... interplay of personal psychic reality and the experience of control of actual objects. This is the precariousness of magic itself, magic that arises in intimacy, in the relationship that is being found to be reliable" (2005, 64). The "significant moment" of *play* occurs when "*the child surprises himself or herself*," and when there is "mutual playing .... *This playing has to be spontaneous, and not compliant or acquiescent* (2005, 68, emphasis in original). It is "helpful to think of the *preoccupation* that characterizes the playing of a young child. The content does not matter. What matters is the near-withdrawal state, akin to the *concentration* of older children and adults" (2005, 69, emphasis in original). Correspondingly among adults Winnicott associates *play* with the "intense experiencing that belongs to the arts and to religion and to imaginative living, and to creative scientific work" (2005, 19).

In a cumbersome fashion, we might summarize *play* in Winnicott's theory of psychological health as a "meaningful interaction with the external world in which a person autonomously assigns importance and meaning to actions autonomously performed and objects autonomously manipulated or experienced, where autonomy signals the absence of coercion and compliance." And according to Winnicott this autonomous process happens in a particular sequence: "(a) relaxation in conditions of trust based on experience; (b) creative, physical, and mental activity manifest in play; (c) the summation of these experiences forming the basis for a sense of self" (2005, 75). Let us call these steps *trust*, *play*, and *reflection*.

Why is *trust* important for facilitating *play*, and why is *trust* important for psychological health? In Winnicott's work, the concept of *true self* is the key term that links *trust* with *play*, and is defined as "the theoretical position from which come the spontaneous gesture and the personal idea. The spontaneous gesture is the true self in action. Only the true self can be creative and only the true self can feel real. Whereas a true self feels real, the existence of a False Self results in a feeling unreal or a sense of futility" (1982, 148). *False Self* in turn arises when a perceived need for compliance and acquiescence generates an artificial presentation of oneself dictated by the terms of the world or audience rather than one's own, and one lives at a distance from the spontaneous gesture of the *true self*. This distance is a powerful source of pain and alienation. And from a clinical standpoint the degrees of false self range widely, from total absorption and total loss of true self (manifest in "actors ... who can only act, and who are completely at a loss when not in a role"); to a false self which recognizes itself as such (and either allows the true self a "secret life" or "[searches] for conditions which will make it possible for the true self to come into its own"); to finally a false self that actually exists "In health" alongside the true self, and is "represented by the whole organization of the polite and mannered social attitude." The latter false self represents a healthy compromise, whereby polite social manners which allow one to get along in the world (false self) combine with a firm and autonomous sense of when compromise "ceases to become allowable when the issues become crucial" (true self) (1982, 143, 150). Winnicott calls this healthy social integration.

Crucially, the theoretical position of *true self* is only realized when *trust* establishes a prior theoretical position which Winnicott calls a *potential space* or *intermediate space* of security and reliability between mother and child. Thus, for example, Winnicott distinguishes between the *good-enough* mother who adapts to the child and provides for the child in a manner that offers full confidence and absolute security, eventually developing a secure *potential space* between the mother and child within which the latter feels free to *play* and assign meaning to the world without being punished or ignored, and the *not good-enough mother* who does not do this, whether through neglect or failing to adapt, and this in a manner that ultimately renders the child too fearful or compliant to *playfully* engage the world in any genuine sense.

To anticipate our next section, a mother's adaptive and nurturing relation with the child—the creation of a secure *potential space* of free and creative activity—becomes a model for Winnicott of larger social and cultural forces which steer adolescents and adults personalities in the same manner. The challenge for the healthy community at large toward its citizens is thus analogous to that of a mother to her child as he approaches maturity—namely, to establish a facilitating environment for play in which the *true self* may not only flourish, but maintain its integrity as it is forced to adapt to the realities of the world. In early child-rearing this represents the gradual movement from a parent's total adaptation to the infant's needs (which initially creates a sense of omnipotence in the infant)to "a series of failures of adaptation" which "are again a kind of adaptation because they are related to the growing need of the child for meeting reality" (1982, 96). The mother's graduated failures to adapt do not destroy the *potential space* because they are (ideally) carefully calibrated to the child's ability to absorb them without trauma or disillusion, while also teaching the child to (mildly) adapt to the world. Indeed throughout, "[c]onfidence in the mother makes an intermediate playground here, where the idea of magic originates .... I call this a playground because play starts here" (2005, 64).

This element of "magic" finally brings us to the third phase of *play*, or *reflection*, which in turn corresponds to those objects—what Winnicott calls *transitional objects*—which mother and child view together and attribute a shared magical meaning that initially comes from the child. For example, a child spontaneously holds a bag and shakes it and finds it funny—the adult's acknowledgment of this humor, laughing with the baby, establishes the bag as a symbolic, magical object that means "funny" and that both stands *between* and *links* them, "simultaneously a symbol of separateness and of union through communication" (2005, 58). Later, a hat or umbrella or other article comes to be associated with a particular family member—the child does not say "umbrella" but rather "Mama!" and the *reflection* of this meaning by others—perhaps the adult's repetition of "Mama!" rather than insisting on "umbrella," establishes firmly the object's newly ascribed and shared meaning. This is the third phase of play—the *reflection* in others of the magical meaning which the child places in an object, and which in turn helps build a shared world of magical and meaningful objects between them.

Transitional objects are thus more than objects of imagination; they are objects of relation which hold a shared symbolic meaning or importance among different people. They are different from random objects in a "state of nature" to which we pay no attention, as well as from private objects which we meaningfully possess but hide from the public. Instead they separate people because they are literally in between them; but they also link people because of a quality that gives them symbolic cultural meaning—namely, the reciprocal common knowledge among those who pay attention to these objects that others are paying attention to them as well, and the reciprocal common knowledge among those who attach symbolic meaning to them that others attach meaning to them as well, even if that meaning might be contested. Viewing transitional objects in *this* manner allows Winnicott to make the transition "from transitional phenomena to playing, and from playing to shared playing, and from this to cultural experiences" (2005, 69).

Winnicott on Culture, Society, and Democracy

In practice, what does the transition from transitional phenomena to playing, and from playing to shared playing, and from shared playing to cultural experience actually look like? Where do we see Winnicott's vision of transitional phenomena and potential spaces in the adult world?

In a recent article, Bonnie Honig (2013) offers one powerful analysis of democratic politics in this regard, "[analogizing] Winnicott's observations about infants' transitional objects and citizens' attachments to public things" (Honig 2013, 62) in a healthy democracy. "In health," Honig argues, "democracy is rooted in common love for and contestation of public things" and "the public love of public objects" (Honig 2013, 60, 65). With this in mind Honig tackles the recent controversy over defunding Public Broadcasting Service(PBS) and the cultural symbolism of public things like Sesame Street and Big Bird. Though these cultural objects lie outside the traditional democratic process, their existence and our joint attention to them establishes a shared sense of culture and meaning. If a majority of Americans grew up with Big Bird, the shared symbolism of Big Bird and whether we continue to support him and Sesame Street is not trivial to our democratic culture. Honig cites other symbolic objects—ranging from a constitution, to a piece of Plymouth Rock, and a public park among others—to illustrate this broader point.

Honig establishes concretely how Winnicott's descriptive thesis regarding how the early development of symbolic capacity in the potential space between child and mother forms the basis of a broader shared social and political culture among adults—that is, how the "intermediate area of experience ... constitutes the greater part of the infant's experience, and throughout life is retained in the intense experiencing that belongs to the arts and to religion and to imaginative living" (2005, 19). Indeed, Honig achieves a level of concreteness that Winnicott often avoided by design. For, as Winnicott readily acknowledges, "I have used the term 'cultural experience' as an extension of the idea of transitional phenomena and of play without being certain that I can define the word 'culture' .... In using the 'word culture' I am thinking of the inherited tradition" (2005, 133). Elsewhere as previously noted, Winnicott associates cultural experience with "the whole area of man's inheritance, including the arts, the myths of history, the slow march of philosophical thought and the mysteries of mathematics, and of group management and of religion .... [I]t is dominated by dream ... [and] starts *in the potential space between a child and the mother when experience has produced in the child a high degree of confidence in the mother*" (1986, 36, emphasis in original).

This latter passage is crucial, for it attaches to cultural experience all of the elements previously associated with healthy play and development during childhood—namely, the *trust* and reliability which established a *potential space* in which *true self* can emerge, play itself engaged within this potential space, and the reflection of symbolic meaning and others' joint attention to intermediate objects to which dream meaning is attached. All of this suggests that if cultural experience is indeed the preeminent playground for adults, it is precisely because the cultural realm plays the analogous role for the adult as the "good-enough" mother figure for developing children. And in this respect what Winnicott says about the individual in *society* overlaps considerably with his analysis of the individual in *culture*—namely, that of a relatively healthy person "his or her relationship to society" is precisely "an extension of the family," and therefore "in health a man or woman is able *to reach towards an identification with society without too great a loss of individual or personal impulse*" (1986, 27, emphasis in original). In this context, the space in which one acts or *plays* is the cultural realm that is recognized, nurtured, and (occasionally, but not too aggressively) challenged by society. Culture in turn is "the inherited tradition ... something that is in the common pool of humanity, into which individuals and groups of people may contribute, and from which we may all draw if *we have somewhere to put what we find*" (2005, 133, emphasis added).

If this is Winnicott's normative-descriptive account of culture and society, what work is left for politics and democracy? What role does political action or public participation play in the healthy and creative human life? Winnicott broaches this topic in a number of essays including "Discussion of War Aims" (1940), "Some Thoughts on the Meaning of the Word Democracy" (1950), "Berlin Walls" (1969), and "The Place of Monarchy" (1970). He argues, or so I will suggest, that politics is not only a realm of dangerous consequences for the world, but also of traumatic risks for the healthy human personality. Political space is no potential space, and politics is no playground. And this holds in even the most stable of parliamentary democracies.

Though Winnicott spends some time comparing the "maturity" and "immaturity" of authoritarian politics in contexts like Mussolini's Italy and Hitler's Germany, the bulk of analysis tackles parliamentary democracy; and Winnicott's idea of *democracy* is in turn richly entwined with an analytical concept of *freedom* that is inherently threatening to the human personality: "Freedom puts a strain on the individual's whole personality," writes Winnicott, for in freedom one "is left with no logical excuse for the angry or aggressive feelings except the insatiability of his own greed. And he has no one to give or withhold permission to do what he wants to do—in other words, to save him from the tyranny of a strict conscience. No wonder people fear not only freedom, but also the idea of freedom and the giving of freedom" (1986, 215). The context of this passage (in "Discussion of War Aims") is expressly political, and Winnicott affirms here in especially direct terms that political space is not a potential space—if anything it's the opposite.

The heavy burdens of political responsibility to one's conscience can trigger a variety of unhealthy responses. One might, for example, adopt hero-worship or stubborn attachment to a principle as a means of transferring responsibility for one's own judgment to another person or entity; or alternatively, one may simply vanish from the democratic space altogether out of inhibition. The first outcome results in false self or "poverty of personality" (1986, 216), an "antisocial tendency" that "is not an identification with authority that arises out of self-discovery," but rather "a sense of frame without sense of picture, a sense of form without retention of spontaneity. This is a prosociety tendency that is anti-individual" (1986, 244). Meanwhile the second possibility—withdrawal from the realm of freedom and politics—threatens to undermine democracy itself by absolving citizens from personal responsibility and leaving power lying in the streets for anyone to grab. So what is to be done?

How can responsible political activity be undertaken without threatening man's healthy conscience?

Winnicott's remarkable solution is the "secret ballot." In a description of British parliamentary democracy, for example, Winnicott writes:

> It is obvious that the working of the democratic parliamentary system … depends on the survival of the monarchy, and *paripassu* the survival of the monarchy depends on the people's feeling that they really can, by voting, turn a government out in a parliamentary election or get rid of a prime minister. It is assumed here that the turning out of a government or a prime minister must be on the basis of feeling, as expressed in the secret ballot, and not on the basis of the poll (Gallup or other) that fails to give expression to deep feeling or to unconscious motivation or to trends that seem illogical. (1986, 264)

Here, the secret ballot allows the average citizen to participate in politics—and in the process assume a light sense of responsibility for the healthy functioning of democracy—while also shielding his or her conscience from attack by transferring the heavy sense of responsibility for political action onto the person they elect. In other words, "[t]he election of a person implies that the electors believe in themselves as persons, and therefore believe in the person they vote for. The person elected has the opportunity to act as a person" (1986, 249). Indeed, the secret election of a *person* (as opposed to, say, a party or policy) is crucial for Winnicott, precisely because it allows for the *conscious* transference of *personal* responsibility—responsibility for the political power which the secret ballot grants to man's *unconscious* drives, which themselves are inexorably tied to personal elements of greed, conquest, and destruction—based on a mature and healthy sense of *trust* established between elector and elected. Via the secret ballot, in other words, democratic citizens allow their real subconscious drives to dominate politics while entrusting others to make the best of their empowerment.

In the long run, this works for democracy because the political actor who wins the election does *not* herself have the luxury of acting in secret—she instead acts in full public view; and where reelection is at stake the elected are even less likely to let their own greedy and aggressive instincts dominate their actions. This also preserves the psychological health of the vast majority of democratic citizens, for whom the thin burden of political responsibility vested in the secret ballot places no great strain on the psyche. These observations help explain Winnicott's otherwise puzzling statement that a "referendum," which is often associated with meaningful direct democracy, in fact "has nothing to do with democracy"—because in a referendum policy proposals are explicit and one's responsibility for policy outcomes more direct and burdensome. Under these circumstances (as they are all the time for the elected politician), one's decisions are likely to be determined by the moral, ethical, or social codes of conduct which one feels *ought* to steer one's decision. In sum, "there is only room for the expression of the *conscious* wish" (1986, 250), because one's conscience is directly involved.

Hannah Arendt on Political Action and Public Happiness

In an influential study, Aristide Zolberg links the recent history of revolutionary enthusiasm in France from 1848, 1871, the 1936 Popular Front, and 1940s Resistance, to the 1968 May Days via the concept of "moments of madness" and "political enthusiasm" in which "the wall between the instrumental and the expressive collapses," participants feel that "'all is possible'," and "politics bursts its bounds to invade all life" (Zolberg 1972, 182–183). More recently, in his account of the 2011 Occupy movement Todd Gitlin writes that "as the encampments endured and grew, a demoralized left shook itself, stood up, and found to its amazement not only that it existed but that it radiated energy, and that energy, in the social world as in the material world, made things happen .... It produced its own satisfactions" (Gitlin 2012, 46–47). Of the same movement Roger Berkowitz wrote that "[t]he protestors are enjoying themselves. For some critics, this is evidence of the lack of seriousness of the protestors and evidence that they are spoiled and naïve elites with nothing better to do with their time. But what is wrong with bringing joy into politics?" (Berkowitz 2011). These observations remind us that for many it is precisely in politics that free and spontaneous action is most meaningful and satisfying. They also remind us that politics is where *play* is most dangerous, for, as André Green suggests in counterpoint to Winnicott, "I am not even sure that play belongs to health," because "the activity of play can become distorted, corrupted, and perverted, in society as well as individuals" (Green 2005, 11). Green mentions "the Roman games, or playing a kind of football with the heads of the defeated enemies in Latin America, or playing Russian roulette; today, even football matches become excuses for assassinations" (Green 2005, 11).

Political theorist Hannah Arendt tried to solve this problem of combining the responsibility of political action with the exhilaration of something like play. She saw in *political action* not only an essential component of the best human life, but an indispensable element of *play* in public action that makes people happy. Like Winnicott, Arendt takes something analogous to play seriously and associates play with the best human life; but contra Winnicott, Arendt insists that we *do* allow play into politics, precisely because it is the most profound and meaningful play available to humans.

In the Preface to an important collection of essays, Arendt quotes French poet René Char recounting his experience in the French Resistance in terms that uncannily resemble Winnicott's.

> Char had discovered that he who "joined the Resistance, *found* himself," that he ceased to be "in quest of [himself] without mastery, in naked unsatisfaction," that he no longer suspected himself of "insincerity," of being "a carping, suspicious actor of life," that he could "afford to go naked." In this nakedness, stripped of all masks—of those which society assigns to its members as well as those which the individual fabricates for himself in his psychological reactions against society—they had been visited for the first time in their lives by an apparition of freedom, not, to be sure, because they acted against tyranny and things worse than tyranny … but because they had become "challengers," had taken the initiative upon themselves and therefore, without knowing or even noticing it, had begun to create that public space between themselves where freedom could appear. (Arendt 1993, 4)

Char's references to finding oneself, nakedness, and moving from an unsatisfying insincerity to its opposite recall Winnicott's dichotomy of the *true* and *false self*. It is as if the experience of resistance under an extraordinary circumstance—being thrown willy-nilly into a crisis in which the old social and political banisters had been obliterated, and the compliant masks once worn in society had suddenly become useless—established precisely those conditions under which the *true* and spontaneous self could surface. Having been set against their will in the extraordinary circumstance of *having to act*, people instinctively rediscovered their *capacity to act*—their capacity to autonomously choose a course, to take an initiative, to speak and act spontaneously, and in the process to create and insert both themselves and their actions into a public world.

Action is another difficult term to define, and as with Winnicott, with Arendt one benefits from something like an inductive approach: Throughout her writings Arendt describes action in terms of "words and deeds," equates action with freedom, locates action in a public space among equals, and insists on action's public character. *Action*'s most intuitive quality is its spontaneity, or what she calls *natality*—the quality of new beginnings which all humans possess (Arendt 1958, 9). Time and again Arendt hammers the point that man by nature is a source of "miracles" with the power to interrupt that "which always happens automatically and therefore always must appear to be irresistible" (Arendt 1993, 170): "The fact that man is capable of action means that the unexpected can be expected from him, that he is able to perform what is infinitely improbable. And this again is possible only because each man is unique, so that with each birth something uniquely new comes into the world" (Arendt 1958, 178).

In a world laced with apparently automatic processes—Arendt has in mind our passive submission to the "forward" thrust of science and the bureaucratization of politics—man's capacity to interrupt these processes and do something entirely unexpected is easily forgotten, and the world simply imposes itself. But the joy of *natality*, the need to experience life as if we could interrupt these processes, and the malaise that results when we cannot is embedded in our nature: "With word and deed we insert ourselves into the human world," writes Arendt, "and this insertion is like a second birth … not forced upon us by necessity, like labor, and not prompted by utility, like work …. [I]ts impulse springs from the beginning which came into the world when we were born and to which we respond by beginning something new on our own initiative" (1958, 176–177). "Because they are *initium*, newcomers and beginners by virtue of birth, men take initiative, are prompted into action" (177).

A second and related impulse which drives humans to *act* Arendt calls the "'the passion for distinction' which John Adams held to be 'more essential and remarkable than any other human faculty'," that "'[w]herever men, women, or children, are to be found, whether they be old or young, rich or poor, high or low, wise or foolish, ignorant or learned, every individual is seen to be strongly actuated by a desire to be seen, heard, talked of, approved and respected by the people about him, and within his knowledge'" (Arendt 2006, 110). As a general matter of fact, Arendt suggests, humans enjoy in a special way the experience of excelling among their peers.

The combination of the two Arendt calls *public happiness*—the extraordinary joy of acting in the public realm among one's fellow citizen combined with the reward of memory, esteem, and distinction. Humans can access many peer groups in work, sports, hobbies, and elsewhere.

But no artificial grouping offers greater potential for more meaningful and extraordinary actions, in front of more of one's peers, remembered and followed further into the future, than the city or *polis*. For, Arendt writes in a passage worth quoting at length:

> The original, prephilosophic Greek remedy for this frailty [of human affairs] had been the foundation of the *polis*. The *polis*, as it grew out of and remained rooted in the Greek pre-*polis* experience and estimate of what makes it worthwhile for men to live together (*syzēn*), namely, the 'sharing of words and deeds', had a twofold function. First, it was intended to enable men to do permanently, albeit under certain restrictions, what otherwise had been possible only as an extraordinary and frequent enterprise for which they had to leave their households .... The second function of the *polis*, again closely connected with the hazards of action as experienced before its coming into being, was to offer a remedy for the futility of action and speech; for the chances that a deed deserving fame would not be forgotten. (1958, 196–197)

The *polis* secures the space among peers in which novel *actions* that are meaningful to the entire community might take place. It also ensures that actions esteemed by one's peers will not be easily forgotten, that one's actions will in effect live on after one's death.

The space in which action happens Arendt calls the *space of appearances*, and it is possible to draw meaningful analogies between Winnicott's notion of the *potential space* and *transitional objects* on one hand, and Arendt's notion of the *space of appearances* and what I will call *public things* (see Honig 2013), on the other. The *space of appearances*, says Arendt, "comes into being wherever men are together in the manner of speech and action, and therefore predates and precedes all formal constitution of the public realm and the various forms of government" (Arendt 1958, 199). In one instantiation the *space of appearances* is a literal gathering of human peers, equals, in the presence of a common political issue or even a physical thing to which meaning (even contested meaning) is generally ascribed and debated among the group. In this case humans on the spot create a space between them for action and deliberation within which symbolic or political objects both link and separate them through a shared experience of meaning. In another instantiation the *space of appearances* refers more generally to the metaphorical gathering of peers, not necessarily face to face but always facing the same thing, that is literally constituted by a long term agreement, or constitution among them that both links and separates them, stands between and joins them in a set of "social rituals, structures, narratives, disciplines, and discourses [which] inform citizens (and non-citizens) about whom to trust and where their loyalties lie" (LaMothe 2014, 293).

These common expectations, particularly when guaranteed by a constitution, help establish a secure *space of appearances*, one might say a *potential space*, within which citizens can feel comfortable *acting* in the political realm—indeed, arguably the principal function of the Bill of Rights today is precisely to guarantee the integrity and security of this *potential space* (albeit with occasional failures) to acting citizens in the same reliable manner with which a mother assures, adapts to, and challenges her child. At the same time, those *public things* to which all (or most) members of a community look, and to which all (or most) attach meaning, and about which all (or most) discuss or deliberate (including the constitution itself)—these are the *transitional objects* which give citizens a meaningful world which links them together despite their separation.

On its face then, an analogy is reasonably suggested between the creative happiness and *play* rendered available to citizens at large in Winnicott's realm of culture and Arendt's political space of appearances. But I am not so sure Winnicott would make this move. All of Arendt's happy positioning of democratic participation and the joys of action notwithstanding, what she proposes regarding political action as a sphere of human creativity, spontaneity, and a realm of distinction is incredibly dangerous. First, it is dangerous to the world—political affairs are high stakes, and the rash pursuit of distinction can easily lead wannabe heroes down a road of rash imprudence and experimenting—indeed treating politics like a game. Moreover, political affairs are themselves extremely unpredictable even for the most prudent, let alone the most playful.

And finally, the potential damage of unpredictable political action affects not only the world, but the self. The citizen who dedicates herself to *acting* in the public suffers an unpredictable fate in at least two respects. The first involves what Arendt calls the unpredictability and "boundlessness" of action: "Because the actor always moves among and in relation to other acting beings, he is never merely a 'doer' but always at the same time a sufferer," Arendt writes, because the consequences of action "are boundless, because action ... acts into a medium where every reaction becomes a chain reaction and where every process is the cause of new processes" (Arendt 1958, 190). We cannot predict the consequences of our actions, and as actors we suffer these consequences not only in the world, but as they ultimately become attached to our public personality without our ever having consented or even conceived of them. Second, and following this point, in entering politics we place ourselves *not* in a secure space in which the *true self* might safely emerge, but rather a dangerous and incredibly unpredictable place in which the identity that is revealed is subject not only to the unpredictability of human affairs, but the subjective and often harsh judgment of our peers: Indeed, "[w]ith word and deed we insert *ourselves* into the human world," writes Arendt—we become *public objects* ourselves—and because of this "*nobody* knows whom he reveals when he discloses himself in deed or word" (1958, 176, 180, emphasis added).

For this reason, and here I will only mention the point—Arendt locates the *ultimate* source of reliability and protection, the security to act spontaneously, in the maintenance at all costs of what she calls the *private realm*, the four walls within which one can always leave the public glare and hide in seclusion. Ironically, then, Arendt like Winnicott advocates a kind of split personality, because for one to suffer the incredible damage to the personality that the harsh light of the public threatens to cast, even as one participates in the most exhilarating and meaningful activities available to humans, requires an absolute dissociation of private from public self, a cognizance of the distance between the *persona* one presents in public, and the private self which can always find comfort and security within the four walls of home and family. It is for this reason, among others, that Arendt showed especial appreciation for the "extraordinary political science" of the Romans, for the "full development of the life of hearth and family into an inner private space we owe to the extraordinary political sense of the Roman people who, unlike the Greeks, never sacrificed the private to the public, but on the contrary understood that these two realms could exist only in a form of coexistence" (1958, 59).

Education and the Qualities of Adulthood

My argument to this point has reached two conclusions. First is that Winnicott and Arendt share an appreciation of play as an essential component of the best human life, and their work draws us to two structural conditions of play—(a) a secure and reliable space which encourages or enables creative and spontaneous action; and (b) commonly recognized symbolic objects which make actions meaningful by establishing a world between people. Winnicott calls these a "potential space" and "transitional object," while Arendt calls them the "space of appearances" and the "public thing," respectively. Our second conclusion is that Winnicott and Arendt, despite these concordant beginnings, diverge in their normative placement of play in adult settings. For Winnicott, adult play properly belongs in a cultural sphere removed from the problems of political responsibility and in which a true self feels free to act spontaneously and creatively. For Arendt alternatively, the most meaningful adult play happens in a political space where adults combine public risk with responsibility and a palpable threat to one's public identity. To conclude, I explain why Winnicott and Arendt, to establish these two very different playgrounds for adults, offer two correspondingly different models of childhood education.

For Winnicott the problem of education—and this from math to morality—characteristically centers on establishing the theoretical position of *true self*. This does *not* entail an absence of challenge or resistance from the teacher, for as already discussed even a healthy personality is typically *split* in social situations, if only to get along in the world. But it does entail special attunement to facilitating the free and spontaneous development of moral and intellectual insight and creative problem solving, while minimizing the salience of authority, compulsion, and compliance.

Notably, even *praise* approached the wrong way can inhibit the child's healthy sense of *true self*. On this point, Winnicott relates the experience of a patient aged ten who "is living in a good home," but who after "having been consistently difficult and unsuccessful" at school "has started to learn and do well. Everyone is delighted and he was referred to as 'a twentieth-century miracle'" (1986, 67). Presumably this praise should make the child happy, but the opposite has happened—immediately after his first "good" grade, the child began dreaming of his own murder and having difficulty sleeping. Soon thereafter he became disruptive at school, deliberately "making the masters at school angry with him" (1986, 68). What happened?

The child's problem began when his academic success shifted from a natural development of his own talent and capacities to a form of compliance: "In one language, he can employ a false self which pleases everyone, but this makes him feel awful .... He is sorely tempted, therefore, to reassert something which is more along the lines of a true self and to be continuously defiant and unsatisfactory, although this too produces no satisfactory answer to his problem" (1986, 68). Winnicott then describes the modern school exam—and one might add the contemporary elementary and high school academic experience *in toto*—as a fount of False-Self cultivation which rewards "the individual's capacity to comply and to tolerate being false, to some degree, in order to gain something in relation to society which can be used while life is being worked out after the phase in which a student's privileges and obligations provide a very special place, which unfortunately does not last forever" (1986, 68–69). The ten-year-old in question was fortunate in that his rapid turn to delinquency signaled awareness of this problem and a sign of hope that leads to recovery. Others will reach this point many years later, prolonging their suffering and compounding with interest the sense of a life long-lived chasing a goal that has lacked personal meaning. Such was the proverbial mid-life crisis which struck a patient Winnicott describes elsewhere, a "middle-aged woman who had a very successful False Self but who had the feeling all her life that she had not started to exist, and that she had always been looking for a means of getting to her True Self" (1982, 142).

All this returns us to the question of how education for Winnicott accomplishes the dual task of supporting *true self* while socializing the young to enter the world with a mildly split (that is to say, only mildly acquiescent and socialized) and healthy personality. And here, in the critical context of moral and cultural education, Winnicott adopts a familiar strategy which prioritizes spontaneity, creativity, and adaptation: "The good alternative [to moral education]," he writes, "has to do with the provision of those conditions for the infant and child that enable such things as trust and 'belief in', and ideas of right and wrong, to develop out of the working of the individual child's inner processes" (1982, 94). Rather than indoctrinate the young with moral and religious ideals—to compel them with the kind of authority that will only lead to projection of a false self—parents should recognize the "good" moral sense that emerges from within a child in its natural development in a "good-enough" environment, and then aid the child by "labeling" the child's natural intuition with such terms as right, wrong, God, and devil: "The labeling socializes the otherwise personal phenomena" (1982, 95).

This same "principle affecting the handing on of moral values applies likewise to the handing on the whole torch of culture and civilization"—whether this involves cultural or religious symbols like the Holy Cross, or the beauty of Mozart, or the general morals, religion, and traditions of family, none can effectively or healthily be imposed upon a child; instead, the best one can do is offer these items neutrally, either figuratively or literally "leaving any cultural phenomena lying round for the child to catch hold of and to adopt" (1982, 101). Indeed, as we have seen, at one point Winnicott applies his reasoning to education in mathematics:

"Why not ask [students] to *guess* rather than to *calculate*, thus using their personal computers? I don't see why, in arithmetic, there is so much emphasis *on the accurate answer*. What about the fun of guessing? Or of playing around with ingenious methods? [...] [I]t must be fascinating to see how, in the teaching of mathematics, *one can catch on to the creative impulse*" (1986, 61).

This method of teaching at a young age is essential for the free and confident development of *true self*—or "unit status, the achievement which is basic to health in the emotional development of every human being," and upon which "the unit personality can afford to identify with wider units—say, the family or the home or the house .... And soon will be part of a social life of an ever-widening kind," including "political matters" (1986, 60). Given this approach to education and development, it is hardly surprising that Winnicott finds inspiration in youthful idealism and immaturity, for "[i]mmaturity is a precious part of the adolescent scene," and, "[i]n this is contained the most exciting features of creative thought" (2005, 198). But importantly, it is the adults' challenge to youth and assumption of responsibility for the world which gives it its "greatest asset: freedom to have ideas and to act on impulse" (2005, 202). Education of this sort is thus not a preparation for political action or responsibility, for its most exciting product does not transfer to the political realm. Winnicott instead prepares the healthy personality to flourish in the less dangerous realm of cultural experience, where such ideals not only achieve social and interpersonal currency, but do so in a potential space of creative action.

Hannah Arendt was no less concerned than Winnicott with the role of play and spontaneity, natality, and meaning in the best human life; but in order to save political action from the destruction of thin liberal proceduralism she turns Winnicott's philosophy of education on its head. Arendt like Winnicott begins her statement on education (in the essay "The Crisis in Education" (1958)) with a basic statement of creative principle, for "the essence of education is natality, the fact that human beings"—and by this Arendt means novel and entirely new human beings—"are *born* into the world" (Arendt 1993, 174, emphasis added). Arendt proffers her philosophy of education with the new and creative in mind, "for the sake of what is new and revolutionary" (Arendt 1993, 196, 192–193). We are always educating "for a world out of joint" (Arendt 1993, 192), she writes, a world of perpetual change. And this is proper, for absent the perennial entry (and exit?) of new people, life on earth would risk becoming a cycle of boredom. Thus it is in terms that first seem ironic that Arendt harshly rebukes philosophies of education like Winnicott's (and John Dewey's), which assign to education what she considers a groundless and ultimately harmful form of play.

For those of Winnicott's ilk, Arendt writes, "[p]lay was looked upon as the liveliest and most appropriate way for a child to behave in the world, as the only form of activity that evolves spontaneously from his existence as a child. Only what can be learned through play does justice to his liveliness .... [L]earning in the old sense, by forcing a child into an attitude of passivity, compelled him to give up his own playful initiative" (Arendt 1993, 183). But Arendt offers at least two forceful objections to this philosophy of education. First is that, in the absence of authoritative standards of judgment and behavior, and the lack of assumption of responsibility for these things by adults, the school environment merely recreates a situation of stress and tension in the child's world that mirrors the adult world. Leaving kids to themselves in what amounts to an unadulterated playground where the children set the standards only creates a new and artificial social space of potential domination. The social world of children and young adults is a cruel and tyrannical world and simply an untenable situation for a child to deal with without damage occurring to the psyche—a Winnicottian false self indeed.

That such a situation is possible, let alone entertained by adults as the institutional norm, manifests a broader problem for Arendt which is the loss of basic standards, tradition, and moral authority on campus and in the classroom that has effectively turned children into adults—those who create and implement values—and the adults into children, precisely when the children are least prepared to do so and most vulnerable to the consequences particularly within their own social world. Put in Winnicott's terms, Arendt argues that by effectively removing, or at minimum emasculating the authority of the most basic and shared norms, rituals, and values of the community—by merely "leaving them lying around," as it were—Winnicott unwittingly destroys the essential *reliability* which basic moral and cultural and intellectual authority would otherwise bring to the child's world. This becomes especially important when children leave the home, for when children leave the home they also leave the reliable potential space provided by their parents for a new world that is fundamentally different and essentially unsafe if only because it exists outside those same four walls. In this new social context, or so Arendt argues, the only way to recreate this potential space, at least among children who are not yet mature enough to fully enter the world as adults, is through authority at the school. Shared cultural authority—what we might call a shared tradition—is pivotal for establishing a *potential space* of creative action and true self because when shared and recognized among students writ large, it provides the security and reliability that in fact does *not* exist in an otherwise tyrannical and potentially nihilistic children's world. Yes Winnicott sets the child free, but only to be devoured (cf. Arendt 1959 [2003]).

Arendt's second and more far reaching objection asks more fundamentally how education can indeed prepare the young to *act* creatively, spontaneously, boldly and courageously, yet also responsibly as mature adults in the political world. And on this point Arendt's answer is unequivocal, that education "[e]xactly for the sake of what is new and revolutionary in every child ... must be conservative" (Arendt 1993, 196, 192–193). In order for students to enter the world responsibly they must not be passively proffered elements of a world "lying around." Rather they must be actively *given* a world. Educators must tell the young what the world is like and where the world comes from. They must actively give the young our inherited cultural and traditional and historical and political symbols, and allow these symbols to rest in between youth and adult alike in order to become the basis of their mutual interest and meaning, discussion and debate. It is the educator's task to *give* the young a world they *can* share, "to mediate between the old and the new, so that his very profession requires of him an extraordinary respect for the past" (Arendt 1993, 193). The young are of course free to alter or change this world as they like, but they must nonetheless *enter* it together and in common with their peers and the adults.

The educator's authority in turn stems not from the grades he assigns or the depth of his intellect—but rather from a place we can only describe as "Winnicottian": for if "the teacher's *qualification* consists in knowing the world and being able to instruct others about it," then "his *authority* rests on his assumption of responsibility for it," for "[e]ducation is the point at which we decide whether we *love* the world enough to assume responsibility for it and by the same token save it[.]" "Vis-à-vis the child it is as though he were a representative of all adult inhabitants, pointing out the details and saying to the child: This is our world" (Arendt 1993, 189, 196, 189, emphasis added). If education can at least bring students to know the world—not *any* world, or a random gathering of worldly artifacts stumbled upon at random, but *our* world; and not by coercion and compliance, but by something more akin to sharing—by putting Mozart on the record player and insisting that *we* listen, rather than leaving him lying on the ground—then the youth will at least be able to enter the world not as naïve idealists with no sense of responsibility for the world (because they know nothing about it), nor stunted false personalities whose blind submission to the world has stifled their capacity to change it. Instead the world itself will come to have meaning, indeed will become the *public thing* par excellence which we share; and the young will judge, conserve, and transform the world with a responsibility that derives from the knowledge that one's actions always occur in a unique position between past and future—that is, in a world that existed before they were born, that will continue to exist long after they die, and which the never-ending stream of newcomers will contemplate with veneration or disgust.

References

Arendt, H. 1958. *The Human Condition.* Chicago, IL: University of Chicago Press.

———. 1993. *Between Past and Future: Eight Exercises in Political Thought.* New York: Penguin.

———. 1959[2003]. Reflections on Little Rock. In *Responsibility and Judgment*, ed. J. Kohn, 193–213. New York: Schocken.

———. 2006. *On Revolution.* New York: Penguin.

Berkowitz, R. 2011. The Politics of Anti-Political Protest: What to Make of OWS. *Democracy: A Journal of Ideas: Arguments Blog.*

Gitlin, T. 2012. *Occupy Nation: The Roots, the Spirit, and the Promise of Occupy Wall Street.* New York: Harper Collins.

Green, A. 2005. *Play and Reflection in Donald Winnicott's Writings.* London: Karnac.

Honig, B. 2013. The Politics of Public Things: Neoliberalism and the Routine of Privatization. *No Foundations* 10: 59–76.

LaMothe, R. 2014. Winnicott and Arendt: Bridging Potential and Political Spaces. *The Psychoanalytic Review* 101(2): 289–318.

Winnicott, D.W. 1982. *The Maturational Processes and the Facilitating Environment: Studies in the Theory of Emotional Development.* New York: International Universities Press.

———. 2005. *Playing and Reality.* London: Routledge.

———. 1986. *Home is Where We Start From: Essays By a Psychoanalyst*, ed. C. Winnicott, R. Shepherd, and M. Davis. New York: W.W. Norton.

Zolberg, A. 1972. Moments of Madness. *Politics and Society* 2(2): 183–207.

PART IV

Intersubjectivity, Justice, and Equality

CHAPTER 12

D.W. Winnicott, Ethics, and Race: Psychoanalytic Thought and Racial Equality in the United States

Alex Zamalin

This chapter argues that D.W. Winnicott's psychoanalytic thought offers a powerful set of ideas that can benefit political theorists interested in devising normative tools for achieving racial justice. Racism, which is structured by emotions of disgust, anger, and fear, as well as a theory of human difference and inferiority, is ripe for psychoanalytic inquiry. Yet, the vast majority of political theorists who have explored race psychoanalytically have largely used ideas like projection, displacement, and introjection to *diagnose* how racism develops and persists, in order to better grasp its roots and causes. Very few, however, have seriously examined how psychoanalysis can be used in a *prescriptive* way: to help diminish those very things—moral apathy, resentment, rage, and guilt—that foreclose serious democratic deliberation, mutual understanding, and collective action between white and black citizens.

Winnicott's work, I argue, not only represents the finest model of psychoanalysis as a normative enterprise, but his unique understanding of freedom, empathy, and creativity is especially valuable for developing an everyday ethics serviceable for racial egalitarianism. The first part of the

A. Zamalin (✉)
University of Detroit Mercy, Detroit, MI, USA

M.H. Bowker, A. Buzby (eds.), *D.W. Winnicott and Political Theory*,
DOI 10.1057/978-1-137-57533-3_12

chapter establishes the unappreciated importance of normative thinking for race. The vast majority of thinkers concerned with racial equality, I show, neglect theorizing the exemplary everyday judgment, communication, self-knowledge, and responsibility necessary for racial justice, focusing instead on structural remedies based in color-conscious public policies. The second part establishes how Winnicott's notion of freedom and what he calls "the capacity for concern" and "holding" and his idea of creativity—in different ways—significantly build upon, challenge, and deepen the contributions of key political thinkers. Turning to an empirical example, the third part argues that Winnicott's ideas were powerfully visible in two contemporary cases in the United States: the Greensboro Truth and Reconciliation Commission (Greensboro TRC) and the Mississippi Truth Project, both of which sought to create a space that allowed citizens to come to terms with past and current racism. Taking seriously Winnicott's work, the final part argues, not only challenges the widespread view that psychoanalysis cannot adequately address issues of timely political importance, but also adds a much-needed normative dimension to critical race studies.

The Evasion of Ethics in Contemporary Thinking About Racial Justice

Over the past several decades, political scientists have begun seriously examining the politics of American race relations. Those concerned with better understanding the nature of American political institutions have stressed the ways in which race has shaped welfare policy (Lieberman 1998), social security policy (Katznelson 2005), the ideology of political parties (Lowndes 2009), and party coalitions (Frymer 2010). By uncovering the way appeals to racially charged images of African Americans in the white mind have often been instrumental for authorizing certain public policies, these scholars have solidified our understanding of the way race has instrumental value in American politics. A smaller group of political theorists, however, more concerned with normative issues, has argued for the importance of taking color-conscious public policies like affirmative action seriously on the basis of equality (Appiah and Gutmann 1996), the value of remembering historical legacies of slavery (McCarthy 2009), and the abolition of white-skin privilege (Olson 2004).

Few scholars, however, have seriously theorized the kind of ethics of everyday life necessary for racial justice. In the Western tradition, ethics is defined as a normative system of acting in the world and treating others.

Among some of the most famous theories are the Aristotelian virtue perspective, which calls for individuals to cultivate such habits like generosity, courage, and truth (Aristotle 2009); the Kantian perspective, which stresses the importance of treating human beings as ends in themselves and ensuring all actions could be universalized (Kant 1998); and the utilitarian perspective, which argues for evaluating behavior on the basis of whether it could promote the greatest amount of happiness for the greatest number of people (Mill and Bentham 1987). There is obvious debate about which system is most effective for justice, but ethics is rarely, and certainly not fully, considered in contemporary discussions of racial inequality. Perhaps this contemporary aversion to ethics is due to the fact that ethics is imagined to be a deeply personal activity that cannot address structural inequalities; or that ethics cannot adequately address the problem of political or economic power, which needs to be confronted with collective, rather than personal, action; or because, given its focus on values as opposed to politics, ethics can easily supply the language for conservatives who want to blame racial inequality on African American moral deficiencies such as lack of industriousness.

Yet, even those few theorists who reject such a dichotomy—understanding that ethics is one essential aspect, if not precondition for collective action—and emphasize the importance of rigorous self-work such as democratic sacrifice (Allen 2004), democratic individualism, which entails recognizing one's complicity in facilitating injustice (Turner 2012), and the importance of self-examination, unconditional generosity and attentiveness to life's tragic essence (Zamalin 2015), do not adequately consider the value psychoanalysis can bring to such a project.

Since Freud, psychoanalysis has, of course, been first and foremost a practice and theory of clinical psychology meant to facilitate individual mental health and diminish pathology, which takes place in an interpersonal setting between patient and analyst. Nonetheless, as a complex system of meaning that deals extensively with aspects of human psychology like anxiety, fear, love, hate, apathy, and desire, psychoanalysis surely seems especially suited to racism, which is a worldview sustained by these emotions and attitudes.

To be sure, in certain political–theoretical key texts, psychoanalysis has been seriously applied to race. The most notable example was Frantz Fanon, drawing on Lacanian psychoanalysis, who famously argued in *Black Skin, White Masks* (2008) that racist language and culture under colonization deprived people of color of a sense of autonomy and dignity. Fanon understood that the feeling of black rage could never be eliminated precisely because people of color would always live within and fail to live up to the white normative standards over which they had no control. Rejecting the existentialist idea, popularized in the 1950s by Jean-Paul Sartre that individuals were simply born to choose, to carve out their own destinies in a world riven by absurdity, Fanon provocatively declared that black is not a man; the racialized subject was a void, a state of non-being. The African American writer, James Baldwin, writing in "Many Thousands Gone" ([1951] 1998), around the same time as Fanon, was himself more optimistic that whites could change their ways. Unlike Fanon, however, Baldwin's interest was in describing how race affected the white ego rather than the black one. But like Fanon, Baldwin never fully extended psychoanalysis in normative direction in order to develop a theory of everyday ethics.

Today, not only has psychoanalysis been regretfully relegated to literary studies and almost entirely expunged from American clinical psychology and academic psychology departments, but there has also been a general failure to extend psychoanalytic thinking to help theorize the kind of ethics necessary for racial justice. In what follows, I am to rectify this gap by turning to work of D.W. Winnicott. It should be noted at the outset that my aim is neither exhaustive nor comprehensive. Indeed, rather than carefully examining the nuances of Winnicott's political thought, I draw out the ways in which certain elements of his thought—elements, which, in a certain sense, are not necessarily inherently political and are sometimes reserved for the clinical context—can enrich contemporary political thinking about racial justice and the politics of racial inequality.

Winnicott, Political Theory, and the Politics of Racial Justice

Winnicott and the Subject of Politics

At the time of Winnicott's writing—especially during the 1950s and 1960s—the dominant academic postwar approach to addressing racial injustice was known as racial liberalism. This so-called approach to racial inequality consisted of compiling a massive amount of data about the demonstrable sociological and psychological effects of racism upon black Americans (Scott 1997). Of course, what at first was present merely as evidence for policies meant to provide black Americans more opportunities—in an effort to combat segregation and ghettoization—

would soon become Daniel Patrick Moynihan's famous argument in his internal policy memo, "The Negro Family: The Case for National Action" (1965) for strengthening black patriarchy—a problematic masculinist argument that was rightly criticized as deeply paternalistic and antifeminist (Rainwater and Yancey 1967).

Although he never directly tackled racial liberalism directly, Winnicott recognized the serious problem with expert knowledge, which aimed to develop a data-driven approach to human life. He commented that "when it comes to having our live planned for us, heaven help us if the thinkers take over. Firstly, they but seldom believe in the importance of the unconscious at all; and, secondly, even if they do, man's understanding of human nature is not yet so complete as to enable thinking things out entirely as to replace feeling" (Winnicott 1990, 170). The problem for Winnicott was that this social scientific approach missed the forest for the trees. In trying to plan for the future and assuming that the rational subject was a fixed truth, he missed the whole and complex human personality. For Winnicott, this personality was composed not only of immeasurable unconscious impulses that continued to frustrate the potential for absolute reason but also contained a great deal of dynamism and unpredictability. He explained: "The material for psychoanalytic research is essentially the human being ... being, feeling, acting, relating and contemplating" (Winnicott 1990, 175). The failure to study such human complexity, Winnicott warned, would not only help promote an unreflective state of being in which individuals would allow their aggression and greed to run rampant. It would also encourage individuals to displace their own difficult-to-digest characteristics upon others: "[N]o help comes to the sociologist through his denying the power of greed and aggression that every individual [experiences] .... The easy way out for the individual is for him to see the unpleasant parts of himself only when these appear in others" (Winnicott 1990, 212).

On the one hand, as a practicing psychoanalyst, Winnicott counseled clinical psychologists to cultivate psychoanalytic techniques to more adequately diagnose and rectify human pathology. On the other hand, as a psychoanalytic theorist, Winnicott, was also concerned with offering a normative-theoretical framework for helping people live fulfilling lives. Three core factors Winnicott believed would achieve this—freedom, empathy, and creativity—are still useful for theorizing and reframing issues of racial justice.

A. The Notion of Freedom: Spontaneity, Against Defensiveness

In some sense, Winnicott's conception of freedom was deeply apolitical. In his essay entitled "Freedom," he suggested that "freedom" "belongs to the psychiatric health in the individual" (Winnicott 1990, 229). If politics is about government and the distribution of goods, freedom for Winnicott was partly an emotional experience. In offering this definition, he eschewed the distinction long debated by political theorists: whether freedom is the negative protection of one's ability to do what they wish or the positive ability to flourish. Winnicott's conception of freedom followed in the footsteps of existentialists like Sartre (2000), who, despite recognizing it as having a tragic essence, thought freedom was deeply a personal experience, but, at the same time, Winnicott, unlike them, cast freedom more as an experience in which internal domination was absent. In the American political tradition, Ralph Waldo Emerson and Henry David Thoreau had famously theorized freedom as self-autonomy; for Emerson (2003) it was self-reliance against society's conventions, while for Thoreau (2004) it was about deep moral conscience, the willingness to stand up for what one thought was right. Freedom, for Winnicott, however, did not mean acting upon what one personally thought was right but—to put the point in psychological terms—was expressed through a lack of defensive organization. Freedom was a condition in which one was not driven by an excessive and monopolizing rigidity and knee-jerk responsiveness ushered forth by fear or anxiety.

The thinker whose thinking about freedom paralleled Winnicott was one of his contemporaries: the African American public intellectual, who was deeply concerned with racial justice, James Baldwin. For Baldwin (1963, 88), like Winnicott, freedom was incredibly hard to bear; it was something that in the words of the critical theorist, Erich Fromm, individuals wanted to escape (1960). As Winnicott explained in a way that would have certainly pleased Baldwin: "It is commonly assumed that we all love freedom and are willing to fight and die for it. That such assumption is untrue and dangerous is recognized by a few .... The truth seems to be that we like the idea of freedom and admire those who feel free, but at the same time we are afraid of freedom, and tend at times to be drawn towards being controlled" (Winnicott 1990, 214). Control gave one a sense of order and security; it provided one safeguards and barriers, orientations for what not to do. Control was, in a certain sense, something of an institution, with rules, regulations and procedures that could be followed. Freedom, in contrast, was something individuals had a hard time practicing or experiencing.

Yet, if Baldwin and Winnicott agreed on what freedom was not, their thinking about what freedom was differed. For Baldwin, freedom was primarily something approximating a Socratic self-examination of one's own unseen commitments and dark emotions (Zamalin 2015, 24–62). For Winnicott, in contrast, freedom meant something of a lightness of being, a weightlessness where one was not, on the one hand, governed by excessive inhibitions, and, on the other hand, a state in which one was not given over to excessive license. Winnicott argued that "the enjoyment of freedom only applies at all simply to the periods between bodily excitements. There is but little bodily gratification, and none that is acute, to be got out of freedom; whereas the ideas of cruelty or slavery are notoriously associated with bodily excitement and sensual experiences .... Therefore, lovers of freedom must be expected periodically to feel the seductive power of the idea of slavery and control" (Winnicott 1990, 214).

If unfreedom, for Winnicott, named a condition in which one was under tremendous psychic strain because of a paralyzing form of anxiety or desire that controlled them, freedom approximated something closer to boredom or radical openness to the new, to the unexpected, to improvisation. Winnicott claimed: "In psychiatric health, for instance, there can be detected a sense of humour as part of the capacity to play, and the sense of humor is a kind of elbow-room in the area of defense organization. This elbow-room gives a feeling of freedom both to the subject and to those who are involved or who wish to be involved with the individual concerned" (Winnicott 1990, 231). At the same time, Winnicott's use of a bodily metaphor ("elbow-room") to describe freedom, which he also found in the embodied experience of play, makes vivid his thinking about the way freedom is itself a counterpoint to scientific rationalism. In other words, one does not achieve freedom through managing and predicting the world—so that it is stabilized. But rather one achieves this like a body immersed in play, which involves "the manipulation of objects," and often certain types of intense interest," which is "associated with certain aspects of bodily excitement" (Winnicott 2005, 69).

For Baldwin, achieving the freedom (which came from self-examination) was essential for racial justice because it brought into relief for white Americans all of their own internal inadequacies of laziness and hypersexuality that they too easily displaced and projected upon blacks. But taking seriously Winnicott's understanding of freedom for racial justice would mean white and black citizens becoming less emotionally defensive and rigid in their ways of being.

Politically, this might mean Americans not being preemptively defensive when African Americans would raise the possibility of racism or racial wrongs. Talk of slavery and Jim Crow is something many white Americans wish to avoid, arguing that, even if both systems of domination were, in fact, obvious moral wrongs, they are events for which white Americans are not currently responsible. After all, so the argument goes, even if their ancestors committed these atrocities, they themselves did not (McCarthy 2002). Yet if white Americans were free in the way Winnicott imagined, then they would not be so preemptively dismissive of such claims. At the very least, they would need to take seriously the possibility of their validity.

B. The Holding Environment: From the Individual to a Caring Relationship

On some level, Winnicott believed that freedom was an individual achievement, a practice that people would have to cultivate in their lives. And yet, he also always insisted that freedom could not exist in a vacuum; its realization greatly depended upon the social conditions within and from which it emerged: what Winnicott understood as a "holding environment." He described the nature of holding as follows: "Holding can be done well by someone who has no intellectual knowledge of what is going on in the individual; what is needed is a capacity to identify, to know what the baby is feeling like" (Winnicott 1990, 28). In developmental terms, a holding environment began in early infancy when the child was actually held and sometimes nursed by their mother, her body providing the infant a source of bodily attachment and physical nourishment. Later on, it extended to what Winnicott called the "good enough" home where parents provided children the basic emotional support that would facilitate healthy psychological growth. To put it in more political-theoretical terms, Winnicott understood the family—or more generally the community—to be essential for individual flourishing.

Winnicott's formulation of the holding environment would have certainly pleased theorists of positive freedom like John Dewey (1991), who believed that freedom was about individual flourishing rather than non-domination, or contemporary "capability" theorists like Amartya Sen (1999) and Martha Nussbaum (1999), who argue for the importance of basic necessities like food, clothing and emotional comfort for self-realization. As with his thinking about freedom, however, Winnicott was not so much concerned with the quantity of specific goods, but the quality of interpersonal interaction. For this reason, Winnicott's theory of a holding environment resonated with the Christian tradition, from Augustine's (1998) call for a capacious brotherly love irreducible to self-narcissism to Martin Luther King Jr.'s (1986) argument for a love of humanity—*agape*—that countered the feelings of animus and rage or even Baldwin's (1992) call that love (a notion that, for him, was much more erotic rather than the familial version espoused by King) was essential for creating a beloved community.

Perhaps the closest analogue for Winnicott's notion of the holding environment, however, would be found in feminist care theory. Against the liberal prioritization of abstract goods like rights and liberty—captured by John Rawls's *A Theory of Justice* (1971)—feminist care theorists argued for making care a supplement, if not a central ingredient for justice thinking. Winnicott's version of care ethics was both developmental and normative. The unconditional love and empathy a mother feels for the infant, wrapping him in her whole being and making herself vulnerable to him so that he is protected from vulnerability, is crucial for the infant's development. Especially at the earliest stages of life, such a relationship is obviously asymmetrical. Viewed from a normative rather than developmental perspective, Winnicott's argument for the importance of asymmetry resonated with Emmanuel Levinas who argued that ethics needed to begin from the idea of being held hostage to the other; as if one was confronted with a stranger at one's doorstep and that the only response was to respond to the sentient face before one (1969).

For Levinas, the asymmetry of what he described as this "face to face" ethics resisted the Enlightenment rationalism that Horkheimer and Adorno (2007) believed constituted the negative side of the dialectic of the Enlightenment, where instrumental reason morphed into the industrial murder brought forth by the Nazi concentration camps. But unlike Levinas, Winnicott asserted that such asymmetry was practically necessary precisely because it provided an individual a sense of self-conscious identity. Being heard, loved, and present for another gives validity to the idea that the person receiving these actions is there: that they matter and are worthy of another person's investment. The mother's love of the infant gives him a sense that he matters, that he is worthy of love and care, that he is understood and endowed dignity by someone who is, what Winnicott called, a "not me," despite the fact that, especially at the earliest stages of holding, the distinction between a "me" and "not me" is often blurred.

Even at such an early infant stage, Winnicott claimed, this recognition gives one a sense of "integration" and stability in a world where the forces that threaten it are widespread and commonplace—especially in a modern capitalist society where one, as a worker, is always subject to the whims of their employers, in a democratic one where their political will is alienated to a larger collective and, of course, in interpersonal relationships where feelings of shame, disgrace, humiliation and insult are always lurking around the corner. Winnicott asserted in "Ego Integration and the Child Environment" (1962) that "[i]ntegration is closely linked with the environmental function of holding …. First comes 'I' which includes 'everything else is not me'. Then comes 'I am, I exist, I gather experiences and enrich myself and have an introjective and projective interaction with the NOT-ME, the actual world of shared reality'. Add to this: 'I am seen or understood to exist by someone'; and, further, add to this: 'I get back (as a face seen in a mirror) the evidence I need that I have been recognized as a being'" (Winnicott 1996, 61).

Around the time Winnicott was writing during the late 1950s and 1960s, King and Baldwin were themselves supplying the arguments for the importance of cultivating an ethos of love when African Americans were beginning to struggle against Jim Crow white supremacy and economic ghettoization during the Civil Rights movement. King insisted that love would help African Americans diminish the rage they felt toward whites and increase their sense of empathy (1986), while Baldwin insisted that it would transform African Americans into prophetic critics who would be willing to tell their white counterparts painful truths about themselves and social realities they wished to ignore (1963). Though not directly involved in that historical struggle, Winnicott kept stressing the importance of holding as that which provided one a sense of intimacy and sense of recognition.

To translate this idea for contemporary struggles for racial justice, holding might mean diminishing the physical distance between white and black Americans. To be capable of holding, Winnicott insists, both parties need to be actually present. Racial segregation militates against this, while integration encourages it. Holding would therefore require black and white Americans working to achieve greater physical proximity: being present together in parks, community centers, schools, or a range of other public places (see LeJeune, this volume).

Second, taking seriously Winnicott's notion of holding might mean white and black Americans cultivating a sense of active listening so that their perspective would be mutually recognized. This process is not entirely dissimilar from the one advanced by deliberative democrats

(Gutmann and Thompson 1996; Benhabib 1992), following Jürgen Habermas (1984/1987), who have argued for the importance of communicative ethics based in cordiality and civility as well as respect and tolerance of another's perspective. Strikingly, Habermas himself abandoned his early interest in psychoanalysis (1972), which he viewed as a self-reflective anti-positivistic science founded upon human values that questioned the primacy of a transparent subject and was interested in human liberation. But Winnicott's perspective not only retains some of Habermas's important early radical insights, but is also not entirely reducible to the deliberative democratic position with which Habermas would eventually became so closely identified. While many deliberative democrats stress the importance of procedure—ensuring that all communication rules are carefully followed—that is ultimately dictated by some standard of reasonableness, Winnicott, anticipating agonistic democrats like Iris Marion Young (2000), described recognition to be contingent upon a variety of standards—rhetorical, physical, as well as nonverbal. What mattered for Winnicott was the substantive goal of recognition rather than encouraged rational agreement that emerged from rational standards.

To be sure, as Winnicott understood, precisely because holding—especially at the earliest stage—was a condition in which the mother's presence simply served to maintain the infant's needs, one might wonder whether holding can ever be useful for justice, especially as it might problematically monopolize the subjectivity of the one doing the holding. Notwithstanding this serious limitation, however, a serious commitment for creating a holding environment for African Americans might entail actually hearing African American perspectives on inequality without attempting to explain why these perspectives are wrong or not fully conceptualized. It might also mean resisting the urge to rationalize one's responsibility for their complicity in racial injustice and work toward always being present in their listening.

It would require deferring to the plural needs of African Americans; if holding is first and foremost based in responsiveness, being vulnerable to what African Americans might need, whether more economic resources, political opportunities or dignity and respect. Viewed from the alternative perspective, however, African Americans would need to work toward cultivating empathy for some white Americans who might be deeply afraid and reluctant to renounce their white privilege and all of the psychological and material benefits it affords them. So too would they need to refuse to engage in a politics of racial separatism and embrace a commitment to the project of interracial living.

C. Creativity: Self-Expression and Enlivening the Self

As much as Winnicott asserted that both freedom and a holding environment were essential for individual flourishing, perhaps the guiding idea that informed most of his work was creativity. To put it simply, creativity, for Winnicott, meant living a meaningful life. Creativity could be found in something extraordinary like composing a symphony or painting a mural, or something much more banal and everyday like cooking or gardening. Like Friedrich Nietzsche who spoke of the importance of individual artistry in life and action (2002), Winnicott's insight was that creativity militated against the idea of compliance, which was associated with a repetition of the same. So too did Winnicott's notion resonate with what Hannah Arendt called "natality"—the beginning of something new, fresh, and exciting—which she insisted was an essential ingredient for creating a robust public sphere (1998). Creativity for Winnicott gave one a sense of purpose, providing orientation in a world. To put it in terms of one famous twentieth century debate over action and identity, if Heidegger famously asserted that being came before acting (2008) and Sartre argued that acting came before being (2007), then Winnicott implied that creativity—as a form of action—itself actually enlivened one's sense of self, providing clarity about who one was, what one's options in life were, and what they might eventually become. He wrote: "Creativity is then the doing that arises out of being. It indicates that he who is, is alive. Impulse may be at rest, but when the word 'doing' becomes appropriate, then already there is creativity … in order to be and to have the feeling that one *is*, one must have a predominance of impulse-doing over reactive-doing" (Winnicott 1990, 39). Creativity did not simply reveal what Winnicott argued was an "authentic self"—the part of one's identity that was genuine rather than contrived—it actually served to activate something fundamental within that self.

Creative living was, for Winnicott, thus essential for individual health, just like creativity was essential for freedom. To put it in a way that distills Winnicott's thinking, spontaneous action is essential for undermining two psychologically debilitating things: one's psychological defenses and proclivity for displacing responsibility away from oneself and unto others. As Winnicott explained, "relaxation is associated with creativity, so that it is out of the unintegrated state that the creative impulse appears and reappears. Organized defense against disintegration robs the individual of the precondition for the creative impulse and therefore prevents creative living" (Winnicott 1990, 29).

For these reasons, the very work of struggling against conditions that perpetuate collective human suffering can be seen as to embody Winnicott's notion of creativity. If we follow Winnicott's observations carefully, then perhaps the creative act of white and black Americans working for racial justice would itself help diminish the very psychological defenses that were a sign of what Winnicott took to be ill health and unfreedom. As Americans invest themselves in struggling against police brutality in the streets, examining their own personal racism, voting for better, desegregated schools, fair-paying jobs, and abolishing racial segregation in all reams of American life they can at once begin to see meaning and purpose in their lives, understand themselves as responsible citizens, and start to see themselves as makers and creators of the world in which they live. Of course, this demand must come from within. It cannot be imposed from external forces like government—as such a move would undermine the individual self-realization that creativity engenders.

Truth and Reconciliation in America: The Greensboro Truth and Reconciliation Commission and the Mississippi Truth Project

As the above sections have demonstrated, there are myriad ways to extend Winnicott's ideas to racial justice projects. But in this section, I would like to turn briefly to two recent projects in the United States in which Winnicott's ideas have found an excellent, if not exemplary, empirical example: The Greensboro TRC, organized in the 2004, as a response to the November 3, 1979 "Greensboro Massacre" in which white members of the Ku Klux Klan (KKK) and American Nazi Party murdered five anti-Klan protestors, and the Mississippi Truth Project, which was organized in 2008 and sought to raise public awareness about racist violence in Mississippi during the Jim Crow period. In discussing both restorative justice projects here, my aim is not so much to argue that they are politically exemplary or even normatively superior to those that are not primarily focused on restorative justice. There is obviously good reason to be suspicious of the very ideal of restorative justice given the way that, as some have argued, it replaces ongoing, future-oriented political struggle and contestation with past oriented, moral recognition, and repair (Torpey 2006; Todorov 2007). Instead, I aim to show how they provide a rich example of the way some of Winnicott's ideals have already been infused in American political projects.

The projects in both North Carolina and Mississippi were modeled on the late 1990s South African Truth and Reconciliation Commission, which was created in the aftermath of South African Apartheid, and were primarily concerned with the ethical project of remembering and discussing the past, which many white Americans in those states wanted to forget. In this basic way, then, both projects embodied Winnicott's notion of creativity because they sought to disrupt people's historical denial, amnesia, and an aversion to excavating the violent and repressive elements of history that do not square well with people's conviction in the liberal values of tolerance and pluralism.

Both commissions also made vivid Winnicott's understanding that the creative act could have the capacity to diminish one's psychological defenses, and thus facilitate individual freedom. Remarkably, the public hearings that were central for providing evidence for the Greensboro TRC not only consisted of testimony from scholars and community organizers, but precisely those who were affected by the massacre, including survivors, former KKK members and police officers. Not all of the participants shared the same narrative or interpretation of the event—some believed it was entirely the fault of Klan members, while others insisted that it was incited by the Workers Viewpoint Organization (Communist Workers Party). Furthermore, some—like Virgil Pierce, Imperial Wizard of the Cleveland Knights Ku Klux Klan (CKKKK)—who was present on the day of the Massacre had very little remorse, arguing that the KKK held little or no responsibility for the event (Greensboro Truth and Reconciliation Commission 2015).

Others, however, took a different approach. For instance, one former participant in the anti-Klan rally, Yonni Chapman, told the Commission that "[t]hroughout history, the voices of those who have struggled against injustice have been silenced and suppressed .... I want to thank the Greensboro Truth and Reconciliation Commission for inviting me to tell my story .... Unless the truth of injustice is acknowledged, there can never be justice or reconciliation, and there will be no peace" (Greensboro Truth and Reconciliation Commission 2015). At the same time, a former Grand Dragon of the Federated Knights of the KKK, Gorrell Pierce, claimed, with a great deal of remorse: "I've had to live with it, I've thought about it every day of my life since then. And you can bet every day I was in the federal penitentiary I thought about it two or three times that day" (Greensboro Truth and Reconciliation Commission 2015). It was almost as if the very creative forum meant to encourage transparent, honest discussion and mutual understanding was precisely what gave these people—ex-Klan members who really had no incentive to tell their story, or victims who could have easily refrained from sharing their painful experiences—to put it in Winnicott's language, a sense of self and the feeling that their lives had some kind of existential value (see Alford, this volume). Something similar can be said for the Mississippi Truth Project's attempt to create a statewide conversation called "The Welcome Table," which featured over three hundred black and white citizens trying to openly discuss race in their communities. Unlike the Greensboro TRC, the Mississippi Truth Project—which was eventually stalled by 2010 because of limited economic resources, lack of political willpower and the US economic recession—despite numerous attempts, never materialized into a full-fledged truth commission, complete with policy recommendations and a written report. Nonetheless, like the Greensboro TRC, by aiming to foster a "culture of truth-telling" (Glisson 2015, 6) in which citizens would speak candidly and intimately about their experience of race and racism, it seemed to embody the spirit of receptive listening and compassion that Winnicott believed would be encouraged by freedom, which he defined as resistance to defensiveness. So too does the very physical proximity of white and black Americans in a common space militate against the fantasy of impenetrability and rigid boundaries that Winnicott thought exemplified psychological pathology.

Especially looking at the transcripts from the Greensboro TRC, however, it is remarkable how citizens aim to both elucidate their perspective and internalize the perspective of those around them. By implicitly understanding that their experiences and truth claims can easily be subject to contestation, they, on the one hand, make vivid the partiality of their experience and, on the other hand, dramatize a capacious awareness and respect about the reality that their experiences may be radically different from those to whom they are listening (Greensboro Truth and Reconciliation Commission 2015).

Such an orientation captures Winnicott's larger idea of a holding environment. Citizens are placed in a condition of mutual vulnerability where they take turns speaking and listening. The important point is that they work to be present for each other: to put it in Winnicott's terms, the presence of a holding environment furnishes the process of recognition and self-understanding, which, in turn, creates the self-efficacy and fearlessness necessary for responsibility and collective action.

Finally, both projects reflect Winnicott's understanding that the durability of keeping alive an ethics of freedom, holding and creativity largely depended upon the resilience of individuals and the social resources afforded to them. While the Mississippi Truth Project's attempted to institutionalize an ongoing oral history project in which individual citizens continued to reflect on their own experiences of racism, the Greensboro TRC issued a series of sweeping recommendations for the city of Greensboro on May 25, 2006—among them, that the city create monuments and exhibits commemorating the massacre and publicly acknowledge the significance of the event, that all city employees engage in antiracist and diversity training, that the city spend more on public health and social services, and that it issue annual reports on racism in the city. The extensive scope of these proposals illuminates Winnicott's view that a healthy and good-enough social environment is absolutely indispensable for individual flourishing, even if that environment is itself comprised of only good-enough individuals. As Winnicott wrote, "[i]ndividual maturity implies a movement toward independence, but there is no such thing as independence. It would be unhealthy for an individual to be so withdrawn as to feel independent and invulnerable [but] social health is dependent on individual health, society being but a massive reduplication of persons" (Winnicott 1990, 22). In sum, if viewed as providing something of an ethical program for care, Winnicott's work teaches us that this project is complex and rife with paradoxes. Not only does his work show us that ethics itself is often uneasily situated between the particular and the universal—the concrete human encounter and the frameworks (whether conscious or not) by which individuals live and interact. At the same time, if, as Winnicott believed, freedom names lack of defensiveness, holding is about recognition and creativity is about self-development, then, following many feminist care theorists (Held 2006; Tronto 2013), the ethic of care implicit in Winnicott's work is at once embodied, physical and deeply emotional and also attentive to the needs of living a life in common with others; deeply personal and subjective (because each encounter is radically different) but also that which requires something of a universal space—a thriving community and society—that actually helps facilitate individual development; essential for individual health and something that can be better facilitated through a more democratic and just political existence.

Winnicott and the Problem of Contemporary Racial Injustice: Addressing Racial Inequality in America

Despite the Civil Rights movement's successful struggle in the 1960s against race-based formal legal and political discrimination, structural racial inequality is still a serious problem today. Perhaps African Americans are less likely to be overtly discriminated against in the voting booth and are no longer forced to endure the humiliation of segregated water-fountains or restaurants, but they are still much less likely than whites to have economic wealth, access to quality education opportunities and health care, and are much more likely to spend some extended period of time incarcerated (Perry 2011). Over the past several years, it has also become clear that African American males—as the ever-increasing list of high profile police-killings of black men by police officers, from Michael Brown, Eric Garner, Samuel DuBose to Walter Scott, Freddie Gray and Tamir Rice, demonstrates—are disproportionately more likely than white Americans to be subject to lethal police brutality (Alexander 2010).

And yet, arguably more so than at any point since the Civil Rights movement, there has been increasing attention to and mass protests against racial inequality today—from the marches in Ferguson, Missouri in 2015, after a grand jury refused to indict the white police officer, Darren Wilson, for the killing of Michael Brown, to the rise of the Black Lives Matter social movement, which, although beginning as a call on social media in 2013, by three young black feminist queer activists, has in the years since made its self-explanatory message that black Americans deserve equal normative status as American citizens and its policy positions about ending police brutality and mass incarceration loud and clear to elected officials. It is precisely in our contemporary moment of renewed attention on racism and racial inequality that Winnicott's insights deserve attention. This is not because Winnicott himself was a theorist of racial justice or because he (or his work) provides direct public policy prescriptions for, or detailed analyses of, racial inequality. It is instead because some of his insights can help enliven contemporary practices and habits of citizenship.

We can obviously debate whether Black Lives Matter and other racial justice protestors should endorse truth commissions or focus their struggles on policy proposals like an end to mass incarceration, more community-policing programs or police body cameras that aim to end police brutality or more socioeconomic programs for black youth. But at the very least, one thing seems clear: these policy arguments could be made more powerfully, persuasively, and potentially more effectively by adopting Winnicott's arguments about understanding freedom as non-defensive spontaneous behavior, taking seriously his notion of cultivating a holding environment of care and compassion that would enable individuals to flourish and of seeing creative action—embarking on the new and unexpected—as something that could actually help create a sense of individual self-efficacy and social health. Doing this might lead to more racial integration, less preemptive dismissals of moral wrongs inflicted upon African Americans, more interracial communication, less defensiveness, and more openness to new collective political projects and spaces for solidarity. Whether at the level of the personal, interpersonal or political, the work of achieving this would, without question, be strenuous and far from easy. But it would also be a crucial and necessary step for remaking America in a way that is more just, equal, and democratic.

References

Alexander, M. 2010. *The New Jim Crow: Mass Incarceration in the Age of Colorblindness*. New York: New Press.

Allen, D.S. 2004. *Talking to Strangers: Anxieties of Citizenship since Brown v. Board of Education*. Chicago, IL: University of Chicago Press.

Appiah, K.A., and A. Gutmann. 1998. *Color Conscious: The Political Morality of Race*. Princeton, NJ: Princeton University Press.

Arendt, H. 1998. *The Human Condition*. 2nd ed. Chicago, IL: University of Chicago Press.

Aristotle. 2009. *The Nicomachean Ethics*. Trans. W.D. Ross. New York: Oxford University Press.

Augustine. 1998. *The City of God Against the Pagans*. Trans. R.W. Dyson. New York: Cambridge University Press.

Baldwin, J. 1992. *The Fire Next Time*. New York: Vintage.

———. 1998. Many Thousands Gone. In *Collected Essays*, ed. Toni Morrison, 19–34. New York: Library of America.

Benhabib, S. 1992. *Situating the Self: Gender, Community, and Postmodernism in Contemporary Ethics*. New York: Routledge.

Dewey, J. 1991. *The Public and Its Problems*. Athens: Swallow Press.

Emerson, R.W. 2003. Self-Reliance. In *Nature and Selected Essays*, ed. Larzer Ziff, 175–204. New York: Penguin.

Fanon, F. 2008. *Black Skin, White Masks*. New York: Grove Press.

Fromm, E. 1960. *Escape from Freedom*. New York: Holt, Rinehart and Winston.

Frymer, P. 2010. *Uneasy Alliances: Race and Party Competition in American*. Princeton, NJ: Princeton University Press.

Glisson, A. 2015. The Sum of Its Parts: The Importance of Deconstructing Truth Commission. *Race and Justice*: 1–11.

Greensboro Truth and Reconciliation Commission. 2015. Statement Archives. http://greensborotrc.org/hear_statements.php. Accessed March 20, 2016.

Gutmann, A., and D.F. Thompson. 1996. *Democracy and Disagreement*. Cambridge, MA: Belknap.

Habermas, J. 1972. *Knowledge and Human Interests*. Trans. J.J. Shapiro. Boston, MA: Beacon Press.

Habermas, J. 1984/1987. *The Theory of Communicative Action*. Trans. T. McCarthy. Boston, MA: Beacon Press.

Heidegger, M. 2008. *Being and Time*. Trans. J. Macquarrie and E. Robinson. New York: Harper Perennial Classics.

Held, V. 2006. *The Ethics of Care: Personal, Political, Global*. New York: Oxford University Press.

Horkheimer, M. and T.W. Adorno. 2007. *Dialectic of Enlightenment: Philosophical Fragments*. Trans. Edmund Jephcott. Palo Alto: Stanford University Press.

Kant, I. 1998. *Groundwork of the Metaphysics of Morals*. M.J. Gregor and C.M. Korsgaard. Cambridge, MA: Cambridge University Press.

Katznelson, I. 2005. *When Affirmative Action was White: An Untold History of Racial Inequality in Twentieth-Century America*. New York: W.W. Norton.

King, M.L. Jr. 1986. An Experiment in Love. In *A Testament of Hope: The Essential Writings of Martin Luther King*, ed. J.M. Washington, 16–20. San Francisco: Harper and Row.

Levinas, E. 1969. *Totality and Infinity; An Essay on Exteriority*. Pittsburgh: Duquesne University Press.

Lieberman, R.C. 1998. *Shifting the Color Line: Race and the American Welfare State*. Cambridge, MA: Harvard University Press.

Lowndes, J. 2009. *From the New Deal to the New Right: Race and the Southern Origins of Conservatism*. New Haven: Yale University Press.

McCarthy, T. 2002. Vergangenheitsbewältigung in the USA: On the Politics of the Memory of Slavery. *Political Theory* 30(5): 623–648.

———. 2009. *Race, Empire, and the Idea of Human Development*. Cambridge: Cambridge University Press.

Mill, J.S., and J. Bentham. 1987. *Utilitarianism and Other Essays*. Ed. A. Ryan. London: Penguin.

Nietzsche, F.W. 2002. *Beyond Good and Evil: Prelude to a Philosophy of the Future*. Ed. R. Horstmann and J. Norman. New York: Cambridge University Press.

Nussbaum, M.C. 1999. *Sex and Social Justice*. New York: Oxford University Press.

Olson, J. 2004. *The Abolition of White Democracy*. Minneapolis: University of Minnesota Press.
Perry, I. 2011. *More Beautiful and More Terrible: The Embrace and Transcendence of Racial Inequality in the United States*. New York: New York University Press.
Rainwater, L., and W.L. Yancey. 1967. *The Moynihan Report and the Politics of Controversy*. Cambridge, MA: M.I.T. Press.
Rawls, J. 1971. *A Theory of Justice*. Cambridge, MA: Belknap/Harvard University Press.
Sartre, J.-P. 2000. *Nausea*. London: Penguin.
———. 2007. *Existentialism is a Humanism*. New Haven: Yale University Press.
Scott, D.M. 1997. *Contempt and Pity: Social Policy and the Image of the Damaged Black Psyche, 1880–1996*. Chapel Hill: University of North Carolina Press.
Sen, A. 1999. *Development as Freedom*. Oxford: Oxford University Press.
Thoreau, H.D. 2004. *Walden: A Fully Annotated Edition*. New Haven: Yale University Press.
Todorov, T. 2003. *Hope and Memory: Lessons from the Twentieth Century*. Princeton, NJ: Princeton University Press.
Torpey, J. 2006. *Making Whole What Has Been Smashed: On Reparations Politics*. Cambridge, MA: Harvard University Press.
Tronto, J. 2013. *Caring Democracy: Markets, Equality, and Justice*. New York: NYU Press.
Turner, J. 2012. *Awakening to Race: Individualism and Social Consciousness in America*. Chicago, IL: University of Chicago Press.
Winnicott, D.W. 1990. *Home Is Where We Start From: Essays by a Psychoanalyst*. New York: W.W. Norton.
———. 1996. *The Maturational Processes and the Facilitating Environment: Studies in the Theory of Emotional Development*. London: Karnac.
———. 2005. *Playing and Reality*. New York: Routledge.
Young, I.M. 2000. *Inclusion and Democracy*. Oxford: Oxford University Press.
Zamalin, A. 2015. *African American Political Thought and American Culture: The Nation's Struggle for Racial Justice*. New York: Palgrave.

CHAPTER 13

Winnicott at Work: Potential Space and the Facilitating Organization

Michael A. Diamond

Introduction

D.W. Winnicott's revisions of the theories of Freud and Melanie Klein are a major force in changing psychoanalysis from a one-person, drives-and-instincts model of mind to a two-person, relational model (Greenberg and Mitchell 1983; Modell 1984). Winnicott's object relations theory is an interpretive and experiential framework for understanding the internal and external world of human relations. Additionally, his object relations theory has become germane to the contemporary psychoanalytic study of organizations, particularly for those researchers who view organizations as relational constructs. This chapter connects Winnicott's ideas on "human maturational processes" and "facilitating environments" to the elucidation of destructive and oppressive, versus constructive and authentic, organizational dynamics (Diamond 1993; Diamond and Allcorn 2009; Allcorn and Stein 2015; Kets de Vries 2006; Stapley 1996; Stacey 1996). My goal in this chapter is to illustrate a theory of organization rooted in Winnicott's assumptions of human nature.

M.A. Diamond (✉)
Center for the Study of Organizational Change, Truman School of Public Affairs, University of Missouri, Columbia, MO, USA

M.H. Bowker, A. Buzby (eds.), *D.W. Winnicott and Political Theory*,
DOI 10.1057/978-1-137-57533-3_13

Winnicott's notions of maturational processes and facilitating environments, transitional and potential space, holding and good-enough mothering, and the true and false self assist organizational researchers in the exploration of conscious and unconscious organizational dynamics and their effects on participants. These psychoanalytic concepts offer theorists, researchers, and consultants a deeper understanding of healthy versus toxic leadership and organizational cultures. Winnicott's theory of object relations focuses on a dialectical and relational medium between self and other, subject and object, me and not-me. The application of this theory highlights the individual's relational and intersubjective experiences and the psychological processes of play and creativity, imagination and curiosity, self-integrity and authenticity. For Winnicott, these psychological processes are essential to nurturing in the holding relationship and attachment between parent and child (mothering caregiver and baby). Yet, these psychological processes by no means end there. They are a prototype of future self- and other-relations, inside and outside healthy and humane work organizations.

In particular, Winnicott's notion of "potential space" serves a central role in his theory of human development (Winnicott 1958, 1960). The realization of potential space is a crucial psychological step in the child's (physical, emotional, and cognitive) maturational shift from a position of total dependence on parents to one of relative independence. Rooted in trust and reliability, the facilitation of "good-enough" holding and potential space is decisive to positive separation and independence (Winnicott 1965). Adequate integrative and maturational processes during infancy and early childhood, I submit, have a profound influence on adult leadership and followership and on efforts to organize people into constructive, participative, resourceful, and democratic collaborations. It is my view that Winnicott's object relational theory helps to explain the perverted political and psychological processes of destructive and oppressive power relations inside and outside organizations and institutions. Consequently, his psychoanalytic theory offers a guide to organization theorists in their desire to assess organizational well-being and humaneness in the workplace.

The Significance of Transitional and Potential Space

Transitional and potential space originates with the mother (parent) and infant, and resides in the zone between fantasy and reality, consciousness and unconsciousness, parent and child, self and other, subject and object. For Winnicott, within this space is the (psycho-geographical) location of culture (Winnicott 1971).When workers say they have adequate space for creativity, innovation, and invention, or that they are free to play at work, they are signifying something profound about the culture and identity of their organization. They are essentially saying: "I'm respected and trusted." In the context of organizations, this means that individual members are trusted and respected by management to carry out tasks effectively and competently. Workers are consulted for their ideas and imagination. Rather than assuming management has the answers to complex problems of organizing and task accomplishment, workers are asked about their ideas for innovation and problem solving. In other words, workers are free to reflect, experiment, innovate, and play at work without the oppressive burden of micromanagement, and the suffocation of hierarchic dominance and submission. In sum, workers are treated as competent and well-informed adults, not as dependent and powerless children.

Trust and respect are delivered out of nurturing potential space. It is from the safety and security of a good-enough holding environment and potential space that childhood curiosity, learning, and exploration are fostered. Affirmative parental response to the child's cues and desires for separation signifies the presence of potential space early in development. This critical relational model for healthy development and maturation persists throughout the life cycle. Thus, in adulthood, micromanagement and coercion at work signify the absence of potential space and a suspicion and mistrust of subordinate workers. This lack of potentiality and facilitation fosters mistrust and disrespect between management and adult workers.

In *Playing and Reality*, Winnicott describes the experience of potential space as follows: "I refer to the hypothetical area that exists (but cannot exist) between the baby and the object (mother or part of mother) during the phase of the repudiation of the object as not-me, that is, at the end of being merged in with the object" (1971, 107). Thus, potential space enables the processes of separation and individuation crucial to the birth of the self. The original sense of self occurs with the child's destruction of the symbiotic bond with the object (mother, father). In describing the essence of this facilitating environment, Winnicott writes: "A baby can be fed without love, but loveless or impersonal management cannot succeed in producing a new autonomous human child" (108). Potential space, therefore, emerges out of the mother's (parent's) ordinary provision of loving and nurturing the baby.

Similar to Erikson's (1963) psychosocial developmental stages, highlighting trust versus mistrust as the fundamental and original crisis of infancy and early childhood, Winnicott writes: "The baby's confidence in the mother's reliability, and therefore in that of other people and things, makes possible a separating-out of the not-me from me" (1971, 109). A sense of mutual trust earned during the attachment phase enables the child to separate and move along her positive developmental path. Winnicott describes this "holding" phase as "a subject-less state" of "primary maternal preoccupation" or what he calls the state of "going on being" (111–112).

Potential space is at the heart of play, imagination, creativity and meaningful work. It is where individuals free associate, construct personal narratives, solve riddles and scientific puzzles, and write good stories. It is, experientially speaking, the location of images and metaphoric processes such as found in musical compositions, poetry, literature and culture, and the construction of self and group identities. Winnicott's idea of transitional phenomena and potential space represents the intermediate or intersubjective third area bordering multiple selves and identities (group, organizational, and political). Thus, potential space is where mutual understanding, consensual validation, and shared meaning transpire. It is a consequence of accepting and embracing paradoxical and dialectical relations as a manifestation of conventional human nature, and the core of forming self- and group identities.

In the psychoanalytic literature, intermediate and transitional, potential space is akin to Thomas Ogden's "analytic third" (2004) and Jessica Benjamin's "intersubjective third" (2004). The third is a position in-between subject and object, self and other, which is located at the boundary between subjects and objects. We might imagine organizing potential space as complementary to Schafer's (1983) idea of "the analytic attitude." From this vantage point, potential space is a frame of mind directing our attention to transference and countertransference experience. It is a process of self-consciousness and reflectivity. Based on the analytic attitude, observers adjust and readjust their psychoanalytic lens so that they might experience the present moment between two or more subjects. In so doing, they shift their awareness and attentiveness toward the area "in-between" and toward the intersubjective structure.

Organizations, generally defined, are cooperative systems, structured around boundaries between individuals (self and others), formal and informal roles, groups, divisions, departments, and organizations. Thus, the translation of what happens in organizations and the workplace cannot solely reside with individuals or organizations, selves, or others; it must dwell somewhere "in-between." To reiterate, the relevance of Winnicottian object relational theory for the study of organizations stems from the perspective of organizations as patterns of intersubjective structures.

Organizing for Potential Space and Organizational Identity

Organizing for potential space requires greater attunement to unconscious processes and intersubjectivity. The meaning and understanding of organizational experience (and membership) resides within the intersubjective patterns of relationships that encompass (what I call) the organizational identity (Diamond 1993, 2016). Organizational identity is located in the psychological and physical space of thirdness or Winnicott's potential space, a phenomenon that also exists outside the relational matrix between mother and baby, and between therapist and patient. It, too, resides in the leader–follower, super–subordinate, and peer relationships.

Organizations are the object as well as the subject of theorizing and observation. Organizations are constructed imaginary spaces composed of structure, strategy, culture, and environment, all of which are secondary to the primacy of organizational identity (Diamond 1993). Organizational identity, the meaning and experience of membership and affiliation, is the articulation of potential and transitional space between self and other, subject and object. It is the location of compromise formations and repetition compulsions, transferences and countertransferences, which, when rendered conscious, represent the possibilities and potentiality of truly cooperative relational systems.

As a psychoanalytic organizational theorist, researcher, and consultant, I ask organizational participants "What is it like to work here?" I do so in order that I might understand the psychological reality of joining and affiliating with a specific organization, and of locating self, what Winnicott (1971) calls "true self" and "false self," within the context of an organization. By true self, I refer to authenticity and relative autonomy of self, and by false self I refer to a compliant self where over-dependency of self on others or on objects, such as hierarchies and authorities, is commonplace (Diamond 2016).

From a psychoanalytic framework, identity comprises a perpetual tension between self (as subject) and other (as object, such as the form and meaning of organizational membership). While resembling on the surface the social constructionist view of organizational identity as interactive and socially constructed, the psychoanalytic concept of organizational identity, in contrast, takes into account the unconscious processes of psychological regression, compromise formation, and intersubjectivity. Moreover, organizational identity evolves from the role and function of transference and countertransference dynamics between individual members, their organizations, and leaders (Diamond 2016).

Deep change in individuals and groups, as in psychoanalysis and psychoanalytic psychotherapy, emerges out of reflective engagement in the dialectical experience of intra- and interpersonal processes. These interactive processes comprise creative and destructive tensions, regressive and progressive actions, paralysis and movement, social and psychological structures, conscious and unconscious motivations, fantasy and reality. The tensions between these psychological processes are experienced among leaders and followers, therapists and patients, consultants and participants, superiors and subordinates, organizational members, and human systems and subsystems. One can say that these social and psychological dynamics of organizational identity are the cognitive and emotional forces of human nature and relational systems—what Winnicott (1971, 102) refers to above as "the actual world with the individual living it."

For Winnicott, the emergence of potential space via playing and cultural experience coincides with the baby's earliest awareness of itself as separate from yet attached to the mothering parent. And it would seem to be the case that the creation of this transitional space or intermediate area of experience, as Winnicott called it, requires some sense of confidence, safety, and security in the presence, empathic attunement, and nurturing capacity of the mother. Potential space originates with primary narcissism and the infant's experience of responsive mirroring and maternal affection grounded in *good-enough mothering (or a good-enough holding environment)*. Here, the baby develops the capacity to be alone and the curiosity to explore her internal and external world (Winnicott 1958, 1960).

For Winnicott, the potential space is where humanity experiences living, neither strictly in fantasy nor reality but somewhere in-between. The notion of potential space is at the heart of what Ogden (1994) calls Winnicott's *intersubjective subject*. For example, consultants may become transitional objects for participants' projections and transferences, particularly during the experience of shifting organizational cultures and the mindsets of leaders from environments of unconscious defensive denial and fantasy to more consciously attuned social and political realities. The idea of potential space in organizational theory, I suggest, frames the subject's experience and perceptions of relational matters as critical to understanding and change.

Potential Space and Benjamin's Intersubjective Third

Jessica Benjamin's concepts of thirdness and intersubjectivity add a deeper understanding of the psychodynamics of organizational hierarchy, power and authority, by highlighting the sadomasochistic interplay of dominance and submission between supervisors and subordinates, executive managers and workers. In "Beyond Doer and Done To: An Intersubjective View of Thirdness," Benjamin states: "Thirdness is about how we build relational systems and how we develop the intersubjective capacities for such co-creation" (2004, 7). The *third* is not a "thing" but a "principle, function, or relationship." "In the space of thirdness, we are not 'holding onto' a third; we are, in Ghent's felicitous usage, surrendering to it" (1990, 8).

The third is, then, that to which we surrender, and thirdness is the intersubjective mental space that facilitates or results from surrender. This nondefensive act of surrender does not refer to submission or compliance; rather, it refers to a letting go of the self, and thus implies, as Benjamin and Ghent suggest, the ability to take in the other's point of view or reality. "Thus, surrender refers us to recognition—being able to sustain connectedness to the other's mind while accepting his separateness and difference: Surrender implies freedom from any intent to control or coerce" (Benjamin 2004, 6). According to Benjamin, *thirdness* is that *intersubjective* mental space that emerges from our capacity to surrender—in the sense of *opening up one's intersubjective field of awareness* and opening up to the emergence of the co-constructed third subject.

We can attend to constructive and destructive, liberating and oppressive relational systems by surrendering to the recognition of mutual subjectivities discovered in the third. Benjamin is acutely aware of the challenges of the oppositional nature of two subjectivities and their separate realities, particularly as it relates to Hegel's master–slave conflict and the relational dynamics of masochism and sadism, dominance and submission. She writes that "the presence of an observing third is felt to be intolerable or persecutory" (2004, 30). The subject may experience the occupying force of the object; unconscious sabotage and collusion may be present. Under such circumstances, the boundaries between "me and you" become confused and inadequately delineated inside the mush of transference and countertransference, projection and introjection. In this case, Benjamin maintains, "malignant complementarity takes hold, the ping-pong of projective identification—the exchange of blame—is often too rapid to halt or even obscure" (30). Benjamin's notion of thirdness enables analysts, theorists, and consultants to observe and claim participation in co-constructed relational systems, similar to Winnicott's view of the psychological and therapeutic processes of potential space. Correspondingly, Ogden's position on the analytic third values consciousness of projective identification and what he calls the "subjugating third" in transference and countertransference. I submit that the theorist's awareness and consciousness of intersubjectivity and thirdness potentially resolves the inevitable trap of transference, and the tendency to engage in splitting the object world into us against them, good versus evil. Ogden's notion of the subjugating third heightens this awareness.

Potential Space and Ogden's Third Subject

The analytic third, according to Ogden (2004, 169), refers to a third subject unconsciously co-created by analyst and patient, "which seems to take on a life of its own in the interpersonal field between them." This third subject stands in dialectical tension with the separate individual subjectivities of analyst and patient in such a way that the individual subjectivities and the third create, negate, and preserve one another (189). The third subject is the product of the *dialectical processes* of the relational unconscious. We confirm, disconfirm, and reconfirm each other in the sense of mutual recognition of our individual subjectivities. The analytic third signifies the analyst's position and consciousness of the intersubjective subject.

Thus, simultaneous surrendering to, and awareness of, the third position enables focus on (without being entrapped by) coercive and collusive relational psychodynamics such as projective identification. Projective identification is the construction of unconscious storylines that contain the fantasy of emptying a part of oneself into another person. This fantasied evacuation serves the purpose of either protecting oneself from the dangers posed by an aspect of oneself, or of safeguarding a part of oneself by depositing it in another person who is experienced as only partially differentiated from oneself (2004, 187).

Consciousness of Ogden's analytic third as that which is co-created between two or more individual subjectivities places attention on the emotional whirlwind of transference and countertransference dynamics. The theory of the analytic third depicts the psychological processes of Winnicott's notion of potential space where, in the middle of projected and introjected emotions, one clarifies and differentiates self and other, me and you, container and contained. Bion's relational model of "container-contained" is derived from a particular aspect of projective identification. According to this model, the infant projects a part of his internal world of uncontrollable emotions (the contained) into the good breast (the container), only to receive them back "detoxified" and in a more tolerable form (Grinberg et al. 1993).

Ogden explains how projective identification operates in the potential space of the analytic third:

> The interpersonal facet of projective identification—as I view it from the perspective generated by the concept of the analytic third—involves a transformation of the subjectivity of the "recipient" in such a way that the separate "I-ness" of the other-as-subject is (for a time and to a degree) subverted. In this unconscious interplay of subjectivities, "you [the 'recipient' of the projective identification] are me [the projector] to the extent that I need to make use of you for the purpose of experiencing through you what I cannot experience myself." (2004, 188)

Ogden describes the recipient in the subjugated analytic third of projective identification as making "psychological room" for the projector's temporary occupation. The projector turns himself over to the recipient and in effect transfers the disavowed unconscious (part self-object) to the outside other. The recipient then participates, according to Ogden, in a negation of herself by surrendering to the "disavowed aspect of the subjectivity of the projector" (189). Thus, the recipient is able to open up her interpersonal field of experience (potential space) between the two subjectivities. From the vantage point of the initially subjugated third the recipient processes and comprehends (identification and recognition) the other's subjectivity as separate from yet linked to his own.

In much the same way as Bion's (1967) notion of container-contained is operationalized, Ogden's analytic third signifies the psychodynamic processes in which the recipient eventually verbalizes and affectively returns to the projector his own disavowed subjectivity in a form the projector can receive, reclaim, and find meaningful. From the vantage point of potential space and the analytic third, one observes and experiences the projector's use of the recipient as a container of toxic and non-toxic emotions. In these psychological processes, split-off and evacuated parts of self are reclaimed and self-cohesion is enhanced along with the capacity to distinguish "me and not-me." Winnicottian potential space might be viewed as the remedy for the destructive forces of psychological regression and splitting.

A more unified sense of self comprising good and bad parts is derived from the psychodynamics of an expanding potential space, or thirdness. What I am referring to here as "an expanding potential space" (or potentiality) is the depth of experience, insight, and self-consciousness that comes from what Winnicott calls a good-enough holding environment. Potential space becomes an antidote to the distorted and frequently polarized boundaries of self and other, subject and object, resulting from unconscious projective identification.

This triangular potential space is the intermediate area of colliding subjects and objects, roles, and divided structures. Organizational identity *is the third intersubjective subject* surfacing above the dyad, solving the problem of duality, as we engage one another in a process of reflective inquiry. The third position signifies participants' capacity to occupy the mental space of observation, reflectivity, and double-loop learning. This reflective learning process and challenge to the status quo enables participants to produce alternative relational structures and more meaningful, productive, inventive and innovative, humane organizations.

During the course of organizational analysis, theorists and scholar-practitioners articulate organizational identity from the vantage point of potential space where participant observations link "here-and-now" interactions with those of the organization, its leadership, and its collective past. Taking up the position of the analytic third as one of occupying potential space lifts awareness and consciousness of otherwise unconscious processes. If trust between participants is ever to be realized, it is hereby understood as originating, universally, out of a good-enough holding and facilitating environment from which authenticity and true selves evolve.

Authentic Organizations: True Selves and False Selves

Winnicott's (1971) concept of the *true and false self* describes the infantile origins of defensive resistance. Unconscious defenses are rooted in infancy and early childhood. However, they are commonplace among adult organizational members as well. The false self tends to be compliant and defensive while the true self is authentic and resilient. Typically, the false self is present at the surface of relationships at work while the true self resides beneath the surface and is hidden from view. Given the defensive and political culture of many organizations, the false self fosters deception, mixed messages, camouflage and the like. The false self is dependent while the true self is relatively independent.

Often in opposition to the prevalence of a false self system, organizational stories (assessments and diagnoses) presented to participants tend to surface a narrative truth embedded in the actual experiences and perceptions of members. By challenging the defensive and ritualistic status quo of organizations, these narratives frequently provide an opportunity for authentic engagements with issues and problems of significance to the organization members. Thus, as a component of psychoanalytically oriented organizational assessment, diagnostic and hermeneutic, organizational stories often call for a more authentic view of the culture as a requisite to moving people and organizations away from hierarchic dominance and submission, defensiveness and deception, and toward less hierarchic, more reliable and authentic collaborative structures. However, such progressive shifts from "not good-enough" to "good-enough" facilitating environments does not occur without resistance to insight and change.

In an effort to illuminate the psychological nature of resistance to organizational authenticity, I offer comments of participants from actual organizational interventions to illustrate what Christopher Bollas, in *The Shadow of the Object* (1987), calls the "unthought known" in organizational analysis:

> Very often the location of freely associated ideas—of those thoughts that spontaneously register the content of psychic life—is in the psychoanalyst. This is so because the patient cannot express his conflict in words, so the full articulation of pre-verbal transference evolves in the analyst's countertransference. The transference–countertransference interaction, then, is an expression of the unthought known. The patient knows the object-setting through which he developed, and it is a part of him, but it has yet to be thought. The psychoanalytic understanding of the transference–countertransference discourse is a way of thinking the unthought known. (1987, 230)

In my application of this concept to organizations, I suggest that it is less the case that participants do not know; it is rather more typically the case that they have not thought of it. The organizational story told by the observer is the enunciation of the unthought known and is a depiction of the organization as a synthesis of themes, patterns, and points of urgency (Kets de Vries and Miller 1984; Diamond and Allcorn 2009). This also refers to the organizational text as a representation of the consultant's listening deeply, observing, participating, and communicating with and back to participants. This depiction of the unthought known is, then, a source of authenticity.

Following the telling of the organizational story (as diagnosis and assessment) observers are known to make pronouncements such as the following: "Oh, so you told them what they already knew." Frequently this implies: "What did they need you for, if all you did was tell them what they already knew?" I think the answer for our purposes of reflection and capturing the paradox of organizational diagnosis and change is to say "yes and no." It may be true that by conveying their observations and interpretations organizational theorists and consultants communicate with the telling of the organizational story something the participants "already know." This is the case particularly because these narrative data are derived from confidential and anonymous, structured, one-on-one interviews, (nonconfidential) group interviews, and other on-site observations. These data are derived from the participants themselves and then *contained*, processed, and organized by the psychoanalytically oriented consultants (Bion 1962; Diamond and Allcorn 2009).

Organizational members had *not thought* of it. They *knew it but they had not consciously thought* about it. Possibly they felt it, but could not articulate it. I often observe behavior and body language contrary to the statement: "We knew it all along." That is, participants appear anxious and defensive. This defensive resistance denotes the struggle of the true self behind the patina of false self. They seem to have an assortment of feelings, ranging from shame and guilt to hostility and shock, about their organizational story. It often feels as if the consultants have surfaced something taboo and too awkward to speak about. Yet, it is written and presented as our best representation of their collective voice.

In fact, frequently the comments (noted above) are followed by: "Yes, but no one has pulled it [the group narrative] all together in this way; we have not seen it or heard it in this form." They seem to be saying it (the unthought known) is different now, as if its form and meaning were previously unclear. Then, some brave souls might say: "Sure, we knew it but now it is out in the open [public sphere] and we have to deal with it." Then, there are those who in an apparent state of amazement say: "I knew there were problems but I didn't know it was this bad!" It is as if the act of surfacing the diagnostic narrative *reminds* organizational members of the emotional shape and sensations of the embodied and suppressed emotions—the true self. Is this an illustration of lifting the barrier of repression and surfacing the unmentionable, and more particularly the unthought known?

Whatever the nature of their response, the process tends to result in enhanced consciousness of participants' collective experiences and perceptions over time. So, I submit that the seemingly contradictory "no" response to the subjects proclaiming that what they heard from the consultants is what they already knew reflects the nature of the response as indicative of the "unthought known."

A psychoanalytic organization theory and practice values participants' willingness to admit that they do not know certain things about themselves and their organization. This personal capacity might be described as the willingness or ability to accept the unknown within the context of *transference and countertransference* dynamics between clients and consultants, as well as between executives, managers, and their employees (Diamond and Allcorn 2003). In organizations, present relationships are often emotionally loaded with personal biographies shaped by past parental and authority relations as well as past attachments.

The concepts of transference and countertransference refer to the unconscious intrapersonal and intersubjective structure of relationships: it is the organizational (structural, typically hierarchical, and relational) context in which emotions and thoughts are consciously, pre-consciously, and unconsciously, shared between two or more people. In some cases, transference and countertransference dynamics are shaped by the combination of a chain of command and individual proclivities in role. Narcissistic and dismissive leaders may be surrounded by underlings hungry for recognition and approval—what is described by Kohut (1977, 7–8) and by Winnicott (1971, 111–112) as a "mirroring" transference. Emotionally (and physically) distant managers may treat workers in a manner that unconsciously mirrored their treatment by a distant and resigned chief executive. Workers at some level "knew" this (they could feel it) but they could not "think it" or discuss it. It was unspeakable and taboo, at least until the consultants arrived and made it public at the feedback sessions.

The concept of "unthought known" helps us to understand defensive initial and common responses from participants to their experience of hearing, seeing, and feeling the consultants' depiction (or *mirror*) of their organizational identity—the intersubjective structure of organization. It is important to point out that, in a psychoanalytically informed organizational diagnosis, by the time consultants' report back to the participants they have established an emotional attachment with members. Consultants and participants carry feelings for one another, and along with these feelings are expectations and some degree of trust reflective of a good-enough holding environment. Defensive participant responses signify genuine resistance to insight and change, which is a consequence of the opportunity through the narrative of language and storytelling to surface the unconscious and preconscious material of collective organizational life.

Psychoanalytic Organization Theorist and Consultant as Transitional and Transformational Object

Profound change has primitive, infantile origins, which affect the capacity of individuals and groups to assess and cope with change in the routine and status quo. As noted above, Winnicott (1965) refers to the parent's holding of the baby as the *facilitating environment*, which in the case of "good-enough" mothering, and the establishment of a secure and safe attachment, produces a child with the confidence and curiosity to individuate and explore both the internal and external worlds—a capacity to move from total dependency toward relative independence. For both Winnicott and Bollas, the parent is a *transformational object* signifying maturation and change processes of attachment, separation, loss, and the baby's experience of transforming from wet to dry, cold to warm, hungry to full, rejected to accepted, anxious to safe and secure, and so on.

If organizational diagnosis unveils a narrative and emotional truth in the otherwise unspeakable story of organizational membership, then inevitably participants will not only have something to say about it, but they will reexperience it in the moment. To say that transference between consultant and participant takes the shape of a "transformational" or "transitional" object assumes human contact and attachment. This emotional tie often takes the form of dependency of the participant on the organizational consultant. This relational link requires potential space, empathy, recognition, and multiple interactions.

Bollas (1987) develops the idea that in adult life individuals search for transformational objects in order to recollect an early object experience, to remember not cognitively but existentially—through intense experience—a relationship which was identified with transformation of the self. This is true for leaders and participants of organizational change. It is acknowledged by many observers that change processes inevitably stir primitive, infantile emotions rooted in attachment, separation, and loss, which then trigger associated participant anxieties (Jaques 1955; Menzies 1960; Kernberg 1979; Diamond 1984, 1998; Stein 1994, 1998, 2001). Executives and their employees somewhat reluctantly open their systems to interventions, exposing their vulnerabilities and admitting to relative strangers their need for help. Consequently, organizational members protect themselves by unwittingly engaging in primitive defensive processes such as psychological regression and splitting.

For example, some participants will not like what they feel or think about the consultants' feedback in the organizational diagnosis. They may displace these bad feelings onto the consultants and project blame onto them for participants' imperfect or dysfunctional circumstances: "Well, it really wasn't so bad until you showed up!" Psychological regression in response to anticipated anxiety about assessments leads to splitting good and bad feelings and then aggressively projecting the bad emotions in the form of blame onto the consultants. This primitive and infantile experience may not meet the unconscious expectations and fantasies of participants to be cured with some magical formula; participants will have to confront processes of change, loss, and grief. Hence, the unthought known of organizational change may very well reside within the participants' unconscious experiences of infantile transformations.

Similar to how members use the organization and fellow members as transformational objects, participants use consultants (and consultants use participants) as transformational objects as well. Observing transference and countertransference dynamics between consultants and participants illuminates underlying forces unique to the organization and its inhabitants, intersubjective dynamics that shape the structure and pattern of organizational identity. In comprehensive and longer term consultations, immersion into the subjects' organizational culture is essential. Inevitably, via transference and countertransference dynamics, organizational consultants become containers of the participants' unconscious emotions. Consultants may be treated unwittingly as spies and invited intruders, saviors and messiahs, jesters and fools, among other covert roles. Unconscious fantasies are frequently displaced onto consultants as transformational objects and rendered outside of the participants' awareness.

In the internal world of organizational members (leaders and followers), fantasies, wishes, fears, and experiences are *transferred* onto organizations and their leaders (as well as consultants) as transformational objects. Different modes of experience are possible due to the collision of subjectivities and social structures of power and authority in organizations. These dynamics have their emotional roots in infancy and childhood. They reside within the adult selves of individuals who assume professional roles and responsibilities within organizational hierarchies.

Before concluding I share a brief case illustration of the consequences of a lack of potential space and absence of a facilitating organizational culture.

Case Illustration: Consequences of Destructive Narcissism, Intimidation, and Conflict at an Entertainment Company

In the instance of one corporation burdened by dysfunction and conflict between two key functions, marketing and operations, workers reported feeling suffocated and intimidated by their CEO. Consequently, conflicted relations and communications between these two functions jeopardized the future of the company, which motivated the CEO to agree with a consultation recommended by his Board of Directors.

From the application of a Winnicottian perspective, I suggest that organizations and organizational identities are relational, experiential, and perceptual systems, and that the heart and soul of their potentiality resides in their capacity to depict the psychological reality, transference and counter-transference, psychodynamics unique to them. In this case, organizational diagnosis revealed a culture and leadership that demanded compliant workers whose primary objective was aggrandizement and idealization of the CEO, leaving as secondary their actual role functions and job descriptions. Directives from the top required compliance. Authority was rarely questioned or engaged by dialog. The executive convinced himself that only he knew the best strategies for marketing and operations. Also, he had a reputation of lecturing staff at weekly meetings where it was highly unusual for him to answer any questions posed by workers. Once the Board learned the company was losing profits, as a result of a dysfunctional relationship between operations in the Midwest and marketing in New York, they insisted on a comprehensive organizational consultation.

While it is apparent that destructive narcissism in the leader is at the center of workers' experience, reparation and change can only occur by opening up the organization to itself and rendering transparent the psychodynamics of intimidation and oppression in the workplace. The establishment of potential space and a facilitating environment means locating a safe space, geographically and psychologically, where members can playfully and creatively articulate problems and invent strategic solutions. These Winnicottian ideas of potentiality and facilitation are crucial to successful intervention in which organizational defenses and dysfunction, resistance to insight and change, are surfaced, confronted, and worked through.

In the case of the entertainment company, which ironically lacked a sense of humor or playfulness at work, the carving out of potential space coincided with the consultants' telling of the organizational story and the opportunity for feedback from workers in a safe environment where humor and authenticity might return.

Conclusion

Winnicott has said about the defensive nature of the false self: "Its defensive function is to hide and protect the true self, whatever that might be." He further states: "Observers tend to think it is the real person in relationships; however the false self begins to fail in situations in which what is expected is a whole person. The false self is essentially lacking, true self is hidden" (1965, 144). Organizational diagnosis confronts participants with the "real self" of the organization, one with a projected self-image of good *and* bad attributes, as opposed to a "false self" following the "party line." This means that participants accustomed to relational systems rooted in suspicious and fragmentary modes of experience in which psychological splitting is incorporated and institutionalized into the status quo (such as illustrated by the previous case) will find themselves having to wrestle, emotionally and cognitively, with the concept of integrated and whole self-objects as opposed to fragmented and part object relationships.

In telling the organizational story, psycho dynamically oriented consultants confront participants with their best articulation of the authentic and actual organizational identity (collective or group self). This confrontation collides with the defensive and false patina of organizational identity, which participants actively promote, although often unwittingly. Frequently, participants respond defensively to the narrative presentation regardless of how balanced, nonjudgmental, and descriptively written and communicated. In fact, many feel judged and respond by saying: "Well, it can't be that bad!" "Don't you have anything good to say?" It is as if the guards at the gate of the false self are reassembling to protect the potentially vulnerable participants from within from unconscious emotions and the unthought known.

Potential space is a metaphor and at best a fluid metaphoric process. Potential space occupies the imaginary location of communication and human contact. It represents the requisite psychological structure and processes for organizational innovation, play, and invention. It is not something we socially engineer. Rather, it is a process that occurs when nurtured and facilitated by leadership and psychoanalytically informed organizational consultants. Potential space requires leadership's acknowledgement and recognition of workers' value, integrity, and competency. Thus, organizing for potential space necessitates "holding" in the Winnicottian sense and simultaneously "getting out of the way" of participants. Analogous to the good-enough facilitating environment between parent and baby during separation and individuation, organizing transformational and authentic organizations implies limiting abusive and oppressive authoritarian practices by managing the excesses of hierarchic dominance, submission, authoritarianism and micromanagement. Facilitating and authentic organizations are substantially more bottom-up in their decision making and strategic implementations, and much less top-down and management driven.

Authentic organizations are possible where leaders attend to and minimize the inevitable emergence of social defense systems (or defensive organizations). Nevertheless, individual members will no doubt engage in self- and other-deceptive and protective practices, which suppress and camouflage their actions, errors, and failures of implementation. Organizational participants will unavoidably defend themselves against anxieties. Social defense systems ostensibly protect participants from having to face conflicts, problems, errors, and the assumption of personal responsibility. These false self systems suppress the capacity to face mistakes and imperfections. Thus, the facilitation of good-enough organizations and leaders entails managing the destructive expansiveness of narcissism and the false idealization of leadership. Demystification and deflation of the idealized narcissistic leader can result from a process of analysis and intervention such as the case illustration above. In some instances, narcissistic leaders accept changes that come with a more facilitating environment where workers offer genuine feedback and engagement in reflective dialog.

Narcissism is inflated and potentially destructive among organizational leaders when hierarchy is manipulated to accentuate immoderate executive power and authority. Potential space is critical to organizational transformation and the movement away from hierarchic dominance and oppression and toward authentic organizing of true selves into collaborative and intersubjective structures. For Winnicott, emotional health and well-being has to do with the reliability and mutuality of relationships. Reproducing Winnicott's holding environment at work implies embracing the dialectical tension between membership and separateness (Diamond 2016), or what Greenberg and Mitchell (1983, 189–190) call the dialectic between contact and differentiation. Hence, ironically, organizing for potential space is both an embrace and surrender to the ongoing tension between belonging and independence rooted in the "primary maternal preoccupation" of infancy and the "me and not me" of the nascent and emerging sense of self. Finally, bringing Winnicottian theory into the organization signifies a movement away from the governing assumption of management by control and dominance, and toward the governing assumption of management by good-enough facilitation and surrender to human nature.

References

Allcorn, S., and H.F. Stein. 2015. *The Dysfunctional Workplace: Theory, Stories, and Practice.* Columbia: University of Missouri Press.

Benjamin, J. 2004. Beyond Doer and Done To: An Intersubjective View of Thirdness. *The Psychoanalytic Quarterly* 73(1): 5–46.

Bion, W.R. (1962). Learning from Experience. London: Karnac.

Bion, W.R. 1967. *Second Thoughts.* London: Karnac.

Bollas, C. 1987. *The Shadow of the Object: Psychoanalysis of the Unthought Known.* New York: Columbia University Press.

Diamond, M.A. 1984. Bureaucracy as Externalized Self-System: A View from the Psychological Interior. *Administration and Society* 16(2): 195–214.

———. 1993. *The Unconscious Life of Organizations: Interpreting Organizational Identity.* Westport, CT: Quorum Books, Greenwood.

———. 1998. The Symbiotic Lure: Organizations as Defective Containers. *Administrative Theory and Praxis* 20(3): 315–325.

———. 2016. *Discovering Organizational Identity.* Columbia: University of Missouri Press.

Diamond, M.A., and S. Allcorn. 2003. The Cornerstone of Psychoanalytic Organizational Analysis: Psychological Reality, Transference and Counter-Transference. *Human Relations* 56(4): 491–514.

———. 2009. *Private Selves in Public Organizations: The Psychodynamics of Organizational Diagnosis and Change.* New York: Palgrave Macmillan.

Erikson, E. (1964). Insight and Responsibility. New York: W.W. Norton.

Ghent, E. 1990. Masochism, Submission, Surrender. *Contemporary Psychoanalysis* 26: 169–211.

Greenberg, J., and S. Mitchell. 1983. *Object Relations in Psychoanalytic Theory.* Cambridge, MA: Harvard University Press.

Grinberg, L., D. Sor, and E. Tabak de Bianchedi.1993. *New Introduction to the Work of Bion.* Rev ed. Northvale, NJ: Jason Aronson.

Jaques, E. 1955. Social Systems as a Defense Against Persecutory and Depressive Anxiety. In *New Directions in Psycho-Analysis*, ed. M. Klein, P. Heimann, and P.E. Money-Kyrle, 478–498. London: Tavistock.

Kernberg, O. (1979). “Regression in Organizational Leadership.” Psychiatry 42: 24-39.

Kets de Vries, M.F.R. 2006. *The Leader on the Couch.* New York: Palgrave Macmillan.

Kets de Vries, M.F.R., and D. Miller. 1984. *The Neurotic Organization.* San Francisco, CA: Jossey-Bass.

Kohut, H. (1977). The Restoration of Self. New York: International Universities Press.

Menzies, I. 1960. A Case in the Functioning of Social Systems as a Defense against Anxiety: A Report on a Study of the Nursing Service of a General Hospital. *Human Relations* 13: 95–121.
Modell, A. 1984. *Psychoanalysis in a New Context*. New York: International Universities Press.
Ogden, T. 1994. *Subjects of Analysis*. Northvale, NJ: Jason Aronson.
———. 2004. The Analytic Third: Implications for Psychoanalytic Theory and Technique. *The Psychoanalytic Quarterly* 73(1): 167–1196.
Schafer, R. 1983. *The Analytic Attitude*. New York: Basic Books.
Stacey, R. 1996. *Complexity and Creativity in Organizations*. San Francisco, CA: Berrett-Koehler Publishers.
Stapley, L. 1996. *The Personality of the Organization*. London: Free Association Books.
Stein, H.F. 1994. *Listening Deeply*. Boulder, CO: Westview.
———. 1998. *Euphemism, Spin, and the Crisis in Organizational Life*. Westport, CT: Quorum Books, Greenwood.
———. 2001. *Nothing Personal, Just Business*. Westport, CT: Quorum Books, Greenwood.
Winnicott, D.W. 1958. The Capacity to be Alone. *International Journal of Psychoanalysis* 39: 416–420.
———. 1960. The Theory of the Parent-Infant Relationship. *International Journal of Psychoanalysis* 41: 37–55.
———. 1965. *The Maturational Processes and the Facilitating Environment*. New York: International Universities Press.
———. 1971. *Playing and Reality*. London: Tavistock.

CHAPTER 14

Winnicott and the History of Welfare State Thought in Britain

Gal Gerson

What view of society and politics follows from perceiving the quest for company as the essential human motivation? The object-relations perspective developed in mid-twentieth-century Britain by D.W. Winnicott and likeminded clinicians such as John Bowlby, Ronald Fairbairn, and Ian Suttie departed from the older psychoanalytic theories expounded by Sigmund Freud and Melanie Klein (Mitchell and Black 1995). The object-relations authors shifted the emphasis toward a more optimistic outlook. It amounted to the formulation in psychoanalytic terms of a distinct, if nuanced, social and political theory, one whose subjects are less isolated and anguished than those entailed by the Freudian and Kleinian models.

Here, I focus on Winnicott and the overlap between his professional stance and a certain historical pattern of British social thought. In stressing the role of attachment, Winnicott matches the perspective offered by early-twentieth-century liberals, social democrats, and other reform-oriented intellectuals who attempted to find a non-selfish basis for political structures. These political commentators saw the core motivation that connects individuals to one another as crucial for justifying the nascent

G. Gerson (✉)
Department of Government and Political Theory, School of Political Sciences, University of Haifa, Haifa, Israel

M.H. Bowker, A. Buzby (eds.), *D.W. Winnicott and Political Theory*,
DOI 10.1057/978-1-137-57533-3_14

welfare state apparatus. The preoccupation with sociability was echoed and given a firmer cognitive basis by Winnicott and other exponents of object-relations psychoanalysis.

The proximity between Winnicott and his allies on the one hand and a certain phase of social organization, along with its ideology, on the other has been noted before. Some correspondences between object-relations thinking and broader humanistic interpretations of Christianity and enlightenment have been explored (Clarke 2006; Miller 2008), as has Winnicott's own particular fitness for providing a basis for an inclusive social theory (Benjamin 1988). The interface between psychoanalytical thought and the welfare state has also been noted (Hoggett 2008). The emphasis here, however, will be placed on Winnicott's concurrence with one particular point in the broader welfare state ideology, namely its historical quest for an explanation of human sociability.

The argument is not causal. Winnicott was not politically engaged and shows scant evidence of being directly impacted by his time's social philosophy. His own work, moreover, was seldom considered by political writers. Instead, I point to conceptual proximities: this was the cognitive world that made Winnicott and the other object-relations writers possible; this is the environment in which they could formulate their theories and in which these theories found resonance; this is the social system in which they made sense. Winnicott's explanation of sociability as a core motivation and his consequent call on society to respect this sociability fit into a universe where such thinking seemed logical and where it served the ideological ends formulated more explicitly and systematically by political theorists.

These authors were primarily exponents of a worldview that formed around the last years of the nineteenth century and combined elements of liberalism and socialism. Not so much an organized movement with formal institutions as a general and loosely bounded trend within educated public opinion, this political segment was known by different names to different participants and later commentators. I use the expressions progressive liberalism or reforming liberalism and their inflections to designate it. This movement provided the basic arguments and motivations that led to the construction of a welfare state from within the premises of liberal democracy. As it produced no authoritative text to match the function that Marx, for example, provided for socialism, this movement relied on a collection of ideas offered by disparate individuals working in an array of fields—journalists, economists, administrators, and others. The growing psychological care sector provided its own theorists, among which Winnicott was central.

His views coach an overall social sensibility in professional terms, and therefore provide that sensibility with another conceptual anchor.

I will first discuss the fundamentals of object-relations thinking and Winnicott's particular contribution to it. I will then explore the challenges that advanced liberal theory met in early-twentieth-century Britain, focusing particularly on its need to assume a core entitlement that justifies welfare measures. I will then argue that Winnicott's psychoanalytic approach could solve some internal and external problems within the progressive liberal debate on sociability, and that, consequently, Winnicott could shore up the progressive arguments for a liberal welfare state.

Object-Relations Theory and Winnicott's Contribution

Winnicott was a part of a broader turn within psychoanalytical thought, one that involved substituting care, attention, and recognition for libidinal gratification. For Freud, sociability was a venue for libido. Social relations were accordingly undermined by the hostility that the scarcity of gratification generates, which Freud shorthanded into the Oedipal situation. Freud's notion of how society works was pessimistic. He warned that the effort to tone down tensions could amount to kicking the can further down the road, as the basic agony could not really be overcome. Hostility, he wrote in *Civilization and its Discontents*, can only be transferred to another group or another context, but it can never be over (Freud 1930). For Klein, similarly, relationships were perpetually marred by the indelible guilt involved in inborn aggression (Klein 1964). Klein wrote little about her overall perception of history and society, but her clinical approach assumes a dark world where any apparent calm is continuously threatened by the fermenting inborn aggression. Object-relations theory, by contrast, perceives sociability as fundamental and independent of other motivations. It distances attachment to family, friends, and the larger community from its earlier associations with shame and suppressed violence (Gomez 1997; Greenberg and Mitchell 1983; Hughes 1989). Accordingly, object-relations theory raises the prospect of rough social harmony.

Since the late 1920s, Ian Suttie had been stressing that, as the mother is usually the first company that a newborn meets, the relationship with her conditions the personality's subsequent development. Inverting Freud's interpretation of the infant's attachment to its mother as primarily physical, and therefore conflicted and troubled by the Oedipal conundrum, Suttie argued that attachment is primarily emotional (Suttie 1952). Maternal influence, he thought, could be strong enough to heal whatever rifts were created in early childhood, if the family is placed within a culture that assigns dignity and agency to mothers. Sexuality gathers its significance from its ability to provide a location for a meaningful relationship rather than from the bodily sensation it involves (Suttie and Suttie 1932, 204–206). Subsequent object-relations theory similarly views the sensory aspect of the child's perception of the parent as a vehicle for the underlying social drive. Ronald Fairbairn was central here (Scharff and Birtles 2014). 'The child's oral relationship with his mother,' Fairbairn writes, 'is the foundation upon which all his future relationships … are based. It also represents his first experience of a social relationship; and it therefore forms the basis of his subsequent attitude to society' (Fairbairn 1952, 24–25).

To these insights, Winnicott adds a reinterpretation of Klein. For Klein, the infant is born with destructive urges directed at part-objects that are largely fantastic. While this may be assuaged by interaction with the real and whole object, the mother, the earlier, 'paranoid-schizoid' element is always present. Together with the later, 'depressive' element that seeks solace and reparation, the paranoid-schizoid ingredient forms a system in which the sociable side of the personality is constantly destabilized by hostility and anxiety. Winnicott formally endorses this model. However, he emphasizes process over positional structure. This process is one through which the various aspects of personality are integrated by contact with an external agent. The mother provides the physical boundary that holds and contains the child's otherwise incompatible elements, thus setting the stage for integration. The destructive urges do not disappear. Instead, they synthesize into a cohesive whole that relates to others while deploying its aggression to test the limits of, and therefore ultimately reaffirm, the relationship (Rodman 2003).

This process involves a certain calibration of parental response. At first, the mother attends to the child immediately and unconditionally. In this way, a sense of continuity in time, stability in space, and trust in others is established. Aggression is tried, but as the mother is not destroyed by the child's attacks, hostility is converted to trust. Later on, however, the mother begins to delay her responses. The child can now withstand the mother's relative distancing because the record of earlier care has been internalized to such a degree that actual close attention is no longer urgent.

The child now simultaneously seeks company and can be confident about its durability: The other is out there, and is valued precisely because it is beyond our control, as we have been shown we cannot destroy it. She is established as an independent subject. One can now relate to an absent mother, as her existence does not depend on her being within one's sight. This relationship unfolds through new channels in objects on which the internalized parental image is projected. Such objects can initially be a blanket or a soft toy, a nursery rhyme or a bedtime ritual. Being external, these objects and activities become means of communication with others, besides the mother: they occupy a transitional position between the subject and external reality (Winnicott 1971, 1–25).

Access to communication venues in work, art, sports, scientific exploration, or public involvement becomes as essential for the adult's health as direct maternal attention was for the child's. To the extent that the individual feels confident about engaging in them, these pursuits can function as transitional phenomena that extend into adult life the function of the blanket or soft toy in childhood: Home is where we start from, and the entire social world is where we capitalize on the health gained at home. Healthy adults perform for others, concrete, internalized, or conceptualized through such broad abstractions as 'society,' 'public opinion,' 'posterity,' or the like. Every meaningful action that is more than mechanical repetition is action within a community that can offer recognition and validation (Winnicott 1971, 6–8).

The theory, however, notes that in some cases, healthy development does not take place. Family situations in which parents cannot satisfactorily respond to children generate illness. Such illness may take several forms. Deprived of comforting internal objects, the individual might be motivated to regain the lost relationship by inflicting pain on others. An individual driven this way might construct relationships in terms of conflict and alienation: these dispositions will be the basis of his or her identity as a person. Aggression and violence are directed at a world that stands for the frustrating or absent parent (Winnicott 1986, 21–22, 242–259). Crime, delinquency and intolerance would ensue. While normal, 'good-enough' social relations are feasible, such distortions do occur.

Sociability and Advanced Liberalism

This clinical perspective has to do with more than purely professional concerns or the internal history of the psychoanalytic movement. It fits into a broader context of British social thought. The idea that disinterested mutual commitment is the primary good that people seek when left to their own devices attracted many late-nineteenth-century authors. The phasing-down of organized religion's prevalence during the latter half of the nineteenth century meant that critics of materialism were left with no footing. The issue, for British thinkers, was not so much capitalism as an economic system, as the morality that participating in a capitalist society implied.

This morality, as it was understood, implied that material reward is the main end that people pursue. It implied a selfish agent living in an atomistic civilization. Those who were taken aback by this prospect had to find a platform from which to criticize and correct it. What was there above and beyond material fulfillment to tie individuals to each other? What other rewards were there on offer for sincere effort and good conduct? How could ethical behavior be defined under such conditions of uncertainty? To address these doubts, commentators developed a rhetoric of public spirit, duty, and altruism. The participationist tradition that ran from Aristotle to Hegel and then from Hegel to local thinkers like T.H. Green, taught early-twentieth-century British authors to value the encounter with the other as the chief educative experience. Within this mode of thought, individuals are never complete or satisfied on their own: They unceasingly cluster together to be morally, intellectually, and emotionally enriched through interaction with their fellows. Acting with and for others is normatively higher and ultimately more satisfying than acting solely for oneself (Collini 1991; Den Otter 1996; Nicholson 1990; Vincent and Plant 1984).

In terms of policy, emphasizing the role of sociability could back up the turn toward 'collectivism,' a term that referred to allowing a larger role for the state in providing social services. Such measures involved a tension within liberalism between, on the one hand, individual entitlements to privacy and property that could be curtailed through the taxation required to enable public services, and, on the other hand, the moral will to address poverty and inequality. In the world of late-Victorian and Edwardian British liberalism, centralizing measures could not be grounded in an appeal to national greatness. British reformers disliked what they saw as the Prussian, statist perception of the nation as a hallowed whole that transcended individual wills. The notion of sociability, however, could legitimize the state's organized intervention in social interaction without recourse to such authoritarianism. It could justify the call for publicly supporting the institutions where such interaction occurs. Individuals were entitled to meet others and bond with them. Maintaining the forums that made such interactions possible could be shored up on liberal grounds. People had rights to life, liberty, and community. Society as a venue for companionship, rather than the state as the holder of military power, could now be perceived as an agent with its distinct interests and rights (Harris 1993, 11–13).

This reaction against what was seen as a demanding capitalist ethic that left little scope for non-economic pursuits and non-instrumental encounters was mixed with a certain degree of nostalgia. In the first decades of the twentieth century, there were those who looked back to the Greek spirit of civil friendship; and there were those who longed for the intimate medieval hearth (Burns 1919; Nicklin 1898). Among political authors, R.H. Tawney's ethical socialism was largely based on the notion that disinterested exchange and 'fellowship' are fundamental needs that go neglected in the 'acquisitive society' (Tawney 1921; Dennis and Halsey 1988, 149–169).

However, the notion of sociability as an independent, primary motivation required a coherent and period-appropriate theory to explain it: Why was the drive to be near others so prevalent? What made it benevolent? The reliance on Aristotle or on ancient virtue could not suffice in a society where classical education was losing its centrality. Additionally, Edwardian progressives distinguished their own claim about the centrality of 'love,' 'fellowship,' or 'relationship' from what was called at the time the gregarious instinct. The turn of the nineteenth century saw a surge in the discussion of crowd behavior. Theorists like Gustave Le Bon (1896) and Gabriel Tarde (1903) suggested that individual conduct changes when put in a group to become herd-like. Reason and the sense of separateness disappear, and imitation takes their place. At the time, these claims enjoyed some scientific credibility, and there were ways in which liberal and social-democratic writers incorporated them into their own views (Wallas 1908). However, the incorporation was limited, as for progressive liberals individual distinction and autonomy could not be abandoned. The solidarity and cooperation that characterizes humans in the progressive liberal worldview had to be a concomitant of, not a contrast to, rational individuality. Liberals could not allow autonomy to be bypassed by a blind drive to imitate.

To address the need for a philosophical backbone to support their beliefs, progressive liberals initially turned to evolution. In spite of its prevalent image as linked to right-wing social Darwinism, the theory of evolution was deployed at the turn of the nineteenth century by most political creeds. If capitalists and imperialists on the right appealed to the harsher aspects of biological selection to justify their support for competition and war, progressive liberals relied on what they thought was evidence for the worth of solidarity, empathy, and cooperation. Progressives argued that humanity's ascent to the advanced level of organization in which weaker members are protected was itself an evolutionary development (Burrow 1966; Jones 1980; Stack 2000). Civilization's refusal to abandon the weak allowed for broader variation, as more types of people survived. Solidarity and tolerance could be seen as both the outcome and source of humanity's supremacy (Freeden 1978, 82–99).

Liberal philosophers like L.T. Hobhouse (1924, 151) noted that individuals are cared for by others from their birth, and so never encounter an asocial condition. Species survive if their individual representatives make it to reproductive adulthood. The more developed species require a longer and more complex period of nurture. The maternal care that makes infants' subsistence possible is humanity's essential condition. But parental care exceeds concerns with nutrition and shelter. It involves an emotional attitude. That attitude, therefore, is the foundation of all social transaction (Hobhouse 1947, 162–163). Individual conduct is conditioned by the experience and anticipation of love. Love's prevalence, Hobhouse argues (1924, 149), is valid even for manifestly destructive behavior:

> The individual mind is inherently a centre of relationships to others, and craves these relationships if it does not find them. Even on its most egoistic side it wants others to feed its vanity, to dominate, to show off to. In its bare formation, then, the community is a product of the general and inherent trend of mind.

Instead of the formless crowd or the classical civil forum, progressive liberals focused on the family. In the home, liberals found both a location for the encouragement and expression of sociability, and a national symbol that drew them closer to broader strands of opinion. Early-twentieth-century commentators of differing political hues compared the English household favorably with what they saw as its more disciplinarian and formalist Continental—especially German—counterpart (Harris 1993, 79–84, 93–94). This perception of the home as a favored site for personal expression and fulfillment could easily be synthesized with the new emphasis on a form of sociability that does not require the dissolution of individual separateness. 'society,' the progressive organ *The Speaker* (1905) remarked, 'is the best of all human pleasures, and the family … must provide the best society.'

The family illustrated the prevalence of sociability in two ways: parental care and marital commitment. Maternal devotion was held up as the primary instance of disinterested benevolence, where keeping company is its own reward. Mothers share their whole existence with their young children, whose company provides them with the overriding satisfaction of their lives. As the family is harnessed to parenthood, and as parenthood consists of sharing one's time with, and devoting one's attention to, another person, sociability emerges as a core interest around which other motivations and satisfactions are organized. Hobhouse urged perceiving 'mother love, paternal love and family affection' as 'the prime examples of an impulse inherent in mind, and potentially as wide as the range of life' (1924, 151).

Marriage, for its part, is the place where evolution, interpreted as the simultaneous development of cooperation and individuality, achieves perfection. Authors such as Patrick Geddes and J. Arthur Thomson (1889) and D.G. Ritchie (1893) found a link, as they saw it, between, on the one hand, the sense of separateness and autonomy that characterizes human individuals, and, on the other hand, people's ability to attach themselves to each other in ever more extensive formations. In advanced species, Hobhouse argued, there is a correlation between the inclination for bonding and cooperation and the existence of individually separate specimens. At the apex of the natural world, humans are more individually distinct than the members of any other species. At the same time, they are more capable of performing tasks together. In marriage, mates choose each other individually, but divide their tasks by gender and so become indispensable to each other (Hobhouse 1906).

Lifelong commitment within marriage also serves to downplay the role of sexuality. This de-emphasis had its own ideological function. Concern with physical pleasure was seen as selfish and material, another aspect of that 'economic man' against which revisionist liberals and social democrats struggled. By describing marriage as based on a sociable drive to which desire is incidental, reforming liberals instilled community and solidarity into what could otherwise be seen as a contract between two individuals for the purposes of using each other's bodies. Hobhouse took care to highlight this point. The 'sex impulse,' he writes,

> is no more than a bodily need or appetite. Fused with the root impulse to give and seek response, it becomes the most intimate personal relation wherein we come most nearly to the ideal of finding another who … will take all that we can give and give all that we need. (1924, 158)

The emphasis on sociability transmitted attention from instrumental relationships to shared pursuits, and highlighted the value of leisure and the domestic life. Humans are powered by a will to associate that pervades all relationships. It may be healthy when addressed correctly, or lead to avarice and aggression when not. Its main location is the family household, and it is best expressed in the mother's relation to the child and in the married partners' commitment to each other. This perspective allowed progressive liberals to incorporate the rational agent of previous liberal theories into a perspective that did not exclude community. Rational individuality could no longer be accepted as a premise, as evolution showed that it was the product of a gradual development. However, rational individuality remained a normative end: Evolution teaches that species move toward greater individual distinction while generating more channels for cooperation and communication.

These ideas underpinned the progressives' policy platform. At its core lay the suggestion that government should be expanded without encroaching on individual rights. The market should be left standing so as to allow individuals to freely pursue their own ends, construct their own households, and weave a fabric of protected private activities around them. At the same time, profits should be taxed to foster more equality, so that gross imbalances would be avoided. Public funds should be channeled to social agencies that support individuals in their everyday lives, in terms of social security, medical services, educational advice, and the provision of a cultural context. These were all thought to be instrumental in maintaining the family-centered civilization that progressives envisaged.

This perspective places no watertight partition between private and public, as all meaningful interactions are motivated by the same social impulse. Involvement with each other's lives—at home and neighborhood, but also through the means of state services and public activism—are primary goods that people seek (Goodin 1988, 70–71). Such goods cannot be assured within a strictly market-oriented order that recognizes nothing but property and its individual owners. Since community is a need and an entitlement, liberal government may be charged with imposing respect for it in the spaces where it most matters—in the region of domestic intimacy. While government intervenes forcibly only in extreme cases, it regards keeping individuals in communication with others as one of its major tasks. The progressive educator and social scientist, Graham Wallas (1914, 373), for example, suggested gearing the social-policy apparatus toward rescuing social isolates like the 'young unmarried artisan, or shopman, or clerk' by offering them public spaces in which they can meet others, as well as the leisure time in which to do so.

Accentuating the role of sociability legitimized expanding governmental control over society without recourse to nationalist or managerial rationales. Individual concerns with solidarity and support, rather than the need for fit soldiers or a greater economic efficiency, could be the basis for the demand that citizens give up some of their income as tax money to be spent on social agencies. This frame of mind could similarly justify opening up the household for some public surveillance. The welfare regime with its assurance of a minimal living standard was thought to function as an enabling space that allowed individuals to develop the confidence required to act independently and to make better use of the opportunities offered by the open market (Meadowcroft 1995, 142–148).

Winnicott and Social Policy

Reforming liberals and their allies reasonably succeeded in their project of extending government's mandate to cover welfare issues. By the 1940s, the comprehensive social agenda formulated by William Beveridge (1942), based on ideas phrased earlier by progressive liberals and social democrats, commanded almost nationwide allegiance. Paradoxically, at that same time the intellectual supports of the welfare agenda began to weaken. While that agenda referred to the existence of the sociable motivation for claiming that government should provide space for interpersonal solidarity, progressives were pressed for accounts of how this motivation worked. Having discarded religion, and faced with a decline of classical education, revisionist liberals were left with an overstretched biological explanation. Applying evolutionary principles to social questions, however, became outdated as the twentieth century wore on. New social sciences developed, in the framework of which the evolutionary plot was marginalized. By the mid-century, German National-Socialism had made any attempt to base social policies on biological considerations deeply suspect. The ideology of the liberal welfare state found itself in competition with Marxism, whose promise of solidarity and equality relied on environmental, rather than biological, factors.

The appearance of object-relations arguments within psychoanalytic debates could fill in the missing details and serve as an explanatory device within the ideological framework of progressive liberalism and welfare-state approaches. With its focus on sociability as a basic drive and on the significance of the family situation, and with its view of aggression as an avoidable pathology, object-relations theory matched the tenets of social-minded liberalism.

Winnicott, in particular, was compatible with the outlook that underpinned the welfare state. His overall perspective echoes the two interlinked elements of that outlook: liberal individualism, and the reliance of individuality on the social environment. Winnicott's central idea—the significance of transitional activity—is a statement about the need to both respect individual separateness and to accept that individual well-being can only be achieved through contact with others. 'The place where we live' is, for Winnicott, a culture that allows us to participate as distinct and integrated units. As he rejects the idea that people can live fulfilled lives wholly on their own, while at the same time insisting on their autonomy and distinctness, Winnicott upholds a socialized brand of liberalism (1971, 104–110).

Winnicott echoes historical forms of liberal thought by imagining a natural, benevolent, and spontaneous order that precedes formal institutions. Formulating his own model of the state of nature, Winnicott writes that complete isolation is abstractly possible, but does not actually materialize:

> At first there is unintegration, there is no bond between body and psyche, and no place for a not-ME reality. Theoretically, this is the original state, unpatterned and unplanned. In practice, this is not true, for the infant is being cared for, that is to say, loved, which means physically loved. Adaptation to need is almost complete. (Winnicott 1988, 131)

In infancy, the original condition that is common to all, humans are dependent. Their initial experience cannot include isolation, as they always already live in groups bound by emotion. 'If you show me a baby,' Winnicott writes, 'you certainly show me also someone caring for the baby' (1984, 99). The weaving of separate psychic parts into a whole can only come through contact with the outside, so that there is no coherent individual before society, and society is immediately structured—'patterned and planned'—by caring. Society is thus natural and precedes both separate individuality and any kind of institutionalized or coercive organization. This mirrors classical liberal stances, such as Locke's, in which government is perceived as an addition to an already existing set of natural relationships (see also Bowker, this volume).

However, there are two major differences between Winnicott's implied politics and classical liberalism. These differences drive Winnicott toward the revised, social-democratic version of liberalism. First, while classical liberals such as Locke acknowledge sociability as a primary, God-given character that underlies sexual and economic interaction, their models of the natural condition make subsistence the first requirement and property an inalienable right, as consuming food entails taking it away from public usage and so making it 'property.'

By contrast, Winnicott focuses on non-material needs. Infantile dependency means that the primary objective is the proximity of another person rather than subsistence. The right it grounds is not property, but company: the thing without which children would not survive. This interpretation impacts Winnicott's perception of privacy and exclusion. Mine and yours can only make sense when a separation between self and other has been established, so that recognizing the other is precondition for property to become a concept. Individual separation in its turn is a product of caring, as the holding parent sets a boundary for the child. Property signifies not exclusion, but sharing. For Winnicott, 'the first possession' is the transitional object, the blanket or soft toy the child treats as special because it carries the projected memory of parental care. The transitional object derives its value from its ability to serve as a vehicle of internal and external communication. Property is never completely private. It is always already social (Winnicott 1971, 2–3).

Second, Locke draws a tight boundary between home and politics. Adam, Locke mentions, was created whole. He had the full array of adult capacities that allowed him to take care of his own life. After Adam, children are not born with full bodily and mental capacities, but are instead deposited with their parents for a limited period during which they mature. Once minority is over, they acquire the ability to assess their own interests, and therefore to bargain and contract with others. They may make a social compact, constitute political society and become subjects of legal rights (Locke 1946, 27–39). Fully grown individuals hold property and raise families which political power may not touch. What takes place in the home is an automatic, natural process. Nurture does not require deliberation or the weighing-in of options, as its functions are biological determined and are therefore roughly identical in all occurrences. The home's product is the adult citizen who can choose, think and act differently from other such adults, and is the subject of instances such as law and politics that mediate between him or her and other such adults. The home is repetitive nature, the public sphere is creative politics.

Winnicott, by contrast, emphasizes the malleability of human character and the precarious nature of rational individuality. People differ in the impact that early attachment makes on them. 'Babies and mothers,' Winnicott writes, 'vary tremendously' (1964, 21). Nurturing cannot be reduced to automatic acts that are identical in all settings. The need to relate and the strategies for gratifying it exist from the first moment of life. Attachment patterns depend on inputs from caregivers. The particular shape they take in each case is neither uniform nor automatic. It is conditioned by the multiple factors involved in the type and size of the family and its relation to the broader environment. One result of this approach is that Winnicott perceives individuality as historical. There were and are social contexts which do not provide for personal integration and therefore do not allow full individuality to arise. Rather than a timeless natural process, the appearance of the separate personality is a human achievement, culture rather than nature (Winnicott 1971, 70).

Accordingly, while the mechanisms that allow physical survival are universal, the factors that make for the benevolent internalization of the parent figure differ. There is no natural realm where cyclical processes take their predetermined course, and no sharp break between the 'natural' sphere of family, on the one hand, and the conventional public world, on the other. Each individual life is political, in the sense of being uniquely determined by the characters, intentions, and liabilities of specific others, from its very start.

The classical liberal perception of the public sphere where rational adults engage with each other in deliberation and contract is reflected in Winnicott's model, but there is less to distinguish it from what happens in the smaller social units. Winnicott encourages school principals to encounter their students with the same holding posture that he attributes to the good-enough mother and the professional analyst (1986, 90–100). When explicitly addressing the political system, Winnicott recommends voting for individual representatives rather than for party lists, as this compels voters to relate to complex and concrete persons rather than to platforms or party names. Politics should ideally replicate and extend the pattern of healthy relating, in which others are valued because we realize that they are imperfect and subjective centers of desire rather than verbal abstractions (1986, 250). In all these sites, activities address the basic social motivation. Whereas Locke pictures a landscape which is split into nature and politics, private, and public, the vision offered by Winnicott is one of concentric circles where the same dynamic repeats itself on all social levels: mother and child, the family, the outside world.

However, a fundamental normative individualism remains. Winnicott stresses that relationships derive their value and ability to be fulfilling from their character of transpiring *between individuals*. The entire account of personal development in his theory centers on the formation of separate autonomy. The newborn 'is not yet a unit' (1988, 116). It is only a collection of limbs and sensations. As there is a Kleinian insight at the background of Winnicott's model, the implication of describing the newborn as incoherent is that this pre-integration phase is one of distress. It is populated with incompatible urges and persecutory part-objects. The integrated self, which is the evaluative end of childcare and therapy, becomes established through contact with a reliable caregiver who provides the infant with a point around which all else organizes. However, the caregiver completes the process by creating distance. When the caregiver or 'mother' begins to 'fail,' the child realizes that the 'mother' is beyond his or her control. She is placed outside the child's subjectivity, in the now-forming objective world. Through the internalization of the comforting maternal image, the child already has a mechanism with which to hold, contain, and integrate itself when the mother is gone (Winnicott 1984, 221–228). The integration of the subject and the realization of the other's distinct existence are achieved simultaneously. Parental constancy and reliability allow the infant to develop an anticipation of the future over which he or she may have some leverage. Thought is related to action, action to consequence. Play and experimentation may now take place, motivated by the need for find new objects and activities that may be used as means of communication. The rational, independent subject owes its existence to the community. The community, however, is valued precisely because it produces such subjects.

Transition and Welfare

What institutional settlement is implied by these professional formulations of the relationship between individual and society? I would like to suggest that this settlement roughly corresponds to the liberal welfare state. Relational analysts issued few explicit statements on public policy. For example, in his 1951 report to the World Health Organization, Bowlby presented a case for governmentally supporting the household. Separation at early age counts as major trauma. Its occurrence leads individuals to attempts to shut themselves off from the world (in order to avoid repetition of trauma), and hence to madness. It drives them to frantic attempts to regain the lost attention, and thus to violence and delinquency; and it leads them to efforts at controlling the environment so as to compensate for the pain (and hence to political fanaticism). By contrast, the healthy person is not haunted by the recurrence of trauma. He or she is not preoccupied with regaining the lost proximity to the mother, as that proximity has never been lost. Confidence is externalized in the ability to think and act independently, take risks, and build one's life around productive activity and reproductive family. Society has a stake in the maintenance of the household (Bowlby 1951).

While less detailed than Bowlby, Winnicott draws similar conclusions. As the basis for these conclusions, one may revisit the previously mentioned idea of the transitional object as the first possession. If this idea is developed, then we should arrive at a concept of property as primarily a means of communication. Through the concrete objects we own, we externalize the self and so make it available for viewing and comment, as for example in assessing its use and worth in trade. However, when seen this way, property should be understood as social in its origin as well as its use. It is not a sacred, untouchable character over which the individual has undisputed control. Rather, it is something that the individual holds by virtue of interacting with others on whom he or she is essentially dependent. Property, in other words, may be legitimately held but equally legitimately taxed. Winnicott's concept thus makes possible a setting in which both the open market and some governmental intervention are intellectually feasible. This corresponds to the basic operation mechanism of the liberal welfare state.

This view of the status of personal property is also borne out by Winnicott's more overt approach to the issue of entitlement. 'The first need,' he writes, 'is for protection of the baby–mother and baby–parent relationship at the early stage of every boy or girl child's development, so that there may come into being the potential space in which, because of trust, the child may creatively play' (1971, 109). Families are healthy when organized to meet the child's demand to be held, which means, at this time and to some extent in ours, the presence of a specialized parent, the mother, and a the presence of a breadwinner to support the caregiver. As the breadwinner faces the harsher world of work and commerce, he, too, should be protected to a certain degree from the uncertainties involved in both the workplace and the household. The family as a unit should likewise be supported in its engagement with everyday difficulties and the occasional misfortune. This may be carried out by providing social services in terms of medical, educational and housing agencies, which extend to the family the same pattern of care that the family gives to the child.

In a concentric, continuous world where there is no sharp break between public and private, Winnicott states, 'social provision is … an extension of the family' (1964, 93).

This is crucial for the well-being, not only of separate individuals, but of the community as a whole. The concern with health is a two-way street. While the societal collective protects and supports families, families produce the individuals who can fit into a free collective. To preserve a liberal society that respects individual entitlements, '[w]e can try to avoid interfering with the homes that can cope … with their individual children and adolescents. These *ordinary good homes* provide the only setting in which the innate democratic factor can be created' (Winnicott 1986, 246–7).

The 'innate democratic factor' is the potentiality for mature health: the personality that values the presence of the other it cannot control. The deliberation over opposing choices that democratic debate involves can only be undertaken by individuals who have learned in their young age to tolerate difference and to accept the separateness of other people. Individuality mutually complements solidarity, as 'in health a man or woman is able *to reach towards an identification with society without too great a loss of individual or personal impulse*' (Winnicott 1986, 27, *emphasis in original*). A society made up of a reasonable majority of such individuals can be stable and democratic, as the citizens can relate safely to others without giving up their own distinct individualities (Winnicott 1988, 152). Making this operative implies taking into account welfare as well as privacy. Individual autonomy is formed through contact, care, and solidarity, which society may institutionalize through public measures such as medical and educational services.

These ideas may also be highlighted by imagining the alternative involved in Winnicott's frame of reference. Drastic parental failure might bring about a situation in which individuals cannot stand the loss of control over their objects, and are therefore attracted to totalitarian ideologies that seem to offer tight control and immediate identification without a remnant of personal separation and autonomy (see also Levine, this volume). Wherever a sizeable constituency exists whose members have not gone through the integration and maturation process, Winnicott warns, 'democracy is not something which can become a political fact' (1988, 152). The necessary abilities both to distinguish oneself from society and to identify with it would not exist, thus laying the ground for a regime that demands complete identification and leaves no room for individuality. To prevent this decline into non-democratic polity, dysfunctional homes should be actively helped so as to bring their performance as close as possible to that of healthy families. Winnicott accordingly stresses 'the vital importance of the environmental provision especially at the beginning of the individual's infantile life' (1971, 66). For this reason, he writes, 'we make a special study of the facilitating environment in human terms, and in terms of human growth' (1971, 66). The essence of democracy, Winnicott writes, 'really does lie with … the ordinary, common-sense home.' The homes, in their turn, 'need help' to tackle issues of physical health in terms of both prevention and treatment; they furthermore require 'instruction in child-care, and help when their children have psychological illness or present behaviour problems' (1986, 247). Democracy depends on individual health, and health on an entire system of services and entitlements that society weaves around the household. Aiding the nurturing environment is existential for liberalism.

In his suggestion that environmental provision supplements, rather than detracts from, individual autonomy and spontaneous community, Winnicott supplies the progressive liberal worldview with a psychoanalytical background, and may be used to provide intellectual and theoretical cover for the measures that this liberalism takes in addressing social issues. The lacuna left open by the demise first of religion and then of the social interpretation of evolution is filled in. Winnicott's theory explains the primacy of sociability through the mechanisms of psychological internalization operative in early infancy.

From Winnicott's point of view, the earlier progressives had gotten most of the picture right, but for one issue. Assessing, correctly as far as Winnicott is concerned, that the mother–child bond is both the paradigm for all other relationships, and that it is the main location of sociability, the Edwardian reformers had focused on the mother and her activity. Mothers, however, are adults. Their lives and experiences exceed their motherhood. Hence, there was the (always implicit) question of why and how attachment suddenly appears in their lives as a key factor that structures the rest of their activities. Maternal behavior could be understood as a particularly feminine and biologically conditioned trait, but that would have harmed the claim that sociability is shared by all people. These difficulties had forced Hobhouse into the uncomfortable assertion that family relations are a mere example of something else, 'as wide as the range of life.' But where does that something else come from? Hobhouse's version of evolution stated the concurrence of cooperation and individual differentiation with biological complexity and ascendance, but it could not determine why this cooperation was so important to humans beyond its instrumental worth, and how it conditioned their behavior. Winnicott, along with the other object-relations thinkers, solves the riddle by turning the picture around: The clue is the infant, not the mother. It is the infant's primary need to associate with others and the infant's view of association as tied to comfort and internal coherence that is so clearly manifest in the nursing couple. As the infant has no previous history and no other pursuits save being an infant, it becomes apparent that its whole life, now and subsequently, will be structured by sociability.

Winnicott provides this explanation with only minimal recourse to biology. Unlike Bowlby, he resisted appeals to natural science and natural-science methods, arguing instead that the premises of psychoanalysis and its methods of narrative and verbalization should be the sole basis of the theory (1971, 79–80; 1986, 37). The centrality of the home, the significance of maternity, the dependence of autonomy and individuality on earlier nurture, the continuity between the domestic sphere and the wider society, and the various pathologies that follow failed attachment are all given an anchor in an unmistakably modern, twentieth-century worldview.

Conclusion

By revising Klein along the lines of the emerging relations-based psychoanalysis, Winnicott arrived at a description of the personality as using both close care and gradual separation, as well as aggression, in its journey toward maturation. As a result, Winnicott pictures mind and society as existing within a process in which self and other, aggression and love, playing and reality, all become parts of a longer development. This development is rooted in the infant's need for parental proximity, for holding and containing. Therefore, the search for sociability and its mutations into transitional space and transitional activities become the key for explaining and structuring social relations. This theory meshed with a broader movement within British social thought, whose aim it was to base the argument for the liberal welfare state on the assumption that people seek each other's company and not merely their own detached and atomistic interests. Winnicott's approach provided social-minded liberalism and the welfare network it produced with a well thought-out model of how sociability conditions behavior. It similarly explained the mutual dependence of individuality and community, which was necessary for tying the liberal and the social-democratic parts of the theory together.

Considered as a political theory, Winnicott's outlook even suffers from the same flaws as historical progressive liberalism and the welfare apparatus it constructed. One of them is that, as it particularly emphasizes the role of caring, Winnicott's model seems to consign women to a function within the home, and so strengthens confining gender roles. Moreover, even if gender roles are reversed or detached altogether from biological sex, the distribution of tasks that ties the caregiver to the home still remains, thus perpetuating strict gender segregation, albeit in a different form. This echoes the overall perception of the family that was promoted along with the welfare reforms of the mid-twentieth century, in which the nuclear and internally differentiated family was assumed as the main recipient of social entitlements (Doane and Hodges 1992; Gerson 2004; Riley 1983).

Another shared flaw is the difficulty Winnicott encounters in addressing the potentiality for unresolved and ultimately violent dispute. Beveridge's welfare state was envisaged as a constituent of an enduring world peace, as it anticipated that lowered tensions within societies would minimize the risk of war and therefore remove the ground from the need to maintain armed forces. Winnicott, similarly, can only see war as a disruption to healthy holding: As it distances the mobilized father and perhaps even threatens the evacuation of children to safer areas, the war experience destabilizes the home and therefore sets the stage for future sickness and the decline of democracy. The cycle is either benevolent or malevolent. The benevolent cycle cannot really contain social controversy beyond a certain level of volatility. What to do during a breakdown or an interruption is therefore not discussed as legitimate politics. These blind spots, common to both social policy and psychoanalytic thought, point to their shared origins in a specific historical context, and to the way in which both apparently separate constituencies had meshed in with each other's premises according to complex social demands and within the context of the developing British society.

References

Benjamin, J. 1988. *The Bonds of Love*. New York: Pantheon.

Beveridge, W. 1942. *Social Insurance and Allied Services*. London: HMSO.

Bowlby, J. 1951. *Maternal Care and Mental Health*. Geneva: World Health Organization.

Burns, C.D. 1919. *Greek Ideals*. London: Bell.

Burrow, J.W. 1966. *Evolution and Society*. Cambridge: Cambridge University Press.

Clarke, G.S. 2006. *Personal Relations Theory*. London: Routledge.
Collini, S. 1991. *Public Moralists*. Oxford: Oxford University Press.
Den Otter, S. 1996. *British Idealism and Social Explanation*. Oxford: Oxford University Press.
Dennis, N., and A.H. Halsey. 1988. *English ethical socialism*. Oxford: Oxford University Press.
Doane, J., and D. Hodges. 1992. *From Klein to Kristeva*. Ann Arbor: University of Michigan Press.
Fairbairn, W.R.D. 1952. *Psychoanalytic Studies of the Personality*. London: Routledge and Kegan Paul.
Freeden, M. 1978. *The New Liberalism*. Oxford: Oxford University Press.
Freud, S. 1930. *Civilization and Its Discontents*. London: Hogarth.
Geddes, P., and J.A. Thomson. 1889. *The Evolution of Sex*. London: Scott.
Gerson, G. 2004. Winnicott, Participation and Gender. *Feminism and Psychology* 14(4): 557–577.
Gomez, L. 1997. *An Introduction to Object Relations*. New York: New York University Press.
Goodin, R. 1988. *Reasons for Welfare*. Princeton, NJ: Princeton University Press.
Greenberg, J.R., and S.A. Mitchell. 1983. *Object Relations in Psychoanalytic Theory*. London: Harvard University Press.
Harris, Jose 1993. *Private lives, public spirit*. Oxford: Oxford University Press.
Hobhouse, L.T. 1906. *Morals in Evolution*. London: Chapman and Hall.
———. 1924. *Social Development*. New York: Allen and Unwin.
———. 1947. *The Rational Good*. London: Watts and Co.
Hoggett, P. 2008. Relational Thinking and Welfare Practice. In *Object Relations and Social Relations*, ed. S. Clarke, H. Hahn, and P. Hoggett, 65–86. London: Karnac.
Hughes, J.M. 1989. *Reshaping the Psychoanalytic Domain*. Berkeley: University of California Press.
Jones, G. 1980. *Social Darwinism and English Thought*. Brighton, UK: Harvester.
Klein, M. 1964. *Contributions to Psycho-analysis*. New York: McGraw-Hill.
Le Bon, G. 1896. *The Crowd*. London: n.p.
Locke, J. 1946. *The Second Treatise of Civil Government*. Oxford: Basil Blackwell.
Meadowcroft, J. 1995. *Conceptualizing the State*. Oxford: Oxford University Press.
Miller, G. 2008. Why Scottish Personal Relations Theory Matters Politically. *Scottish Affairs* 62: 47–62.
Mitchell, S.A., and M.J. Black. 1995. *Freud and Beyond*. New York: Basic.
Nicholson, P.P. 1990. *The Political Philosophy of the British Idealists*. Cambridge: Cambridge University Press.
Nicklin, J.A. 1898. Ideals of Friendship. *The Westminster Review* 149(6): 680–687.
Riley, D. 1983. *War in the Nursery*. London: Virago.

Ritchie, D.G. 1893. *Darwin and Hegel.* London: Swan Sonnenschein.
Rodman, F.R. 2003. *Winnicott.* Cambridge, MA: Perseus.
Scharff, D.E., and E.F. Birtles. 2014. From Instinct to Self: The Evolution and Implications of W.R.D. Fairbairn's Theory of Object Relations. In *Fairbairn and the Object Relations Tradition*, ed. G.S. Clarke, and D.E. Scharff, 5–25. London: Karnac.
Stack, D.A. 2000. The First Darwinian Left: Radical and Socialist Responses to Darwin 1859–1914. *History of Political Thought* 21(4): 682–710.
Suttie, I.D. 1952. *The Origins of Love and Hate.* New York: Julian Press.
Suttie, I.D., and J.I. Suttie. 1932. "The Mother: Agent or Object?" Part II. *British Journal of Medical Psychology* 12(3): 199–233.
Tarde, G. 1903. *The Laws of Imitation.* New York: H. Holt.
Tawney, R.H. 1921. *The Acquisitive Society.* London: Bell.
The Speaker. 1905. (Editorial) 17 June: 274–275.
Vincent, A., and R. Plant. 1984. *Philosophy, Politics and Citizenship.* Oxford: Blackwell.
Wallas, G. 1908. *Human Nature in Politics.* London: Constable.
———. 1914. *The Great Society.* London: Macmillan.
Winnicott, D.W. 1964. *The Child, the Family, and the Outside World.* Harmondsworth: Penguin.
———. 1971. *Playing and Reality.* London: Tavistock.
———. 1984. *Through Paediatrics to Psychoanalysis.* London: Karnac.
———. 1986. *Home is Where We Start From.* New York: W. W. Norton.
———. 1988. *Human Nature.* Philadelphia, PA: Brunner/Mazel.

CHAPTER 15

Vulnerability, Dependence, Sovereignty, and Ego-Distortion Theory: Psychoanalyzing Political Behaviors in the Developing World

Robert C. Chalwell

Classical psychoanalytic theory maintains the premise that behaviors are products of drives and the conflicts that arise from these drives (Van Ginneken 1988). Grounded in the Freudian school, Dr. D.W. Winnicott both expanded and narrowed the lenses of his work to focus on ego psychology, where the psyche of children is viewed as developing in relation to a real, influential parent (Winnicott 1960, 1965, 1992). While remaining true to the study of ego development in children, the trajectory of his theories have since been interpreted to, at times, serve as a bridge between the Viennese school, which relied heavily on play therapy and interpretive techniques, and the London school, which held that the psyches of children were not developed enough for classical analysis and advocated for a more educative role for analysts.

Applying Winnicott's focus on the early interactions of a child with a primary caregiver to the socialization of nations, similar relational patterns can be observed, particularly in the dynamics of imperialism, decolonization,

R.C. Chalwell (✉)
Broward College, Pembroke Pines, FL, USA

M.H. Bowker, A. Buzby (eds.), *D.W. Winnicott and Political Theory*,
DOI 10.1057/978-1-137-57533-3_15

the pursuit of individual and collective security, and the management of collective goods (Pevehouse 2002a, b). Where national wealth creation and resource acquisition might be seen as the most logical counterpart to the pleasure principal of classical psychoanalytical theory, Winnicott's theories of ego-distortion, maturational processes, and specifically the concept of the "holding environment," are herein asserted to have significant application to analyzing the behaviors of the countries to be discussed.

Domestic, regional, and international conflicts recurrently result from disputes over how resources and wealth are distributed. Aggressions, directed inward or outward, are often characterized as projections of the sovereignty afforded to all nations. Winnicott's theory of true self/false self is applied to analyzing antagonistic or defensive projections of sovereignty which evidence being self-harming and counterproductive to development goals, while serving alternative national pursuits, such as prestige seeking (Braveboy-Wagner 1985). Moreover, this work situates the role of intergovernmental organizations (IGOs) as agents of policy intervention within states and regions as central. Winnicott's treatment of the concepts of transference, countertransference, and the role of the effective analyst is applied to the policies of multilateral institutions (IGOs) as the forum where a wide variety of development interventions are prescribed and delivered, in seemingly futile attempts to resolve tensions when sovereign-nation behavior runs counter to existing norms and legal obligations (Pevehouse 2002a, b; Lyotard 1974).

The Discipline of Political Science, and specifically international relations (IR), facilitates the study, analysis, and understanding of systems of government and the interactions of an increasingly wide array of political actors. Traditionally, IR has narrowly investigated the security concerns, economic well-being, trade flows, and interactions of nation-states. As a branch of the social sciences, the investigation of political phenomena has, out of necessity if not deliberateness, exhibited to be an interdisciplinary endeavor. The dynamic interactions of geographical, environmental, psychological, sociological, and context-specific variables, has conditioned political scientists to acknowledge the impacts of diverse influences on political outcomes. However, unlike other social science disciplines, mainstream political science continues to be very wedded to the analysis of macro-level quantitative data that are easily accessible and comparable across like units of analysis. Although terms such as dependence, identity, sociology, and psychology are regularly utilized in the varied subdisciplines of political science, scholars continue to be wary of the difficult-to-quantify nuance operationalizing these variables invites. Winnicott was an ardent proponent of data-driven analysis and utilized his many years of pediatric practice as a source for developing his theories. With the adaptation of Winnicott's theories, and perhaps his practice-driven theoretical lens, an opportunity is presented to look at the interventions of development agencies in varied attempts to remedy the vulnerability of developing countries as a source of data able to drive desired macro-level generalization.

Toward the end of expanding the IR postcolonial development toolkit, this essay endeavors to adapt Winnicott's theoretical typologies and insights to the analysis of the political behaviors of the subgroups of Commonwealth African–Caribbean–Pacific (ACP) countries that achieved independence after World War II (WWII). The threshold problem of political psychology theory or the adaptation of psychoanalysis theory to political behavior proposed herein is to identify the facilitating environment dynamics and resulting political structure of individual, or groups of, nations which influence observed political behaviors.

Popular models of behaviorism employed in political science and political psychology include Game Theory (Basar and Olsder 1995) and the Rational Choice Theory (Riker 1995). The fundamental assumption of behaviorism is that intentions are unobservable and unknowable. Political scientists in the field of IR are restricted to observe state behavior and outcomes, and make causal assumptions as to intentions or how leadership will act. With nations being collectivities of human beings—as is common in the effective psychoanalysis of individuals, couples, and small groupings—there arguably exists the facility to employ empathy and introspection to infer intentions from behavior (Van Ginneken 1988). Moreover, where understandings of geopolitics treat geographical and resource-driven animus among and within states as a starting point, Winnicott's conceptualizations of "maturational processes" and "facilitating environment," broadly, are apropos to unpacking observable variation in the frequency and degree of regional cooperation versus conflict exhibited amidst national development pursuits as evidence of "healthy development" or the need of informed and effective intervention.

Maturational Processes and Development in Commonwealth ACP

Winnicott's fundamental work on psychoanalysis and child development between the years of 1926–1964 details the maturation process of a human being step by step from early childhood to adolescence stage. The main themes are heavily influenced by Freud's theories on infancy and establish a paradigm for an infant's growth from dependence toward independence. There are three stages. The first stage is absolute dependence, which is the early stage of emotional development. The infant is dependent on the mother's womb and care. Winnicott states that "this term "maturational process" refers to evolution of the ego and of the self" (Winnicott 1965). Winnicott also wrote that "case histories showed me that the children who became disturbed, whether psycho-neurotic, psychotic, psycho-somatic or antisocial, showed difficulties in their emotional development in infancy, even as babies" (1965, 171). The next step is relative dependence where the infant is aware of the presence of her dependence (Winnicott 1965). The last step is the infant's journey to toward independence.

Winnicott's theories differed from his peers as his pediatric practice brought him in close and regular contact with mothers and infants. He emphasized the importance of parent and child relationship by defining the "holding environment." This conceptualization of a psychic space between the mother and infant, neither wholly psychological nor physical, was for Winnicott the "holding environment," which allows for the child's transition to being more autonomous (Winnicott 1960, 1989). The infant is dependent on the holding environment where the mother holds the infant physically, emotionally, and in her mind. For a child to develop a healthy, genuine self, as opposed to a false self, Winnicott felt, the mother must be a "good-enough mother" who relates to the child with "primary maternal preoccupation."

The Crown Colony era can be asserted as encompassing the "facilitating environment" for a colony's preparation for independence. The "holding environment" is then a period where the colony is absolutely dependent and must be "held" in all ways. Winnicott further states that infant development should be facilitated by "good-enough" maternal care in order for the infant to survive. The good-enough care in the context of preparing former colonies for decolonization was clearly varied across the empire, with divergent outcomes and causality attributed by some scholars along racial, geographic, and resource endowment lines (Williams 1944). The following adaptation of Winnicott's maturational processes is proposed to add depth and contextual nuance to the shallow UN classifications of Most Developed Countries (MDCs), Less Developed Countries (LDCs), and Least Developed Countries (LLDCs) traditionally utilized.

Chalwell Adaptations of Winnicott's Maturational Process Stages and UN Classifications

I. Winnicott's Stages of Maturational Process

- Absolute Dependence
- Relative Dependence
- Independence (successful ego integration)

II. UN Classifications for Country Development

- Least Developed (LLDC)
- Less Developed (LDC)
- Most Developed (MDC)

III. Adapted Typology for the Commonwealth ACP

- Crown Colony
- Neocolonial Dependence
- Economic Independence (successful integration into the global economy)
- Sources: Winnicott 1960; United Nations 2016

The dependence of the ACP countries is not questioned. Since independence, each region has relied on the willingness of former imperial powers to continue preferential trade relationships and economic development aid. The Lomé Agreement of 1975 embodied the acceptance of postcolonial dependence among ACP counties and categorized newly independent states according to stages of economic development that would entitle them to preferential trade. Lomé, as the agreement is regularly referred to, was a trade and aid agreement between the European Economic Community (EEC) and 46 developing ACP countries. The agreement was revised and renewed three times, with a total of 70 ACP countries being signatories to Lomé IV (1989). The agreement provided for most ACP agricultural and mineral exports to enter the EEC duty free, and a preferential quota system for the import of products, such as sugar, bananas, and beef. Additionally, the EEC committed almost 30 billion ECU to development aid and investment in the ACP signatories to Lomé. While dependence was seemingly not questioned, the variation in types of dependence was not accounted for. My proposed adaptation of Winnicott also provides the adapted typology proposed to capture the true positioning of the Commonwealth ACP. Consequently, critical analysis of the impacts of Lomé find that the agreement did more harm than good by not promoting diversification and fostering economic resilience in ACP countries (Ogbonna 1982; Hurt 2002).

In short, the extensions of parent-like care by Europe did not facilitate the hoped for transition of the Commonwealth ACP from dependence to relative dependence, and certainly not to independence, in the economic sense. Despite ample evidence to this reality, ACP countries fought ceaselessly to maintain the preferential trade relationships that historically supported their mono-crop driven economies. Through the lens of classical psychoanalytic theory, this behavior could be viewed as point of arrested development at the Oedipal stage, where reliance on the mother figure is extended, resulting in an inability to act with appropriate levels of autonomy. Few ACP countries were prepared for the stark changes that the Single European Act (1993), the World Trade Organization (1994), and US economic aggression under the Clinton administration (1992–2000) would wreak on their already tenuous position in global trade. Through application of Winnicott's theory, sovereignty, like "self," would not be debated, but the quality of sovereignty would be a site for analysis and intervention. Did the "holding environment" facilitate the necessary levels of care, trust, and empowerment to facilitate a sustainable trajectory toward independence and integration into the global economy? For all the willingness to grant independence, had the former imperial power been a "good enough mother"? What would be the impacts of the European metropole turning its collective attention inward and away from its far-flung former children, as prescribed by deepening integration on the continent?

The Maastricht Treaty of 1992, meant the deeper integration of Western Europe and the establishment of the European Union (EU) in 1993. This evolution resulted in the creation of a consumer market that is 50 percent larger than the United States (in population though not actual consumption), and a pooling of resources and political influence that put into question America's preeminent positioning in atheorized unipolar post–Cold War international system. Utilizing the then new World Trade Organization (WTO) multilateral platform, the United States aggressively pushed for even greater reductions in trade barriers, and specifically targeted the postcolonial trade preferences afforded to ACP countries by Lomé, which were perceived as discriminating against American agricultural interests in Latin America and the Asia-Pacific region. With the coming into force of the Cotonou Agreement in 2003, the structures of ACP–EU cooperation changed significantly (Hurt 2002). Due to the non-reciprocal nature of the arrangements under Lomé, EU–ACP, trade relations were deemed to be in conflict with the WTO Article I principle of non-discrimination. Bowing to political pressure from the United States and the European Union all but ended long-standing preferential trade relationships with ACP countries. The new reciprocal arrangements are founded on the creation of regional and subregional free trade agreements (FTAs). The goal of the FTAs is to make ACP trade (intra-regional and extra-regional) WTO compatible (Chalwell 2013; Huffer 2006; Hurt 2002). The pursuits of fully liberalized trade and the integration of the developing countries (economic independence) into the world economy are also central goals of the Maastricht Treaty.

Imperialism and the Commonwealth ACP

Under the US-driven international system established in the wake of WWII, nation-state sovereignty has become cemented as the standard unit of analysis in IR and international development (Camilleri and Falk 1992). Even as scholarly attention has been increasingly drawn to other global actors, the state and state sovereignty continues to be the bedrock of international law and the organization of global society. Most importantly, as independent nation-states chart courses for national development and holistic security, the evidence of asymmetry and deficit of adequate resources for sustainable development is overshadowed by the constructed sanctity of sovereignty. This empowers political leaders to pursue policies that are contrary to their country's long-term best interest. Analyzing these behaviors is confounded by the near inability to isolate varied national motivations from responses to diverse exigencies, or from the extra-national pressures of former colonial powers and hegemonic influence such as that exerted by the United States.

Most of the member-countries included in this study were initially founded as economic ventures, or trading colonies (Williams 1944). These private, often corporate ventures afforded investors significant autonomy over early colonial affairs. Chartered Company governance gradually transitioned to Crown Colony status once local populations grew and evidenced to require a more intimate association with the British Parliament (Bissessar 2000). The transition to Crown Colony status was projected by Britain as the act of a beneficent mother embracing her far-flung children throughout the empire. For white colonials, Crown Colony status meant the loss of autonomy and the measure of self-rule previously enjoyed. For slaves, freed Blacks, and indigenous populations, Crown Colony status was welcomed, initially, as a refuge from exploitation and marginalization. Some scholars assert that the legacies and intersection of imperialism, slavery, and racism are what have contributed most to the pervasive vulnerability of the Commonwealth Caribbean and Commonwealth Africa (Williams 1944). Their arguments are supported by observing, in comparison, the trajectories of Canada, South Africa, Australia, and New Zealand, which all transitioned from dependence to independence at varying times between 1867 and 1953. By the early nineteenth century, among other differences, these colonies exhibited structurally marginalized indigenous populations, as in the case of South Africa or significantly smaller slave and freed Black populations than compared to white colonials, as in the case of Australia and New Zealand (Holland 1981; Williams 1944).

Over the course of the UN led decolonization period (1945–present), more than eighty former colonies have gained independence. The decolonization agenda was driven first by the Atlantic Charter (14 August 1941), punctuated by three individual UN Declarations. Although there was no one process of decolonization, in Africa, the Caribbean, and the Pacific, along with the promise of continued preferential trade and development support, imperial Europe sought to perpetuate or superimpose parliamentary style government institutions in their former colonies. Pursuant to claiming sovereignty many Commonwealth ACP countries established stable governments almost immediately (Braveboy-Wagner 1985). However, as will be discussed in more depth in the pursuant comparative analysis, each has, since independence, undergone some measure of constitutional reform. Additionally, postcolonial Commonwealth Caribbean development has, since early gains, exhibited marginal economic development and decades of economic stagnation (Chalwell 2013; WEF 2009; Braveboy-Wagner 2007; Page 2002). Postcolonial Commonwealth Africa has been plagued with spates of authoritarian leadership, civil wars, ethnic conflict, and health epidemics (Hartzenberg 2011; Lee 2002). The Commonwealth Pacific has had to contend with its small island developing state (SIDS) status and the varied environmental and development concerns baring that status in the Pacific brings (Tarte 2014; Poling 2013). This essay looks at postcolonial political projects, with specific attention to regional integration as a necessary path to sustainable development, and assesses enduring impediments to its pursuit.

Commonwealth ACP Decolonization Through the Lens of the "Facilitating Environment"

Until WWII, and for some British subjects even longer, Great Britain was perceived as a far off mother, who though not perfect, cared for and wished the best for her children. This maternal projection was promoted through the Crown Colony system that from the mid-nineteenth century endeavored to transition trading colonies with large disenfranchised slave or indigenous populations into integrated overseas Britons (Williams 1944). This era, and through decolonization, is asserted to be the counterpart to Winnicott's state of "primary maternal preoccupation" where mothers are preoccupied with the care of their baby, starting from the last few weeks of pregnancy and couple of weeks after the birth (Winnicott 1960, 1965).

Winnicott (1960) highlights the importance of the parent and child relationship by also defining the "holding environment." He further establishes that the infant's development should facilitated by "good-enough" maternal care in order for the infant to survive. Winnicott felt that a good-enough mother allows herself to be used by the infant so that he or she may develop a healthy sense of omnipotence that will naturally be frustrated as the child matures. The baby is completely dependent and with the care received during this dependency his ego develops and paves the way for the construction of a separate self in the maturational sequence which leads to relative dependence, and finally independence. Winnicott holds that when development progresses normally and the child has passed both phases normally, he/she will be prepared to best integrate with the world and face its inevitable hardships. As will be expanded more thoroughly in pursuant sections, this maturational process of dependence to independence, where functional integration into a wider community is achieved, is proposed to be analogist to the postcolonial goal of transitioning from dependence (colonial and neo-colonial) to economically developed (Page 2000), resilient, integrated in the global economy (Sala-i-Martin et al. 2009; Shadlen 2005), and fully sovereign. As will be evidenced by the historical narrative to be presented, regional integration, supported by a regional IGO was promoted as an extended "holding environment" for the vulnerable colonies. Membership in these organizations, and the support and resources that membership would afford could be perceived as an attempt to further development and self-governing capacity. However, the limited success of these integration projects and the perpetuation of vulnerability will be found consistent across the Commonwealth ACP.

Decolonization of Commonwealth Africa

By virtue of the sheer size of the continent of Africa, the colonial era and decolonization has not been a straightforward process. Though the presence of Europeans and imperialism in Africa dates back millennia, the official partitioning of Africa, known as The Scramble for Africa (1881–1914), resulted in 90 percent of the continent being colonized by Britain, France, Germany, Spain, Italy, Belgium, and Portugal. The decolonization of British Africa was achieved, in rare instances, peacefully, but primarily with protracted violence and bloodshed. The period is officially recognized from the independence of South Africa in 1910 to the independence of the Seychelles in 1976. Some scholars also include the creation of South-West Africa in 1990 and Southern Sudan in 2011 as part of decolonization in Africa (Ndlovu-Gatsheni 2012).

During the colonial period Africa was strictly organized under individual colonial powers. Regional groupings along linguistic lines have existed officially and unofficially for hundreds of years. Pan-African regionalism is most frequently counted post-WWII from the establishment of the Organization for African Unity (OAU) in 1963, succeeded by the African Union in 2000 (Worger et al. 2001; Springhall 2001). Other subregional multilateral projects now exist to promote solidarity, self-reliance, and an endogenous development strategy through industrialization (Hartzenberg 2011). African leaders have long-held regionalism as a means to uniting the continent both politically and economically. Though regionalism in Africa has taken on different forms to accommodate national, regional, and international evolutions (Awad and Youssof 2013). Increasing intra-regional trade through market integration is a primary component of the strategies employed by all organizations with the aim to integrate regional economies in Africa. As is the case with so many postcolonial projects, the model for such integration is the EU Market integration efforts in Africa have been deemed a dismal failure (Lee 2002; Economic Commission for Africa 2010). More than 80 percent of Africa's exports are still destined for outside markets, and the continent imports more than 90 percent of goods from outside (WTO 2011).

The North American Free Trade Agreement (NAFTA) and the creation of the Eurozone, only served to reinforce the commitment of African leaders toward market integration. In 1991, the Abuja Treaty was signed, creating the African Economic Community (AEC), with the goal of total integration of African economies by 2025. The AEC came in the wake of the failure to meet the objectives of the 1980 Lagos Plan of Action, the creation of an economic community in Africa by 2000. The marginalized positioning of Africa in the modern global economy is currently being exacerbated by unresolved political instability, a legacy of imperialism which leaves the continent vulnerable to recurrent economic, health, and security threats (UNCTAD 2011). Critics of market integration in Africa, advocate instead for individual economies to be integrated in the global market place through FDI and trade with extra-regional trade partners in the Americas, Europe, and Asia (North 2005). For this reason, intra-regional capital and trade flows are dwarfed by those from other capital rich regions. For critics, market integration in Africa is a distraction from more lucrative extra-regionally focused trade policies, not a solution to economic under performance and vulnerability (Awad and Youssof 2013; Lee 2002; Page 2002). Neither strategy clearly prescribes the path of transition from dependency to independence.

Decolonization of the Commonwealth Caribbean

Recognizing the vulnerable positioning of the former colonies in a rapidly changing international economic system that emphasized market openness and large-scale competitiveness (Sala-i-Martin et al. 2009), the United Kingdom supported the creation of a political and economic union among its Caribbean colonies. The ill-fated Federation of the West Indies was established in 1958 and survived for four years, amidst in-fighting, insular nationalism, and weak federal institutions (Bobb 1966). The union was finally dissolved in April of 1962, following the secession of Jamaica and failed attempts to salvage the Federation. Jamaica claimed its independence from the UK and national sovereignty on 6 August 1962, followed by Trinidad and Tobago on 31 August of the same year. The remaining Federation members claimed independence from the UK between 1966 and 1983. The newly independent nations remained members of the Commonwealth (then the British Commonwealth) and in 1965 once again pursued integration through the Caribbean Free Trade Association (CARIFTA) which was superseded by the Caribbean Community (CARICOM) in 1973.

The Organization of Eastern Caribbean States (OECS), a subset of CARICOM, has gradually achieved degrees of integration seen only in the United States of America, and currently being forged by the European Union. In attempts to mitigate the historic vulnerability, the OECS a trade and monetary union was established in 1981 was formed to further the Eastern Caribbean Common Market (ECCM) agreement of 1968. However, the efforts of CARICOM to promote broader Commonwealth Caribbean integration, as a counter to the historic vulnerability of the region, has exhibited to be pervasively entrenched. Many of the intra-regional tensions and institutional weaknesses that destroyed the Federation of the West Indies remain unresolved more than half a century later (Chalwell 2013; Rohlehr 2001). A September 2009 report by the UN Economic Commission on Latin America and the Caribbean (ECLAC) shows that the Latin America and the Caribbean economy grew an average 4.1 percent from 1950 to 2008, while its average annual inflation rate from 1970 to 2008 reached 15.4 percent. Anticipating the region's high level of vulnerability to the ongoing transformations and realignments in the global economy, a 2005 World Bank Report on the Caribbean region, also citing ECLAC, stated:

> The Caribbean region is at a development crossroads and its member nations must take significant and concrete steps to improve productivity and competitiveness and face up to a more global competition if they are to accelerate or even maintain past growth. (ECLAC 2005, 1)

Arguably, the writing has been on the proverbial wall for the Commonwealth Caribbean for at least two centuries. Small scale is not optimally competitive in the modern global economy (WEF 2009). Indeed, the region's disjointed geography, small scale and general disadvantage was only surmounted through the extension of unsustainable colonial and postcolonial trade preferences, which have been effectively eroded by an aggressive push for freer trade (Chalwell 2013). Intensifying regional integration, however challenging and costly to individual national pursuits, is the best option for regional resiliency and sustainable development. How then do we account for the continued reluctance to cede the sovereignty required to harmonize regional political, trade, and economic institutions? Defensive posturing, the perpetuation of intra-regional colonial era rivalries, and parallel failed market integration projects in the pervasively economically vulnerable Commonwealth ACP are all deemed "normal projections of sovereignty" through the lenses of traditional political science theory (Chalwell 2013; Braveboy-Wagner 2007, 1985).

That pervasive vulnerability has been exhibited by the region for many centuries, or that the region is dependent on the ability to trade in goods and services in demand in larger wealthier economies is not in question (Chalwell and Iliev 2016; Chalwell 2013; Braveboy-Wagner 2007, 1985). However, the evidenced aversion to reducing barriers to trade intra-regionally and the unwillingness to negotiate from a stronger unified position could be assessed as irrational. Winnicott's theory of true self and false self will be further developed to characterize the antagonistic projections of sovereignty in the developing world as harmful distortions of national ego and counterproductive.

The Decolonization of the Commonwealth Pacific

The postcolonial trajectory of the Commonwealth Pacific is notably different from its African and Caribbean counterparts. In 1947, a significant contributor to regional cooperation was initiated by colonial powers in the creation of the South Pacific Commission (SPC). Between 1962 and 1980, ten British Pacific colonies attained independence and joined the Commonwealth (Jayasuriya 2009). In 1971, the independent nations of the Commonwealth Pacific formed the South Pacific Forum (renamed the Pacific Islands Forum in 1999), mandated to be a multilateral platform equipped and empowered to address political, social, and economic issues. A number of agencies including the Forum Fishing Agency, Pacific Forum Line, and the South Pacific Regional Environment Program now cooperate with the UN, and other organizations to promote sustainable development throughout the region. The SPC was renamed the Secretariat of the South Pacific Community in 1997, and over 22 island governments now belong to this primarily technical assistance oriented organization (Huffer 2006).

The South Pacific was generally regarded as a quiet, isolated backwater. However by 1988, Melanesia, the Pacific's largest and most economically dynamic island states have intensified regional cooperation through the creation of the Melanesian Spearhead Group (MSG). The IGO has in recent years expanded its purview to include environment, geoscience, tourism, education, and security, and is leading the process of regional economic integration. The Polynesian Leaders Group was created in 2012 to facilitate similar pursuits. Further advancements in regional cooperation have come through the UN where Pacific Island states renamed the regional bloc the Asia-Pacific Small Islands Developing States (PSIDS) grouping (Tarte 2014; Poling 2013). This grouping has successfully caucused on issues of sustainable development and climate change, rather than as the Pacific Islands Forum group, whose future remains uncertain since the 2009 suspension of Fiji, PIF's host-country.

Opinion is divided on the broader and long-term significance of these regional developments. One view is that these new institutions fill gaps in the region's architecture, but do not challenge the dominant position and authority of the PIF, primarily due to the presence of Australia and New Zealand as PIF members. Debate notwithstanding, these regional IGOs have been and continue to be important mechanisms for asserting sovereign identities and establishing rights as states. For some former colonial powers, regional institutions are mechanisms used to perpetuate continued Western hegemony over the Pacific Island region (Huffer 2006). As members of some or all of the key regional organizations, Australia and New Zealand hold special places in the regional order as the only non-Pacific Island members of PIF. Firth (2014) highlights "a shift to a new, Australian-directed regionalism." Similarly, Poling (2013) argues that the PIDF (of which Australia and New Zealand are not members) "is not and is unlikely to become a competitor to the Pacific Islands Forum in anyway meaningful, but particularly as the coordinating hub for Pacific development."

Though different, the tensions, conflicts, and general challenges of regional development pursuits across the Commonwealth ACP exhibit to be ubiquitous while dynamically diverse. As already argued, this diversity of endowment, challenges, and positioning is not adequately accounted for in classical political theory. The following section will liberally apply Winnicott's theories as a means of enhancing the assessment of regional development needs and to fill in significant gaps in the international development architecture that serves as the tenuous lifeline for beleaguered Commonwealth ACP countries. Winnicott's true self and false self will be a unifying theoretical thread that characterizes the discussed antagonistic projections of sovereignty in the developing world as harmful distortions of national ego and counterproductive. From the historical narrative foundation provided, along with the critical characterization of sovereignty, this work will conclude with insights for regional IGO-driven development interventions.

Commonwealth ACP and Sovereignty: The True Self/False Self Problem

Classical political theory would have us accept a *de facto* fungibility across sovereign national pursuits. Rational Choice, in particular, assumes that group members are myopically concerned with maximizing private goods and the collective good produced by the group (Bicchieri 2003; Riker 1995). In large groups, however, myopic members are expected to be unwilling to pay for the collective good (which, by definition, they can always use), resulting in free-riding. This, of course, is a formula for group disaster. In the theory, groups solve this problem either by producing private goods of sufficient value to induce membership or by coercing others to join. The application of Winnicott's theories to the political behaviors of the Commonwealth ACP complements Rational Theory, and other classical approaches to IR, trade and development, and fills in glaring gaps in the core–periphery paradigm. Specifically, adapting Winnicott's theories centers the primary colonial-era relationships of developing countries. This focus holds the continued structures of dependency and vulnerability to be outcomes of "not good enough care" by metropolitan powers of former colonies during the time of political dependency and subjugation (imperialism).

In the context of sustainable national development and effective integration in the global economy, causal attributions to history must be further specified according to the range of established regional and national institutions and the kinds of actions guided by them (Jayasuriya 2009; Przerworski 2004;Przerworski et al. 2000; Pevehouse 2000). In the context of the Commonwealth ACP, these institutions may be established to promote integration, trade, development, education, health, or other areas of policy intervention. This awareness notwithstanding, the aversion to overt interference has restricted regionally or internationally funded policy intervention projects to what sovereign nations will consent to. As exhibited by the perpetuation of Lomé and the concerted, though ineffectual resistance to the Cotonou Agreement, consent more often than not, did not extend far beyond the expectation of development aid and continued preferential trade terms for mono-cash-crop exports (Chalwell 2013; Hurt 2002). These precise behaviors are what seem to invite the adaptation of Winnicott's typologies.

Winnicott used the concept of "true self" to describe a sense of self based on authentic experience, and a feeling of having a "real self." "False self" by contrast Winnicott described as a defensive façade, behind a mere appearance of being real. When what Winnicott described as "good enough parenting" was not in place, the infant's authentic self was in danger of being encroached on by the need for compliance with the parents' wishes and expectations. The result for Winnicott could be the creation of a false self, where "other people's expectations can become of overriding importance, overlaying or contradicting the original sense of self, the one connected to the very roots of one's being" (Winnicott 1965, 142–143). Furthermore, Winnicott asserts the utmost importance for the child to experience full dependency, relative dependency and independence, in order to integrate the ego. The integration of the ego in the context of this essay is analogist to ACP countries achieving "true sovereignty" via market integration, and scaled, competitive and resilient integration in the global economy.

In political theory, sovereignty is understood as the full right and authority to self-govern without interference from outside sources or bodies. Dating back to the Westphalian model of state foundation (1648), broadly defined, sovereignty is supreme authority over some polity, its geography, resources, people, and national pursuits. Since WWII, the foundation of sovereignty, particularly of new states, has been recognition by other states and membership with voting power in the UN. The concept and prototypes of the sovereign nation-state are found in the imperialist polities of Western Europe. Up until the colonial era, the movement of people and goods, in Western Europe, was less restrictive. As access to the wealth of the New World was determined restrictively, we find an impetus for the consolidation of national identity—one different and arguably greater than the "spontaneous awakening of national consciousness, yearning to express its revolutionary desires" most traditionally discussed (Chalwell 2013, 47).

Viewing nation-state sovereignty thus, we must contend with the disparate processes of its attainment since the Peace of Westphalia. What informed British, French, or Dutch nationalism was arguably the culmination of at least a millennium of migration, resisting pressures from imperial Rome, clan warfare, warring monarchies, and civil wars. Where the objectives of imperial Europe gave rise to nationalism and the nation-state were clear, no such universality can be attributed to the tidal wave of new nation-states that proliferated in the wake of the postcolonial era. This difference of environment and motivations to sovereign nationhood is arguably at the root of the inconsistent performance of many ACP countries.

Through the theoretical lenses of Winnicott informed psychoanalysis, applied to understanding and ultimately prescribing for the behaviors observed: *variation in the facilitating environments of ACP countries have resulted in wide variation in the necessary "good-enough care" that promotes healthy development of self, resulting in a distorted projected national self.* Through the lens of an adapted true self/false self theory, we see clear evidence of a false projection of sovereign independence, a national false self.

In Winnicott's depiction, a dependent child subject to a non-empathetic mother will gradually develop a "false self," give up his/her needs and demands and will quickly try to form himself according to the demands and expectations of the mother or others. Exploitative colonial and neo-colonial policy could be argued to be one such example of non-empathy. With further adaptation of Winnicott's theory, the national "false self" will preoccupy itself with its appearance to other political actors (prestige seeking) and will be inclined to present a superficial concordance. Winnicott suggests that a false self adapts to outside influences in order to protect the true self (Winnicott 1975). Application of the concepts of true self and false self to analyzing the nationalist projections of Commonwealth ACP countries are centered on the political identity construct of sovereignty. "True sovereignty," which has not been achieved, will be enveloped, encapsulated and hidden by the false self or "sovereign but pervasively vulnerable." "True self" in the context of the nation-state is the projection of strength in proportion to power leveraged from alliances that expand or optimize resource endowments (see McIvor, this volume). False self, on the other hand, is a futile, continuous effort to embody and project the power history and the environment has not provided.

In further analysis of a false projection of sovereignty, again adapting from Winnicott, the fact must be recognized that the intervening development agency can only negotiate with the false projection of the state-client about establishing the state's "true sovereignty" through a transition to economic independence. Further, the development agency must also recognize that the engagement establishes a link, whereby investment in the success of the state-client introduces a measure of collateral dependence. At the point of transition to "true sovereignty," the development agency and the state-client should be in a fully transparent awareness of their mutual dependence. Winnicott draws parallels between the infant–mother relationship and the patient–therapist relationship. Like the psychoanalyst in an occurrence of transference, the development agency serves as a surrogate for a figure from the patient's past (often a caregiver). In the context of the Commonwealth ACP, Great Britain's care was not in line with the needs of its colonies, and upon decolonization and the *de jure* achievement of sovereignty, a false projection of sovereignty, or dependent sovereignty, is observed. The policy expertise, resources, and assistance by the development agency must then be understood to be a part of a relationship of dynamic transference. The overarching goal would arguably be to assist the state-client in reworking early developmental disruptions and to provide the opportunity to fulfill unmet development needs and combat vulnerability through effective integration into the global economy.

Conclusion

In critical analysis of the postcolonial performance of the Commonwealth ACP we see that political behaviors and the intersection of numerous endogenous and exogenous factors have contributed to stagnation and hampered prospects of transitioning from dependency to true sovereignty, independence, and effective integration into the global economy. The overarching assertion of this work is that the failure of integration projects in the regions discussed are due to inadequate preparation for independence during the colonial era (holding environment) resulting in distorted perceptions of sovereignty and projections of self-sabotaging false sovereignty (false self).

In politics, however, there are always losers as well as winners (Riker 1988). Even without the recurrently prescribed economic diversification, coordination, and integration, benefit continues to be garnered by the limited domestic actors in the import/export sector of individual countries, and of course to large exporting economies such as the United States and the EU. These political actions, processes, and resultant outcomes have effects on all citizens, and regional groupings. Vulnerability to global economic shocks and the limitations of restrictive scale has left the Commonwealth ACP without the infrastructure or resources to effectively meet the needs of burgeoning youth populations (Chalwell 2015) and national development goals broadly (UNCTAD 2009). This awareness is but a starting point. The re-equipping of intervening agencies with legitimate insights as to the source and varied manifestations of aggressive posturing and an unwillingness to cooperate and coordinate as members of regional IGOs (the projection of false sovereignty) is where the true value of this adaptation lies.

Attempts of a cookie-cutter approach to the postcolonial development projects of countries in differing regions of the world and with disparate resource endowments have exhibited to be ill-fated. This essay promotes the liberal adaptation of Dr. Winnicott's psychoanalytical theories to the analysis of postcolonial political projects in the Commonwealth ACP, with specific attention to regional integration. Assertions made herein, establish a high utility for the nuanced understandings of dependency and vulnerability influenced political decision-making afforded by the adaptation of Winnicott's theories. The primary utility is asserted to be found in the legitimizing of a therapeutic relationship between an intervening development agency and the developing country. In numerous contexts, the success of the intervention is measured by relatively superficial evidence of transformation or change within the behaviors or policies of the state-client. This superficiality is dually perpetuated by the requirement of the development agency to exhibit success and the state's denial of its vulnerable position. Along the lines of the more educative role prescribed by Freudian approaches, the agency–state-client relationship must be one where

1. the expertise, and the utility of engaging with the development agency, is not questioned;
2. the state-client is deliberately pursuing a remedy to its vulnerable position, and sees value in agency intervention (therapy);
3. the goal of achieving true sovereignty and effective integration into the global economy is a transparent and desired goal.

However, this reorienting of thinking is complex and outside of theory, and will antagonize the dynamic behavioral phenomena at play on the levels citizen, state, and region. As with the processes of psychoanalysis, the political scientist or development practitioner cannot simply equate his or her own intentions with the intentions of others. Nor can he or she arrive at those intentions entirely by empathy, or control how well intentioned interventions are perceived and received by states, politicians, and the average citizen. There is a requirement to work back and forth among outcomes, actions, actors, and intentions to discover specific development goals nation-states actually have. The recommended applications of this approach proceeds as follows:

1. Drawing from existing empirical data, the social scientist assumes goals for relevant subjects and then predicts choices and outcomes on the basis of assumed goals.
2. If the scientist then observes that predicted actions and outcomes occur, he or she has in fact explained the outcomes and the research is complete.
3. If, however, the scientist fails to observe the predicted outcomes and actions, then he or she must reconsider the attribution of goals. With a new attribution, a new prediction, if observed, completes the research.
4. If, however, prediction fails again, the process must be repeated and repeated, until finally the prediction is correct and the explanation is satisfactory.

Such testing and revision is not possible for behavioral generalizations divorced from theory. Further, a key component missing from the development agency-driven intervention model is the recognition of collateral dependence. Proponents of deepening integration as a means of sustainable regional economic development and security are equipped with insights to enhance existing policy toolkits. Future development of the adapted paradigm presented, include deeper application of Winnicott's theories to social, cultural, security, and other national and regional pursuits, and the deliberate identifying of behaviors as "appropriate to the stage of development" and "contributing to advancement," or "harmful." Scholars and practitioners must build capital with stakeholders and exercise great care to respect the interactions with, and projections of, national "false self" by state-clients. Progress will only come from deliberateness in the reconceiving of the intervening agency–state-client relationship as therapeutic, and the process of integration as one that is beneficial and desired. The strategies found to be effective in developed economies have not and will not facilitate the transition from dependence to independence necessary for scaled, competitive and resilient integration in the global economy, deemed crucial for the survival of developing economies. A great opportunity exists to equip practitioners with the specialized skills to effectively engage with vulnerable state-clients, informed by understandings of the impacts of having come to sovereignty bereft of the "good enough care" from metropolitan colonial authorities, required for resilient integration in the global community.

References

Acemoglu, D., S. Johnson, and J. Robinson. 2003. The Rise of Europe: Atlantic Trade, Institutional Change and Economic Growth. *American Economic Association* 95(3): 546–557.

Acemoglu, D., and J.A. Robinson. 2006. Paths of Political Development and Our Argument. In *Economic Origins of Dictatorship and Democracy*, 1–47. Cambridge: Cambridge University Press.

Austin, G. 2010. African Economic Development and Colonial Legacies. In *International Development Policy Series*. Geneva, Switzerland: The Graduate Institute.

Awad, A., and I. Youssof. 2013. Africa's Economic Regionalism: Is There Any Other Obstacle? Paper prepared for the African Economic Conference, 2013: "Regional Integration in Africa." October 28–30, 2013. Johannesburg, South Africa.

Barratt, B.B. 2010. Somatic Psychodynamics. In *The Emergence of Somatic Psychology and Bodymind Therapy*, 79–87. London: Palgrave.

Basar, T., and G.J. Olsder. 1995. *Dynamic Noncooperative Game Theory*. London: Academic Press.

Bertram, G. 1987. The Political Economy of Decolonization and Nationhood in Small Pacific Societies. In *Class and Culture in the South Pacific*, ed. A. Hooper et al., 16–29.

Bicchieri, C. 2003. Rationality and Game Theory. In *The Handbook of Rationality, The Oxford Reference Library of Philosophy*, ed. A.R. Mele, and P. Rawling. Oxford: Oxford University Press.

Bissessar, A.M. 2000. *Crown Colony Administration, Structural Adjustment and New Public Management: The Agony of Reform*. St. Augustine, Trinidad: School of Continuing Studies, UWI.

———. 2005. Governance in a Small State. In *Globalization and Governance: Essays on the Challenges for Small States*, ed. A.M. Bissessar. Jefferson: McFarland and Company.

Bobb, L.E. 1966. The Federal Principle in the British West Indies: An Appraisal of Its Use. *Social and Economic Studies* 15(3): 239–265.

Braveboy-Wagner, J. 1985. *Interpreting the Third World: Politics, Economics, and Social Issues*. New York: Praeger Publishers.

———. 1989. *The Caribbean in World Affairs: The Foreign Policies of the English-Speaking States*. New York: Westview Press.

———. 2007. *Small States in Global Affairs: The Foreign Policies of the CaribbeanCommunity (CARICOM) (Studies of the Americas)*. New York: Palgrave.

Camilleri, J.A., and J. Falk. 1992. *The End of Sovereignty? The Politics of a Shrinking and Fragmenting World*. Aldershot, UK: Edward Elgar Publishing.

Chalwell, R.C. 2013. *The Political Economy of Trade and Development in the Commonwealth Caribbean*. Dissertation. Ann Arbor, MI: UMI/ProQuest.
Chalwell, R.C. 2015. 'Big Up Yourself My Yute!': Investigating the Impacts of Youth Majority Populations on Politics and Policy in the Anglophone Windward Islands of the Caribbean. Paper Presented at the Conference on International Development Fairfax, VA.
Chalwell, R.C., and I. Iliev. 2016. Trade Wars in Paradise: The Legacy of Intra-CARICOM Economic Conflict and Prospects for Deepening Integration. Paper Presented at the Midwest Political Science Association Annual Conference, Chicago, IL.
Economic Commission for Africa (ECA). 2004. *Unlocking Africa's Trade Potential*. Economic Commission for Africa, Addis Ababa, Ethiopia.
———. 2010. *Assessing Regional Integration in Africa IV: Enhancing Intra-African Trade*. http://www.uneca.org/aria4/index.htm
Firth, S. 2014. Security in Papua New Guinea: The Military and Diplomatic Dimensions. *Security Challenges* 10(2): 97–113.
Hartzenberg, T. 2011. Regional Integration in Africa. https://www.wto.org/english/res_e/reser_e/ersd201114_e.pdf
Holland, R.F. 1981. *Britain and the Commonwealth Alliance, 1918–1939*. London: Palgrave.
Huffer, E. 2006. Regionalism and Cultural Identity: Putting the Pacific Back into the Plan. In *Globalization and Governance in the Pacific Islands*, ed. S. Firth, 43–58. Canberra: Australia National University Press.
Hurt, S.R. 2002. Co-operation and Coercion? The Cotonou Agreement Between the European Union and ACP States and the End of the Lomé Convention. *Third World Quarterly* 24(1): 161–176.
Jayasuriya, K. 2009. Regulatory Regionalism in the Asia-Pacific: Drivers, Instruments and Actors. *Australian Journal of International Affairs* 63(3): 335–347.
Kahler, M. 2000. Legalization as Strategy: The Asia-Pacific Case. *International Organization* 54(3): 549–571.
Lee, M. 2002. Regionalism in Africa: A Part of Problem or a Part of Solution. *Polis/R.C.S.P./C.P.S.R.* 9(Numéro Spécial): 1–24.
Lyotard, J.-F. 1974. *Libidinal Economy*. Paris: Les Éditions des Minuit.
Ndlovu-Gatsheni, S.J. 2012. Fiftieth Anniversary of Decolonization in Africa: A Moment of Celebration or Critical Reflection? *Third World Quarterly* 33(1): 71–89.
North, D. 2005. *Understanding the Process of Economic Change*. Princeton, NJ: Princeton University Press.
Ogbonna, M.N. 1982. An Analysis of ACP-EEC Trade After Lomé I Convention. *Acta Oeconomica* 29(3/4): 341–360.
Page, S. 2002. *Regionalism among Developing Countries*. London: Overseas Development Institute/Macmillan.

Pevehouse, J.C. 2002a. With a Little Help from My Friends? Regional Organizations and the Consolidation of Democracy. *American Journal of Political Science* 46(3): 611–626.

———. 2002b. Democracy from the Outside In? International Organizations and Democratization. *International Organization* 56(3): 515–550.

Poling, G. 2013. *The Pacific Islands Development Forum: Keep Calm and Carry On, Commentary*. Center for Strategic and International Studies. http://csis.org/publication/pacific-islands-development-forum-keep-calm-and-carry-on/. Accessed 1 September 2013.

Przerworski, A. 2004. The Last Instance: Are Institutions the Primary Cause of Economic Development. *European Journal of Sociology* 45(2): 165–188.

Przerworski, A., M.E. Alvarez, J.A. Cheibub, and F. Limongi. 2000. *Democracy and Development: Political Institutions and Well-Being in the World, 1950–1990*. New York: Cambridge University Press.

Riker, W.H. 1995. The Political Psychology of Rational Choice Theory. *Political Psychology* 16(5): 23–44.

Rodrik, D., A. Subramanian, and F. Trebbi. 2004. Institutions Rule: The Primacy of Institutions Over Geography and Integration in Economic Development. *Journal of Economic Growth* 9(2): 131–165.

Rohlehr, G. 2001. A Scuffling of Islands: The Dream and Reality of Caribbean Unity in Poetry and Song. In *New Caribbean Thought: A Reader*, ed. B. Meeks, 265–305.

Sala-i-M, X., J. Blanke, M. Drzeniek Hanouz, T. Geiger, and I. Mia. 2009. The Global Competitiveness Index, 2009–2010: Contributing to Long-Term Prosperity Amid the Global Economic Crisis. In *The Global Competitiveness Report 2009–2010*, 3–47. Geneva: World Economic Forum.

Shadlen, K.C. 2005. Exchanging Development for Market Access? Deep Integration and Industrial Policy Under Multilateral and Regional-Bilateral Trade Agreements. *Review of International Political Economy* 12(5): 750–775.

Springhall, J. 2011. *Decolonization Since 1945: The Collapse of European Overseas Empires*. New York: Palgrave.

Tarte, S. 2014. Regionalism and Changing Regional Order in the Pacific Islands. *Asia and the Pacific Policy Studies* 1(2): 312–324.

US Economic Commission for Latin America and the Caribbean. 2011. *Economic Survey of Latin America and the Caribbean 2010–2011*. Economic Division. ECLAC, Santiago de Chile.

Van Ginneken, J. 1988. Outline of a Cultural History of Political Psychology. In *The Psychology of Politics*, ed. W. Stone, and P. Schaffner. New York: Springer.

WEF (World Economic Forum). 2007. *The Global Competitiveness Report 2007–2008*. Hampshire: Palgrave.

———. 2008. *The Global Competitiveness Report 2008–2009*. Geneva and Hampshire: World Economic Forum and Palgrave.

———. 2009. *The Global Competitiveness Report 2009–2010.* Geneva and Hampshire: World Economic Forum and Palgrave.

Williams, E. 1944. *Capitalism and Slavery.* Chapel Hill: University of North Carolina Press.

Winnicott, D.W. 1960. The Theory of the Parent-Infant Relationship. *InternationalJournal of Psychoanalysis* 41(6): 585–595.

———. 1965. In *The Maturational Processes and the Facilitating Environment: Studies in the Theory of Emotional Development*, ed. M. Khan. London: Hogarth.

———. 1989. *Holding and Interpretation: Fragment of an Analysis.* New York: Grove Press.

———. 1992. *The Child, the Family, and the Outside World.* Boston: Da Capo Press.

———. 2014. *Through Pediatrics to Psychoanalysis: Collected Papers (1958).* London: Routledge.

Worger, W., N. Clark, and E. Alpers (ed). 2001. *Africa and the West: A Documentary History from the Slave Trade to Independence.* Phoenix, AZ: Oryx Press.

World Bank. 2005. A Time to Choose: Caribbean Development in the 21st Century. http://www.unicef.org/lac/spbarbados/Implementation/SP%20 Poverty/Regional/Timet ochoose_WBCARreport_2005.pdf. Accessed 9 March 2013.

World Trade Organization (WTO). 2011. Regional Integration in Africa. Economic Research and Statistics Division. Staff Working Paper No. ERSD-2011-14.

Index[1]

[1] Note: Page numbers followed by 'n' refer to footnotes.

M.H. Bowker, A. Buzby (eds.), *D.W. Winnicott and Political Theory*,
DOI 10.1057/978-1-137-57533-3

Q

R

GPSR Compliance
The European Union's (EU) General Product Safety Regulation (GPSR) is a set of rules that requires consumer products to be safe and our obligations to ensure this.

If you have any concerns about our products, you can contact us on

ProductSafety@springernature.com

In case Publisher is established outside the EU, the EU authorized representative is:

Springer Nature Customer Service Center GmbH
Europaplatz 3
69115 Heidelberg, Germany

www.ingramcontent.com/pod-product-compliance
Lightning Source LLC
LaVergne TN
LVHW052026200926
848481LV00005B/1601
* 9 7 8 1 3 4 9 9 5 4 1 8 6 *